D1230187

THE CRITICAL TWILIGHT

The International Library of Phenomenology and Moral Sciences

Editor: John O'Neill, *York University, Toronto*

The Library will publish original and translated works guided by an analytical interest in the foundations of human culture and the moral sciences. It is intended to foster phenomenological, hermeneutical and ethnomethodological studies in the social sciences, art and literature.

JOHN FEKETE

The Critical Twilight

Explorations in the ideology of Anglo-American literary theory
from Eliot to McLuhan

ROUTLEDGE & KEGAN PAUL
LONDON, HENLEY AND BOSTON

595313

First published in 1977
by Routledge & Kegan Paul Ltd
39 Store Street,
London WC1E 7DD,
Broadway House,
Newtown Road,
Henley-on-Thames,
Oxon, RG9 1EN and
9 Park Street,
Boston, Mass. 02108, USA
Photoset in Compugraphic Times Roman
by Kelly and Wright, Bradford-on-Avon, Wiltshire
and printed in Great Britain by
Lowe & Brydone Ltd
Copyright John Fekete 1977
No part of this book may be reproduced in
any form without permission from the
publisher, except for the quotation of brief
passages in criticism

British Library Cataloguing in Publication Data

Fekete, John

The critical twilight.—(The international library
of phenomenology and moral sciences).
1. Criticism—United States
I. Title II. Series
801'.95'0973   PN99.U5   77–30187

ISBN 0–7100–8618–0

Harriet Irving Library
AUG 28 1978
University of New Brun...

To my parents, Lily and Stephen Fekete,
with love and appreciation

Contents

Contents

Foreword

For some forty years, from the 1920s to the 1960s, literary criticism occupied a place of quite exceptional importance in the intellectual life of the English-speaking countries. Its exceptional character, in comparison with the situation in otherwise comparable cultures, is now often remarked upon. It has been explained as a result of the absence of certain elsewhere important intellectual practices: classical sociology; philosophy in a mode wider than that of logical analysis; Marxism. Alternatively it has been explained as a specific consequence of the powerful intellectual traditions of 'Anglo-Saxon' empiricism. There is some substance in each of these explanations, but it is impossible to reach any adequate interpretation unless the practice in question is directly studied. And this, in any full sense, has for different reasons been very difficult to do.

One major reason follows from the standard definition of this work as Literary Criticism. If that title is taken at face value, to indicate critical analysis and evaluation of 'literary texts'—poems, novels and plays, it is easy to see why it has a place in a culture but very difficult to see why it should claim, sometimes successfully, a central and even dominant function. The claim, it is true, has always provoked some bewilderment, and often some scorn. But this has been largely because, taking the practice only at face value, observers have noted only its assumed specialism and, in all its other manifestations, been able to diagnose no more than rash extension or effective displacement. Moreover such observers have been notably strengthened in this habit by the standard presentations of 'Literary Criticism' itself. Throughout this period there has been strong emphasis, in defining the practice, on the analysis and evaluation of '*texts*': to be sure as a necessary argument against other more 'peripheral' kinds of literary study, but also as a description of the central 'discipline' of more extensive kinds of analysis. Faced with this reiterated definition of 'attention to the words on the page', observers have been surprised and even practitioners mystified that the result of this attention has so commonly been a form of discourse about social life as a whole. That such discourse was valued and influential, in the period of its major importance, is now, indisputably, a fact about the culture in which it occurred. But, in the last ten years especially, it has become impossible either to accept the proffered relation between the specialist discipline and the general discourse, or, which is equally important, to react to the problem with a merely generalized bewilderment and scorn. Increasingly it is the practice itself, and the body of theory which in spite of some denials it so evidently carries, which needs study, analysis and evaluation. And then the starting point of this work is the realization that what has been called, in English, Literary Criticism has in this major period always and fundamentally been something more than the specialized practice which the term seems to indicate. There are several possible alternative descriptions. Dr Fekete, interestingly, suggests 'Critical Theory', but as his remarkable study shows, even this has to be taken in a very wide sense.

In its earliest phase, modern critical theory was predominantly situated in England. It had complex relations with the specifically English tradition which is now usually called the culture-and-society argument, but it was also defined within a very specific contemporary cultural situation. Dr Fekete is surely right to identify its fundamental concern as a problem of *order*, within a very deep social and cultural crisis in which the limits of current religion and science, but also the probable disintegration of an inherited social and cultural order, were being sharply experienced. The stress on order can indeed be noted as early as Matthew Arnold, in what is probably the major turning-point in the culture-and-society tradition. Arnold, we remember, consciously opposed culture to anarchy, and the anarchy there immediately in question was a lively popular campaign for the suffrage. But the setting was always wider than a merely political crisis. It was a major crisis of the whole human social order, and the specific response, in modern critical theory, is to be found over a very wide range, from its directly social and political implications (which were to become more and more explicit, and to change internally, as the movement developed) through to its specialized emphases on the *organization* of responses and on the literary text as the objective medium of such an organization.

From about 1930 the English and North American forms of this movement began processes of separate though still related development. In the 1920s the two leading figures had been an American in England, T. S. Eliot, and an Englishman who was subsequently to work in America, I. A. Richards. In the immediately subsequent phase there are interesting points of comparison, for example between the reliance of F. R. Leavis and early *Scrutiny* of an idea of 'Old (rural) England' and the Agrarianism which Dr Fekete traces as a phase in the work of John Crowe Ransom. But thereafter, at least until the sixties, the English and North American developments diverge, and it is significant that from the years after 1945 English literary criticism, in its more specialized sense, came increasingly to rely on the later phases of North American theory and practice.

Dr Fekete has chosen to study, centrally, the North American development. His most remarkable contribution is his analysis of what he describes as a 'paradigm in motion', in which, through what appear at first sight to be no more than shifts in critical position and method, there is a decisive movement from defensive reaction through capitulation to a new phase of the social order to active agency in its service. His detailed analyses of the work of Ransom, Northrop Frye and of Marshall McLuhan, chosen as nodal points of this development, form the basis for a revaluation which is of the first importance, not only within literary studies but in the broader area of cultural and social analysis which this powerful tradition has sought to dominate.

Its importance to English and North American readers is then clear. But it has a further relevance. Since the middle sixties, and with gathering pace, there has been a form of apparent rejection of this critical tradition which is in fact only a new, more powerful but also more alienated version of its fundamental problematic of objectivist organization. Critical structuralism, often in confusing association with an objectivist form of Marxism, has indeed to be seen, as Dr Fekete argues, as a phase of this destructive tradition, rather than as any kind of alternative to it. Thus, instead of easy contrasts between 'Anglo-Saxon' and 'European' modes, we have to face the reality of a continuing internationalized dominance of critical formalism, now in complex and interpenetrating relations with deeper forms of the social crisis.

Dr Fekete's argument speaks for itself. I would add only, for the record, my memory of the years of friendship and collaboration while he was preparing and writing this work in Cambridge. Other work is now being done here, by other writers, on the English version of this movement, through to the sixties. But I can speak of the exceptional thoroughness and seriousness with which Dr Fekete approached his task, and also of the deep human warmth and commitment which, again exceptionally, underlies a work of such marked theoretical rigour. It is still in these terms that an alternative movement, in this vital area, will form and develop.

Raymond Williams

Preface

This study can be described as a 'theoretical critique.' If equal emphasis is put on each of the two words, together they define both the nature of the study (as that specific mode of appropriation we call 'theory') and its social disposition (as that specific orientation we call 'critique'). All theory structures phenomena and constitutes meaning. In other words, the relation of theory to its object (which it can never exhaust) is partitive and non-symmetrical, and its principle of selection or particularization (alternatively one could say, totalization) is unavoidably embedded in a historical nexus. The theoretical task of this study is to discover and elucidate the features of the historical interests that play a formative role in articulating the conceptual schemes of modern bourgeois critical theory[1]—specifically, articulating them in terms of selected sets of categories and types of interdeterminations that serve to distort or exclude those structural variables that are essential for any meaningful project of social and human liberation. Consequently, my own particularization of the modern tradition of critical theory aims at those theoretical elements which provide access to and most sharply reveal the immanent intentionality developing at the heart of the tradition; and, in its own turn, my argument seeks to mediate critical activity toward a *telos* of human emancipation.

In its self-image as a 'critique,' this study seeks to embody both the semiological aspect of discourse about discourse, and the epistemological aspect of knowledge of the limitations and necessities of its object. These define the field of attention of the book. But if its theoretical task is to be achieved, then this study must realize itself as a critique in terms of two further dimensions, one methodological and one ontological. As a critique, in the sense of unfinished, non-scientific discourse or contribution, it needs to reject that typical enterprise of reified science which has the result of stabilizing a congealed reality from the assumed point of view of Truth, and needs to affirm its own epistemological stance from within the motion of a totalizing project of struggle. And as a critique in the sense of negativity, the study must oppose modern critical theory for being the theoretical face of capitalist transformation, identify it as neocapitalist practice, and affirm itself as a moment[2] of revolutionary praxis, thus providing the social ontological ground for its methodological attitude in the struggle for the historical validation of its truth.

Contemporary philosophy of science is beginning to recognize that different theories are ontologically incompatible, and that the the choice among them is ultimately not a formal problem but embodies a choice among historically produced values. Bourgeois critical theory in its development (like the type of humanism to which it gives form) is both a sensitive index of the social reality which it expresses and an important constitutive part of that reality: it is deeply involved with our most fundamental ideas about who we are and about how we relate to each other and to nature. And the choice among alternative theories—a choice that invariably reanimates the past, shapes the present, and chooses a future—is resolved into questions of engagement and comportment in relation to the historical ensemble of human interactions and the social metabolism with nature.

In North America, the diffusion of bourgeois humanism as a specialist cultural activity has for decades been ensured through an elaborate network of ideological apparatuses: the formal and informal educational systems. At the same time, the spontaneous revolt of many people against social and academic sterility has repeatedly left them susceptible to the promises of the ideologies thus diffused. There are two related reasons for this which have for long together determined the balance of ideological forces. Firstly, modern critical theory, in each phase of its development, has always worn a mask of protest and rebellion in its polemics against the old orthodoxies that were to be displaced again and again in favor of new ideological formations, progressively more adequate[3] to the dominant social imperatives of a capitalism integrating its spheres of material and spiritual production and reproduction, and progressively more firmly entrenched in ideological institutions. Secondly, the failure of 'The Left' to move beyond an obsolete theoretical level to grasp the new human possibilities that the movements of history are forever opening up—the failure to develop and build upon rich and liberating cultural insights into the 'superstructural' or subjective side of history—has left a more or less open field for the official ideologies of the prevailing 'positive' culture. None the less, the monumental social crisis that erupted in the 1960s has radically undermined the cultural base of the system. The vast human possibilities contained within the profound orientational crisis that characterizes the 1970s can be brought one step closer to realization if, in the struggle for orientation, popular consciousness can genuinely liberate itself from the remnants of conservative ideological hegemony and from the persistent institutionally sustained appeal of false prophets.

The natural history of this book has its origin in a situation of direct relevance to this problem. In the late 1960s, the political culture of the student movement found a point of contact with the cultural politics of critical theory: the two constellations converged over the category of participation. The universities were a realm in which the contradictions of a culture in the processes of manipulated integration into the sphere of social production were experienced acutely and could be temporarily exploded. Everywhere the slogans of participation in the decision making processes carried the anti-authoritarian struggle. Marshall McLuhan had great attraction in such a context since he not only stressed participation, involvement, as a central coordinating concept, but appeared to locate it as a progressive category of reality, a genuine tendency of the future, thus lifting it beyond the level of a tentative ethical imperative. With the achievement of participation in the governing bodies came the awareness of continuing manipulation, powerlessness, and subordination to goals that were alien in their definition and implementation. As the contours of effective power came more clearly into focus, it also became remarkable that McLuhan did not talk about power. Nor about freedom, self-determination, truth, or value. And nowhere in his concept of man or society was there room for associated human beings who wanted to gain control over their own destinies. There was no field of possibility for a historical subjectivity; the very composition of the theoretical system precluded a social ontology based in self-constituting, creative human praxis and, with it, all potential of liberation from actual domination.

Two central fetishes appeared to govern McLuhan's view of the world: form and technology. In this perspective, people became objects in a world where human objectifications functioned autonomously and divorced from all dimensions of value and substance. McLuhan's work seemed, in effect, an ideological embrace of reification, built around a formalism that impoverished the reality it approached. At the same time, his name and ideas were rising to prominence on the waves of Utopian renaissance that characterized the late 1960s. Here was a cultural and sociological phenomenon of great importance, and the need to understand it posed the necessity of undertaking to investigate the historical development of bourgeois critical theory.

This inquiry could strategically be narrowed to modern theory and, within that, to the major North American pedagogical tradition, that is, the tradition derived from I. A. Richards and T. S. Eliot, which could, it seemed, be studied with justification as a unit through its key figures, John Crowe Ransom, Northrop Frye, and Marshall McLuhan. Not only does fetishism recur as a decisive common feature of this tradition; the tradition also takes on features of a maturing social-scientific paradigm. This opens up the areas of the relation of science to social ontology, and of 'scientific' criticism to art. Most importantly, the tradition is not static but displays internal evolution along several axes of relationships involving art, criticism, and social reality. If, for example, the New Critics import technicism from the social sphere to the aesthetic sphere, McLuhan subsequently projects aesthetic categories into a social analysis centered in technology. Ultimately, the development and structural features of modern critical theory can be illuminated by the Marxian methodological principle that the anatomy of man is the key to the anatomy of the ape. While one has to understand how deeply each phase is rooted in earlier phases, it is important to see the tradition as leading to its contemporary culmination in McLuhan (and pointing beyond, to systematic structuralism). Though its development is in some respects uneven, this is a tradition united throughout by an overwhelming ideological coherence and an irresistible theoretical motion toward social stabilization and the elimination of the active ontological level of human subjectivity.

Sociologically, the successes of the New Critics, the near-canonization of Northrop Frye in institutional literary circles, and the international vogue of McLuhanacy, suggest a relation of deep adequacy[4] between these ideologies and essential dynamics of the historical epoch within which they have been active. In the present period, within the most advanced capitalist countries, the contradiction between production expansion and consumption deferral that had characterized the classical liberal phase of capitalism no longer applies, in principle. The Utopian possibility of the material satisfaction of all human needs and their infinite development is within reach as a function of social and communal criteria beyond the realm of strictly economic necessity. If living labor power were released from immediate goods production, as is tendentially possible, and from the relations of domination that have spread from production to all of society, then alienation could be abolished and labor power reappropriated as the creative human life activity and teleological force that freely creates, exchanges, and enjoys a human world. Through conscious historical praxis in control of our technical-economic processes and our social and cultural forms, we could transcend the economic domination of social relations entirely and move to a higher stage in the historical evolution of the human species, beyond the point of immersion in the immediate production and reproduction of the material means of life.[5]

Within the capitalist socio-economic formation, however, these potentialities are not being realized and their future depends on the success and orientation of developing revolutionary struggles. The primary commitment of administered societies to the retention of relations of domination means the inhibition of these possibilities, an abuse of productive capacity, a prodigious extension of rationalization, and the degradation of culture. Capitalism has not resolved its contradictions in the shift from the entrepreneurial to the monopoly stage; to survive the structural crises in the early part of this century, it has displaced them and it now faces new crises. Economically, it must artificially generate new forces of accumulation, it must artificially generate effective monetary demand, and it must artificially generate employment. Politically, it must artificially generate legitimacy for the established forms and relations. And culturally, it must artificially generate a creative and dynamic subjectivity to guarantee the continuing viability of the system while ensuring that this subjectivity (in all its technical, analytic, speculative, and affective forms) is effectively instrumental-ized within the safe boundaries of a readily manipulable code of social values and meanings.

These social exigencies have become linked decisively to an institutional cultural matrix and to an all-pervasive information environment through the growth of a huge education system (organized ideological centers that also function partly to train personnel, partly as a form of disguised unemployment) and a giant mass consciousness and communications industry (involving advertising and media) that promote, coordinate, and control a whole new way of life: *life as consumption*, particularly the consumption of information, of the signs, the social meanings which adhere to all our physical and spiritual products and which acquire their value in the framework of a manipulated sign system, a systematic code that bears no organic relationship on any one-to-one basis with a given object or need to be satisfied.[6]

A crucial role in the new phase (which we may call simply neocapitalism) is played by the state which during this period is brought into symbiotic relation with the economy. The role of the state becomes indispensable both to ensure demand and to ensure employment; its taxation, monetary, and credit politics, its imperialist expansion of markets and fields of operation, and a host of other interventions locate the state as the embodiment of the corporate capitalist class's plans to enforce a system of unnecessary and perverted production and labor domination. State intervention in the ecoromy from the 1930s and 1940s onwards—the historical domain of the present study—is no longer occasional, designed to forestall or resolve any of a great variety of menacing crises, but rather a permanent regulation and direction of the economy. At the same time, jointly with the culture industry, state apparatuses also penetrate the realm of everyday life and seek to effect the total administration, bureaucratization, and surplus normatization of community and personality.

What we learn from these changes in economy, polity, and their interrelation, is that an indispensable key to this new period becomes the drive for stability, for controlled change, for order. And, from the point of view of cultural investigation, the following point is essential: instead of realizing the now materially plausible supersession of political-economic society, neocapitalism attempts its complete regulation. This means the extension of capitalist rationalization to the whole of society, involving the subordination of the whole of society, in all the spheres of its life, to categories of domination. What occurs, instead of the elimination of the economic character of the economy, of its self-determination based on its historically specific independent laws (thereby gaining the prerogative of conscious historical subjectivity for associated human beings), is that commodity fetishism reaches beyond the sphere of production into areas previously exempt from or even in opposition to its domination, such as non-economic personal or cultural activity. This further rationalization aims to effect the manipulated integration of all aspects of existence into a stable and ordered totality articulated by the independent and irresistible operation of neocapitalist rationality, a social form fetishized as a law of nature that consequently cannot be superseded but can be regulated, controlled, and used to advantage for the partial satisfaction of the immediate manipulated needs of particularized consumers.

In general, within this framework, the production, movement, and distribution of information take on central significance. This context, which is so clearly the historical ground of McLuhan's vision of technologized change and cybernetic programming, makes it imperative to pay attention to the new role (and to the history) of cultural ideologies and to situate them as integral parts of a unified social reality. One significant conclusion that seems inescapable from a careful study of the categorical development of bourgeois critical theory is that traditional humanistic criticism has been fully integrated into that world which is the putative object of its criticism. One immediate consequence follows from this: if we are to develop a critical bearing on our world and a voice in our future, then we have to reject the claims made by the specialist humanities to be the champions of value in a world they believe to be composed of disturbing, absurd, or inhuman scientific and technological fact. Their position represents no real *alternative* in a world structured in the way that ours is.

Ideas change their meaning as their historical context changes. The doctrine of the privileged virtues of art as a superior reality (for example) signalled, in the Renaissance, a progressive confidence in the creative potentials of human artifice that was to produce a world increasingly free of the bounds of nature and emancipated from extra-human limitations. The same doctrine in the nineteenth century expressed the defensive and increasingly abstract romantic aesthetic protest against both their exclusion from the dominant mode of social production and the utilitarian values of the dominant material culture. The same doctrine in the formulations of modern humanists is a hollow mockery that barely disguises their obscene complacency at having found a comfortable specialty far from the madding crowd where they can serve—unchallenged by the cry from the present or the call from the future—as the *official* pessimists or the *official* 'consciences' of a permanently established order.

On one hand, under the conditions of attempted neocapitalist regulation and direction of the totality of existence, at controlled work or at controlled play, where culture becomes a commodity and knowledge an industry, where the merger of traditional 'base' and 'superstructure,' of material and cultural production, steadily solidifies, there the rigid separation between ideal-cultural reality and material-social reality no longer has a basis in real life. Indeed, the manipulation of meaning and of subjectivity are now structured into the core of our social processes. On the other hand, within the growing corporatism that institutionalizes an assigned, structured, and limited place for every special interest—and which characterizes the manipulated social integration that has replaced the liberal capitalism of the last century—the humanist stance as professional representative of true value is in fact an ineffective, integrated, specialist posture that takes up its harmonious place next to the specialist representatives of other isolated elements of contemporary life. By virtue of its pretensions within a framework that protects the absolute authority of the given order, such humanism can hardly fail to exert a profoundly repressive ideological influence. There is limited merit in bemoaning the decay and disintegration of the values and meanings achieved in the course of human civilization unless one allows for their renewal and realization through the radical projects of human self-activity.

The main tradition, in any case, celebrates achieved form and order. In our time, when the existing social forms stand between the possibility of realizing the dreams of humanity (the hopes of the past) and the actuality of the nightmare evolving daily within those forms (the shapes of the past): the fetish of achieved form bears an affirmative relation to the ideology of perpetual domination, and it must accept responsibility in the reproduction of a counter-revolutionary society.

The whole Richards–Eliot tradition becomes increasingly complicit in the unfolding nightmare. This tradition of critical theory can be located on the road from the Nietzschean-existentialist death of God to the death of man announced by structuralism. It encompasses a movement from the transcendence of God to the transcendence of Man and, finally, to the transcendence of Structure and System—all set over against *historical human beings* who are denied our capacity to unite the historical and the transhistorical in a revolutionary praxis that could change history and change ourselves. It is within these coordinates that the developing theoretical paradigm matures, until it reaches, in the writings of Marshall McLuhan, the most complete fusion of all the elements of the tradition in the form of a secular religion for cyberneticized men-machines.

It is when we relate the changes in the critical tradition to their particular antecedents in literary-social history that we may be most forcefully struck by their dramatic significance. Modern critical theory represents in part the assimilation, after a long period of tension, of romantic anti-capitalist 'culture' to reified capitalist 'civilization,'[7] and the collapse of negativity into the positivity[8] of neocapitalist rationality. This is perhaps the most important analytic argument concerning the modern critical tradition that this study seeks to present, and it underpins all the formulations of evidence. Romanticism, for a long time an outsider to the positivist/utilitarian temper of the social order, has come to prevail, over the course of time, at the very centers of social ideology. It has become absorbed into the dominant discourse, but at a high cost. In the process, romanticism has been stabilized—a literary critic might say 'classicized.' The organicism peculiar to the romantic project, for example, has been preserved and sanctioned within the corporate reality of our epoch, but stripped of whatever emancipatory content or form characterized it at the source. Our own period testifies each day to the systematic *reintegration* of the culture/civilization or art/life divisions that shaped the romantic problematic and animated aspirations within it. Yet this process of reintegration, with its neoromanticizing justificatory ideology, does not occur in such a way as to make beauty and truth govern the social process but rather so as to instrumentalize image and meaning and sensibility. In consequence, any neoromanticizing outlook today, such as that embedded in the ideology of modern criticism, in so far as it accepts or embraces the prevalent social or cultural forms and their interrelationships, tends, paradoxically, not to sustain but rather to obliterate the truth of the romantic position and its intrinsic links with that Western tradition whose goal has been and continues to be full and authentic human emancipation. It appears likely, in fact, that both the modern critical tradition and the social totality to which it belongs and which in part it expresses present the development of a counterrevolution that presupposes 'the long revolution' since the Enlightenment that has been charted by

Raymond Williams but degenerates it and strives to evolve theoretical and practical forms and categories that would preclude its renewal on a higher level.

This study attempts to develop these points through a close examination of key aspects from the works of Ransom, Frye, and McLuhan. In effect, with social ontology as its framework, the study looks at theoretical responses to historical changes, and moves from the defensive reaction embodied in Ransom's theory through the capitulation that structures Frye's, to the counterrevolutionary theoretical engagement constructed by McLuhan.[9] In Part I, I examine the historical development from the roots of the tradition in the romantics, through its ground in Arnold and Pater, and its foundation in Richards and Eliot, to the North American critical theory itself. In Part II, I trace Ransom's movement toward accommodation through the Fugitive and Agrarian periods to the subsequent academic professionalism of the New Critical period, analyzing this ideological motion through his metaphysics, poetics, and theory of science. In Part III, I investigate the specific form of capitulation involved in the three components of Frye's world, namely, the poetic universe, the critical universe, and the social-cultural-educational universe. In Part IV, I argue that McLuhan's own development consists of three phases which recapitulate the development of the whole critical tradition with which they coincide in chronological time from the 1940s through to the 1960s. This reinforces the argument that these theories and their evolution are dialectical parts of a deep and far-reaching social evolution. A thorough analysis of McLuhan's cybernetic semiotic, and its relations with social, historical, and mental life, challenges on the ontological level McLuhan's counterrevolutionary religion of reified technological transcendence. In the Conclusion, I pursue the specific features of modern North American critical theory to their ideological linkages with French structuralism, and argue the connection of these technocratic ideologies with material tendencies and social struggles. Finally I suggest some essential determinants for a liberating scholarship that would be active in the revolutionary transformation of our reality.

I must stress that my interest in modern bourgeois critical theories is primarily methodological: I am concerned with the ideological way that socio-historical reality is addressed and formulated on the metaphysical, epistemological, and ontological levels, that is, in the questions that structure the theoretical appropriations, and in the assumptions that control the formulations. My substantive interest in the specific validity of the answers provided to the questions is secondary and subordinated to the exigencies of my methodological interest. In other words, the book is not primarily an attempt to replace each of Ransom's, Frye's, and McLuhan's substantive theories with one of my own. It is, on the contrary, a theoretical critique: an interrogation, a challenge, a polemic, a constitutive struggle.

Acknowledgments

I wish to express my appreciation to Donald Theall and Raymond Williams, whose confidence and encouragement have been a great help; and I want to thank Carolyn Tate, Brian Turner, and other friends who have listened to my reflections with patience, and whose responses and work have stimulated further thoughts. I am also sure the book has been much improved through the editorial interventions offered by John Nicoll. And, in particular, I want to signal my gratitude to my close friends Susan Wheeler and Mark Wilson, who have been very generous with their time and efforts throughout the processes of revising, typing, proofreading, and indexing. Also, I would like to thank *The New Republic* for their kind permission to reproduce the article 'How to Criticize a Poem' by Theodore Spencer. It is difficult to assess what goes into the writing of a study of this kind; but, as the lion's share of research and writing were done between 1969 and 1972, I should like to record my belief that without the social and cultural politics of the late 1960s this book would not have been produced.

J.F.
Toronto, June 1976

Abbreviations

A single author is examined in each of Parts II, III, and IV, and the majority of references are to the works listed below. With regard to these, I have dispensed with the full apparatus of chapter notes and have adopted the following conventions. The first reference to a work listed below is noted among the chapter notes at the end of the book according to standard procedures. In the case of subsequent references to that work, the abbreviated title and page number follow the quotation in the text and are written thus: (GWT 358). If further quotations from the same work follow closely, only the page number appears in parentheses, for example (385). In order to limit the number of abbreviations the reader needs to bear in mind at any one time, references to the works of a given author outside the part devoted to him are given in the chapter notes according to standard procedures. References to any work that has no abbreviated title are also noted according to standard procedures.

Part II: John Crowe Ransom

GWT *God Without Thunder: An Unorthodox Defence of Orthodoxy*
NC *The New Criticism*
SP *Selected Poems*
WB *The World's Body*

Part III: Northrop Frye

AC *Anatomy of Criticism: Four Essays*
CP 'The Critical Path: An Essay on the Social Context of Literary Criticism,' in *Daedalus*

Abbreviations

FI *Fables of Identity: Studies in Poetic Mythology*
FS *Fearful Symmetry: A Study of William Blake*
MC *The Modern Century*
MS 'The Knowledge of Good and Evil,' in *The Morality of Scholarship*, ed. Black
SS *The Stubborn Structure: Essays on Criticism and Society*

Part IV: Marshall McLuhan

CA *From Cliché to Archetype*
CB *Counterblast*
COB *Culture Is Our Business*
EC *Explorations in Communication: An Anthology*
GG *The Gutenberg Galaxy: The Making of Typographic Man*
LC *The Interior Landscape: The Literary Criticism of Marshall McLuhan, 1943–1962*, ed. Eugene McNamara
MB *The Mechanical Bride: Folklore of Industrial Man*
MM *The Medium is the Massage*
PI 'Playboy Interview: Marshall McLuhan . . . ,' in *Playboy*
TN 'The Place of Thomas Nashe in the Learning of His Time' (diss.)
UM *Understanding Media: The Extensions of Man*
VP *Through the Vanishing Point: Space in Poetry and Painting*
WP *War and Peace in the Global Village*

PART I

General Introduction
Structures and Genesis

CHAPTER 1
Nineteenth-Century Problematics 1

A Romantics

Modern critical theory in the Anglo-American tradition has theoretical and historical roots in the period of eighteenth- and nineteenth-century romanticism. When we seek to illuminate the scope and pattern of change by comparing the two problematics, we find on every significant level that the strategic relation between romanticism and modern critical theory resides in the radical modern inversion of the romantic framework. The decisive feature of the romantic period (in regard to this inquiry) was that historical reality was producing itself in the determinate form of a duality between 'culture' and 'civilization.' During the period of modern critical theory, this bifurcation is being resolved by the reunification of 'culture' and 'civilization' under the extended categories of neocapitalist production relations. In relation to the dominant social forms, the structural reality at the heart of romanticism was tension, negation; at the heart of modern critical theory, it is identification, affirmation. It has taken more than a hundred years to stabilize and integrate this cultural opposition, and it is valuable to record it at its source.

It is helpful to understand the romantic movement as a historical movement associated with the dynamic of liberal capitalism deep in the transformations of the Industrial Revolution. Its early revolutionary impulse was part of the struggle to liberate the productive forces, material, intellectual, and emotional, from the stultifying forms of the past, and could speak for all of humanity. The linguistic aspiration to the use of the 'natural' language of real men and the smashing of the ordered structure of neoclassical language embodied this force. Romanticism was revolutionary

3

because it sought new, post-feudal social forms; moreover its social ideal was (organic) communitarian and resisted the homogenization of social relations under the logic of the market. In the context, at first, the revolutionary energies admired and desired by Blake, Wordsworth, and others, were to be fully committed to the realization of a new society, as *The Prelude* indicates:

> Not in Utopia,—subterranean fields,—
> Or in some secret island, Heaven knows where!
> But in the very world, which is the world
> Of all of us,—the place where in the end
> We find our happiness, or not at all!

However, the deformations of the French Revolution, evidenced in the static political organicism of Jacobin justice, and of the capitalist social relations being entrenched in urban-industrial England, occluding the possibilities of creating a world of direct, unmediated personal relations in an urban life form, eventually led the romantics essentially to recoil from social and political aspiration. This is not to deny that Blake, Wordsworth, and Coleridge, Southey, Byron, and Shelley, for example, all had political experience or that they were all deeply involved in the social questions of their age. That has been adequately established by the relevant scholarship. The argument here is that their work, which came to stand in humane and imaginative cultural opposition to the oppression and exploitation of a capitalism based on factory and machine production—to the new forms of stultification and impoverishment produced by the new social rationality—came also to incarnate *contracting* claims. Their value-based notions of total social revitalization receded as the values they represented came to be expressed in terms independent of the ongoing daily advance of the society. The cultural opposition they presented took the form increasingly of a value alternative or surrogate experience outside the dominant social practices rather than the critical edge of transformations within the frame of progress; more a means of evaluation than a means of orientation for social leverage.

Of course, the basic contours of this problematic of contraction are not biographical or psychological. The problem, in part, was that while, historically, the critique of old forms was embodied in concrete forces, the romantic critique of the new capitalist forms and practices, by contrast, found no significant social force to carry it in this period, even implicitly, much less consciously and articulately.

Although certain universal values of human development were thus incarnated in the romantic movement and opposed to the class-determined material developments, historically this opposition could be only an abstract negation (with equal emphasis on 'abstract' and 'negation'). This contradiction determined the philosophically and politically uncertain attitude of the romantic critique. And as the cleavage in the historical practice of the age took shape in the form of a split between the spheres of the material production and reproduction of life, the social progress of empirical 'civilization,' and the sphere of 'culture,' of secondary objectifications and abilities, of cultivated values, the romantic critique became increasingly faced with its powerlessness and could only degenerate.

The problem became complicated as cultural distortion accompanied cultural autonomy and isolation. It could only deepen as it moved further into the nineteenth century. At the same time that the aesthetic subjectivity was precluded from active participation in the construction of the social forms, the artistic objectifications of this subjectivity entered the social sphere in the form of commodities. On one hand, the alienation of the products of his work produced the artist as alienated subjectivity and, in defensive protest against his partial proletarianization, led to a withdrawal into craft consciousness with concomitant fetishization of the form-giving function. On the other, the exclusion of the artist from socially significant contact with rich material experience and possibilities produced an impoverished aesthetic subjectivity and, in direct consequence as well as in defensive protest, led to a withdrawal into the historically enforced autonomy of the cultural sphere, with concomitant fetish of the formal elements of art. This double fetish of form had its own dynamic, and the critical quality of artistic opposition became itself progressively more abstract in the absence of adequate material expression.

The romantics were aware of the basis of capitalist production in the commoditization of human labor power, or, as Coleridge saw it, the alienation of the inalienable, 'the labourer's health, life and well-being,'[2] and over two generations they did maintain an 'uncompromising humanism.'[3] But, for them, this never meant adopting backward-looking perspectives. We find Shelley still taking joy in the results of capitalist accumulation, the prodigious development of productive forces and understanding, even while bewailing the wrongs of the world. But his revolutionary idealism already displays a social revolt forced to turn inwards. The idealization of cultural production as 'unacknowledged legislation' disguises the divorce from the social world enforced by a hostile public. Meanwhile, the abandonment of the effort to change the structure of reality appears clearly in Keats. Nature, which in Wordsworth had stood as an alternative to the ugliness of urbanization and as a response to the town-country division and the alienation of fragmentation, expresses a new disaffection from society in Keats. The privatization of the artist, the commoditization of his work, and the contempt for the audience produce a shift from social communication to formal integrity and inaugurate in Keats a defensive phase of the romantic critique.

E. P. Thompson's analysis of Keats delineates there a new conception of the relation between art and social life within which art is no longer an agency of man's struggle with nature and with himself in his development. In order to defend art in a world that excludes it, Keats redefines 'beauty' as something not found in reality but having its source in the separate world of the imagination, the subjectivity of the artist. 'Art (if we set aside a lingering faith in its refining moral influence) was conceived as a compensation for the poverty of life.' In Keats the two worlds are opposed but he continues to struggle for their reconciliation and his work is defined by the tension.[4] Subsequent work cannot keep the balance and vacillates between escapism or moralizing sentimentality—irony at best.[5] The ideal-reality division is accepted as given, the revolt declines, and values are evoked with a sense of nostalgia for the unattainable.[6]

The position of Keats is an important turning point. The idea of freedom recedes from social theory to aesthetics. Yet, given the historically produced culture-civilization duality, it was possible for the sphere of culture to become the home of an ensemble of elements that reached beyond the socio-economic world of industrialism and formed a critical dimension of reality which, in Marcuse's words, was 'in aesthetic incompatibility with the developing society,' and preserved 'images of a gratification that would dissolve the society which suppresses it.'[7] But the position is contradictory and it contains two serious internal problems.

In drawing attention to the first problem, Raymond Williams argues the crucial point that the idea of art as separate and superior reality, in reducing culture to 'art,' precludes the realization of imaginative culture as a whole way of life. Consequently, however valuable art may be as a symbol for a whole range of general human experience, it remains 'an abstraction nevertheless, because a general social activity was forced into the status of a department or province, and actual works of art were in part converted into a self-pleading ideology.'[8] In this specialization, aesthetics absorbs an element of positivity.

The second problem is that the position involves the beginnings of a consistent formalist subjectivism, the great structural crisis of modern art. Art is indeed the highest, richest, most developed form for the manifestation of human subjectivity, but this is in no way reducible to the subjectivity of a single subject. The power of art to express and intensify and evoke human subjectivity beyond that accessible in ordinary life is the power of an objectification, a formation of significant content. The escape into the subject, the displacement of attention and interest in the direction of formal, technical questions of 'how' dissociated from historical questions of 'what,' destroys the coherence of the world and impoverishes the subjectivity. This subjectivism, too, contains elements of positivity, the corollary of abstract negation: its ultimate posture towards historical reality is passive.

This passivity is an important shift, and a serious contradiction in the romantic position, one of the key contributions of which was to bring to consciousness the new mobility in the life of bourgeois society. The romantics introduced a dynamic sense of history in the view that all institutions of social and cultural production are moments of historical practice, and in their affirmation that man makes his world. Yet Hauser is right to note the other side of this historical consciousness, 'its historical mysticism, its personification and mythologization of historical forces, in brief, the idea that historical phenomena are nothing but the function, manifestations, and incarnations of independent principles.'[9] The capitalist reality that produces the historical consciousness also mystifies it in enforcing its separation from the material developments.

The same contradiction of dissociation and impotence is involved in the questions of rationality. Confined within the ideal sphere of culture, in the absence of mediations of social action, the romantic protest against the alienation of rationality necessarily collapses into irrationality. I want to stress this complementary character of rationalism and irrationalism, two one-sided tendencies internally in conflict within bourgeois development. It is the separation of bourgeois cultural practice from bourgeois social practice that reproduces the dichotomy. Precisely because it was locked into the structure of these divisions without access to significant social forces for leverage, romanticism was cut off from any historical resolution of the problem of alienated reason such as could be possible in a joint supersession of both conflicting tendencies through the praxis of socio-cultural revolution.

Here I have to pose once more the problem of this culture-civilization split, because understanding it as a historically produced structure is indispensable for understanding the problematic of modern critical theory. What I have been trying to do is to penetrate through the reified categorical duality and to see it as a determinate unity.[10] In other words, I am arguing that it is not satisfactory simply to pose the social sphere as some kind of basic reality and the cultural sphere as simply a reflection or response or derivation from it, a critique or judgment on it, a superior or inferior reality which should or should not have had a different relation with the other reality. It is only by refusing to assume these as permanent categories, or their relation as a permanent relation, that we can see the *bifurcation* of culture and civilization as *itself* the specificity of the determinate historical practice of a social formation in a given epoch. Within the duality, cultural production was to remain a persistent if contradictory and progressively weaker and more abstract and reactionary critique of the social realm. But *within* the duality, there is no solution for the increasingly problematic character of culture. It is rather a question of moving to a different level of the historical practice of the social formation as totality, that is, of superseding the duality.

This precisely is what becomes possible and necessary in the present epoch with the tendentially increasing release of human labor from productive activity combined with increasing immediate consumption.[11] The supersession of the bifurcation of 'culture' and 'civilization' *could* take place in a liberated social formation where the imagination could be a unifying principle of the production and reproduction of the totality of life. Instead, the supersession of the duality *is actually* taking place as the neocapitalist manipulative integration of all aspects of social and cultural life under its categories. And it is essential to understand that this unification is a determinate historical practice with a specific character, if we are not to fall into the abstract longing for unity that is the characteristic feature of modern critical theory. In the present context, an abstract longing for unity is increasingly counterrevolutionary in so far as it is bound to be seduced by the unification currently being realized within increasingly counterrevolutionary historical forms.

B   Post-romantics

Matthew Arnold, and then Walter Pater, Oscar Wilde, and Symbolism represent an important mid-way position in the development toward modern theory. In the post-romantic phase, 'culture' and 'civilization' are stabilized into autonomous realms. This position, in all its subsequent variations, accepts the established order as unalterably permanent. Within this stabilized division, culture attains exaggerated prominence as a superior reality. This overemphasis asserts itself in two related tendencies that restate but move beyond the romantic position of radical counterimagery[12] to the realm of social life, and anticipate the modern forms of integration in critical theory where culture re-enters social life as a key determinant. On one hand, an independent culture is susceptible to the illusions of self-determined autotelic formalization. On the other hand, once its formal integrity is ensured, an independent culture can be posited as the truth of life, its source of authority, or its governing principle, and can press the claims of its superior reality on the life of society. What makes possible for post-romantic criticism the *external* attachment of a moral or social significance to culture is the commitment to an *internal* principle of formalization, that is, precisely the deformation inherent in the achievement of cultural autonomy. The active humanist concerns and the closed formalist aesthetics of such critical theory are thus complementary.

Matthew Arnold defines 'culture' for the tradition as the study and pursuit of perfection that must be generalized to all the individuals in the society.[13] This is close to the type of cultural position that Marcuse calls 'affirmative culture,' 'the assertion of a universally obligatory, eternally better and more valuable world that must be unconditionally affirmed,'[14] a world that can be realized without changing the state of material reality. Arnold's 'culture' is still a critical negation of the prevailing 'civilization' to the extent that it raises standards in terms of which the utilitarian social and economic relations of the latter can be judged; but it does not seek seriously to intervene in those areas. Perfection, valued in opposition to 'the mechanical and material civilization,' is preserved as 'an *inward* condition of the mind and spirit,'[15] however generalized it must become, and is said to develop 'our humanity proper' over 'our animality,'[16] a distinction that remains with the tradition as a renunciation of the historical unity of human self-development. For Arnold, culture in principle does involve the effort to make perceived perfection prevail, and in this resides 'the moral, social, and beneficent character of culture.'[17] But Arnold's activism in trying to generalize perfection, in educational matters specifically, only highlights the contradiction of the tradition: the social character assigned to culture is external to the structure of culture. The internal character of culture is defined by the priority of the cognitive passion that seeks knowledge of the universal order and acts as a check on the passion for doing good which, says Arnold, is 'apt to be overhasty.'[18] Whatever its worth, agitation on behalf of 'culture' is by no means the same as social intervention in all the ways of life in the name of cultural values. The moment of historical practice, of realization on the level of the fundamental relations of human existence in society, is therefore postponed in infinite regress.[19]

In terms of this conception, the ultimate Arnoldian image of 'the harmonious expansion of *all* the powers'[20] of human nature—an anthropological vision that might legitimately point to a future supersession—is vitiated and transformed into an isolated ideological priority for the present that leaves unchallenged the forms of bourgeois class domination even as it criticizes some of its results. For by the time Arnold is writing, the bourgeoisie has seized political control and abdicated its progressive dynamic, while a proletariat has developed that cannot be easily ignored. But Arnold's view of culture, introduced into the realm of social reality, poses for the working class the idea of internal perfection as their primary need, even over a political or economic consciousness of their life activity.[21] During this period, in Arnold and even more later, culture is linked to what effectively is the class oppression of civilization. As Marcuse writes:[22]

> To the need of the isolated individual it responds with general humanity, to bodily misery with the beauty of the soul, to external bondage with internal freedom, to brutal egoism with the duty of the realm of virtue. Whereas during the period of the militant rise of the new society all of these ideas had a progressive character by pointing beyond the attained organization of existence, they entered increasingly into the service of the suppression of the discontented masses and of mere self-justifying exaltation once bourgeois rule began to be stabilized. They concealed the physical and psychic vitiation of the individual.

The *fetish* of spiritual culture falsifies the *genuine* need for spiritual culture and invalidates the truth that 'man does not live by bread alone.' E. P. Thompson rightly criticizes Arnold for expecting 'the workers to fight the battles for culture and refinement before they had fought those for bread and health' and the tendency to incorporate the working class as a vehicle for realizing objectives derived from discontents 'which had little relevance to the immediate grievances under which the class itself was suffering.' But I cannot agree that 'it was, indeed, a *great* thing for Arnold . . . to . . . turn for aid to the workers, as the least corrupted, most hopeful, element in . . . society.'[23] (My italics.) For, in relation to the subsequent tradition the ideological features of this appeal seem to me more to the point. Arnold's view is that culture, the sweetness and light which he places as objective before the workers, 'seeks to do away with classes; to make the best that has been thought and known in the world [a class-determined affirmative orientation, this] current everywhere. . . .'[24] Indeed, he contends, culture raises people out of their class to their *humanity*.[25] Even more specifically, within each class 'there are a certain number of *aliens*, . . . —persons who are mainly led, not by their class spirit, but by a general *humane* spirit, by the love of human perfection. . . .'[26] These people with culture represent our 'best self' and should constitute the 'source of authority' in the society. Thus Arnold's attempt to carry this culture to the workers involves a profound and far-reaching ideological bias in substituting the abolition of class consciousness and class identity for the abolition of class society. This Arnoldian view of a culture within which is superseded the structure of class conflict in social existence both disguises and reinforces real class domination. It has been, needless to say, a very influential view throughout the modern tradition and, in relation to the realities of social antagonism and oppression, and the possibilities of real liberation, it is a fundamentally passive position.[27]

The final point I want to bring to attention in this section about Arnold concerns his views of art and criticism. Both are seen as part of the process of culture, as expressions of the 'best self.' 'The future of poetry is immense,'[28] Arnold claims, because it resists the disintegration that has affected religion, and poetry can be our salvation as everything else fails. This perspective, which anticipates I. A. Richards and, indeed, plays the role of a central, secularized eschatology in the tradition, is again beyond the structures of social division and conflict. There are no historical specifications on poetry as 'a criticism of life'—only the 'conditions fixed for such a criticism by the laws of poetic truth and poetic beauty.'[29] In regard to criticism, Arnold defines an autotelic form which anticipates much modern theory and embodies that pure cognitive bias of neutrality that characterizes the withdrawal of theoretical activity from its role as mediator of the transformation of human life. Criticism becomes the exercise of curiosity, the 'disinterested love of a free play of the mind on all subjects, for its own sake': 'it obeys an instinct prompting it to try to know the best that is known and thought in the world, irrespectively of practice, politics, and everything of the kind, and to value knowledge and thought as they approach this best, without the intrusion of any other considerations whatever.'[30] The view is close, even in diction, to Pater and aestheticism, and finds its conditions of possibility in Arnold's view of a unified culture of class aliens whose perspectives are free of the distortions of special interest or class ideology. Such a view feeds logically into the modern streams of intellectual elitism generated by the neocapitalist production and structural integration of intellectual labor.

Walter Pater's own views are largely derivative from the tradition, and from Arnold especially, but some moments of his work need to be considered to focus the specific development of the tradition. Structurally, the art for art's sake theories still represent a resistance to the utilitarianism of the social realm, but the cost of confining aspirations to the realm of culture is the fetish of form as an end in itself, which, paradoxically, feeds back to reinforce the capitalist specialization in the division of labor. The new theory accepts the place of the artist in the division of labor and, in that context, what had been rebellion moves toward hedonism: the heightening of the intensity of the aesthetic experience. Adopting a Heraclitean stance of seeking the fleeting truth of the moment, Pater seeks experience itself as the goal, obedient only to the laws of art, devoted to art for its own sake. 'For art comes to you, proposing frankly to give nothing but the highest quality to your moments as they pass, and simply for those moments' sake.'[31] The greatest good in this aesthetic reduction of ethics is the intensity of the 'hard, gemlike flame.'[32] But where romantic passion had been a historically determined antagonistic response of individual integrity to the relativity and order of the bourgeois world, Pater's subjectivism is reduced to a non-militant personal positivism that allows the world to be no more than 'his' experience, 'his' sensation. In the attitude of an observer concerned only with his own impressions, a tear has no more meaning than a raindrop. 'Every moment some form grows perfect in hand or face; some tone on the hill or the sea is choicer than the rest; some word of passion, or insight or intellectual excitement is irresistibly real and attractive to us—for that moment only.'[33]

Three aspects of this position deserve attention. Firstly, that whatever awareness these moments produce, Pater intends to live them only on the aesthetic level. This novelty in the tradition is a building block of a general tendency (that becomes important later) to classify all realms of life into aesthetic categories: distinctions are blurred, with corresponding distancing from vital human purposes. Secondly, this is a subjectivism where all is form: there is no attempt (and no criterion) to differentiate between the human 'face' and the 'tone on the hill.' The collapse into the formalism of immediate subjectivity produces an abstract and inhuman objectivity. This paradox is fully preserved with the formalism of modern critical theory. Thirdly, although this subjectivist aestheticism will exhaust itself by reaching a dead end in its internal logic before modern critical theory begins, it does contain here a moment of the transition. For although Pater's range is limited, he wants to respond to things for what they are. The immediate consequence of this positivism has been noted: 'It is enjoyment that he is looking for, but in great part it is enjoyment that has an objective source and is controlled by the object.'[34] This leads into the fetish of the art object in modern critical theory during the period of neocapitalist subject/object inversion when reality becomes an object of contemplation and consumption.[35]

Perhaps the most distinctive feature of Pater's aesthetic is the belief in life as an art, lived as an end in itself. His aesthetic categories, including that of the typical or ideal, are projected from art to life. In *The Renaissance*, he still speaks of living intensely in the beautiful present. The essay on Wordsworth in *Appreciations* softens this ethic to living in impassioned contemplation of man and of nature. The goal of life is found in contemplation rather than action—the characteristic passivity of modern aesthetics. Two years later, in *Child in the House*, for the first time life is envisioned in terms of the ideal. Florean Deleal, the child in question, comes to conceive of religion as an idealized representation of daily life in the light of which one may orient the details of existence. This positivism, under the category of 'myth,' becomes central from Eliot to McLuhan. The climax is reached in *Marius the Epicurean* where the philosophic aspiration is to live in the 'ideal present.'[36] The function of education in this conception is to teach us to live so 'exclusively' in the ideal that 'the mere drift or *debris* of our days comes to be as though it were not.'[37] The highest goal, then, is to live in a constructed imaginative vision of the ideal.[38] This is a position of full flight; the ideal is refuge not stimulus.

Ultimately, we are dealing not with the aestheticization of life but with the reduction of life to aesthetics and, specifically, to a determinate alienated bourgeois aesthetics. A genuine transposition of aesthetic categories to life would mean the realization of aesthetics in life, that is, the imaginative, defetishized subject/object unity that is peculiar to art. It would presuppose the end of reification, of the autonomous power of objects, so that people could appropriate fully their human essence which now exists largely or only in the form of generic objectifications, including art.[39] It would take the form of the conscious relation of concrete individuals to themselves, to other people, and to human objectifications in a world remade on aesthetic-ethical-scientific principles by a conscious and self-conscious humanity. Neither Pater nor later bourgeois theorists can even approach such a conception in the absence of an interest in and commitment to revolutionary historical praxis and social liberation. Instead, Pater takes consolation in the contemplative posture of being rather than doing, a lifeless caricature of man reduced to the pitiful role of humble spectator of an illusion. In this, Pater anticipates the attitudes fostered by the modern society of the spectacle.[40]

This, in fact, is the common feature of the aestheticism at the beginning of the imperialist period and records both the decadence of upper class preference for perfect illusion to imperfect reality, and the feeling of crisis, the fear of change, of the disintegration of the known world.[41] Life is generally renounced in favor of art, and justification for life is sought in art. The significant shift in the tradition that this position represents is that the hedonism, as Hauser remarks, is no longer anti-capitalist, though it remains anti-bourgeois and anti-philistine.[42] This latter category itself is a typical reduction of the period, and expresses the deformations of the aestheticist response to reality.[43]

Oscar Wilde's 'new aesthetics,' later embraced and incorporated by Frye, is the *reductio ad absurdum* of the autonomy of art position. Its four doctrines express a profound alienation from history and society: 1 'Art never expresses anything but itself. . . . In no case does it reproduce its age.' 2 'All bad art comes from returning to Life and Nature, and elevating them into ideals. . . . The only beautiful things are the things that do not concern us.' 3 'Life imitates Art far more than Art imitates Life. It follows, as a corollary from this, that . . . external Nature also imitates Art.' 4 'Lying, the telling of beautiful untrue things, is the proper aim of Art.'[44] If Wilde can combine his sparkling but impoverished aesthetic with a general humanism, as Raymond Williams argues,[45] then that is an example of the specific contradiction I noted earlier:[46] a contradiction whose primary aspect is the cultural fetish which presupposes the abrogation of historical praxis and the resignation to the isolation of culture, and conversely, to the immutability of social reality. The humanist caught in this framework is severely limited, and lacks effective historical bearings, irrespectively of the moral depth or intensity of the humanist.

Finally, let us consider briefly some relevant aspects of Symbolist theory, influential in the English tradition since the late nineteenth century. Symbolist theory expresses a total alienation from the social world that is transfigured into an uncompromising aestheticism. It escapes into pure subjectivity, and consequently expels both genuine objectivity and rich mediated subjectivity from art. The negation of history and society is absolute and therefore absolutely abstract. The search for the transcendent reality beyond the socio-historical is the sheer despair of total frustration and impotence. Symbolism is aesthetics in crisis, protesting hysterically against commodity pressures.[47] Poetry becomes for Mallarmé the power of denial, the expression of the Idea which is absent from the empirically actual. This is, of course, the perennial ambivalence of an idealism that wants something other than what actually exists: it is both a negation of the existing reality and an accommodation to it in so far as it fails to challenge it and does not pose its material supersession.

The point of significance, however, which connects Symbolism with the modern tradition, is the problematic of language. Again, as in the case of Pater, the specific form of Symbolist subjectivism expressed in pure poetry is rejected by modern critical theory and converted into its determinate opposite, the fetish of the object. The element that is preserved is contained in the Symbolist emphasis on words. 'Poetry,' in Mallarmé's famous specification to Degas, 'is made with words, not ideas.'[48] But Marcuse has defined the shift in the problematic evocatively: 'The spectre that has haunted the artistic consciousness since Mallarmé—the impossibility of speaking a non-reified language, of communicating the negative—has ceased to be a spectre. It has materialized.'[49] The Symbolists tried to divorce meaning (signifiers) from what was meant (signifieds) in their search for an authentic language,[50] and destroyed the structure of traditional discourse in the desperate protest against the social dehumanization of language. Modern critical theory makes a fetish of language, and embraces its principles of order. In the end, both arrive at principles of transcendence.[51] The great difference between them can be sensed in the contrast between Rimbaud's insistence that the poet's function is to arrive at the unknown by the '*disordering of all the senses*,'[52] and the pursuit of unity characteristic of the contemporary ideologies of order.

CHAPTER 2

Foundations of Modern Critical Theory

A Introduction: Hulme, Richards and Eliot

Impressionist criticism presupposed shared tastes and became increasingly difficult to sustain once the unified bourgeois culture of Victorian England began to disintegrate through the dynamics of bourgeois division, proletarian development, progressive specialization, and artistic alienation. Two alternatives developed: an arbitrary and desperate open subjectivism, and a subjectivism disguised by a shift of attention to the object or objective medium. My argument is that, as this latter alternative came to prevail, the cultural sphere (which earlier had become isolated from the socio-economic sphere) then itself became split—between the subject of cultural production on one side, and the object produced, on the other. Critical interest, concentrating on the object, grew indifferent to the author's problems, practices, and purposes. The human subject, earlier stripped of historical praxis within the cultural sphere, was now expelled from the aesthetic realm even in his capacity as a conscious, purposive producer, as the subject of cultural praxis. His place there was assured only in the form of a frozen subjectivity inherent in the aesthetic object itself. The internal values of this object, meanwhile, were considered independent of the problems and historical struggles of mankind. In general, criticism developed anti-liberal features,[1] thus correlating to other features of the ongoing transformation of liberal capitalism into organized, and then programmed, monopoly capitalism.

For our purposes, T. E. Hulme's work is an important early manifestation of the change. His *avant-garde* interests and search for new forms and methods are combined with explicitly professed reaction.[2] And his prophecy of 'a classical revival,' in voluntarist

17

dismissal of the historical fact of 'a hundred years of romanticism,'[3] is itself part of a historical event.[4] There are two aspects of his work that I want to stress in particular. The first is Hulme's identification of language as the key to the poetic process. In his Bergsonian view of artistic intuition, art aims 'to see things as they really are,'[5] to achieve the precision of a classical 'dry hardness.'[6] Ordinary language, he contends, is an inadequate instrument which permits only approximations like the 'architect's curves.' It is only the poetic dislocation of this language which changes its shape and forces it into the exact curve of things as they are.[7] Although the logical separation of intuition and expression remains, the emphasis on language points toward modern critical attitudes.

The second aspect, perhaps even more characteristic of the bias of the modern tradition, is rooted deeply in Hulme's anthropology. He rejects the anthropology he associates with romantic rationalism: the view that man is naturally good but suppressed by social conventions. In its place, he substitutes the traditional Christian anthropology of man as an intrinsically limited being who cannot escape original sin.

Both positions mystify the social ontology of historical praxis which involves, at each historical level, concrete anthropological determinations, that is, limitations that man has produced and may supersede, and possibilities that man has also produced and may realize. But the significant point for this inquiry is that Hulme's renunciation of the bourgeois revolution has close connections on the ontological level with the systematic exclusion of praxis from modern critical theory. The connection is in the eternalization of the rule of man-made systems of objectification over the concrete human beings themselves. Thus we find Hulme arguing that man, 'a very finite and fixed creature,' can be 'disciplined by order and tradition to something fairly decent.'[8] In this perspective, existing conventions and order—and this latter category in our epoch has always carried the content of oppression—become the main elements of value and creativity.

At this point, before beginning the examination of the foundations of modern critical theory in T. S. Eliot and I. A. Richards, I must enter into radical dispute with Frank Kermode's influential interpretation in *The Romantic Image*.[9] In general, Kermode rejects the proclamations of war against romanticism by modern theorists, along with the latter's explicit classicist bias, by arguing that their attitudes derive with no fundamental variation from the romantic tradition of the isolated artist, separated from action, with unique access to reality through the truth of the Image, and are intelligible only in terms of this romantic tradition. Kermode's argument, I would contend, is the type of formal liberal elementalism which mystifies and distorts all its comparisons in the pursuit of isolated elements of theories. It seems to me difficult to ignore both the self-image of the modern critics as being different from the romantics,[10] and their theoretical self-consciousness in categorizing as classical the chief axis of their work: the order-disorder, or unity-multiplicity axis.[11] But it is not a question of choosing one or the other. To the extent that the romantic/classical terminology is at all useful in determining the specificity of the modern tradition, what is at work there is precisely the classicization of romanticism, the rationalization of irrationality, the socialization of individual isolation, the conventionalization of individual energy: in general, the resolution of romantic contradictions in the collapse of critical negativity into a formative positivity.

Romanticism had been a negative, critical philosophy, and modern critical theory is a positive, affirmative philosophy. That many of its elements are drawn from the romantic tradition is not in dispute. But if romanticism becomes the raw material of modern theory, its (critical) nature is transmuted in the course of integration into the new uncritical configuration. In particular, as I have argued, the commotive[12] determinations of the differential historical situation of the romantic and modern traditions are decisive. Romanticism was located in the period of exclusion of culture from the social realm. Today, cultural production is collapsing into the categories and practices of social production, and the increasingly total reification[13] of an increasingly total society is, in Adorno's words, 'preparing to absorb the mind entirely.'[14]

Modern critical theory, it is generally agreed, is founded on the work of I. A. Richards and T. S. Eliot who produced the basic perspectives for reorienting criticism toward a new object, new methodological forms, and new epistemological structure. Richards' materialism and Eliot's idealism combine to form a modified scientistic objectivism that displaces the subjectivist Bloomsbury approaches in favor of an object-centered criticism. It may be true that 'to divert attention from the poet to the poem is a laudable aim,'[15] yet, ironically, the new fetish of the text abstracted from its context in the end reintroduces the subjectivism that was meant to be avoided. Still, the New Critics themselves record a change at the source of the modern tradition. 'The net effect' of Richards' criticism, writes Cleanth Brooks, 'has been to emphasize the need of a more careful reading of poetry and to regard the poem as an organic thing.'[16] And John Crowe Ransom regards Eliot as the type of the 'intensive' critic in his methodological fixation on the text itself, as opposed to the 'extensive' or 'dogmatic' critics 'whose equipment consists in one or two ideas apiece.'[17] In other words, the modern critical tradition, from the New Criticism to McLuhan and others in the present day, inherits an intensive criticism, and entrenches general agreement with Eliot's critique of the 'lemon-squeezer'[18] view of the poem which sees it as the vehicle of a single, extractable, and communicable meaning. As the linear progress of liberal capitalism turns into the complex stabilization of change, so criticism supersedes notions of linear rationality and seeks to find the rationality of the object in the very complexity of its system.

In the study of the object, the stress falls increasingly on its material medium, the language. Modern criticism becomes part of a general tendency to fetishize language as the source of intelligibility and of social life, and the locus of the solution to all problems. In the chaos of change, it appears as the one focus that is ordered and can be controlled. Language, for Eliot, shapes experience. For Richards, the universe as known to us is a fabric constituted, continued, and maintained by language.[19] Language, in this conception, is the means to mental order, and 'the instrument of all our distinctively human development, of everything in which we go beyond the other animals.'[20] This fetish of language which abstracts it from the work process is part of that reduction of human life to epistemological dimensions that characterizes the tradition, especially in the later stages.

I want to draw attention to this linkage of the epistemological problematic with that of order. The same linkage is reinforced by the integration of epistemological strategy around myth. Much of twentieth-century thought, in drawing back from the alienation of rationality, takes refuge in mythopoeic consciousness. I cannot even outline here the many dimensions of the problem that are relevant to this study; I shall do so in examining the place of myth in the theories of Ransom, Frye, and McLuhan. For the moment, I want only to indicate the interrelation of mythology and order in the problematic bequeathed by Richards and Eliot to the tradition. For Eliot, myth is a parallel structure that serves to make 'the modern world possible for art' by bringing order: 'It is simply a way of controlling, of ordering, of giving a shape and a significance to the immense panorama of futility and anarchy which is contemporary history.'[21] And as we shall see, for Richards, for whom the true task of words is 'to restore life itself to order,'[22] epistemological space—in the second, post-scientistic, stage of his strategy to preserve for art its role as our savior—is totally occupied by myth. 'All is myth,'[23] he declares, and without his mythologies man is 'a congeries of possibilities without order and without aim.'[24] And, to add Richards' central preoccupation, it is the poetic function which bears 'the burden of constituting an order for our minds.'[25] These concerns, and Eliot's aspirations to reunify our dissociated sensibilities, combine to structure the initial matrix of modern critical theory—and the entire fabric of questions relating to the sensorium, or poetry, myth, and language, or culture, civilization, and history—as the problematic of organization, balance, and order.

One aspect of difference between Eliot and the early Richards must also be mentioned: the dispute concerning the locus of aesthetic structure. Richards' psychology stresses the process of appropriation (experience); Eliot, the object itself (language). Ultimately, as Murray Krieger has argued, the Hulme–Eliot side of the tradition succeeds in modifying the Richards side toward 'objective criticism.'[26] In any case, both sides of the dispute, *mutatis mutandis*, are explorations in the problematic of organization, balance, and order. Moreover, from the point of view of this tradition of literary criticism as a whole, what is most important about this dispute is that, in the process, drawing on both sides, the tradition becomes locked into an ideological subject/object dualism that *separates* experience and expression, instead of seeking significance precisely in their *relationship*.[27]

B T. S. Eliot

Eliot's relation to Arnold's definition of the poetic function as a criticism of life reveals the unilateral disarmament that comes to characterize modern critical theory in the face of the imposing immediacy of the world. 'If we mean life as a whole,' writes Eliot, '. . . from top to bottom, can anything that we say of it ultimately, of that awful mystery, be called criticism?'[28] This type of position, as Lukács has commented, is stuck at the level of the given immediacy of fetishized forms of life, and accepts their surfaces as permanent truth no matter how dehumanizing these are revealed to be.[29]

Eliot's view of art as 'impersonal' points up another side of the same problem. In hostility to the earlier subjectivist attitudes, Eliot aspires to 'arriving at something outside of ourselves,'[30] and proposes to assess the progress of an artist in terms of 'a continual self-sacrifice, a continual extinction of personality.'[31] The poet, he claims, has 'not a "personality" to express, but a particular medium, which is only a medium and not a personality, in which impressions and experiences combine in peculiar and unexpected ways.'[32] In this perspective, Eliot grasps one-sidedly a part of the process of homogenization that is necessary in order to rise from the heterogeneous life of particular man, living pragmatically in the everyday world according to his immediate needs, abilities, and possibilities, to the level of the human genus at a determinate historical point: the 'suspension' of particular, ego-centered subjectivity.[33] In art, as Lukács explains throughout the *Aesthetics*, this process in which the 'entire man,' artist or receiver, consciously appropriates 'man's entirety,' is effected through a homogeneous medium that draws all capacities, feelings, cognitions, and experiences into a single specific mode of concentration and permits a new, defetishized grasp of relations.[34] This aesthetic subjectivity, however, is in no way that of the particular individual of everyday life. Moreover, in concentrating all that there is of the generic within the creating subject into an objectivity, the work of art remains a personal product that bears the indelible mark of a personality in determinate relation to the human genus.[35]

Art, in other words, is not impersonal, though it is non-particular. But the fetish of immediacy and the acceptance of alienation reduce reality to the level of givens, and leave Eliot, and modern bourgeois theorists in general, incapable of grasping the full process of totalization involved in genuine artistic creation. They are unable to distinguish the privatized particularity (that must be suspended) from the personality concentrated in the conscious relation to the generic sphere. In this context, the *escape* from privatized particularity, or the *escape* from depersonalization, is confusingly itself called 'depersonalization' by Eliot and described in terms of 'surrender' to the work and to unconscious determinations in the presence of the poet's mind as catalyst. Indeed, there is a general displacement toward the unconscious in the tradition, and the impersonality theory serves in this regard to enforce transcendent factors beyond the range of conscious human powers.

This emphasis in Eliot is combined moreover with a formalist bias that exaggerates the process of the combination of elements, in the presence of the catalytic 'receptacle' of the poet's mind, over the substance or significance of these elements. It is 'the intensity of the artistic process, the pressure, so to speak, under which the fusion takes place, that counts.'[36] Marshall McLuhan, who himself makes much use of this position, notes that for Browning the immortal moment had still been one of 'ethical choice and assertion,' while Eliot's aesthetic moment is 'an affair of zoning.'[37] Aesthetic value, therefore, is divorced from the content and achieved by purely technical means. Together with the 'objective correlative' category, whose apparent neutrality makes it specifically available to manipulation, we see here the contribution to the tradition of a specifically technological aspect.

The relation of the artist to his work constitutes one side of the impersonality theory; the relation of the work to all other works constitutes the other. In this respect, Eliot shares with Hulme the stress on the fundamental formative role of tradition. It is undoubtedly true that the already existing human objectifications which each generation inherits from the past and shapes to its own needs, both material and spiritual, provide the transhistorical continuity of human existence and the indispensable condition for advance in human development. But uncritical stress on tradition falsifies this truth. It is a choice, a choice against the future, and that becomes another pillar of modern theory (reinforced by the causality in Richards' psychic contexts). The orientation is explicit and worth noting: the struggle between the old and the new is replaced by 'conformity between the old and the new.'[38] The new is from its moment of appearance situated in a continuum which it alters by the variation it introduces: a new equilibrium is reached. There is no room here for revolutionizing the existing culture. The conception is static and its main thrust is to contain and stabilize change.

To perceive this affirmation of tradition as a form of historical consciousness[39] is to miss the point. Eliot's poet who 'lives in what is not merely the present but the present moment of the past'[40] is locked into a fetish of immediacy that will vitiate his art. Only the perspective of the future provides the possibility of grasping the totality of the determinations and the nature of their motion in the present, and only the perspective of a radically different future provides the basis for a critique of the present, and for a totalization of the past, present, and future of the worlds within and without the work of art on grounds other than the static chronological continuity of what is presently given. Modern bourgeois critical theory is not opposed to time and change: it stabilizes time and change. What it abolishes is historical time, future time, time which is not the perpetuation of the present.

A central aspect of this problematic is the notion that the whole of literature (at least, of European literature) forms an ideal order of simultaneous existence, persistently adjusted, if slightly, and forever preserved as a complete order.[41] That the present epoch has opened up the past for us in new ways is true. That from this past we may appropriate values that can serve to sharpen the cutting edge of our resistance to the present and of our attempts to supersede it is also true. But it is equally true that in Eliot, and modern critical theory, the past plays no such role. Simultaneity, which in Frye is further broken down to an order of words, and is in McLuhan generalized to include all history, operates in the tradition as a formal principle that stabilizes the objects of its application into a docile system that can be contemplated and controlled. It is a scientist and technological conception, evolving toward notions of structure and system. On the methodological level, it implies antagonism to causality. In this respect, it expresses an increasingly totalitarian society in which it seems to matter little what depends on what, and also prevents the comprehension necessary to move beyond that society. Like mythic parataxis, the simultaneity principle is, on the ontological level, mired in immediacy. On the epistemological level, it stumbles among appearances. On the ethical level, it disguises the choices from the past that keep the present to its course, and deflects the choices that would link the present to a new future. And on the metaphysical level, it is a search for order within the given facts of the world.

This brings us to Eliot's famous 'dissociation of sensibility' which, in this phrase he borrowed from Rémy de Gourmont, has seemed to become a fixed star in the constellations of modern theory. As a historical explanation of psychic or aesthetic change it is feeble and inadequate. A quarter-century after introducing the category, Eliot himself admitted its weaknesses, exonerated Milton and Dryden from the terrible burden of responsibility for this evil, voiced his suspicion that the causes of the change in sensibility may not be accountable in terms of literary criticism, concluded that even the national history was too limited to explain the mystery, for which causes were to be sought in Europe, and finally abandoned the whole project by taking refuge in irrational agnosticism: 'And for what these causes were, we may dig and dig until we get to a depth at which words and concepts fail us.'[42]

As a programmatic imperative for the reunification of sensibility, however, and as a call for order, the dissociation formula remains a powerful and influential invocation which, like so many aspects of the Richards–Eliot tradition, finds its most complete development in McLuhan's reformulations. Eliot himself, in his discussion of Milton, speaks of 'the hypertrophy of the auditory imagination at the expense of the visual and the tactile.'[43] This implies that poetry requires a proper ratio of the senses, and Eliot commits his poet to balancing the senses. If dissociation is an unbalanced ratio of the senses, the function of the poem is to fuse the sensorium and, at a higher level, to fuse thought and feeling.

The following points of importance to the tradition seem to me particularly significant. The analysis reaches deeply into the human body—the alternative focus of attention to social determinations. The analysis is formalistic, posing problems in terms of proportionality, and does not relate in any serious way to the deep alienation of sensory life in capitalist society. And, finally, as I have already noted above, the problematic of organization, balance, and order structures the question of the sensorium, as it structures questions of poetry, myth, language, culture, civilization, and history.

C I. A. Richards

In turning to I. A. Richards' contributions to the modern tradition, we may observe that his concerns, at first with mental equilibrium and the internal organization of experience, and later with linguistic and mythopoeic activity, dovetail with Eliot's interests in such a way as to constitute a powerful orientation for critical theory. The epistemological and methodological shift in Richards' theoretical development toward the neo-Kantianism of his mid-1930s writings never dislocates the problematic of order as his theoretical center of gravity. Within that context, Richards' chief contributions are the religion-art-science triad, a psychological-philosophical orientation,[44] a scientistic thrust, components of a practical criticism, a linguistic-educational program, and a sense of urgency.

In the first phase, Richards provides a historical location for his theory by positing a contemporary 'biological crisis,' that is, a crisis of mental organization that can be resolved 'partly by thinking, partly by reorganizing our minds in other ways.'[45] The distinction suggests that it will be a question of something operating on our minds, and we shall note that the solution does not involve practical or social action. In general, there is an extraordinary passivity built into this founding theory of the modern tradition. What has caused the crisis of our world, according to this historical idealism, is the decline of the Magical View with the rise of science; that is, the crisis of religion. The problem, Richards tells us, has its source in the nature of science. 'It can never answer any question of the form: *What* is so and so? It can only tell us *how* such and such behaves.[46] And it does not attempt to do more than this.'[47]

This position involves a practical and technical relation to reality;[48] it is skeptical with respect to a genuinely cognitive role for science and redefines the task of science in terms that reduce the substantiality of reality to manipulable relations that can be handled through *how* questions. The positivist philosophy of science expressed in this view embodies traits of the alienation of science. It is true that there is a crisis of humanity in relation to science. However, this is not simply a crisis of religion but, indeed, a crisis of the nature, activity, and orientation of science itself. Even beyond the specific forms of complicity of modern science in serving and justifying the technical practices of class domination, its general epistemological posture (with its claims of agnosticism in relation to questions of substance and, by corollary, its claims of neutrality and indifference as regards its uses) defines its general ontological standing as an instrument that finds its logical home in the present technological order. Such alienated science loses the capability to realize the historical goal that generated it to mediate the emergence of the human world out of nature in a context of self-understanding and self-determination. This goal collapses into the self-validating rationality of capitalist science, into problem-solving on the grounds of actuality. Science abrogates the formation of a world picture that is essential to mediate historical practice beyond the present stage, subordinates cognition to the achievement of practical results, reduces ontology to technological dimensions, and thus accepts a limited function.[49]

'Nor, indeed, can more than this be done,' Richards insists, validating an alienated science for all eternity in terms of the methodological habits of positivist practice current at the time. 'Those ancient, deeply troubling formulations that begin with

"What" and "Why"—as contrasted with "How"—prove, when we examine them, to be not questions at all; but requests—for emotional satisfaction.'[50] In so disposing of religious metaphysics and of teleology as a cosmological category, Richards' methodology also happens to eliminate questions relating to the social ontology of labor, 'the only point at which a teleological project can be ontologically demonstrated as an actual instance of material reality.'[51] Thus, in effect, his position ends up obscuring the contexts in which questions regarding purpose and meaning, deep moving forces of human life, can be given historical, non-metaphysical answers referring to the production and reproduction of the totality of social existence. In consequence, he subverts the argument that problems of meaning can be resolved only through or in relation to human praxis. He himself will seek the solution in questions of mental organization.

If science will not satisfy the demand for a cognitively credible world picture, nor can philosophy or religion do so any longer. Scientific criteria, notes Richards, are in total occupation of the realm of cognitive knowledge. 'And, with that, all the varied "answers" which have for ages been regarded as the keys of wisdom are, for many minds, in danger of dissolving together.'[52] At the same time—and this is the other side of this problem for Richards—our minds must be organized, and 'we do not and, at present, cannot order our emotions and attitudes by true statements alone. Nor is there any probability that we ever shall contrive to do so. This is one of the great new dangers to which civilization is exposed.'[53] Scientific knowledge simply cannot be the basis for 'an equally fine organization of the mind'[54] as alternative modes of belief.

This distinction provides the outlines for a separation of verifiable and non-verifiable knowledge, each assigned a specific function. The argument is made on the level of linguistic discourse. From the context of alienated science and from a metonymic miscategorization—interpreting objectified forms of social consciousness (art) as merely forms of language[55]—develops a role for art as 'pseudo-statement,' determined as 'a form of words whose scientific truth or falsity is irrelevant to the purpose in hand.'[56] Thus, from the start, art is situated under the shadow of scientific categories and absorbed into the ground of its alleged polar opposite. The duality, consequently, is inherently unstable, and this strategy for 'finding a place for poetry in a scheme of things where science was the norm'[57] was bound, even by its internal logic, to fail.

27

The interpretive debates about Richards' 'pseudo-statement,' concerning whether poetry merely refers to the author's feelings and whether the emotional power of poetry depends on objective reference to something other than emotion itself,[58] tend to miss the point. As it happens, Richards accepts that a cognitive component is necessary for poetry, at the same time that he emphasizes that the cognitive component is necessarily subordinate to other factors in the functioning of the whole. But what is most important in this relates to the definition of pseudo-statement as 'a form of words which is justified entirely by its effect in releasing or organizing our impulses and attitudes (due regard being had for the better or worse organizations of these *inter se*)'.[59] This view of art raises magical or technological expectations, and reduces art to the same everyday pragmatism that, as I suggested earlier (p. 26 and n. 49), alienated science in decisive respects failed to move beyond. In this regard, Richards' 'continuity doctrine' linking the poetic activity to everyday life, embraced so enthusiastically by Stanley Hyman as 'the view that revolutionized criticism and began its modern movement,'[60] is based in the fetish of immediacy. This controls an alienated aesthetic derived from the problematic of alienated science with a basis in the alienation of everyday existence.

Richards asserts that scientific statements and non-scientific pseudo-statements are functionally different but both necessary. In his reasoning, the danger lies in our myths defiantly challenging scientific cognition on its own grounds and destroying themselves in the process of fighting a lost cause. Pseudo-statements must be recognized as *pseudo*-statements whose primary function is not the provision of verifiable knowledge but the ordering of our attitudes. 'Their work is not that of science; as they do not give us what science gives, so science cannot give us what they give.'[61] The whole crisis can be resolved through correct categorization: 'The remedy . . . is to cut our pseudo-statements free from that kind of belief which is appropriate to verified statements.'[62] The crisis, of course, like every other problem in Richards, is interpreted as a problem of misunderstanding and hence is accessible to resolution on the level of consciousness.

'The conflict should never have arisen,' he writes, but if it goes on, with all our organizing myths crumbling around us, 'a moral chaos such as man has never experienced may be expected.' But all is not lost. 'Our protection is in poetry. It is capable of saving us, or since some have found a scandal in this word, of preserving us or rescuing us from confusion and frustration. The poetic function is the source, and the tradition of poetry is the guardian, of the suprascientific myths.'[63] This apocalyptic faith in the power of art (and in the power of the critical theory that talks about art) to effect our salvation has been preserved in the tradition in Ransom, in Frye, and in McLuhan. And if Richards has tried to eliminate (typically, by changing signifiers, substituting 'rescuing' for 'saving') the stigma of eschatological scandal, he has neither tried nor managed to eliminate the stigma of passivity that structures the whole conception.[64]

Before leaving this stage of Richards' aesthetic theory, there are several more aspects to consider. Like all ideological analyses that use biological models, Richards' formulation of the mind projects a social paradigm. The mind for him is a system of interests which 'must come into play and remain in play with as little conflict among themselves as possible.' Each impulse of experience is to have 'the greatest possible degree of freedom.'[65] Conflicts of interests are to be resolved not by conquest but by conciliation.[66] At the same time, we want the kinds of experiences that will involve the greatest number of impulses. 'For if the mind is a system of interests, and if an experience is their movement, the worth of any experience is a matter of the degree to which the mind, through this movement, proceeds towards a wider equilibrium.'[67] This is the first approximation to a functional equilibrium that will find its speculative elaboration in Frye and its full development in McLuhan. It is a balance and conciliation model that posits an infinity of particulars held together in perfect equilibrium as the ideal. The units of this system are not seen as the condition for the realization of the freedom of the other units, but only as the source of possible interference with other units. With its stress on integration, the logic of this liberal model points toward mass society. On the literary level, its static concern with a state of equilibrium and reconciliation of opposites will find its first renewal in the New Critical theories of irony.[68]

The theory of value involved here is important, for that is the decisive connection between Richards' psychology and aesthetics. It has often been noted that this value theory is a purely quantitative model stressing the degree of organization of impulses. The optimum number of impulses an experience organizes and the increased capacity for impulse organization it may produce are the criteria of value.[69] At the same time, communications, for example poems, embody a certain combination of impulses which can be transferred.[70] W. H. N. Hotopf argues that the indifference to the content of what is organized means that this communicative transfer 'has unlimited scope, and Man can be saved by the right kind of education, one which by the economical means of symbols will make Man's structure correspond to that of the Universe.'[71] This formalization, that excludes action, purpose, and the social context from its considerations, and always looks to education for improvement, comprises, in embryo, the whole development of the tradition up to McLuhan.

Now, the poet, in Richards' view, gives order and coherence to experience through words that adjust the impulses to one another.[72] 'The greatest difference between the artist or poet and the ordinary person is found . . . in the range, delicacy, and freedom of the connections he is able to make between different elements of his experience.'[73] The artist connects more impulses in a broader field of stimulation than the ordinary person,[74] and, value being the optimum satisfaction of impulses, the works of these experts 'in the "minute particulars" of response and attitude'[75] occupy a key place in the hierarchy of value. The aesthetic experiences are 'ordinary experiences completed,'[76] 'the most formative of our experiences because in them the development and systematisation of our impulses goes to the furthest lengths.'[77]

There are three points to be made about this position. Firstly, Raymond Williams is surely right to argue that 'the idea of literature as a training-ground for life *is* servile';[78] but one must add that there are in any case, no case histories in Richards of any actual lives being enriched by literature and then being objectified in liberating practice. The input-output cycle is blocked at the level of the hypothesized input. This is a historically motivated blockage that persists throughout the tradition. Secondly, the position manifests a contempt of and an alienation from social-practical life. On one hand, this expresses the real impoverishment of life in this epoch where, indeed, the appropriation of the human essence by each individual is impeded, and the already developed values of humanity do exist primarily in the form of such objectifications as art. But, on the other hand, it accepts and theorizes the alienation and, in ideological practice, perpetuates it forever. This naturalization of alienation is also reproduced, *mutatis mutandis*, at every stage of the tradition.

Thirdly, we come to the most important point. This theory brings together, *in a new unity*, a view of art as a superior reality on one hand and, on the other, the fetish of immediacy[79] that characterized utilitarian value theory. Polarities that had been opposed for a hundred years, since the romantic protest against the logic of industrial capitalism, are blended together in this quantitative value theory[80] that sees art as its highest realization. What is more, the valorization of art now finds its basis at the level of immediacy (in the pragmatism of organizing the optimum number of everyday impulses and of increasing to the optimum the capacity for impulse organization). The position is the first major step in the social assimilation of the romantic tension. What results from this new combination is a demoralization of aesthetics and an aestheticization of morality which remain and intensify as the tradition develops.

In the remainder of this section, I shall briefly indicate the outlines of Richards' second stage of theoretical development. Since the detaching of poetry from science in the way proposed failed as a convincing foundation for the poetic function, Richards shifted to absorbing science in myth: the inverse of the earlier position. Meaning, in the first phase, was treated as a psychological problem. In the second phase, Richards makes the transition to an epistemological problematic, and this part of the theory stands in the tradition as the initial moment of epistemological reduction.

Richards now explains that[81]

> while any part of the world-picture is regarded as not of mythopoeic origin, poetry—earlier recognized as mythopoeic—could not but be given a second place. If philosophical contemplation, or religious experience, or science gave us Reality, then poetry gave us something of less consequence, at best some sort of shadow.

Consequently, Richards turns to the neo-Kantian epistemology of a formative consciousness that constitutes and maintains the world of our experience through mythopoeic linguistic activity.[82] This new orientation is taken to be a shift toward a cognitive role for art and is welcomed by the tradition that follows Richards. For us, its valuable moments are cancelled by the reduction of human reality, in its production and appropriation, to the epistemological level. Although it posits an active role for man in relation to his universe, it is a theoretical Trojan horse in the tradition: a treacherous gift that eliminates the historical praxis without which there is no active man. 'For what is there,' asks Richards, 'of which we can think or speak, which is not a hypostatized abstraction?'[83]

It should be clear that in the new orientation Richards retains the problematic of order. Mythology, in his analysis, unifies our powers, orders our possibilities, and controls the growing order of the mind in response to the Universe.[84] And as in the earlier stage, poetry and this centrality of order bear a special relationship. 'If we grant that all is myth, poetry . . . becomes the necessary channel for the reconstitution of order.'[85]

In this period, very significantly for my argument, Richards adopts for his dominant image Coleridge's aeolian harp (wind harp), which he takes to exemplify the coalescence of realist and projective epistemologies. Prose discourse, he claims, invariably slips into one or the other fallacy, either realist or projective. Either it represents percepts and concepts as identical to the things themselves, or it represents them as embodying mental projections that display only the mind and not nature at all. It cannot speak without error the unity of objective nature and mind. It cannot express accurately the object from whose relations with us originate our needs, but which we know only through the projection of a subjective sensibility.[86] Our needs come from our relation to nature, but our categories of cognition come from the mind, projected in response to independent objective nature, in order to satisfy our needs. This unity of object and subject is linguistically embodied all at once only in poetry. It alone is able 'to preserve us from mistaking our notions either for things or for ourselves.'[87] On the basis of this subject/object unity which it speaks, comes the formulation: 'Poetry is the completest mode of utterance.'[88]

What has to be emphasized here is that the subject/object problem, the problem of unity, cannot be resolved by a sleight-of-hand reduction to an epistemological moment. It is a problem that has to be addressed on the level of historical ontology, and consists precisely in the abolition of reification, in the reappropriation of human subjectivity, of productive praxis, now alienated and sold as a commodity, and in the conscious appropriation of the already developed human powers presently reified in our objectifications that today rule over us. In other words, the subject/object unity is a question of changing our relation to the world.

Genuine art, Richards perceives correctly, is a subject/object unity. But this is so because it makes sensible a defetishized world, a man-made world. And every genuine work of art offers an ethical perspective on the future in that it gives objective form to a generic value hierarchy that is chosen and structured with a view to the destiny of mankind. This aesthetic ontology is not preserved when the aesthetic subject/object unity is represented as merely an epistemological attitude in the world at large, and even less when human comportment in the world is pictured on the model of the aeolian harp. The aeolian harp, whether in Coleridge or in Shelley's *Defence*, is primarily an instrument, and only in an alienated reality does man behave as an instrument. Even more significantly, any aeolian harp type of behavior is hopelessly anchored in the never-ending present; it dissolves everything into the moment; it has no bearing on the future.[89] In this respect, of course, the aeolian harp is an appropriate image that incarnates the specificity of the theory: the fetish of immediacy.

I have been examining the structure of the foundation that Eliot and Richards built for modern critical theory. In concluding this section I want to review some of the explicitly programmatic imperatives that Richards left for the tradition. Positivist philosophy in general was very excited about the possibilities involved in the analyis of linguistic statements, in the belief that all genuine questions were answerable. Richards himself throughout his writings retains an interest in language and its influence on the mind, and has an abiding faith in education as a means of bringing linguistic awareness that will eliminate the chief problems of mental organization. If incorrect linguistic theories and linguistic distortions can cause errors in thought, two possible cures come to mind, Hotopf argues: change the language or change the user—that is, make the user more aware. Richards' position, typically, was that 'one must only interpret, never try to change, which would be interfering.'[90] In consequence, throughout his work, there is a focus on the theory and practice of language. The search for meaning in the world is transferred from the realm of concrete life to the realm of words.

In this context, Richards raises the problematic of communication which, especially in connection with mass culture, becomes so important later on in the tradition. 'A large part of the distinctive features of the mind are due to its being an instrument for communication';[91] 'the arts are the supreme form of the communicative activity';[92] and 'the two pillars upon which a theory of criticism must rest are an account of value and an account of communication.'[93] In *Practical Criticism*, Richards offers the strongest formulation of this position, anticipating the subsequent elimination from the tradition of all valuation, by posing that as a logically and chronologically secondary activity:[94]

> That the one and only goal of all critical endeavours, of all interpretation, appreciation, exhortation, praise or abuse, is improvement in communication may seem an exaggeration. But in practice it is so. There is, it is true, a valuation side to criticism. When we have solved, completely, the communication problem, when we have got, perfectly, the experience, *the mental condition* relevant to the poem, we have still to judge it, still to decide upon its worth. But the later question nearly always settles itself. . . .

How much a principled emphasis on communications always means in practice a distraction of attention from the substantive and structural problems and antagonism involved in the communications situation, we shall see later in this study. For the moment I am concerned only to note the program.

Once this kind of attitude was generalized, it needed only specifications that Richards supplied amply and repeatedly. In *The Meaning of Meaning*, Richards and Ogden discover defenses 'against the pitfalls and illusions due to words.' It becomes the task of Grammar to train 'every user of symbols' in these as 'preliminaries for the right use of language as a means of communication.'[95] Richards discovers in *Practical Criticism* 'the inevitable ambiguity of almost all verbal formulae,'[96] and calls for 'the diagnosis of linguistic situations, systematic ambiguity and the functions of complex symbols,'[97] and for 'a systematic discussion of the forms of meaning and the psychology of understanding.'[98] He makes the recommendation 'that an inquiry into language . . . be recognized as a vital branch of research, and treated no longer as the peculiar province of the whimsical amateur.'[99] The institutionalization of literary studies that Eliot recognized as a cause of the transformation of literary criticism[100] is here explicitly demanded and becomes realized with the New Critics, accompanied, as we shall see, by the disastrous effects that accompany specialization.

Richards further contributes to the New Critics a stress on metaphor, 'the omnipresent principle of language':[101] 'A better understanding of metaphor is one of the aims which an improved curriculum of literary studies might well set before itself.'[102] Then, having announced that 'an absence of syntax is a favourable condition for Imagination,'[103] Richards again defines the task of criticism, making the orientation unmistakable: 'to recall that poetry is the supreme use of language, man's chief co-ordinating instrument, in the service of the most integral purposes of life; and to explore, with thoroughness, the intricacies of the modes of language as working modes of the mind.'[104] Indeed, 'the study of the modes of language becomes, as it attempts to be thorough, the most fundamental and extensive of all inquiries.'[105] In this way, the modern tradition, right at its inception, has a fully contemporary ring, linked at the extremities with the Russian formalism that preceded it and the French Structuralism that now dominates the field, and, through the course of the development of the tradition, with the emphases of Ransom, of Frye, and, especially, of McLuhan.

Finally, Richards contributes *Practical Criticism* to the tradition: perhaps the first example of close reading of individual texts on a large scale. Analogous to the practice of anthropological functionalists such as Malinowski, whose work appeared within the covers of Ogden and Richards' *The Meaning of Meaning*, the study of these protocols was Richards' fieldwork. In Richards, as in the New Critical contextualisms, the character of the new practical criticism bears close similarities to the functionalist practices of fieldwork. The interdependence of all the parts of the object under examination is postulated so that no priorities can be specified. The heresy of paraphrase and other evils are methodologically excluded. All facts are presumed equal. The whole is to be studied as an organic unit. There is a general functionalist theory of coherence (of impulses, of verbal units, of oppositions), but the approach to each specific object is in terms of *ad hoc* specifications. The exclusive focus on the formal integration of the object, the extreme empiricism of method, the elevation of practical criticism to the level of a *sine qua non* for criticism, the isolation of the resulting studies from their historical context, their negligible comparative value owing to the stress on internal empirical criteria—all these, plus the establishment of the problem of order as the key 'scientific' problematic, are ideological similarities in two different fields of modern theory at a determinate historical time. The second phase of critical development, in Northrop Frye (as in Radcliffe-Brown), seeks to develop a theory to coordinate the fieldwork and guide it, to link individual units on the basis of a single structural variable, the archetype, as the key to integration. And the third phase of the tradition, as in McLuhan or Parsons, develops a full hierarchical paradigm with systematic organization and specified linkages.[106]

In practical criticism, too, Richards was programmatic for the tradition, and I offer these comparisons for their heuristic value. In closing this section, perhaps the most important point is to recall that in Richards, as in Eliot, it is always the problematic of order that structures the theoretical formulations as their immanent finality. And, in this sense, the most decisive feature of the Richards–Eliot foundation for modern critical theory, a feature that reverberates throughout the tradition, is the programmatic mystification of totality.

CHAPTER 3

Paradigm in Motion

My purpose in this section is to make some introductory remarks in the nature of a kind of overview of Ransom, Frye, and McLuhan, their interrelation, and their theoretical development from what I have called defensive reaction to counterrevolution. At every level this tradition involves paradoxes composed of permutations and combinations of the relations of art, science, and religion. It is the initially anti-rationalist, anti-scientific Ransom who introduces the scientific outlook into American criticism and prepares the ground theoretically for the entry of technicism. Frye becomes the main advocate of scientific criticism, which he attempts to found theoretically for the modern tradition. But his bias is mythological, his writing mythomorphic, and his critical system is erected on a religious medieval exegetical schema. And McLuhan, starting from an explicitly religious and anti-technological position, eventually emerges as the most influential modern spokesman for technological rationality. Art and science, which are complementary and convergent forms of social consciousness, are explicitly opposed to one another, while literary criticism itself seeks to become science. Art and religion, which are, in principle, irreconcilably opposed forms, are merged.[1] In the text of this study I try, on one hand, to situate these paradoxes in a continuous theoretical and ideological tradition, and, on the other, to indicate the character and development of this tradition as the inescapable *prise de position* of determinate theoretical attitudes in regard to the prevailing social reality.

The movement of the paradigm in the process of its formation manifests an increasing rationalization and systematization. In its later stages, with Frye and McLuhan, critical theory breaks new ground in evolving new strategies, based on analogy and myth, for overcoming the problems that contingency and quality have customarily posed for logical, quantitative rationalization. But in the course of such increasingly comprehensive formalization, the place of the aesthetic principle in the social totality is distorted because isolated formal and technical elements are given priority.

In terms of the development as a whole, in Ransom's writings art is still sustained in opposition to the prevailing reality. In Frye's conception, art is radically separated, on the genetic level, from history; history, it is said, has no role in its production. Meanwhile, on the structural level, as a central structural principle *within* civilization, it is constitutive of the prevailing reality. The unity of this position, as we shall see, is a surrender to what exists. Finally, in McLuhan's work, art re-emerges explicitly on the other side, at the service of the given order, actively helping in the consolidation of its operations. The function of art becomes to navigate our adjustment to the independent technological transformations of the whole of our internal and external life. In the movement from Ransom's art (as the cognition of 'the world's body'), to Frye's art (as a 'power to be possessed' in its capacity as the language of social ideology), to McLuhan's art (as the navigational guide that shows us 'how to ride with the punch instead of taking it on the chin'), modern critical theory makes its transitions from Richards' and Eliot's concerns with the role of art in the integration of the personal psyche to defining a role for art in the problematic of social cohesion. While Ransom's work still testifies to a certain awareness of the falsity of established life, Frye's awareness is ambivalent and absorbed, and McLuhan is a conscious apologist.

The New Critical fetish of the object, which abstracts it from the process of aesthetic homogenization in both its production and appropriation, produces a false critical dualism that opposes a view of the object as a closed, self-contained language construct against a view of the object as a transparent expression in language of some antecedent content. Both views distort the form-content problem and obscure the decisive questions related to the specific and historically determinate relations among experience, expression, and appropriation.[2] From this methodological depravity, it is an easy step to the complete separation of form from content in Northrop Frye, and to postulating, as he does, that the primary context of literary objects resides in their formal interrelations within a rationalized field, an order of words. The next major transition is to the work of Marshall McLuhan, in which the accumulated notions of the tradition of literary theory are employed in new and powerful ways designed for the broader field of communications and social theory. Here, cultural technology forms a socio-biological language whose formal determinations shape and rule over people who are regarded as servomechanisms, and the new role of aesthetics is to enable the human servomechanisms to function appropriately. An ever-deepening renunciation of value and content in strategic areas is a gauge of the successes of modern critical theory in assimilating the moments of anti-capitalist tension in its heritage.

The scope of the changes in the historical orientation of the tradition can be indicated, for example, through the changes in the category of 'contemplation.' For Ransom, contemplation stands, despite the reactionary character of his categorical framework, in subjective opposition to any instrumental logic. For McLuhan, contemplation becomes a subordinate category at the service of, and indispensable for adaptation to, the prevailing and autonomous instrumental rationality. In the course of such a radical transformation of the category, although this may appear as a paradox, the contemplative, reified attitude to the given actuality is powerfully fortified. The distance between these two forms of the 'contemplation' category is the ideological distance between reaction and counterrevolution.

The contemplative attitude, I should add, is a significant feature of a formalist tradition in its appraisal of separated structures and functions, forms and contents. Like earlier humanists, these modern critics are not formalists in any sense of limiting their attention to artistic form and excluding social reality from their field of vision. They write profusely about their concerns in a social dimension. What situates modern critical theory as a formalist tradition is the formal-ism manifest in the escape from the historical character of objects in the direction of fetishized form, with the consequent violation of specific form-content relations and, through the generalization of specific forms, the dissolution of human possibilities within the established modes of actuality. Ultimately, ultra-formalism expresses the epistemic decadence associated with the contemplative comportment that is displacing defetishizing historical praxis within the 'society of the spectacle.'

PART II

John Crowe Ransom

The Critical Theory of Defensive Reaction

CHAPTER 4

Introduction to John Crowe Ransom

The response of American capital in the 1930s and 1940s to its structural crisis was a great, manipulative social integration based on Keynesian transformations. This was made possible, not only by economic factors, such as a vast scale of production able to rely on a vast internal market, but also by cultural factors, such as the absence of effective interference from any major anti-monopolist cultural forms or traditions. The neocapitalist rationalizations involved, not only the efficient organization of working class energies as labor power, stabilized in the new labor groupings, but also, among other things, the assimilation of such cultural/ideological opposition, coming from radicals on the right, as was cast in pre-capitalist forms. In this historiographic context, the study of the development and categorical structures of the New Criticism is a case study in the ideological evolution of a right opposition, and in the dynamics of social integration.

The New Criticism, so called after John Crowe Ransom's book in 1941 with that title, was not the first 'new criticism'[1] but by far the most significant one. It produced consciously a transformation of literary ideology which had the effect of inaugurating, on the level of the theory and practice of literary criticism, the process through which 'culture' was to occupy a new place within the realm of neocapitalist 'civilization.' The New Critical movement was very successful and vastly influential. It dominated the field of theory for over a decade (roughly from the time of the disintegration of US Communism in the second half of the 1930s, that is, the beginning of social integration under Roosevelt, to the anti-Communist hysteria in the late 1940s, that is, the beginnings of consolidation under Truman), and the field of critical practice for several further years. It built an institutional basis so broad and firmly entrenched that to this day, although no longer the dominant form, New Criticism constitutes a substructure of modern critical theory.

Its methodological principle of close attention to textual detail, adopted from T. S. Eliot and I. A. Richards and intensified as a fetish, was hailed as early as 1941, even by a severe critic, as an impressive and unprecedented achievement,[2] and has remained a permanent contribution to the tradition. Some have viewed the New Critical success as primarily the success of an attempt, 'for the sake of our complete humanity,' to formulate 'a new "apology for poetry"' in opposition to both scientism and aestheticism.[3] Others have hailed it as the success of a 'rebellion, in the cause of literature, against unliterary and uncritical academicism,' and of a humane response to the 'modern necessity' for creating 'a structure of value in the midst of chaos.'[4] Such perspectives, however, allow the self-image of the New Critical project to take the place of an analysis that might penetrate below the surface of immediate description. I am going to try, in what follows, to situate the New Criticism in the context of commotive changes.[5]

The key figure is John Crowe Ransom, poet, teacher, critic, theorist, and editor. He was the leading member not only of the New Critical phase of the development, but also of its two antecedents, the Fugitive and Agrarian phases.[6] Foster is right to call him 'philosopher general to the New Criticism';[7] and it is in that capacity that Ransom acted for over a quarter of a century as navigator of the transition, not only of a group of Southern intellectuals from Fugitive to Agrarian to New Critic, but, in the process, and more significantly, of critical theory to a new social location. It is this movement that is decisive for the history of literary ideology, and it was primarily Ransom, not Tate, Brooks, or Robert Penn Warren (the other major Southern critics) who prepared and operated the transition to new corporate accommodation. It is for this reason that Ransom becomes the focal point for this stage of the analysis.

István Mészáros has noted the major role of 'outsiders' in the history of philosophy, ranging from Socrates to Lukács. 'Philosophical generalizations always require some sort of *distance* (or "outsider-position") of the philosopher from the concrete situation upon which he bases his generalizations.'[8] In view of the precedents, we should not perhaps be surprised in principle that what became the dominant literary ideology of the whole of the United States should have been developed in the economically backward South. What we must look into, however, are the homologies that account for the fullness with which this specific theory satisfied the requirements of the whole cultural and ideological field.

To understand the New Criticism, we have to understand the contribution to it of the Fugitive and Agrarian phases. Examining the development phenomenologically, we shall find, in the chapters that follow, first of all an escapist Fugitive moment. This comprises the self-image of an outcast seeking refuge in an ideal realm, in the idealization of an interiority that is externalized and shared in the form of works of art. The position is characterized by rootlessness, hence the search for a cold technical objectivity. Subsequently, in the Agrarian phase, this moment modulates into a militant interiority that is externalized in the form of the ideal life (called 'the aesthetic life') in place of the real one that is severely criticized and rejected. Thus the escape into the ideal is replaced by the attempt to make an ideal real. This Agrarian challenge to the overpowering reality is not only a complete failure; *it is anticipated to be a failure, and is fought as a lost cause.* In consequence, the failure is irrevocable and becomes the condition and motor for a new reconciliation in the third, New Critical, phase.

Where Agrarianism seeks to present itself as socially and economically programmatic for an aesthetic life as a totality to which art as such is to be subordinated, the New Critical perspective, as we shall see, confines the broad scope of Agrarian ideology within the bounds of a literary criticism that champions art in safety from *within* the non-aesthetic life of the existing society. All possibilities of reshaping the exterior world are renounced to gain social sanction for the perfection of the interior world, the sensibility, through the strictly literary experience of life. We find, too, that the strong Agrarian critiques of industrialism are reduced to a critique of science, then to a critique of abused science, until, finally, peace is made altogether in the New Critical period, and the primacy of science is acknowledged. The New Criticism becomes widely known and influential as the defender of art by virtue of its view that art is necessary for truly human life and for knowing the world; but this is both knowing and living with the *established* reality through the contributions that the aesthetic sensibility can make. From the time of the Agrarian failure, the progression is an inexorable one toward the integration of critique into dominant rationality.

We can now penetrate to the deeper historical forces prompting these changes, and identify the ground for the adequation of the theory to the dominant social *telos* in a way that will account for Ransom's reversals of position, for the integration of his critique, and for the thrust of his defense of art. The interwar period saw a rapid industrialization of the South—an invasion by Northern monopolies. Both urban and rural traditional petty bourgeoisie were being declassed. The South was changing its forms of existence, and Ransom and the others were a minority with no significant links to the social life of the present. As Fugitives, they sought refuge in poetry and metaphysics; as Agrarians, they attempted one last struggle for the survival of the traditional social class to which they belonged by background and social position. But Ransom and the Agrarians developed no organizational forms for their aspirations. When, inevitably, their ideological endeavors failed to translate themselves into the material results they desired, Ransom was able to lead them to a new social location as part of the new professional (academic) intelligentsia. There, within new boundaries and positive social sanctions, the group could define their position as representatives of metaphysical and aesthetic value.

As Fugitives, they had tried to resist their social dislocation on the grounds of culture, for which, as Agrarians, they attempted and failed to gain a socio-economic basis. Their defense of culture, in the absence of socio-economic content, was empty reaction referring back to an idealized past. In their integrated relocation, they could now press their cultural claims with new substance and new authority deriving from their newly acquired place in the social process. Their methodological (and ultimately historical) range, however, was now limited to the confines of their new home, the neocapitalist totality. Their work gained historical validation at the expense of scope and critical edge.

Simultaneously, a structural transformation of the social formation was taking place, including the capitalization of culture. It was precisely this transformation that made it possible for the New Critics to emerge as a significant group. Art and values, in this context, were in internal crisis, but also threatened from outside by conflict with an ascendent scientism, and hence in need of a base for defense. But this defense would have to facilitate the transition of art and values to their new place in social life, and relieve the strains of the whole transformation.

The convergence of the two sides of this commotive problematic finds material realization in the academic humanities, itself made possible by the neocapitalist requirements for the expansion of education. As we shall discover, the New Criticism, as an academic specialization, preserves the escapist Fugitive moment, no longer as an abstract negation but as integrated tension. It preserves as well, as constitutive moments, the Agrarian protest (now evolving into a harmless, smug or helpless, scorn for a science that is no longer challenged), and, especially, the Agrarian failure (now translated into a rejection of all socio-historical dimensions). In this form, the New Critical cultural apology can serve as the adequate ideology for the changing role of culture in the 1930s and 1940s. Both sides of the convergence embody a contradiction between the inexorable magnet of integration and the cultural opposition to this integration[9]—an opposition that cannot succeed in the absence of social forces that can bring about the supersession of the whole historical problematic. The important point is that through his concerns with a traditional ontology slipping away from him in the social, economic, cultural, and religious spheres, and through his search for a new ontology, Ransom is able to develop out of the internal dialectic of his own historical position outside and somewhat distanced from the society as a whole, the adequate cultural ideology for a social formation itself in transition of social ontology, of the basic forms of its life, of the production, reproduction, and communication of its world. And as Ransom's long Odyssey terminates in finding a new place within the social pattern, so too the even longer Odyssey of 'culture' back to the realm of 'civilization' from which it had been separated in the nineteenth century begins to come to an end.

To round out this analysis, I want to indicate very briefly an aspect of the ideological situation that contributed to the concrete possibility for the New Critical ideology to assert itself and prevail. The structural crisis of liberal capitalism that produced the First World War also meant that the following decade was a time of spiritual crisis, of disillusionment, disaffection, and dissent. The traditional reference systems of religion, morality, social mythology, and ideals were disintegrating. Personal escape combined with social protest, and both cynicism and the search for an alternative, non-bourgeois future, were important determinants of the culture profile of the period, in literature as in literary theory. The 1929 crisis and the years following it effected a change in this picture. Roosevelt at the head of the US government, in the interest of the capitalist class as a whole, introduced the first major phase of the regulation and integration of social forces through the intervention of the state. In the field of aesthetics, by the 1930s, liberalism had declined as a creative force, and the reactionary Neo-Humanists were experiencing a second phase of influence, defending gentility through pre-capitalist standards developed earlier by Paul Elmer More and Irving Babbitt. They condemned everything from humanitarianism and feminism to labor unions and popular education.[10] The main point is that their position was extra-literary and non-aesthetic. By the same token, as capitalism was seen to be unstable, the possibility of radicalism in literary criticism as in economics arrived, and Neo-Humanism disintegrated. Marxist criticism, 'a negligible force at the beginnings of the '30s,'[11] became influential, and, although it was doctrinaire and failed to deal with the decisive formal aspects in the relations with content, it established important social dimensions for literary study.

But Marxist criticism was fatally tied to the Communist Party, and fatally undercut by the latter's surrender to New Deal capitalism after 1935. The anti-fascist common front policy of the Party, and their newly developed position that capitalism would be able to realize the Communist goals of peace and prosperity, imposed a general impotence on Marxist aesthetics. Philip Rahv noted at the time that Marxist criticism lost its function if it was to be abolished as critique by an enforced cooperation with the bourgeoisie:[12]

The orientation towards capitalist democracy has deprived the proletarian writers of those political values which alone distinguished them from the non-proletarians. . . . As for Marxist criticism, it finds itself with less and less work on its hands. All that the Marxist critics can do is write conventional pieces with a slight social edge or else compose political polemics against the 'counterrevolutionary fascist-aiding Trotskyites.'

In other words, the internal inadequacies of the Marxist criticism of the period, in combination with the disastrous consequences of the surrender of the Party in the United States and of the politics of the Soviet Union in its domestic purge trials, its policy in Spain, and its pact with Hitler in 1939, produced the complete ideological collapse of the Marxist movement and of Marxist criticism by the end of the decade.[13]

It is useful to emphasize this development for two reasons. On one hand, it is valuable to bear in mind the moments and forms of ideological struggle and stasis that are an important part of modern US history, and to situate the New Criticism as an ideological alternative to the Marxist criticism. On the other, it helps to recall that the New Criticism which, in its Fugitive form, first developed in the 1920s, gained its real influence only after the 1930s with the collapse of the Marxist movement in the United States and the collapse of Agrarian politics. In the 1920s, the form of Fugitive literary theory was aesthetic, disillusioned, and traditional. In the 1930s, in the economic transition and under pressure of the struggle for the future of the society, the Agrarians, like Eliot, emphasized extra-literary considerations in opposition to those of Marxist sociologism. The New Criticism was able to move in, not to combat a strong left-wing position, but rather to occupy the vacuum left by the failure of socialist criticism to realize its opportunities.[14] At this point, the New Criticism introduced a technicism and an accommodation with science, and it mercilessly attacked and destroyed left-wing aesthetic forms, including the totally reformist forms of historiographic or sociological criticism. In other words, the cultural politics of the New Criticism are linked with the political culture of the period, and, as in the rest of the modern critical tradition, the cultural methodology reveals its politics directly.

We must once again examine the romantic-classical argument to relate the New Criticism along a certain salient axis to antecedent aesthetic polarities. With respect to the New Critics, the major bourgeois interpretations are divided. Krieger claims that these critics are significantly different from the romantics, that for them the unique poetic knowledge is controlled by the mode of discourse and not some transcendent psychology or intuition.[15] Foster insists that behind certain classicist principles lies a romantic sensibility 'which most truly constitutes . . . the "real" identity of the New Criticism as a literary movement.'[16] These are not satisfactory conceptual approaches. I shall merely reaffirm here that, methodologically, the decisive factors in the relation of the New Critical to the romantic problematic (regardless of borrowed elements) are the internal categorical transformations, and the radical changes in social location.[17]

The issue can, in any case, not be reduced to either Krieger's categories of the type of knowledge involved or to Foster's categories of emotion, faith, and metaphysics.[18] New Critical theory also involves a whole set of categories structuring attitudes to nature and society, which all testify to an attempt to 'classicize' and integrate the 'romantic' alienation. And it is noteworthy in Ransom that, in addition to the 'classical' mimetic attitude to nature, the attempt to reconcile the state and the individual, and the formal restraint of his poetry, he attempts, even in regard to rationality, to combine anti-rationalism in metaphysics with rationalism in aesthetic criticism. Moreover, a methodologically comprehensive and unified rationality becomes increasingly prevalent in his writings as the proffered social critique (defensive and reactionary though it was) declines.

I have argued that the romantic critique of the alienation of reason, unable to link itself to historical forces, could not avoid the collapse into irrationality, a complementary bourgeois form.[19] It is precisely the *reverse* situation which obtains with Ransom. His position is a right-wing and irrational critique, abstract at the outset, *until it is relocated on the grounds of the dominant social rationality*. In the course of reintegration with the concrete historical realm, the position becomes increasingly rational, but the cost is the loss of its negative moments.[20] To maintain a romanticizing thesis, the evidence has to be seriously misinterpreted. Thus Foster argues that Ransom's eventual stress on structure and logic is a move toward mystical religious Truth.[21] This is a gross distortion; the move toward logic is the move toward rationality.

One more point has to be added. Robert Penn Warren observes:[22]

> Both [Eliot and Ransom] have experienced a necessity for order, and, in consequence, have concerned themselves with disorder as the overt subject matter of their poetry. Both have diagnosed the disorder in terms of dissociation of sensibility, although Ransom, on this point, has been more general.

Stewart notes that Ransom's prose is concerned with developing the appropriate epistemology and ontology for a pluralist cosmology where reason and sensibility would have their proper roles and satisfactions.[23] In other words, the Ransomian universe is structured by the same problematic of order that was central to Eliot and Richards.

As will become apparent, however, this problematic, in the case of Ransom, is in motion. Within the context of a search for order, the terms and internal relations of the problematic continually change so that it undergoes a radical alteration in its social character. In the earlier self-definition *against* the society, the search is for an equilibrium defined in terms of the conflict of art *against* science. In the later self-definition from *within* the society, the equilibrium is proposed in terms of a biological model. Art and science are viewed as *functionally complementary* with respect to what they do for the human organism; indeed, in this conflict-free frame of thought, even the claims that science is primary are considered valid. This motion of the problematic of order structures and expresses the incorporation of a defensive reactionary critique into a corporate liberal framework that seeks ideally to eliminate conflict through coordinating specialized functions within a hierarchical organization governed by a universal rationality.

CHAPTER 5

Fugitive and Post-Fugitive

The Fugitive phase contains in embryo many of the features of the later phases; it is the first stage of a dynamic continuity, and I shall review it here very briefly. The Fugitives were based in Nashville, a city which considered itself the Athens of the South,[1] even to the extent of building a concrete reproduction of the Parthenon—full size. They had discussed metaphysics for years before actually founding their magazine, *The Fugitive*, in 1922. This concern with metaphysics, with poetic production, with literary criticism, and with their location in the South in a period whose driving impulse was 'progress,' together essentially define the Fugitives. Their work, it seems agreed,[2] initiated the Southern Renascence. But they wrote without being at home in a South in transition, feeling no sympathy for the New South and rejecting the Old South. The name of the group accurately expressed its members' alienation. Their self-image of the moment included the neoromantic posture of the outcast with access to special knowledge. And Ransom's unsigned editorial for the first issue of the magazine fixed their social position, with reference to the Southern past, as being in flight 'from nothing faster than from the high-caste Brahmins of the Old South. Without raising the question of whether the blood in the veins of its editors runs red, they at any rate are not advertising it as blue.'[3]

In relation to formal aesthetics, Ransom, 'the first modern' among the group, 'castigated sentimentality whenever it showed its simple head and first set up the Baal of complexity for worship.'[4] Ransom's own poetry, 'deliberately minor' in the tradition of Donne, Marvell, and Yeats,[5] has been ranked among the truly distinguished poetry of the twentieth century.[6] In the nineteen issues of *The Fugitive* from 1922 to 1925, he published fifty-nine poems, a

greater number than any of the other fifteen members produced.[7]
The poems pose the themes that will later be worked through in the
prose: for example, the poet versus the man of instinct, art versus
reality; love versus lust in 'April Treason'; the head-body dualism in
'Painted Head'; nature versus science, that is, 'a most celestial rose'
versus 'dreary unbelieving books' in 'The Rose'; frigid rationality in
'Spectral Lovers'; the unknowableness of the universe in
'Necrological'; or the attack on rationalism or idealism in 'Our Two
Worthies':[8]

> And this is how the Pure Idea
> Became our perfect panacea,
> Both external and internal
> And supernal and infernal.

In general, the poetry embodies the dualistic structure that is
to characterize the prose. It is, moreover, a sophisticated poetry with
philosophical thematic unity and a texture derived from exploiting
the English language's affinity for noun constructions. But the
range is limited, and the compositional purity of classical restraint
and irony ultimately makes a static, passive poetry.

The critics analyze Ransom's irony as the acceptance of human
limitations, in place of romantic escape from the individual's
predicament;[9] as the ethical reference to a constant center in the
unified sensibility, in the principles of order, in place of romantic
flight from centrality in irresponsible negations.[10] In this connection,
one might observe that the source of this irony in the poetry is that
same perceptual phenomenology that will emerge in the prose in a
contradictory role. It appears both as the grounds for the critique of
scientism, in the stress on the sensuous richness of reality; and also as
the grounds for the surrender to the established reality, in the
allegiance to the concrete, here and now, without the mediation of
subverting social dimensions. The exegesis of a poem such as
'Morning' (SP 74), with its attack on the fetish of familiarity, and its
contraposition of the aesthetic against the scientific-practical-
moral, of the perceptual against the categorical, reaching its climax
in Ralph's devastating surrender to 'Simply another morning, and
simply Jane,' could display Ransom's entire theoretical position in
all its strengths and weaknesses. Yet the poetry remains a type of
alienated art that fails to embody concrete typicality. It does not
develop a rich social typology, so that the attempt to present
perceptual depth dimensions of common situations results in an

abstract and fabricated simultaneity of particular details and symbolic generalities brought into direct contact. The articulations of the prose compound this inability to supersede immediacy, by elaborating the features of a *contemplative* attitude as the material embodiment of the perceptual attitude, in putative opposition to a *technological* embodiment of the categorical attitude.

Ransom's first important article on poetics, 'Waste Lands' in 1923, raises significant issues, still with a neoromantic coloring. Art is seen as 'gently revolutionary' in contributing the 'free and unpredictable associations discovered for the thing.'[11] This becomes a permanent theme. But the artistic work is done by the imagination, inspiration, and genius. The artist must be non-partisan and yield to 'an agent more competent than reason.'[12] This one-sided opposition illuminates an important feature of the bourgeois paradigm—its inability to unite partisanship with aesthetic autonomy, and its insistence on excluding partisanship from totality.[13] If all genuine totality is totalization, historically always in the process of being produced, then it presupposes partisanship as its principle of totalization, its mode of giving meaning and structure in the construction of a world, whether in philosophy or in art. And this partisanship is not a barrier to objectivity; in fact, it is the condition of objectivity because it is the necessary link with the future. The position exposes that the fullness Ransom seeks from the gift of art no longer constitutes a criticism of life, but only a criticism of scientific partiality.

The next significant essay, a turning point in the development of Southern criticism, was 'Thoughts on the Poetic Discontent' written for *The Fugitive* in June 1925. The article is a rejection of romanticism and a defense of a sophisticated dualism that Ransom calls 'irony.' He rejects first the romantic humanist rationalism, the 'naive dualism' of subject and object which expects nature to be capable of being molded by the subjective will materialized in work. The world, Ransom argues, cannot be so controlled. Next he rejects the attempt to seek a mystical community with nature, and adopts the Hulmean point of view that there is no such continuity between man and nature. What this sequence of punctured illusions produces—and we should note that the definition involves a motion of the mind for Ransom that it does not later for Brooks—is a new mature dualism involving 'a mellow wisdom which we may call irony.'[14] And then come the famous and influential definitions of irony as 'the ultimate mode of the great minds':[15] 'Irony is the rarest of the states of mind, because it is the most inclusive; the whole mind has been active in arriving at it, both creation and criticism, both poetry and science.'[16]

We notice that 'the whole mind' has been involved in a contradiction: the rejection of the work project of civilization on the grounds of a principled submission to limitation. The position is built on both criticism and passivity: the paradox of right-wing alienation. It is like the writer's irony that Lukács calls 'a negative mysticism to be found in times without a god':[17] the certainty that the ultimate has been encountered and grasped precisely in the skepticism of self-limitation.

In further work Ransom attempted to provide an epistemological and aesthetic foundation for this three-stage sequence that reached its climax in ironic dualism. For two years, between 1926 and 1928, he worked on a book to be called 'The Third Moment.' It was never published, but partly incorporated in other writings at the end of the decade, and known otherwise only through his letters to Tate. He argued that experience contains a *sequence* of three moments: a first moment of concrete precategorical experience; a second moment of categorization, of conceptualized knowledge aimed toward a pragmatic *telos*; and a third moment, a mixture, which recovers through images, coexisting with concepts, the qualities lost in the second moment. The thrust of Ransom's formulations is aimed at the second moment which he associates with science, technology, and instrumental logic—all of which, in his view, serve our animal instincts. This, he sees as the dominant pattern in civilization, but one he rejects.

We can see in the three moments the methodological roots of a fundamental political instability that builds into the theory the internal conditions that make possible a dialectic of accommodation. For the rigid separation and opposition of the sensuous (first moment) and the categorical (second moment), the elimination of all conceptual (second moment) elements from what is considered the world of actual experience (first moment), means, in effect, the elimination as well of all linguistic elements, and, ultimately, the paradoxical reduction of that world to a state which is not human at all. The subject/object differentiation that is the condition for a human historical world is impossible in the absence of all abstraction—here relegated to the second moment. The attempt to duplicate experience in the first two moments, in order to distinguish a level of experience free from or prior to the alienation of contemporary consciousness in actual alienated existence, means, effectively, the elimination of historical experience altogether, and the collapse of the human world into precisely that prehistorical realm of complete biological-instinctual domination that Ransom associates with reason and seeks to avoid. The other side of his paradoxical dissolution of historical ontology is that a solution appears available on the purely epistemological level—in the third moment, where sensuousness and reflection meet in the poetic image. In this context, the articulation of the third moment in terms of the axes of inclusion and fullness, that is, in terms of a mixture that includes in full all the aspects that were separated into two moments in Ransom's artificial duplication of experience, confines the critique of science to the level of immediacy, and leaves no place for questions regarding the historical alienation of both everyday perception and higher-level categorization. Moreover, since Ransom blames the wrongs of the world on science, his critique remains contained on the epistemological level, and abrogates the challenge to alienation on the ontological levels of experience. Indeed, the effect of this phenomenology is that, in identifying alienation and loss of quality with a second moment of science and production *as such*, in themselves, Ransom, in seeking restoration of lost quality, rejects not only alienated science and alienated production, but this entire second moment, and in the process, the development of productive forces in human history in general.

If 'what we require always is to return simply to the sense'; if 'every Sensible is a source of inexhaustible sensation'; and if, therefore, 'reality means simply inexhaustible quality,'[18] then two alternative ways exist to achieve a balanced third-moment dualism. If the problem is a disproportion between the first two moments caused by scientific/technological usurpation; if the first moment of qualitative relations with sensuous nature has been displaced historically by a second moment of quantitative, scientific/technological relations of production with nature, then to re-establish a balance between them, one can have again less of the second, or (if that proves impossible) somehow more of the first. The expansion of needs and their satisfactions, the realm of the scientific-practical second moment, can be inhibited, and a life constructed that will enhance contact with inexhaustible reality and recover the appropriate balance between the first two moments in objectifying the third moment as a way of life. Or, the continuing expansion of needs and satisfactions can be accepted, and third-moment balance can be established through the parallel intensification of our symbolic contacts with inexhaustible reality. The first solution is that of Agrarianism, the second that of the New Criticism, which here picks up the threads from Richards leading to our salvation. It should be emphasized that both solutions naturalize capitalist alienation as the unavoidable product of the materialist orientation; they differ only in considering materialism unnecessary (and retractable) or necessary (and tolerable), respectively.

To recapitulate: the critical alienation in Ransom's response to reality leads to the methodological retraction of history that is inherent in his phenomenology, and finds itself susceptible to alternative resolutions: either in the reactionary critique represented in the Agrarian renunciation of the specific historical situation, or in the uncritical integration represented in the New Critical submission to the specific historical situation. The choice of one over the other, and the transition from one to the other, is a function of the historical and ideological determinations that have already been discussed.

Art is situated in this process by Ransom as an embodiment of the third moment. 'Essentially, Poetry is always the exhibit of Opposition and at the same time Reconciliation between the Conceptual or Formal and the Individual or Concrete.'[19] It combines the aspects of quantity and quality, while leaving the latter 'free and contingent.'[20] Art includes a necessary moment of science. The romantic position of artistic superiority to reality is modified, and the 'wildly romantic' denial of science is considered 'suicidal.' Purity is exchanged for mixture:[21]

An important detail is, to show why, with our formal cognitive habit or apparatus, we cannot have *fresh experience* of first moments; because they disintegrate as fast as they come. And this corollary: In Nature as compared with Art, our sense of Wholeness is extremely vague and unsatisfying; the artistic contemplation of Nature is better, a very advanced state, in which we are conscious of the scene as we might have conceptualized it, and at the same time of the scene as we actually do persist in intuiting it. But this is quite like Art; a Mixture.

Moreover, Ransom insists, art has many relations with the world and it is 'a species of idolatry'[22] to treat it as a formal absolute, as Tate following Eliot advocated. Already in September 1925 he had written for *The Fugitive* that 'good poetry is that which fits our own passionate history, and expresses that which needs expression from our private deeps.'[23] To satisfy this vital need, he had sought to unite past and present and to establish, as Frye was to do later in a different historical context (more antiseptically and without the force of value concerns), the traditional conventions as the source of form. 'Poetry is saved from being utterly licentious and chaotic by having a form and content based closely (as a general thing) upon Tradition. . . . Its privacy consists perfectly with its conventionality, its formality.'[24] In the second half of the decade, with the discontinuation of *The Fugitive* in 1925, Ransom's concerns were filtered through a developing sectional or regional consciousness and a search for social location.

1925 was the year notable for the Scopes Monkey Trial where John T. Scopes was convicted at Dayton, Tennessee, for teaching Darwinian theory in the public schools, contrary to state statute. Ransom was outraged at the ensuing ridicule of the South and felt caught up in the general polarization. The issues that were raised involved centrally the questions of nature and rationality and seemed to Ransom to focus the whole historical commotion. The Fugitives had tried to avoid sentimentalizing the Old South; now it seemed that the real danger was the continuing economic conquest and spiritual humiliation of the South by the North. To defend the South, Ransom and the others had to oppose a whole alternative conception of life to that of the North. To ground that conception, they revived the culture of the past, its codes and ceremonies, and posited it as the embodiment of a mythopoeic, anti-rational, anti-progressive metaphysics. The position took years to evolve, but eventually it developed into the Agrarian defense.

What tends to characterize right-wing ideologies, which have no real social basis for using the future as their point of reference and thus necessarily turn toward the past, is the idealization of the past, the abrogation of the effort to liberate tradition from conformism,[25] and the exaggeration of custom, which, as Frantz Fanon says, 'is always the deterioration of culture.'[26] It is important to be aware that the Agrarian position is a deep mystification of the Southern past. It is, first of all, a racist history for which black people are either passive or invisible. Secondly, it fails to record and interpret the fact that the South controlled national politics from the Revolution to the Civil War, and, especially in the last quarter-century before the Civil War, once the planters had won decisive supremacy in the South, in order to protect the slave institution. Thirdly, it ignores that behind the ideal of egalitarian yeoman society up to the Civil War lay the politics of racism, class, and power, that slavery was the power base for the plantocracy's subordination of the white yeomanry. Fourthly, it neglects the effects of slave resistance in corrupting the moral typology of the white culture. Fifthly, it not only forgets the internal divisions among whites but also that racism was the operative principle of the unified culture in so far as it cemented white solidarity under planter hegemony. Sixthly, it perpetuates the lie of the gracious South, a lie finally being torn to shreds as historians incorporate the reports of the oppressed; and it disguises the fundamental feature of Southern culture: that it was a *culture of control* involving the social, political, and ideological aspects necessary for dominating black slaves and keeping non-slave-owning whites in line.[27] Where any of these factors are acknowledged at all, they are acknowledged only to be approved.[28]

All this notwithstanding, Ransom's philosophical dualism adopts the explicitly social, political, economic, and cultural dimensions of an ostensibly irreconcilable North-South polarity. During this period, Ransom articulates his specifically truncated dialectic with reference to art:[29]

> Art is our refusal to yield to the blandishments of 'constructive' philosophy and permit the poignant and actual Dichotomy to be dissatisfied in a Trichotomy; our rejection of third Terms; our denial of Hegel's right to solve a pair of contradictions with a Triad. And here's a slogan: Give us Dualism, or we'll give you no Art.

The sterile conflict of hypostatized schematic oppositions marks all of Ransom's writings. During this period, the historical correlatives are the postulated Northern and Southern ways of life. The South, in Ransom's view, clearly could not absorb the North; at least it must preserve its own autonomy. The methodological consequences derived from this defense of the South are that the state of opposition is essential, dualist stasis a value, and Hegelian motion a danger. Conversely, once integration is accepted, much later, on the historical plane, dualism leaves the aesthetic realm as well in favor of a new monistic 'Concrete Universal.' What follows, of course, from the affirmation of Dichotomy and the 'rejection of Third Terms' is a truncated two-term dialectic. Such a dialectic (whether in Ransom's dualistic oppositions or in something as totally different as, for example, democratic centralism) is an inherently unstable dialectic, and the weaker term invariably becomes subordinate to the stronger. The relative strengths are, here again, a function of historical determinations.

For the moment, however, what is worth noting is how Ransom unites his aesthetic and historical concerns. In the same letter to Tate in which he had rejected a rigorous aesthetic formalism, he writes:[30]

'I subordinate always Art to the aesthetic life; its function is to initiate us into the aesthetic life, it is not for us the final end. In the Old South the life aesthetic was actually realized, and there are the fewer object-lessons in its specific art.'

This notion of 'the aesthetic life' provides for Ransom the key to the Agrarian defense of the South, and, as a relation to nature and to work, carries the full weight of his critique of modern capitalism. It is the failure of this critique that leads to its integration. The Agrarian aspiration to achieve balance through the aesthetic life is reduced to the New Critical satisfaction with aesthetic symbols.

CHAPTER 6

Agrarianism

A General Metaphysics: *God Without Thunder*

God Without Thunder, Ransom's first book, published in 1930, contains the assumptions of the preceding and subsequent periods. The aim, to explain 'the function of the myths in human civilization,'[1] and the demand, to 'restore to God the thunder' (GWT 358), define the ideological program of Agrarian metaphysics. Essentially, the argument is structured in terms of three interlocking sets of dualities: the opposition between two teleological ontologies, two anthropologies, and two political economies. The position expresses alienation, criticism, and futile reaction. It is locked into the peculiar posture of an anti-capitalist critique filtered through petty bourgeois interests into precapitalist forms; and the critique is in permanent internal tension with undercurrents pulling toward accommodation.

Ransom begins by positing religion in a causal relation to the whole of human life.

> We mean by religion, usually, a body of doctrine concerning God and man. But the doctrine which defines God, and man's relation to God, is really a doctrine which tries to define the intention of the universe. It is therefore his fundamental philosophy, it expresses the conviction he holds about his essential destiny, and it is bound to be of determining influence upon his conduct. (3)

This theorizing is a search for meaning in everyday life, and assumes a transcendent (extra-human) design in the universe, beyond the intentionality embodied in the human labor process. Consequently, it requires the transformation of reality into myth and the assumption of human limitation as the corollary of extra-human

61

transcendence. Religion, then, provides supernatural knowledge 'not accessible to science' (11); it is 'a system of myths, upon the scientific knowledge of nature as its base' (13).

Roland Barthes observes that there is only one language which is not mythical, the language of man as producer or revolutionary, speaking 'in order to transform reality and no longer to preserve it as an image.'[2] We find that Ransom's position, in reaction against the alienated life forms of modern capitalism, displaces the entire problematic of production and transformation. He writes: 'The mind must accept the world order' which, moreover, is discontinuous with the 'secular enterprise' based in the moral order (49). As in the fascist theories that contended the spiritual determination of the economy,[3] for Ransom 'the religion of a people is that background of metaphysical doctrine which dictates its political economy' (118).[4] A critique of contemporary forms of life on that basis must be contradictory and unstable.

Opposed to the religious perspective that reminds man 'to remember his limits, and be content with his existing conditions' (118), Ransom sees 'the new religion of science,' which conceives man's relation to the universe as if God had invited man 'to profiteer upon the universe' (16). This secular program 'spins its projects for human improvement at the expense of nature, which it scorns, and of God, who is its spirit' (118). Thus, scientific teleology in Ransom has an ontological character which we must remember in interpreting his arguments through their various transformations. This opposition between science and religion is founded on a view of reality that we have seen before:[5]

> Reality . . . consists in a fulness of quality, not permanence of quality. A real thing is a bundle of complementary qualities and an inexhaustible particularity. Anything else is less than real, an abstraction from the real, though it may seem as precious and noble as a Platonic Idea, writ imperishable in the heavens.

Science, in Ransom's view, mutilates nature for our practical objectives, brutally destructive in practice and in theory, and always involves 'abstracting some arbitrary essence from the whole' (140). 'Science is quite willing to lose the whole for the sake of the part' (139).

Meanwhile, the religious relation to reality involves the categories of fear, respect, enjoyment, and love; it conserves the object unselfishly. In its cognitive aspect, which shapes our beliefs and conduct, 'the myth of an object is its proper name,' and aims at the object's 'fullness of being' (66–7). Art and religion, in this conception, share a basic metaphysical identity. Where they differ is in the stability of the single religious myth by contrast with the mythic versatility of art (98). It is to be noted that here (as throughout the modern tradition of critical theory) the ontological hostility between art and religion is systematically mystified.[6] A general hostility to the secular productive enterprise (in the context of a failure to distinguish between an alienated and a non-alienated production and reproduction of social existence) means the elimination of the real problematic of alienation—even though, in fact, Ransom's polemic is very sharply critical of certain actual forms of alienation. Since the problematic of alienation is the real domain of the opposition between art and religion, in its absence art can be drawn onto the ground of religion, and the anthropomorphic similarities in them can come to prevail in their characterization.

On this general basis, Ransom constructs two opposing anthropologies. In the scientific view, he argues, man is an animal with reason, which serves his instincts and desires and 'permits him to live a life more animal than that of animals' (195). In the religious view, man is more than a reasoning animal, he also has sensibility: 'In order to be human, we have to have something which will stop action, and this something cannot possibly be reason in its narrow sense. I would call it sensibility' (197). What is important in this construction is that both terms of the opposition are one-sided embodiments of alienated aspects of actual capitalist social life, and hence the critique remains abstract and incapable of pointing to supersession of the established reality. Against the utility fixation of alienated man, blocked in this society from appropriating the full human essence that is materialized in human objectifications, Ransom opposes a contemplative comportment that is itself, as Lukács has shown, the alienated product of the progressive rationalization of labor.[7]

In arguing against the capitalist relation to nature in terms of mastery (that is, against an ontology and an epistemology that set the subject against the object), Ransom joins the Schopenhauer tradition of condemning the active life altogether and reducing man's world-creating subjectivity based in objective praxis to the interiority of a contemplative subject. In other words, in seeking the rejection of actual forms of alienated activity, Ransom's anthropology internalizes this relation as a general principle. Alienation thus becomes fixed as an inevitable and permanent product of any strategy of production for the satisfaction of needs and the creation of new needs. Ransom takes refuge in the contemplative stance generated by capitalist reification. This stance is offered as solution, however, in the form of the precapitalist relation of man to nature characterized by the dependence of the subject (man) on the object (nature), which converges, in certain respects, with the reified structure of modern social forms, where objects rule over man. Thus, the same vantage point that allows Ransom at times a sensitive and incisive critique of aspects of capitalist alienation, also, by virtue of its backward orientation and its affirmation of a key aspect of reification, makes that critique necessarily ineffective and cut off from any alternative future.

The decisive error would seem to lie in Ransom's failure adequately to understand that the universalization of the exchange relation, that is, the general principle of utility, has been a contradictory phase in the social evolution of human powers and activities.[8] In this context, the transformation of the production process into 'a scientific process, which subjugates the forces of nature and compels them to work in the service of human needs,'[9] does indeed tend to turn all quality into quantity and increasingly to impoverish living labor power at the same time as producing an ever greater objective world of values that stands opposite it in the form of alien property.[10] On one hand, there is 'the great civilizing influence of capital; its production of a stage of society in comparison to which all earlier ones appear as mere *local developments* of humanity and as *nature-idolatry*. For the first time, nature becomes purely an object for humankind, purely a matter of utility; ceases to be recognized as a power for itself.'[11] On the other, capital diminishes the living worker, transforms him into an accessory of the machine,[12] and structures a process where 'forces of production and social relations—two different sides of the development of the social individual—appear to capital as mere means, and are merely means for it to produce from its limited foundation.'[13]

Ransom, however, does not separate the historical necessity of the *objectification* of the powers of social labor from the necessity, under capitalism, of their *alienation* in relation to living labor.[14] He confuses objectifying praxis with reification, and in rejecting reification, also rejects the universal development of human productive forces, which is its other side. This is an attack on history, a regression to the idolatry of nature, and a glorification of passivity, in the context of which the critique of capitalist alienation takes on the character of a strictly abstract negation, vitiated by its reactionary standpoint. The alienated theoretical attack on the alienated anthropology of capitalist society succeeds only in obscuring the possibilities for liberation from the relations of capitalism.

This difficulty is evident in the bearing of Ransom's dualisms on economics. His anthropological opposites clash materially on this plane. Ransom argues that in the scientific life, 'man is reduced to being the tender of machines' (GWT 172), that our existence is 'mechanized, but not necessarily filled, not made more intelligent,' but subordinated to the dictates of machines (173). And he offers a sharp perception of the manipulation of desires and needs, in part through the seductive and unscrupulous sales effort (202), and of the new responsibility imposed on man 'as a regular consumer' to buy and use a 'multitude of clean, shining, effective products' that he does not really need, while deep desires, for example, for 'ordering our geological and climatic environment on a large scale,' go unrealized. 'For what it fails to give us, mechanical science would like to make up by giving us plenty of things that we do not want' (176–7). He links the two sides of the process in the claim that 'there is little to choose between the indignities of modern man as a laborer and as a consumer' (207). And he sees the process as inexorably dynamic: 'This is not merely an age of machines but an age of progressive machinery. . . . There is no economic stability. There is progress' (208). And what Ransom opposes, in recalling again the classicizing problematic of order and balance, is the excess of science, the unbalance between appetite and appreciation, the tendency of science to usurpation and monopoly.

> It is because industrialism gives an undue encouragement to science, and too much right of way to appetite, that we have to take the position that industrialism is far too dangerous a thing for us to indulge in. But for a similar reason we have to oppose the cult of science on its purely theoretical side, when it tries to monopolize our intellectual life. (216–17)

The alternative, again, is the religious view which, although not proposing a reversion to primitivism, does defend the *status quo* at each step of progress, and challenges 'any fresh and sweeping developments' (124). The religious theory of life, assumed to be and

65

argued as identical with the aesthetic theory of life, is a critique of industrialism, 'and bids us halt the industrial progress' (195). The programmatic opposition for Ransom becomes the *aesthetic* life versus the *anaesthetic* life, developed theoretically through the decisive mediation of man's relations with nature.

The products of science for a mechanized life, Ransom argues, reinforce dimensions of speed and power, and their use is the practice of 'a technique of anaesthesia' (181) where we fail to observe 'the sensible infinity which constitutes the landscape of our world' (180). Scientific anodynes remove our attention from our inability to manage our material and social environments, and direct it to fields where our 'force is visible and certain' (181–2). This is the area of productive work, allegedly a universal panacea, but effectively an anaesthetic for people 'afraid of the fullness of the inner life' (184). In general, science knows only the uses of nature, 'does not credit nature with having any life of its own,' and 'is possible to us only on condition that we anaesthetize ourselves and become comparatively insensible.'[15]

The full interiority that Ransom sets up in opposition to external activity is based on a specific alternative relation to nature. This is 'the purest esthetic experience,'[16] the contemplation of the infinite particularity of the objective world. 'The aesthetic attitude is definable with fair accuracy in the simple and almost sentimental terms: the love of nature' (180); 'and that means the love of anything for itself,'[17] a relation of Kantian–Schopenhauerian 'desirelessness.' In the rejection of contemporary historical forms, Ransom turns sentimentally to nature. He posits a '*rapport* with environment' (180) as a fundamental human need, and the arts as primary means of access to it. 'The works of art are psychic exercises which are just so many rebellions against science';[18] and while one type of art criticizes science by its own standards, another 'suspends the whole purpose-and-attainment process.'[19] Such art, he claims, 'exercises that impulse of natural piety which requires of us that our life should be in loving *rapport* with environment.' It permits us to 'revel in the particularity of things, and feel the joy of restoration after an estrangement from nature.'[20]

The aesthetic life is a crucial Ransomian category, both in its Agrarian affirmation, and its subsequent New Critical abrogation. The exposition above should make possible the elucidation of three important aspects concerning the structure of the argument and each of its two main terms. Firstly, the position involves a far-reaching rejection of the values and life forms of Ransom's society; it is offered as critique. But the mediation of nature poses ambivalence. On one hand, as Lukács has shown, nature becomes 'the repository of all these inner tendencies opposing the growth of mechanisation, dehumanisation and reification';[21] while on the other, the longing for nature mystifies the dehumanizing social institutions and blunts the critique by not directing the challenge at the social structures themselves.

This links with the second aspect, the love of nature as the love of anything for itself. The alienation from a given form of social rationality translates an aesthetic disinterest into a general ethic without social *telos* or points of reference. If science (which Ransom opposes, even while leaving unchallenged its positivist definitions) ultimately leaves the established order (which it organizes as given) unchanged in the name of rationalism, Ransom's aesthetic life leaves the same order unchanged in the name of anti-rationalism. The farther the critique moves from the social forms that must be its target, the less concrete it becomes.

Thirdly, the anaesthesia, which is the object of the critique, does not in fact flow, as Ransom suggests, inevitably from the machines, from a specific mode of objectification inserted as mediation in the man-nature metabolism. This error—structurally the same fetish as McLuhan's, but here, significantly, with opposite (critical) value sign—consists in ignoring the embeddedness of human objectifications in the social relations of capitalism. This precludes theoretically the perspective of moving beyond capitalism to a new mode of social existence, initially defined by the possibility of all-round appropriation of the already developed full human essence at no lower level of human powers, capacities, abilities, and activities than, at least, that which exists in the present social formation. This point is especially significant in terms of Ransom's own problematic. The *rapport* with nature that he formulates, representing the nostalgic desire to feel at home in the world, embodies a precapitalist relation. In this respect, precisely what distinguishes the capitalist mode of production from precapitalist modes is a shift—of world-historical significance—in the man-nature relationship, that is, in the labor process. This process becomes, for the first time, purely social, with the separation of the inorganic conditions of human existence from that active existence (as the objective conditions of labor take the form of capital, and individuals become propertyless wage laborers).[22] Man takes control of this essential metabolism: the man-nature relation becomes a strictly historical form of the social relations among human beings. That Ransom attempts to bypass this whole sphere of social determinations keeps his critique within the bounds of bourgeois ideology and prepares for its failure and integration.

Since Ransom cannot offer solutions on the level of social transformation, he seeks to incorporate social and economic dimensions directly within a metaphysical basis for the human metabolism with nature. Not only does he stress 'contact with the elemental soil' (GWT 127), he also specifies that 'the best labor is the one which provides the best field for the exercise of sensibility—it is clearly some form of pastoral or agrarian labor' (201). In consequence, agriculture serves Ransom and other Agrarians as the economic center of social-ideological agitation, intended, as I have argued, as the delineation of a viable historical location for the protagonists through the specification of a suitable relation with nature. In other words, the solution is sought in a different level of technical relation to nature, and not in an alternative social and ecological articulation of an advanced technical interchange with nature.

B Economics: *I'll Take My Stand*

Most Agrarian articles appeared in Northern publications: *Hound and Horn*, *New Republic*, *The American Review*. This latter, especially, was founded to provide a base for the 'traditionalist' critique of 'Radicals of the Right' or 'Revolutionary Conservatives' who sought to remedy modern chaos through a return to discarded fundamentals. It promised sympathetic exposition to fascist economics and politics, and planned to draw on four main groups: Neo-Humanists, Neo-Scholastics, English Distributists,[23] and Southern Agrarians.[24] Indeed, the Agrarians adopted a traditionalist standpoint, emphasized the moral cohesion of an inherited quality of life, and expressly held up as a value the Southern tradition of leisurely work and play reproducing the established European conservative forms of living 'along the inherited lines of least resistance in order to put the surplus of energy into the free life of the mind.'[25] Ransom recalled the eighteenth-century South in terms of the[26]

social arts of dress, conversation, manners, the table, the hunt, politics, oratory, the pulpit. These were arts of living and not arts of escape; they were also community arts, in which every class of society could participate *after its kind*. The South took life easy, which is itself a tolerably comprehensive art.

And this South, Ransom insisted, was to remain Southern 'in the pure, traditional, even sectional sense.'[27]

Critics such as V. F. Calverton[28] and Dudley Wynn[29] noted during the Agrarian period the contradictions of an appeal to tradition, in that the most fundamental tradition in the South was in fact the Anglo-Saxon Dissenter tradition, the progressive Protestantism of the yeoman class, the tradition of a petty bourgeoisie oriented to capitalist technological advance. Yet the Agrarians elaborated their idyllic versions with such confidence that it seems almost crude to raise the ugly blemish of the slave system,[30] the profit fixation, or the ruthless exploitation of natural resources. In the event, the programmatic question could be phrased by Ransom in terms of his favored dualisms: 'How can the Southern communities, the chief instance of the stationary European principle of culture in America, be reinforced in their ancient integrity as centers of resistance to an all-but-devouring industrialism?'[31]

When the Agrarian campaign was fully launched with the publication of *I'll Take My Stand*, the *New York Times* review of the book, 15 February 1931, called the twelve essayists 'twelve Canutes, . . . without any Saxon conquests to their credit, bidding the waves of the industrial North Sea to fall back.'[32] The polarization is not in dispute; but, in retrospect, D. Davidson adds an important clarification:[33]

We did not, of course, mean that the term industrialism should include any and every form of industry and every conceivable use of machines; we meant giant industrialism, as a force dominating every human activity: as the book says, 'the decision of society to invest its economic resources in the applied sciences.'

Although this strategy took some time to crystallize, the point is well taken. Despite characteristic vacillations, the case of the Agrarians, by background, by occupation, by social position, by allegiance, and by point of view petty bourgeois, was directed ultimately against the monopolization of capitalist production and was not, in essence, an advocacy of non-capitalist relations. The critique was historically specific to a period of growing agricultural and industrial concentration: it attacked a specific form of capitalist production while, at the same time, worshipping capitalist property ownership.[34] This is the decisive contradiction of Agrarian anti-capitalism which situates it as a struggle against change. Although they were writing at a time of profound economic crisis, Davidson stresses that they were disturbed by the boom period as much as by the spectacle of disorder;[35] in general, they 'were fighting against a development, not just trying to sentimentalize the past.'[36]

It was for that reason, too, that Andrew Lytle, Tate, and Warren wanted to title the book 'A Tract Against Communism,' to stress the ideational polemic in the conflict with developmental tendencies rather than simply the aspects of Agrarian revival. Their early diagnosis of Stalinist Russia along a single axis, as superorganization, regulation, and control, and their identification of Russian development, at the extreme, with US trends, provided a powerful two-pronged strategy for Agrarian agitation in the 1930s. The basic position served their struggle against both the system itself and possible left alternatives to it.[37] 'The escape,' Andrew Lytle wrote, 'is not in socialism, in communism, or in sovietism—the three final stages industrialism must take. These change merely the manner and speed of the suicide; they do not alter its nature.'[38] And Ransom:[39]

We therefore look upon the Communist menace as a menace indeed, but not as a Red one; because it is simply according to the blind drift of our industrial development to expect in America at last much the same economic system as that imposed by violence upon Russia in 1917.

In addition to criticizing the brutalization of labor and of consumption, and the 'general decay of sensibility' through the wrong attitude to nature[40] in the 'evil dispensation' of industrial civilization,[41] Ransom attempts to argue his critique on the structural levels of the internal contradictions, thereby differentiating his position from the apologist stance of the subsequent tradition. He criticizes Sidney Lanier for making superficial, if accurate, objections to capitalism, of the kind that can only lead to ineffectual liberal 'reforms of the heart' such as 'fair play' or 'social justice.'[42] His own critique points to inevitable overproduction,[43] and 'that dangerous, or possibly that fatal, flaw in the capitalistic system . . .: its expansive principle, which does not permit of stability' and produces inevitable periodic breakdowns.[44]

But Ransom's metaphysical determinism betrays the economic critique in both instances. In the first, it leads him to see overproduction in relation to 'the rate of natural consumption,'[45] rather than as the overproduction of exchange values, that is, the inadequacy of monetarily effective demand rather than of demand as such. What could have been a genuine critique of capitalism, indicating a rational redistribution and liberating redevelopment of priorities, thus becomes again an obfuscating critique of 'industrialism' from a basis in natural anthropology. The mystification of the historical development of the level and nature of basic human needs leads from there to a construction in terms of subsistence farming. In the second instance, in relation to crises, Ransom is led, like many critics working from a left-wing metaphysics, to underestimate the abilities of capitalism to modify itself with relative success in pursuit of stability. The New Deal sought to create political conditions for precisely that transition to a crisis-free economic operation of the system. Roosevelt's strong politics carried the intervention of the neocapitalist state into the key problems of unemployment, economic development, effective demand, and so forth.

In consequence, Ransom proposed land as the means to 'stabilize our economy' against the 'inherent tendency' to 'overcapitalization and overproduction.'[46] 'Those who have lost their places in our ordinary capitalistic society may begin all over upon the land'[47]—the land as a direct source of subsistence. He emphasized that there was too much land in the United States for a money economy; that only commercial farming was doomed, not farming as such. 'The apostasy of American farmers from primary subsistence farming is the greatest disaster our country has yet suffered; it is fortunate that it can still be undone.'[48] Of course, Ransom did not expect Agrarianism to prevail over the industrial section of the United States, but thought it could flourish by its side.[49] The irony, which it is important to notice here, is that the kind of primary private economy with secondary commodity production that Ransom envisages requires substantial intervention of the state to direct and regulate the transformation. Ransom himself proposes a series of necessary taxation, appropriation, education, and service measures. In other words, Ransom's precapitalist program for 'happy farmers' depends on the neocapitalist state. Already at this point the Agrarian position hides a tendency toward accommodation which becomes fully manifest in the New Criticism.[50]

Naturally, the Agrarians could not find any social force to embody and carry their position, that is, their program was politically empty. Without the working class, no transformation of the social system was possible, and for all their outrage at the ignominies of work in a machine economy, at the brutalization and lack of dignity of factory labor,[51] the Agrarians were no friends to the workers.[52] It has been noted, too, that despite assertions that virtue derives from the soil, the Agrarians saw no virtue in the blacks and poor whites closest to the soil, and, evidently, had no real contact with their struggles.[53] And while Ransom and others carried on their reactionary ideological agitation, radical popular attempts to intervene in the social and economic situation in an active, organized, and liberating way, as in the case of the Southern Tenant Farmers' Union in 1934, were being crushed or assimilated into the rationalization of the capitalist economy.[54]

While the politics of real social struggles were unfolding around the Agrarians, their position remained ideological, and politically totally bankrupt, in spite of the extensive social and economic scope of their concerns and priorities. The only agency Ransom could suggest as the bearer of the Agrarian program indicates clearly the non-transferability of the Agrarian critique into the practical dimensions:[55]

> No Southerner ever dreams of heaven, or pictures his Utopia on earth, without providing room for the Democratic party. Is it really possible that the Democratic party can be held to a principle, and that principle can now be defined as agrarian, conservative, anti-industrial? It may be impossible, after all.

The Democratic party, under Roosevelt, became instead an agency for the rationalization of the capitalist economy. The Agrarian ideological critique had failed, but the neocapitalist rationalization in part coincided with, and in part assimilated, the Agrarian position. In particular, the rationalization offered a new framework from within which Ransom's New Criticism could operate comfortably. This, we shall see, meant abandoning the basic socio-economic dimensions of the position and repudiating the critique; effectively, it meant the adoption by New Critic Ransom of a theoretical comportment which Agrarian Ransom had, in advance and explicitly, abjured.

C Poetics: *The World's Body*

Most of the essays in *The World's Body* originate in the Agrarian period, and it is convenient and appropriate to examine them in this section. The book was highly influential in the New Critical stage. It criticizes science, defines the nature, function, and mechanisms of the aesthetic sphere, and attempts to provide access to the concrete substantiality of objectivity by establishing the objectivity of art as a mode of cognition. The defensive polemic against science, articulated in *God Without Thunder*, is again pursued, but now through art rather than religion.[56] And the general indictment of the modern world which, as John Bradbury points out, can serve as a pretext for casting off systems of reference, permits the elaboration of an aesthetic that focusses on the isolated work itself.[57] During the Agrarian period, however, this aesthetic self-reliance is only one aspect of a whole series of social, economic, ethical, and metaphysical concerns. When Ransom argues that poetry is a make-believe 'showing what might have been,' a perfect restoration to our minds of 'freedom and integrity' for the duration of the experience, even though subsequently it releases us back to the real world, again 'fallen men' (WB 249–50), he is at the same time fighting an acute ideological struggle for the permanent realization of an 'aesthetic life.' The point can be stressed in a general form. On one hand, Agrarian poetics is a full preparation for New Critical poetics and carries with it an elaborate ideological baggage, developed under the pressure of a historical situation, which enters constitutively into the later constructions. On the other hand, the failure of the Agrarian campaign, and the New Critical relocation, manifest in not only the retraction but also the repudiation of the essential extra-aesthetic dimensions, produce internal modifications and external effects that radically alter the character of the whole poetics. Both aspects should be borne in mind during any consideration of Ransom's poetics. I shall now examine some of its major moments.

i Philosophy of art against philosophy of science

The search for totality structures Ransom's poetics, as it structures the other spheres of his interests. His philosophy of art is defined in relation to the inadequacies of science. His critique of science (GWT 217–32) relies on Bergson and Hume; science, he argues, is caught between the Scylla and Charybdis of telling less than the truth and telling more than the truth, the Bergsonian and Humean errors respectively. In the first respect, science is partial, abstract, and incomplete (232). It is 'always *a science*, and committed to a special interest' in relation to which it selects out of many properties the one

73

relevant property (WB 115). It can never present the concrete whose essence is *variety* (GWT 287). In the second respect, science assumes more 'machinery' (225), for example, causality, than it can demonstrate. In general, science cannot embody the concrete whole and cannot deal with the contingent detail that it finds 'irrelevant to the pattern, and distracting' (217).

This critique operates in the matrix of classical philosophy, and poses the problematic of systematic rationalization. In fact, the two aspects, scientific specialization on one hand, and a contingency irreducible to lawfulness on the other, are related. Scientific signifiers as a whole cannot be symmetrical with the totality of signifieds; the contents of reality, especially sensuous contents, are not reducible to a systematization of rational form. Irrationalities, inescapable contingencies, always surface; content intervenes in the form and dissolves the system.[58] Lukács has shown that, in its drive toward rationality, classical philosophy avoided the impasse of this form/content contradiction only by directing its attention to partial formalizations in delimited areas 'by means of abstract rational special systems,' and by renouncing attempts 'to achieve a unified mastery of the whole realm of the knowable.' Indeed, according to this argument, 'the origin of the special sciences with their complete independence of one another both in method and subject matter entails the recognition that this problem is insoluble.'[59] To transpose this into Ransom's terms, the Humean problematic produced the Bergsonian.

Continental philosophers since the First World War have been writing of the crisis of science. The most original study was made by Edmund Husserl, who developed a critique of the objectivistic outlook of modern science that substitutes for the real sensuous world of nature and society, a world of lawful, abstract, quantitative categories artificially constructed.[60] He traced this fetishistic consciousness[61] from the initial Galilean attempts to mathematize reality in order to control nature, through Cartesian and Baconian formulations, to modern positivist scientism. In the course of the development, objects of knowledge come to be identified with objects of nature, reality is frozen into fixed categories, and the concrete subject is eliminated from the object. Ransom's critique has important points of contact with this phenomenological critique. He protests against the 'ruthless reductions' of positivism, 'the extinction of experience in the blank indifference of a universe which is not even mechanical but only mathematical' (GWT 263).

The difficulty with Ransom's position begins in that he accepts the false utilitarian rationalism of positivist scientism as inherent in science. In other words, he permits to alienation in its immediacy the full and permanent occupation of the realm of science. Two immediate consequences follow: in opposition to abstraction (which in fact is a necessary mediation for reaching the concrete), he insists on elevating the experience 'above any explanation' of the experience (263); and in opposition to what he sees as scientific pragmatism in the service of the appetites, he places disinterested contemplation.

But this position precludes criticizing scientistic objectivism for being itself contemplative, and thus it obstructs the path to unalienated science. In addition, paradoxically, in counterposing sensuous experience to categories of explanation, it impoverishes culture, which we cannot in fact strip of all categorical and linguistic elements and which is not reducible to the perceptual world. Ransom's theory gets locked into an alienated utility/contemplation dialectic with disastrous consequences. Creative historical praxis is expelled from the very categorical articulation of the theory, and has no way to appear, and no role to play, in the constitution of either the ontological or the epistemological fields. The 'desperate ontological or metaphysical manoeuvre' (WB 347) that the poem is said to be is cut off from the genuine social ontology that is the basis of art. It is with an aesthetic, then, that is effectively the counterpart of that alienated modern poetry that seeks to escape from an unbearable historical reality and to reach the world of objects in themselves without social mediation, that Ransom tries to attain to substantial concreteness. If, however, genuine concreteness is produced and appropriated through the determinations of human social life, then with Ransom we are confined to the immediacy of pseudo-concretions.

All of Ransom's aesthetic formulations flow from a strategic opposition to science, as was the case with Richards. This dualism contains here a moment of critical negation, but methodologically the negation is vitiated in the contraposition of an *alienated* art against an *alienated* science. Ransom stresses the imaginative ability 'to contemplate things as they are in their rich and contingent materiality' (116). '*Science gratifies a rational or practical impulse and exhibits the minimum of perception. Art gratifies a perceptual impulse and exhibits the minimum of reason*' (130). This reconstitution of the world of perception is made possible by a variety of technical devices. In art, 'we make a return to something which we had wilfully alienated' (116); contemplation through artistic form provides the innocence of Schopenhauer's 'knowledge without desire,' which renders 'the body of the object' 'for its own sake' (45). It is this aesthetic knowledge of the world's body that becomes the central and most influential thesis, not only of Ransom's work, but of the New Criticism as a whole.

ii Poetry as a form of knowledge

Ransom's strategy involves an attempt to establish art as a 'deliberate career' like science, just as serious, official, studied, consecutive, difficult, and important (53). The stress falls on the authority of objectivity. Ransom is critical of romantic expression of self 'rather than an object' (145), as of modernist expression of 'what is near the subject-pole of the subject-object relation' (145). In criticizing Richards, Ransom stresses the object-pole and insists that the complexity resides in the object experienced rather than in the experiencing mind; it is 'constitutional to nature' (150). In general, Ransom, like all the New Critics, asserts again and again that poetry offers true knowledge, that it is a tough-minded intellectual activity that cannot be treated as soft or subjective emotionality. In a tactical affirmation of the need to analyze meaning, to understand poetry before being moved by it, to participate in poetry actively with all one's knowledge and intellectual resources, Allen Tate deplores the loss of the ability to read difficult poetry, and observes: 'But it is very hard for people to apply their minds to poetry, since it is one of our assumptions that come down from the early nineteenth century that our intellects are for mathematics and science, our emotions for poetry.'[62] At the same time that they rail against Platonic or ideational poetry (120–8), these critics place a very high premium on intellectuality.[63]

The real problem with this form of emphasis on the intellectual cognitive elements of art is the distortion produced in the subject/object relation by the implied presupposition that the concrete world is independent, preconstituted, and available to the contemplative subject. But knowledge is not contemplation, and objectivity, as Antonio Gramsci argued, except from the point of view of transcendence, always means human objectivity and is always a moment of 'a struggle for objectivity.'[64] The contemplative comportment, Ransom's false alternative to alienated utilitarianism, demands its appropriate object, and finds it in a stabilized nature 'having its own existence' (WB 45). Ransom's ontology sets the individual of everyday life face to face with nature and, therefore, necessarily conceives the subject/object relation as cognitive. The position is itself a product of the reified social relations of capitalist society; its irony is that Ransom's aesthetic thus takes as its structure the same objectivistic and naturalistic attitude that distinguishes alienated science.

For Ransom there are two modes of 'formal cognition,' 'two ways of transcribing nature.' Science delineates its universal relations; art 'makes imitations or full representations of nature' (205). A key to the notion of cognition involved is the view that 'the things are constant, and it is the ideas that change—changing according to the latest mode under which the species indulges its grandiose expectation of subjugating nature' (124). The object is separated from the categorical modes of its appropriation, and this independence of the object serves as the basis for a thoroughgoing empiricism that becomes most explicit in New Critical practice.

The exclusion of historical praxis from Ransom's aesthetics leads to positing an objectivity that could not possibly have any significant meaning for us. The truth that art deals with the man-nature metabolism is falsified once that relation is abstracted from the social metabolism. Nature exists for us only in its socio-historical appropriation, and art depicts, not nature, but the human experience of nature, that is, nature as a moment in the totality of the social life of human beings. Art is not science; it is always subjectivity that is determinant in poetry, not the bare object in which it recognizes itself.[65] The task of literature to depict man without fetishes, to make sensible the socio-historical human essence, to objectify and make possible the appropriation of the memory and self-consciousness of human development, is precluded in Ransom's poetics. What takes its place is a phenomenology whose role is to reconcile us with the established reality through the worship of the facticity of things, to teach us that 'the way to obtain the true *Dinglichkeit* . . . is to approach the object as such, and in humility' (124), and to assert that 'knowledge is appreciation' (GWT 216).

Of course, Ransom is aware that art is anthropomorphic, but the persistent subject/object duality of his empiricist attempts to justify the ways of art to alienated science produces a paradox that haunts the poetics: objectivism turns into its corollary subjectivism. In art alone, anthropomorphism is not subjectivist; concentrated subjectivity unites with concentrated objectivity through the homogeneous medium. But Ransom posits a two-step process for the cognition of the world as particularity. The first step, the primary order of poetry, is a perceptual reportage of the 'objects in detail without ever exceeding actual observation' (WB 158); this, he says, is analogous to painting. Next, he argues, the poet goes beyond painting, beyond visibility,[66] 'animates nature,' investing organic and inorganic forms 'with his own mentality' (159). The gratuity of this object-directed increment added to a base of scientifically verifiable observation reveals the transformation of artistic anthropomorphism—and of the theoretical truth that we know objects only under historically created human categories—into empiricist subjectivism.

In general, the acceptance of science as the defining frame of reference for the construction of a poetics leads to a categorical error. While 'cognition' is an adequate category for comprehending the specificity of science, and finds in science its most appropriate methodology, it is not the appropriate category for grasping the specificity of art, although art does contain cognitive elements. Lukács observes: 'What the work of art offers can be simultaneously more and less than cognition.'[67] More, in that it may discover facts and dimensions about the world and ourselves that disanthropomorphic modes of cognition, like science, have not been able to approach or express. Less, in that its rendering of these essential determinations remains on the level of phenomenal detail, sensuous concretion, without rising from immediacy (albeit a new level of generic immediacy) to objective knowledge. Art enriches and deepens our awareness of the human universe, and artistic perception, directed by the homogeneous medium, is different from that of science or everyday life, and presents a different experience of the same realities.

Ransom's ideological elaborations find a springboard in experience. Through the homogeneous medium, art concentrates the fullness of its determinations into sensory evocation; the task of mimesis is to bring to life reality as it really is; and objects appear as if newly born, with fresh innocence, so that art breaks with pragmatic abstraction.[68] But what is crucial is that art always refers to the subject, that the immediacy it puts in place of everyday immediacy is that of generic self-consciousness, that the world it makes available is a defetishized world of rich potentialities made sensible at a concrete point in human historical development. And the point is that in presenting this human essence as immediate human existence, art offers to raise both the artist and the receiver above the level of the particularized everyday world. It is not a question here of the idealist reproduction of the world's body, or of a full and preconstituted non-alienated reality: art is the objectification of a non-reified relation to the world—a non-reified relation that exists for and is lived by the aesthetic subjectivity in the course of both creating and appropriating the aesthetic world.

This defetishizing function of genuine art, which is not simply looking behind the veil, or filling in variety and body, involves a collision with everyday subjectivity. Lukács has established that all genuine art involves this cathartic collision, and that it is based on the generic value hierarchy, appropriated in the artistic construction, which serves as a standard against which everyday life is critically measured. Hence, it carries the imperative to change one's life. In other words, the elevation beyond the everyday happens in the artistic catharsis, and art, precisely because of the specificity of the self-contained aesthetic world, can influence human life. As Lukács notes, catharsis shows the individual, in the mirror of the generic essence, the fragility and heterogeneity of his normal life, incapable of realizing itself in coherent fullness. Catharsis is a liberating shock where the individual affirms this generic essence in his own life.[69] (It is, I cannot emphasize too strongly, this experience which is ideologically reduced in all bourgeois formalist aesthetics to 'formal and technical perfection' contrasted with unformed life.) In other words, the contrast of the cathartic experience with ordinary experience is the means to the possibility of transition from aesthetics to ethics.

Ransom's aesthetic theory is completely unable and unwilling to come to terms with this crucial finality of art. It takes refuge in the pristine positivity of prolonged contemplative cognition. The contemplative attitude and catharsis are irreconcilable, and Ransom mischaracterizes catharsis as the agency that prepares for scientific-utilitarian efficiency. In his long essay 'The Cathartic Principle' (WB 173–92), and again in 'The Mimetic Principle' (210–11), he dismisses Aristotle's catharsis superciliously and contemptuously,[70] and insists that it is a partisan of the non-aesthetic relation 'between man and his environment' (210) and thus the enemy of the simple mimesis that he takes to mean 'the love of nature' (210). Although the analysis, as always, derives its impetus from a negative relation to science, its result is that catharsis, the truth of aesthetic mimesis, is posited as its antagonist. Ransom's assumptions are like a distorting mirror, and the closer he comes to the aesthetic object in that mirror, the farther away he moves from it in reality.[71]

iii Mimesis, memory, and form

The notion that art is imitation is of central importance to Ransom. Not only does it stress the object, but it founds the interpretation of disinterested cognition: 'not being actual, it cannot be used, it can only be known' (196–7). In this respect, art is actually better than nature, which is 'an object both to knowledge and to use' (197).

> As science more and more completely reduces the world to its types and forms, art, replying, must invest it again with body. The one technical process requires the other. The artist resorts to the imitation because it is inviolable, and it is inviolable because it is not real. (198 n.1)

In *The World's Body*, the scientific habit of mind is no longer as clearly the symbol of 'industrialism' as in *God Without Thunder*; in consequence, the general idealism of the position is much more apparent. If the world of objectivity cannot resist scientific aggression, artistic imitation becomes indispensable because it not only can resist, being 'one degree removed from actuality' (132), but in addition, can even save the world and restore its body, being faithful to the phenomenal world (132). The claims made for art, typically in this tradition, are vast. The cost of this particular strategy, which relies on an overemphasis on 'knowledge without desire,' is the insulation of art from the active life of normal existence.

Of course, a certain disinterest *is* involved in the aesthetic suspension of the pragmatic teleologies of everyday immediacy, but the exaggeration of this aspect entails an idealist distortion of essential features of art. On one hand, such a position ignores the change effected in the recipient's attitude to reality by the surrender to the formed content of the work which is enforced by the very nature of a homogeneous medium. This change puts an end to the disinterest *within* the aesthetic sphere, regardless of how elaborately mediated the *subsequent* effect may be, depending as it does on the needs and experiences of the recipient before and after the appropriation of the aesthetic experience. On the other hand, the aesthetic experience has an effect in human life beyond the experience itself, an effect which devolves from the essence of art.

This social significance of art has long been recognized and established, and it is a regression to dismiss it, to neglect it, or to retain it suitably modified to accord with the cult of disinterest.[72] In general, the separation of the object from the modes and nature of its appropriation and reception is an expression of the triumph of commodity fetishism over aesthetic defetishization.

In Ransom, the fetish of disinterested contemplative cognition truncates the aesthetic dialectic at the point of suspension of pragmatic immediacy via the medium. As far as Ransom is concerned, memory and form are the two agencies that make it possible to establish the aesthetic distance required for 'disinterest.' Ransom blends Wordsworth, Bergson, Proust, and Freud in a psychology that serves his aesthetics. The general idea is that aesthetic experience is compelled by recollection; it is 'based on second love, not first love' (116). Our attention in the first experience of reality, he concludes, is dominated by the scientific-practical drive for efficiency; the fulness of sensibility is registered 'only upon the faithful and disregarded camera of memory' (250). The 'body and solid substance of the world' can be found only in 'the fulness of memory, but out of this we construct the fulness of poetry, which is counterpart to the world's fulness' (x). And, since memory itself 'is relegated to the dark, or the unconscious . . . the poet's intention becomes the intention of finding access to the unconscious. It takes a poet to find it.'[73]

We might note that Freudianism is generally brought into the modern critical tradition as a means to find either permanent typologies, or levels of signification that offer an escape from the history that has yet to be made. The powerful subversive possibilities in Freudianism are suppressed. Memory, for instance, could be a radical category. Memory not only conquers the separation of the external and internal worlds, but it conquers time as well. It could yield, as Marcuse says, 'critical standards which are tabooed by the present.'[74] It could explode the rationality of repression; regression could thus be progressive. But this is not possible in Ransom's phenomenological problematic of a dissociated sensibility that seeks to regain a lost original unity. The poet's search for the 'way back to those whole states of mind in which the world is originally experienced, and from which every pure intellectual achievement had to take its start'[75] is merely the defensive maneuver of a regressive phenomenology that will not struggle with the problems of the present and has no perspective on the future. The truncation of the aesthetic dialectic at the point of contemplation makes the conquest of time false and meaningless, since it cannot pass to the mediation of activity in time, and therefore will not supersede the boundaries of the present.

The same situation arises in the case of artistic form, the means to the realization of an 'inviolable' imitation based in the fullness of memory. Where the Russian formalists emphasized the subversive aspects of form, here the stress is on its conservative aspects as another constituent of order. 'The aesthetic forms are a technique of restraint' (31). Through the restraints of forms, codes, and rituals, conventions which prevent immediacy (whether in art, manners, or religion), we come 'to respect the object' (34). Form impedes the natural man from hurting or disrespecting the object (38); in other words, it precludes intervention in objectivity. 'The object of a proper society is to instruct its members how to transform instructive experience into aesthetic experience' (42). The word for his generation, Ransom ventures, is 'formal' and 'reactionary' (42). Artistic form is the body the poet gives to his passions (40); it is the means to the innocent knowledge of the world's body for its own sake in all its contingency (45).

Ransom has been criticized for limiting cognition to fidelity of perceptual representation, and ignoring the artist's selective, interpretative contribution.[76] Meanwhile, Cleanth Brooks has argued that the poet is a *maker* not a *copyist*, that his mirror is a 'distortion mirror' that brings focus.[77] But Ransom's poetics in fact resolves this problem; his poet is both maker and mimetic, maker *through* mimesis. If both ordinary and scientific perception distort, then the poetic imitation (of what is, for Ransom, the real world of fullness) has the poet in the role of maker, since art in effect refocuses and restores. And he states that technical form orders the thing-content, develops it beyond being 'a solid lump' (119–20). It is the technical devices that provide aesthetic distance and increase 'the volume of the percipienda or sensibilia' (130). Art is hypothetical[78] or fictive, so that action and scientific interest are inhibited (131). Meter gives anonymity (257), inhibits the prose function (259), and releases the aesthetic function (259). And tropes, such as metaphor, invite perceptual attention and free the senses from science (133).

Aesthetic form for Ransom always opposes the scientific. This recalls the problematic in classical philosophy of systematic rationalization that I discussed earlier. Artistic form seemed uniquely able to unite contingency and necessity, and the problem that was insoluble for formal rationalism was referred to art. Art became a cornerstone of Kant's system, a crucial moment of the search for totality. And, as Lukács showed, the Schillerian extension of the aesthetic principle beyond art was a contradictory attempt to solve social fragmentation by mental reconstruction.[79] Ransom, in effect, operates in this matrix, but he now divides the Kantian complementarity of art and science, and turns art and science into opposing moments. The search for totality by Ransom's contemplative subject in the fullness of sensibility leaves the other two-thirds of the Kantian triad, theoretical and practical reason, alienated. Ransom's trajectory moves through the available forms of established culture. The real fullness and totality that have to be created through the historical praxis of the concrete historical subject against the established realities are inaccessible to Ransom. Neither that subject nor that praxis is available within the terms of his theoretical construction. None the less, at least the Agrarian strategic complex involves the prospect of a pseudo-totality appropriate to the contemplative subject. In the New Critical resolution, the aesthetic sphere simply becomes a partial sphere among other partial spheres.

iv Sentiment

Sentiment is an important concept for Ransom; it is the point of contact between the capabilities of the ordinary person and the artist. Like Richards, Ransom is unable to differentiate adequately between the everyday and the aesthetic. 'Sentiment is the totality of love and knowledge which we have of an object that is private and unique.' It is responsible for a 'vast increment of diffuse and irrelevant sensibilia' that obstruct science and action (WB 36). The specification of value in terms of 'irrelevance' expresses a *defensive* negation of the prevailing rationality; in the New Critical phase its domain will be progressively invaded by that rationality. Sentiments and the formal arts are 'alternative forms of aesthetic knowledge' (230); the differences lie mainly in the smaller volume of the latter, the greater explicitness of its knowledge, and the intense concentration needed to produce it, versus the fairly universal and less precise character of the former. Sentimental knowledge of the object 'simply grows' (231).

The exclusion from aesthetic theory of the concrete connections between the individual and the society, of the cathartic elevation from everyday heterogeneity, through the medium, to the homogeneity of generic immediacy, leaves no grounds for differentiating between aesthetic and everyday forms of contemplative subjectivity. Once the aesthetic is no longer understood as the objective formation of subjectivity determined by a comprehensive and intensive relation to man's human essence, aesthetic immediacy collapses into everyday immediacy.

Ransom writes:

> Love, respect, tenderness, fixation upon the object, all these terms would define an attitude in subjective or emotional terms, but they mean nothing until we study what we are really trying to do with the object. We are only trying to know it as a complete or individual object; and, as a corollary undoubtedly, to protect it against our other and predatory kind of knowledge which would reduce it to its mere utility. Sentiment is aesthetic, aesthetic is cognitive, and the cognition is of the object as an individual. And this, I imagine, is all the mystery that will be discovered in sentiment. (216)

We find here again the characteristic irony of the contemplative objectivity of Agrarian poetics; it turns into an aesthetic subjectivism, a psychology. All the stress on fullness has failed to specify the aesthetic object; the aesthetic relates and refers to an *attitude* in opposition to the scientific. Whether he calls it appreciation or sentimentality, or enjoyment or celebration or love or respect or humility, whether he defines it as disinterestedness or desirelessness, Ransom is describing a mental approach to the object, a psychology. Everything, by virtue of its infinite fullness, can become an aesthetic object if only we have the right attitude to it: a position of pure empiricist subjectivism.

Ransom's subjectivist stress on attitudes expresses an absence of objective norms, a lack of social location. The discovery of a new social location in the New Critical period produces a new type of stress on the object, a new localized criticism, and a deepening of reified scientism. It is the sentiments, Ransom writes, which keep us 'up to the decent level of our historic humanity' (232). Once the Agrarian social matrix is gone, the New Critical period is left with an ideology of submission and an abstract humanism based in an integrated, object-dependent sensibility.

CHAPTER 7

New Criticism

A The Rise of New Criticism

The New Criticism dates from the latter part of the 1930s. The failure of Agrarianism was followed by abandonment of the Southern problematic along with the neoromantic absolutist attitude, and led to reduced claims, geared to the actual possibilities for realizing a 'fullness of sensibility' within the *given* historical forms. This meant the discovery of a new geographical and social location, and involved a move to the North and the development of a program and an institutional basis that would provide a place for art and a place for its proponents appropriate to the historical commotion. Ransom was the decisive figure in this transition. While Tate (for example) retained for a long time the posture of absolutist reaction and finally wound up in the arms of the Catholic Church, Ransom, who had since Fugitive days always been less doctrinaire and tortured, was able to lead the integration under the categories of secular authority, make peace with the prevailing rationality, and prepare the theoretical ground for the literary technicism corresponding to the Keynesian technicism that was concurrently transforming social life.

Ransom recalls that after the 'red fury' of Agrarianism had subsided, he lived without harm in a 'minority pocket of the culture,' that is, 'educational institutions, with pockets of "humanities," whose interest has identified itself increasingly with ours,' and publishers, and so forth.[1] It is important to remember the joint growth of, on one hand, the institutional power of critical theory, involving, with the rise of mass education and mass culture, a broad and dense fabric of educational and journalistic interrelations, positions, and influence, with control over decisions affecting the

85

direction, orientation, and priorities of a whole field, and, on the other, the great ideological influence of a key system of reference for notions of our relations to the objective world, to other people, and to ourselves. In this context, Louise Cowan is surely right that the 'greatest impact' of the New Critics 'has been in establishing a profession of letters.'[2] I would add a dimension familiar to historians of science—that this professionalization was to be linked with both the immense restriction of vision and the consequent precision of detail that are characteristic of New Criticism.[3]

I want to sketch briefly some of the main elements in the theoretical and institutional formation of New Criticism. On the programmatic side, there is the beginning, in the post-Agrarian essay in *The World's Body*, 'Criticism, Inc.,' of a new focus on criticism itself, increasingly seen as an independent entity that can stand as the object of attention. Criticism, in this view, is empiricist and non-partisan. The critic is to deal with both the prose core and the 'totality of connotation' (WB 348); and criticism is said to involve the technical study of poetic devices (347), within the context of the 'first law' of criticism, that it must focus on the nature of the object (342) and identify the poetic 'ontological or metaphysical manoeuvre' (347). There is a general insistence in the New Critical period that priority belongs to the poetic object, not to its effect; that the poem is autonomous, closed, self-contained, complete, and to be contemplated as a pattern of knowledge. Only 'the hardest close analysis of the actual poems,' Ransom writes, can establish their content;[4] the New Criticism is a specifically 'literary criticism,'[5] that is, in contrast with the 'business of the moralist,' 'the business of the literary critic is exclusively with an esthetic criticism.'[6] Ransom rejects the 'shapeless miscellany of all prior criticism' and expects that the new criticism, as a kind of collaborative effort, will arrive at something 'radically new, and fertile' and 'proportionately as definitive' as the new physics or the new logic.[7]

In every crucial respect, these manifesto-like statements point in the direction of the development of bourgeois scientific formalism. Moreover, Ransom's theoretical program was consciously linked with a program of institutional entrenchment that was to provide it with a viable place in social life. In 1937: 'the whole enterprise might be seriously taken in hand by professionals;' 'criticism must become more scientific, or precise and systematic, and this means that it must be developed by the collective and sustained effort of learned persons—which means that its proper seat is in the universities'

(WB 329). In 1939, in the opening issue of *The Kenyon Review*: 'The colleges have really not had an available body of critical theory to teach. But now it is the Age of Criticism.'[8] And in 1940, having put the case for the study of 'the structure and mode of construction of the object' against the 'official policy of the professors,'[9] Ransom contends that a 'tough, scientific' critical attitude must take the place of the 'nearly accomplished' historical, linguistic, and editorial work of orthodox literary scholarship:[10]

> I should think that the future of the professorship of literature is immense. But that is because I judge that the revolution will presently occur, rather peacefully and in the course of nature, and the professors start in upon a new order of studies: the speculative or critical ones.

Ransom's new rationalism is in sharp contrast with his Agrarian anti-rationalism. I shall shortly examine some of the new relations it involves. For the moment, I would note that the changes for which Ransom prepared the way far exceeded his own wishes. By 1952, he reports not only that 'in the academy the verbal analysis has pretty well secured its place and tenure' but also that it has 'bogged down' in an 'excruciating impasse: with cold-blooded critics of poetry working away at what sometimes appear to be the merest exercises with words.'[11] By the latter 1950s, the New Criticism was being displaced by mythological structuralism, but its program of technological positivism, and its advocates, remain entrenched at various levels of the field.

In 1939, Ransom moved to Ohio and founded *The Kenyon Review*,[12] which he edited for twenty years (until his retirement in 1959) as a permanent manifesto of the New Criticism. The whole Kenyon College complex, with the *Review*, 'The Kenyon Review Fellowships,' and 'The Kenyon School of English'[13] provided a central base to focus the efforts of an increasingly powerful literary movement under the general shaping influence of Ransom, whose books and articles offered a theoretical foundation, as well as a name, to the New Criticism. Several other journals constituted additional means of production under New Critical control, the most important being *The Hudson Review* (from 1948), *The Sewanee Review*, which Allen Tate edited from 1944 to 1946, and *The Southern Review*, founded by Cleanth Brooks and Robert Penn Warren in 1935 following the death, in the previous year, of *Hound and Horn*, which Richard Blackmur had edited in 1929, and of which Yvor Winters and Tate were regional editors in 1942. *The Southern Review* was absorbed into *The Kenyon Review* in 1942. By the end of the 1940s, New Criticism could be found in most North American literary reviews. During this period, too, New Criticism succeeded in effecting an educational transformation, and became established as the dominant pedagogic tradition. It is generally accepted that the vastly influential textbooks published by the New Critics (widely welcomed, used, and imitated) deserve credit for this, especially Cleanth Brooks' successful anthologies.[14] On the whole, New Critical institutional penetration of the ideological realm through teaching, literary journals, and publications of theoretical, practical critical, and pedagogic interest, provided a broad and solid structural basis for the diffusion of ideology.

B The Novelty of New Criticism

To understand the ideology of the New Criticism, it is essential to view it in the light of its relation both to its Agrarian antecedents and to its social context, that is, to situate it with respect to its past and present. Characteristically, the novelty of the new position is most clearly manifest in the attitude to science which, in terms of the ontic structure of Ransom's work, is always the determining feature, in that science represents for him the dominant form of social rationality. We find that, compared to earlier positions, a new balance is offered: 'The scientific and aesthetic ways of knowledge should illuminate each other; perhaps they are alternative knowledges, and a preference for one knowledge over the other might indicate an elemental or primary bias in temperament' (NC 294). Gone is the urgency of the differentiation between man and animal, gone the crisis of civilization. The whole framework of the opposition is drastically reduced to the level of discourse where, although the issue of the difference cannot be dodged, Ransom declines to 'ride either hobby, the scientific or the literary.'[15] Poetry still tells us more about the world than science 'needs to tell,' but 'this truth is not unfriendly to science nor need it be fatal to the practical structure' (93).

Coming after the Agrarian formulations, it is strikingly apparent that this new position aims to preserve much of the substance of the developed poetics, while neutralizing its critical form—its moments of negativity. Indeed, to contain the critique, Ransom has now to penetrate even to the most essential feature of his poetics, the contemplative Schopenhauerian poetic 'knowledge without desire': 'That doctrine also seems too negative and indeterminate.'[16] The positive version of the doctrine stresses the 'increment of meaning' in art, without stressing the combat with science. In general, Ransom moves from a conflict model to a functional complementarity model, one that is ideologically adequate to the integrative tendencies of the historical period. On one hand, in seeking at the expense of his 'old-line education' to conceive human activities 'naturalistically,'[17] that is to look, not for social, but for biotic motivations, Ransom increasingly views art as a secondary of 'leisure' interest that promises 'not to interfere with the organic interests, which are primary.'[18] On the other, he comes to declare himself opposed to rescuing the 'humanities' by disparaging the natural and social sciences, both of which he now considers to be valuable and humane forms of our adaptation to nature and to society.[19] The relation of art to scientific-practical life is fully pacified.[20]

> Poetry is an organic-and-inorganic activity; first and last it is organic, or Positive and in the service of the organism; in between, but discreetly and in less than subversive measure, it is inorganic, or unrelated to the organic interest. It has a commanding identity with prose, and a radical but not inimical difference.

Biological models applied to social forms always carry an implicit bias toward the positivity of the established order. Ransom makes the inclination explicit. At a time when Tate is still explicitly rejecting the successes of public education in teaching adjustment to the given society,[21] Ransom, impressed by the 'honesty' of the positivist forces of social construction, proposes 'to have commerce with the world.' He also claims to 'admire the moderns for the honesty and rigor of their analytical methods.'[22] The most illuminating formulation of this new attitude is in a letter to Tate dated 23 May 1941:[23]

> I am forced to regard poetic theory as science, though a new science, because about a new or 'different' kind of discourse. That's why I don't want any taboos, restrictions, philosophical censorship, against the analytic work. If that is positivism, I guess I'm a member of the tribe. But so far as the absurd emphasis on scientific discourse as the only discourse goes, I'm far from being one.

We should now be in a position to locate this change in position as the commotive specificity of New Critical ideology. What Ransom's new position means is not the obliteration of earlier anti-rationalist poetics; it means the transplantation of neoromantic irrationality onto the new ground of neocapitalist scientistic rationality. It means, therefore, precisely the assimilation of all critical aspects; they are integrated and contained.

It is important to understand that, if an earlier sharp antagonism can now take the form of a docile, contained antinomy, then the ontological foundation of this containment, that is, a location within the social integration, has been accepted. Again, we must refer the New Critical world to the Agrarian. The passivity and submissiveness of Agrarian poetics was contradictory; it retained a critical aspect in relation to reality as long as it was held within the broader Agrarian project for a different reality. In one sense, its passivity expressed a withdrawal from the given reality, and its submission was oriented to the alternative that was to be made available through the aesthetic life. The New Critical retraction, the repudiation of the broad Agrarian social matrix, retains the passivity and submission only as a surrender to the existing alienation.

In the Agrarian period, the critic and poet Donald Davidson had written: 'Harmony between the artist and society must be regained; the dissociation must be broken down. That can only be done, however, by first putting society itself in order.'[24] And, in sharp contrast to the educational program of the New Criticism and of the subsequent tradition, the Agrarian Ransom had explicitly rejected education as an adequate solution to the problems. As he wrote:[25]

> The trouble with the life-pattern is to be located at its economic base, and we cannot rebuild it by pouring in soft materials from the top. . . . Humanism, properly speaking, is not an abstract system, but a culture, the whole way in which we live, act, think, and feel. It is a kind of imaginatively balanced life lived out in a definite social tradition. . . . We cannot recover our native humanism by adopting some standard of taste that is critical enough to question the contemporary arts but not critical enough to question the social and economic life which is their ground.

By contrast, the New Critical Ransom abdicates the social critique, forgets the 'anaesthesia' of scientific machine efficiency, and reduces a profound problematic to the typically modern fetish of a language abstracted from material reality. He now writes:[26]

> I cannot think the difficulties are social, or economic, or

material, for these difficulties are perennial. It is true that we have plenty of trouble adjusting to an Age of Machines, but it hardly paralyses us. I find myself more and more imagining that the epochal thing that has happened to us is a sudden crisis of language and expression.

And, in this period, Ransom goes even further than this in renouncing the possibilities of supersession. He adopts the view that progress is irreversible and considers a return to an agrarian economy 'a heavy punishment.' Art and science, he argues, would have been impossible without the division of labor, and he regards the specific form of the capitalist division of labor as identical with socio-economic advance in general. In consequence, he believes, it is enough that there should be in society a few men 'strong enough to complete their experience eventually' and hence be able to produce art. The project of creating the conditions of possibility for everyone to complete his experience has been abandoned as impossible fantasy. Ransom sees no way of going back; and he has at no time been able to conceive a way of going forward to a genuinely liberating and fulfilling future. So the position is this: specialized labor 'has become our second nature;' salvation comes through art. 'In the forms which this salvation takes, we do go back into our original innocence, but vicariously or symbolically, not really. We cannot actually go back, and if we try it the old estate becomes insupportable.' Works of art (or religious exercises) are thus viewed as 'compensatory concretions' to help us 'manage as we are': 'they return to primitive experience but only formally; by no means do they propose to abandon the forward economy.'[27]

In other words, the structure of alienated reality is accepted even at its surface as being permanently unchangeable. The project of humanizing our concrete existence is ruled out; it is argued that we can humanize only our thought, symbolically, by way of 'compensation.' It is important to understand the historical meaning of this New Critical humanism. Ransom's values as such have not had to change. Once an alienated reality is eternalized, the die is decisively cast, and all critical values from an earlier opposition take on a different significance. The attempt to affirm values within an alienated totality without attempting to explode that alienation simply reinforces the alienation and, as in this case, subordinates the realm of aesthetic humanism to the reified categories of neocapitalist production relations. Values need not be abrogated; they can be incorporated. This is the strategy of a social formation tending toward a corporate reality and the total administration of life, and Ransom's self-satisfied assertion that the former Agrarians are now 'defending the freedom of the arts whose function they understand'[28] expresses the New Critical surrender to that strategy.

It cannot be emphasized too strongly that the bourgeois sanctification of humanist symbolization denies humanism in the flesh. The romantic reduction of culture to the special province of art has already involved an element of positivity in precluding the realization of imaginative culture as a whole way of life.[29] The polemical defense of art by New Critical specialists[30] is a second order specialization that reintegrates the position assumed by the romantics in the capitalist division of labor. This critical but isolated position, which had been assumed during the grand bifurcation of the historical practice of the social formation, is now reintegrated into the neocapitalist corporate functionalization of different social spheres on the grounds of a unifying positivity.

We have yet to consider the scientistic aspect of New Critical specialization. The stress on scientific analysis in an intrinsic aesthetic criticism is a rationalization of artificially isolated partial functions that are made autonomous and isolated from other partial functions. In the process of this specialization, totality is not reached but destroyed; the new 'scientific' sphere is from the start a fetish, an internally coherent formal system that is also increasingly abstract and empty. 'An IBM could probably simulate with equal interest'[31] the practical criticism of the 1950s. As an alienated special system it is a specific alienation with its specific alienated language and methodology; the New Criticism even develops its specific vocabulary.[32] The stress is on the integrity of the object, but since bourgeois-scientific integralism is arbitrary, New Critical analysis is exclusive, not inclusive, and remains so in the development of the formalist paradigm throughout the tradition.

The Agrarian Ransom had criticized science for being always *a* science, hence partial. The New Criticism is now open to the same critique. The more developed and established the New Criticism and its subsequent tradition become, the more it happens that 'the world lying beyond its confines, and in particular the material base which it is its task to understand, *its own concrete underlying reality* lies, methodologically and in principle, *beyond its grasp.*'[33] Such a scientific approach is necessarily tied to reified reality; it is a positive study of forms in abstraction from their real essence. This is the irony of Ransom's 'ontological criticism.' The fetish of immanent moments of form occludes the real art-object/reality relation, and cuts the criticism off from its genuine ontological problematic.

C Ontological Criticism: *The New Criticism*

> The differentia of poetry as discourse is an ontological one. It treats an order of existence, a grade of objectivity, which cannot be treated in scientific discourse. . . . Poetry intends to recover the denser and more refractory original world which we know loosely through our perceptions and memories. By this supposition it is a kind of knowledge which is radically or ontologically distinct. (NC 281)

With this view of poetry as a language in the service of the phenomenological immediacy of everyday perception, Ransom defines poetic signs as iconic signs which, as *signs, refer* to objects, but which, as *iconic* signs, also 'resemble and imitate these objects' (285). Iconic discourse embodies whole, concrete objects, including their value properties *inter alia*, and necessarily involves indeterminacy since the embodied particulars always exceed definition.

The link between Ransom's view of the poetic function and his influential call for an ontological criticism that will gain access to the substance of poetry through a study of its structures, is the notion that the structure of poetry resembles the structure of the world. This point has been controversial and often criticized.[34] Yet this most important point in Ransom is the basis of his endlessly repeated assertion, in various permutations of correlated pairings (including, on one side, structure, or constants, or design, or argument, or prose, or logical core or scientific core, and, on the other side, texture, or contingents, or residue, or increment, or sensibility, or tissue of irrelevances), that the poem embodies both necessity and contingency.

In 1929, Ransom gives a clear formulation of this resemblance between the poem and the world: 'Art, as a representation of nature, represents it in its dual capacity as composed in part of constants and in part of contingents. If it were lacking in either feature, it would fail in realism, . . . and it would forfeit our confidence.'[35] And even more explicitly, in 1952, Ransom argues that 'the little world [the artistic imitation] sets up is a small version of our natural world in its original dignity.'[36] The argument is broader than some sections of *The World's Body* would suggest, and bases the mimetic theory, beyond the empiricist level of copying detail, in the structural continuity of categories on the ontological level.

Potentially, this is Ransom's most important methodological insight. It could lead to a social and historical view of a unified reality within which art and science could be located according to their division of labor as forms of social consciousness. Instead, given Ransom's metaphysics, the formalism of the theory, and the exclusion of social-historical mediation, the ontological continuity (that finds a basis for the internal articulation of the work of art in the articulation of objective nature) serves only to entrench a mechanical separation of universality (constants) and particularity (contingents), to exclude notions of catharsis in favor of notions of mimesis or of linguistic/technical closure, and to provide support for reducing aesthetics to the fullness of everyday perceptual immediacy.

From this basis, Ransom views the poem as a body of language bounded by two arcs of indeterminacy (semantic and metrical), and defines 'the vocation *par excellence* of criticism' as the distinction of the determinate and indeterminate elements of meaning in the work of art (NC 300–2). In abrogating judgment of social and artistic significance in favor of a technical study of 'the coexistence and connection' of these elements, Ransom seeks to bring criticism to a 'level of professional competence' (301–2). The interest of this kind of study, Ransom insists, is more profound than a merely ethical interest; it is ontological.

Ransom's recognition of the refrangibility of the initial subjectivity and the refractivity of the medium (that is, that the medium of literary language does something different from simply expressing, transparently, an author's conscious intention) is a significant moment for the tradition. However, deflection from the real homogenization effected by the medium to an assertion of heterogeneity—the coexistence of constants and contingents, structure and texture—as being 'the specific, the characteristic mode of poetry' (130) distorts the discovery. The New Critical 'linguistic revolution' in reading poetry is to be achieved by emphasis upon 'the total connotation of words.'[37] Yet, notes Ransom, 'we cannot attend to all the meaning behind any poem, and we must have some sort of schedule of priorities in what we do attend to' (128–9). Although, he stresses, the differentia of poetic discourse is the texture, the 'non-structural increment of meaning' (220), nevertheless, this must attach itself to the logical structure that is found in every poem, and which is there for the purpose of supporting the texture (129).

Ransom's structure-texture formulation is a rationalist deduction from his notions of the nature of reality and from the axiom of ontological resemblance. The methodological significance of this position for the present discussion lies in the unusually strong sanction it affords for an investigation of the ideological core of these aesthetic formulations, a sanction reinforced by Ransom's own explanation of the genesis of the analysis. Ransom claims to have been unable for years to see how 'real particularity could get into a universal,' how concrete and universal could form a single unit.[38] 'But it was the political way of thinking which gave . . . the first analogy which seemed valid. The poem was like a democratic state, in action, and observed both macroscopically and microscopically';[39] 'a democratic state, so to speak, which realizes the ends of a state without sacrificing the personal character of its citizens' (54). The ends of the state are realized by organic, purposive, economic human activities, and, of course, the poetic universals are 'paradigms of rational human processes'[40] in this sense.

We cannot fail to read in this characterization the ideological form of a historic change. The aesthetic function is interpreted as an accretion of contingency to the primary 'organic' functions on which it depends and with which it coexists and co-constitutes the democratic—in the present analysis, corporate—state. Culture is located as an internal aspect of a more comprehensive integration, and there is no question of changing either other aspects or the arrangement itself. This contingency may be a localized escape from the law of necessity, but it neither subverts nor explodes it. Within this framework, it is true, Ransom still resists complete logical rationalization. Indeed, he has often been criticized for going too far in the structure-texture separation.[41] What would appear to be at work here is that, within the framework of the specific categorical structure of the theory, such mechanical pluralism is the most suitable response to the pressures of the period; and although some shifts in emphasis occur during the second decade of the New Criticism, a higher level of rationalization is not in fact reached until the further formalizations on the basis of myth and analogy in Northrop Frye's extension of the realm of Ransom's category of 'structure.'[42]

In this context, we should examine briefly the chief internal dispute within the New Criticism: the 'heresy of paraphrase' discussion. Ransom, like all the New Critics, grants that 'the poem is not included in its paraphrase.'[43] Indeed, he raises as the 'Number One problem for poetic theory,' the question of what is excluded from the argument, and repeatedly he locates this differentia as 'the imitation-element of the poem, . . . its free natural imagery,'[44] and the goal of poetry. But Ransom adds the second proposition that 'the poem must include its own paraphrase, or else a logical argument capable of being expressed in a paraphrase,'[45] since 'a pragmatic occasion is required for an act of attention.' The romantic attitude of witnessing and reporting, he holds, arrives at nothing; 'the logic of a human purposiveness is necessary for poetic as for any other discourse.'[46] Against Ransom's dualism, Cleanth Brooks insists that the text of the poem is a total context of organic interrelations. He emphasizes a lack of logical structure in the poem, which exists in its metaphors. Only the poem can speak the poem, no statements about the poem can be taken for its essential core, and the organic relation of all the elements means that nothing has primacy. Brooks operates in the neo-Kantian matrix of symbolic form theories proposed by W. M. Urban and Suzanne Langer. The poem is said to have a unity that is the reconciliation of all disparities and tensions. Everything is subordinated to 'a total and governing attitude. . . . The unity is achieved by a dramatic process, not a logical; it represents an equilibrium of forces, not a formula.'[47]

This is an irrational holistic theology which, if carried through consequentially, would stop criticism entirely. It is a contradictory unity; it both reaches backward to the Agrarian irrationality and forward to the post-logical forms of rationalization.[48] It is perhaps most useful for this discussion to see it as an ideological face of New Critical practice. The stress on the interrelation of all elements with no possible priorities recalls the programmatic practical criticism of I. A. Richards and the methodology of empiricist functionalism. From a point of view outside the New Critical framework altogether, the Ransom–Brooks dispute may be less significant for the immediate theoretical conflict between pluralism and organicism than for the general ideological unity of the two positions. Brooks' assertion that all irrelevancies are functional to the total attitude in the search for unity[49] is as much (or, indeed, even more) a surrender to the governing rationality as Ransom's position. And neither theory is able to deal with the gains and losses involved in the critical project of translating a generic form of self-consciousness (art) into a generic form of consciousness (criticism), that is, in raising to the level of objective knowledge the generic immediacy of the world of the art object.

Such too is the case with the related issue of irony. For Ransom, since his Fugitive discovery of irony as the inclusive third moment that expressed humility in face of objectivity, the category has remained a category of submission to the domination of the given world. Its role is to parry the blow of a triumph of the realm of 'is' over the realm of 'ought to be,' and to suspend for a moment the decision.[50] It is a flight from resolution, and, Ransom claims, a special type of poetry (NC 95). For Brooks, the category is a universal category of poetic order which includes and reconciles oppositions, tensions, incongruities.[51] Again, what we need to see is not so much the internal dispute in which, in any case, the definitions and intentions are largely shared, but that the whole dispute already takes place on the ground of positivity; and both poetics, in effect, are ideologies of functional equilibrium.

In this connection, it is informative to look at the reformulations in the second decade of New Criticism, especially with respect to meter. On the whole, if the first decade of development had its center of gravity in the scientistic side of Ransom's New Criticism, the second saw a shift to the humanist side, the two being structurally linked in the poetics through the 'prose humanism' (versus an innocent aesthetic naturalism) or moral design or logical scruples, that is, the human purposiveness of the discourse.[52] Ransom announces in this second decade that modern society does not seem destitute of its normal humanity and that he has 'hopes for it, even on its own terms.'[53] At the same time, there is, firstly, a new stress that the defense of poetry 'will have to be a defense of its human substance.'[54] Indeed, Ransom criticizes Richard Blackmur for being too technical in his studies, for a lack of 'ideological emphasis,' and for appraising social and religious ideas only for their 'function within the work; even though they may be ideas from which, at the very moment, out in the world of action, the issues of life and death are hung.'[55] This is the kind of repressive value-incorporation I discussed earlier. To note it here is important if a complete picture of Ransom's developing theories is to be traced, although this type of referential imperative survives only in a very deeply modified form in Frye. Secondly, the call for a study of 'substantive as well as formal values in the poem'[56] is accompanied by a corollary emphasis on the prose side of the poem, to the point of insisting that poetry can be read as prose at will, since 'the prose is there too, and easily intelligible.'[57] In the Kantian pairing of the understanding and the imagination, Ransom now finds it strategic to reinforce the former, as in his attack on symbolism: 'The understanding . . . keeps ever awake . . . in order to be ready to restrain the imagination if it tries to be free.'[58] In other words, the dominant rationality is ever more powerfully asserted in the aesthetic realm.

Meter is the third, and perhaps most important aspect of the reformulations. In a major attempt at theoretical revision in 1947, Ransom proposed a Freudian id-ego problematic that was still a two-term dialectic.[59] But in 1952, meter is established as an independent third term. The enormous pressures under which Ransom's dualism had operated for thirty years proved too much, and the two-term dialectic finally cracked. A three-term dialectic is a move toward the synthesis that earlier Ransom had tried to avoid. None of the revisions, the last important attempt at which is the pair of 'Concrete Universal' essays,[60] is theoretically momentous; their interest for us is in this ideological movement toward a unified rationality.

In 1952, Ransom remarks that logic and metaphor have strived in vain to dominate each other; 'but now I suggest that we must reckon with the meters too, and the poem assumes a trinitarian existence.'[61] Meter is enforced against both and provides an overall equilibrium. And most clearly, in the same year in 'Humanism at Chicago,' in addition to its aspect of social, ethical, rational, and useful denotation, and its aspect of inviolable, formless, free imitation beyond denotation, the poem is established in a third aspect, as a metered construct. This third aspect encompasses and envelops the first two aspects, and makes an 'elemental, cosmic, and eternal object;' that is, meter permeates the other two worlds (of logic and metaphor), and lets us 'have them *sub specie aeternitatis*.'[62] The aesthetic rhythms, of course, are formal generic moments of the transhistorical human world produced in the course of the elevation of mankind out of nature; the characterization of the metered object as 'elemental, cosmic, and eternal' reflects the ideological valuation of permanent order.

CHAPTER 8

Conclusion to Ransom

Herbert Marcuse has repeatedly remarked on an endemic tendency to reduce the tension in the two-dimensional logic of capitalist thought to a one-dimensional and authoritarian system. We have seen above the trajectory of Ransom's truncated two-term dialectic in the progress of a philosophical attitude that first advocated one side of the dualism, then embraced the dualism as a whole. Eventually, Ransom experimented with trinitarian formulations and unified constructions. By the time he observed that evil was 'too well established in nature ever to fail us,' but that its party was 'in the minority' and would 'never prevail,'[1] the issue was decided and the dualism had the character of a shame-faced monism. At the end of his official career in 1959, Ransom no longer sided with the 'Old Order' but talked 'for the other side,' in arguing that 'not the dull sheltered Garden, but the unknown forbidding world at large, is what we must identify in all piety . . . as "the best of all possible worlds."'[2] And he cautiously turned toward the 'vitality and power' of mass media.[3] The transitions in his position have been remarkable, they really have, and the personal career heroic, but these are comprehensible if we find their locus, as I have been arguing, in the historical trajectory whose significance resides in the transformation of social ideology in the cultural realm.

An important part of this totality is its moment of reified humanism. The question posed is the relation with nature, which is not to be challenged but embraced. The controlling notion, embodying a nostalgia for a non-alienated human existence, while retaining the material forms and bases of alienation, is that 'if we can obtain the sense of community with the infinite concretion of the environing world, we may cease to feel like small aliens, even though busy, cunning and predatory ones.'[4] Naturally, the solution is offered in terms of the symbolic subject/object unity of the aesthetic experience. It is proposed that the social function poetry fulfills is to 'lend us morale; it is an excellent effect in an Age of Anxiety; and so far as we know every age is an age of anxiety.'[5] The projection into the past from a disaffection for the present serves to eternalize alienation in the future as a transcendent law of life. But it is said to be bearable because 'an acute pain has become chronic and low-grade'[6] since the Romantic tradition. Now, morale is to take the place of a morality actualized in practice; through the salvation of art, as we have seen already, 'we manage as we are.'[7]

The indelible positivity of this program is explicit.[8]

> We can't have any effect on the economy, and . . . what results is that humanism is a way of life; and the people who practice it might as well call it a metaphysical society or a mode of life; . . . it's a minority group and it can even be operated by people who are thoroughly attuned to the new economy, because that's the only thing that saves us.

Such a humanism is integrated, bankrupt, and cut off from the ontological possibilities for its material realization. The New Critics, in becoming the official, authorized defenders or representatives of a tradition of values, achieved an ideological adequation to the commotion and, in consequence, an influence disproportionate to their numbers. But, in becoming integrated professional specialists, they also stabilized the form and content of their vocation, and neutralized its critical possibilities. The position is very clear in Ransom's discussion of 'the communities of letters.' 'How much more tolerant, and more humane, is this community than the formal society!' If we add them all up, we get a 'secondary society.' 'But the group has no organization, and no revolutionary intentions.' Aesthetic culture simply provides 'release for the oversensitive.'[9]

The complementary counterpart of New Critical reified humanism is the reified scientistic objectivism of the New Critical aesthetic. Ransom asserts that art relates to a different order of reality, a different grade of objectivity, from science. This is a distortion. It would be more accurate to point to a division of labor between art and science as different forms of consciousness, different active ways of organizing our responses to the world on levels of mediacy specific to their respective categorical structures. But they relate to a unified reality; and in the neocapitalist commotion they are both alienated. The New Critical science replaces the real world with its own ideological-metaphysical categories (for example, a core of constancy, or the fullness of the world's body) that are then assumed to *be* the reality and are duly investigated with rigorous precision. In this fashion, the work of art is insulated and fetishized, and the problem of historical relation to the world is reduced to the problem of cognition of preconstituted objectivity.

This purely cognitive comportment abstracts from the process of aesthetic production and reproduction, that is, from the process of cathartic homogenization in the creation and appropriation of the art object via the homogeneous medium. In consequence, it posits the world as rigid subject/object duality which, if one or the other pole is not to be violated, can be linked only by a tenuous bridge of innocent contemplation. We must note the consequences of such a position:[10]

> As long as man adopts a stance of intuition and contemplation he can only relate to his own thought and to the objects of the empirical world in an immediate way. He accepts both as ready-made—produced by historical reality. As he wishes only to know the world and not to change it he is forced to accept both the empirical, material rigidity of existence and the logical rigidity of concepts as unchangeable. His mythological analyses are not concerned with the concrete origins of this rigidity nor with the real factors inherent in them that could lead to its elimination. They are concerned solely to discover how the *unchanged nature* of these data could be conjoined whilst leaving them unchanged and how to explain them *as such*.

This attitude results in the New Critical close reading, which is a liquidation of the whole world outside the magic circle of the individual critic facing the individual text. Like econometry or other technologies, New Critical technicism is never innocent of the determinations of the conceptual systems which, implicitly or explicitly, control it. The position is structurally subjectivist. John Holloway's perception that the method gives results of variable quality, because it is not clear 'when to take it further and when to stop,'[11] yields only a partial truth. The implication that it may be a case of a sound method occasionally forced beyond its proper parameters is not acceptable because the ideological specificity of New Critical close reading lies precisely in the absolutization of the methodology, and, therefore, of the subjectivism. It follows from this that the quality and nature of the results depend on and vary with the individual critic.

Although it is by now almost commonplace to observe that much of the work produced by this formalist subjectivism is arbitrary overreading or distortion of the text,[12] the epistemological basis of this error is by no means equally clear. I have argued earlier that a theoretical conceptualization can never be symmetrical with its object, that the relation between concept and object is mediated by another relation, that of the concept to its teleological basis, which itself bears a determinate relation to the socio-historical context. In consequence, the conceptual realism of the close reading, like that of the contemporary structuralist reading, in aiming at the 'totality of connotations,' at an exhaustive positive apprehension of the object, cannot fail to be dogmatic, and to project an extraneous problematic into the object and then proceed to analyze that projection.[13]

The operation of the problematic on the formal-technical level is in one aspect a historical regression in aesthetic study. But in a number of respects, with which I shall conclude this examination, the New Critical position is an advance. Ransom's insistence that the work of art is a construct, a real, dense object, a closed structure of objectification, is a genuine advance of critical theory over all earlier biographical, 'historical,' sociological, philological, or other scholarly methodologies. Until the aesthetic status of a work of art is established, there can be no aesthetic discussion, strictly speaking, and Ransom and the New Critics are important in bourgeois theory for asserting the ontological status of art as aesthetic. If they have helped to establish that art is not an inferior reality produced by or traceable to some other sphere of the social totality, and if they have helped to resist the popular nineteenth-century reductions of art to some social or economic 'factor,' to that extent they have made a genuine advance. At the same time, art must be seen as a moment of the historical practice of the social formation, intimately involved, within the categories of that totalization of praxis, with the essentials of human development at a concrete moment in space and time; and Ransom and the New Critics failed to locate art in these terms.

In consequence, the embryonic New Critical scientific paradigm remains an alienated scientific paradigm that deepens the reification of subjectivity. This scientism, in precluding the historico-specific consideration of symbols, points ahead to Frye; in the focus on the linguistic medium, to McLuhan. Ultimately, the New Criticism is a step forward precisely in its most profound vocational project. The positivist empiricism of New Critical practice, which accepts the object as a given, is directed to the assimilation, the consumption of the art work. Professionalization in this cultural role locates the New Criticism, in terms of the commotive changes involving extensive new rationalization, as a novel productive force of the neocapitalist integration. And, in its ideological role, it prepares for even further rationalization, for even broader and deeper reification.

PART III

Northrop Frye
The Critical Theory of Capitulation

CHAPTER 9
Mythological Structuralism

A Introduction

Northrop Frye's reputation and influence in the realm of bourgeois critical theory are secure beyond challenge. Volumes could be written discussing his substantive system of literary theory, much of which in complexity, sophistication, erudition, and level of insight—hence in scope of ideological efficiency—far exceeds earlier formulations. At what was evidently a canonization session of the English Institute's 1965 meeting at Columbia University, Geoffrey Hartman, although disclaiming the aim of 'premature deification,' described Frye with the Copernican image of the 'virile man standing in the sun . . . overlooking the planets' in order to indicate his 'new vantage point with its promise of mastery and also its enormously expanded burden of sight.'[1] Angus Fletcher, meanwhile, expressed his admiration for Frye's systematic design by comparing it to the Haussmann plans for the layout of Parisian streets.[2] Frye himself graciously accepted this conceit of the Haussmann boulevards, 'which enabled Parisians, so to speak, to see Paris,' as comprehending his ambitions for criticism.[3] It is appropriate to recall another aspect of Haussmann's designs: that they represented an attempt at political control by promising to check the subversive strategies of street fighting. Frye's theory, in the present analysis, embodies aesthetic capitulation to the commotive forms of domination; it proposes a view of culture structurally articulated to preclude radical historical praxis.

Frye 'has had an influence—indeed an absolute hold—on a generation of developing literary critics greater and more exclusive than that of any one theorist in recent critical history.'[4] His speculative systematic construction, the representative form of bourgeois critical theory in the Anglo-American tradition in the latter 1950s and 1960s, with its intimidating symmetries testifying to what Kenneth Burke called 'his frenzy, or orgy, of rheostatic classifying,'[5] is the appropriate moment of cultural ideology for a historical period of immobility.[6] Frye is a Janus-faced interlude between John Crowe Ransom and Marshall McLuhan: on one hand, a consolidation and extension of the formalization of the literary realm, and, on the other, a preparation for a dynamic refocussing of critical theory aimed at the formalization of the totality of social communications. Frye's critical theory, to the extent that it is a scientistic criticism operating on a closed poetic universe, is arguably the last phase of the New Criticism; but in so far as it presents a structural linguistics and communications, in its analysis of the 'verbal universe,' it is arguably the first phase of that reorientation of the literary tradition that is associated with McLuhan. I shall suggest that Frye's work represents a static moment of integrated capitulation between the two dynamic moments of, firstly, the New Critical disengagement of critical theory from social interest and, secondly, the reengagement of critical theory, this time militantly on the side of the prevailing social motion, in the counterrevolutionary position of McLuhan. These two discontinuities, with respect to Ransom and to McLuhan, are situated, I would argue, within the continuity of a tradition of critical theory intelligible as the ideology of progressive cultural rationalization. In this study, the treatment of Frye is comparatively brief; what I want to indicate are the key aspects of Frye's theory in their relation to the present argument.

In retrospect, Frye writes: 'The critical path I wanted . . . was a theory of criticism which would, first, account for the major phenomena of literary experience, and, second, would lead to some view of the place of literature in civilization as a whole.'[7] Frye attempts to satisfy this double aim by formulating a critical theory that views literature as an order of words organized internally by recurring forms independent of history, that stresses, at the same time, the structural centrality of literature in civilization as a primary means (language) of mental production, and that regards the critical theory itself as synthetic and scientific. My argument is that Frye's theory represents in the modern tradition of critical theory that moment when the romantic cultural sphere (which, for over a hundred years, had been located by theorists in opposition to, or in tension with, utilitarian material developments, with what nineteenth-century diction called 'civilization') is reintegrated—

structurally, but not (until McLuhan) with real *historical* reference—as a decisive *internal* principle at work in civilization. This is an important move from the uneasy accommodation to the dominant social patterns that became embodied in New Critical aesthetics, and a prelude to the emergence, in McLuhan's writings, of the absolute dominance of cultural technology over the fate of civilization.

Frye's position implies two major arguments against the New Criticism, and expresses the development from empiricism to a unification of the cultural field by means of a single structural variable, the archetype. The critique of New Criticism is explicit in Frye's *Anatomy*. On one hand, it is said, empiricist close reading, although ingenious, is bound to be futile without a 'sense of the archetypal shape of literature as a whole.'[8] Frye, himself, aims 'to give a rational account of some of the structural principles of Western literature in the context of its Classical and Christian heritage' (AC 133), structure being understood as the recurring principles of literature, such as convention and genre. On the other hand, empiricist close reading is said to neglect such moments of structure as genre because it is concerned with the work of art in itself and 'not as an artifact with a possible function' (95); in consequence, it is insensitive to certain analogies of form. These analogies of form recover for Frye that most important thing he claims the New Criticism lost: 'the sense of context' (CP 272). This context is 'literature as an order of words'[9] whose structural principles recur in individual works. The analogical methodology, in general, becomes the basis in Frye for a much more extensive scientistic rationalization of the literary world than was possible for the New Criticism, and for an educational program that claims that 'the archetypal or conventional element in the imagery that links one poem with another' is essential for the possibility of 'systematic mental training' through literature (AC 100).

The second, and more far-reaching, development from New Criticism involves rejection of Ransom's notion of ontological continuity between literature and the objective world. The New Critics had already attempted the elimination of historical dimensions from criticism, but Ransom had still persisted in adhering to an existential phenomenology, 'ontological' cognition, and categorical continuity between art and the rest of the world. Frye eliminates these in arguing the complete autonomy of the poeᵗic universe through a radical form/content distinction. He repudiates the 'fallacy' of 'existential projection,' and insists that 'the poet never imitates "life" in the sense that life becomes anything more than the content of his work. In every mode he imposes the same kind of mythical form on his content, but makes different adaptations of it' (63). In consequence, critical theory takes up residence exclusively in the realm of the transhistorical, in the realm of permanent or recurring forms. Once transhistorical forms are abstracted from their dialectical unity with the historical realm, they become socially devitalized, and fetishized as idealist essences active at the heart of phenomena. This point is extremely important with respect to Frye's attitudes. The results are evident in Frye's transcendental humanism, idealist notion of civilization, categorical, non-normative scientism, cyclical typology of literary history, and mythic typology of literary structure and cultural unity.

Frye embraces the romantic principle of the human origin of human civilization,[10] but this shift from a religious transcendence to immanence none the less preserves transcendence in secular form. The transhistorical becomes prehistorical; 'desire,' an idealist anthropological principle, is posited as the motor of the development, pre-existing its forms of manifestation. This is the category that links, on the formal level, culture and civilization.

> Civilization is . . . the process of making a total human form out of nature, and it is impelled by the force that we have just called desire. . . . Desire is . . . not a simple response to need, for an animal may need food without planting a garden to get it, nor is it a simple response to want, or desire *for* something in particular. It is neither limited to nor satisfied by objects, but is the energy that leads human society to develop its own form. . . . The form of desire . . . is liberated and made apparent by civilization. The efficient cause of civilization is work, and poetry in its social aspect has the function of expressing, as a verbal hypothesis, a vision of the goal of work and the forms of desire. (AC 105–6)

We should note that if 'work is man's response to his own desire . . . to see the world in a human form,'[11] then work is simply the realization of a meaning that precedes it. In such a one-sided dialectic, a superhistorical principle is set against historical activity. Desire becomes the subject of which the forms of historical praxis, and the objectifications of such praxis, are predicate determinations that can never fully express or realize it. It is not only that the categorical context is static and religious, in that 'the major components' of this human form of nature—the city, the garden, the sheepfold, and so forth—are identified as 'the organizing metaphors of the Bible and of most Christian symbolism' (113, 141), but that, methodologically, a principle of eternity, pure and invariable, has priority over historical principles, which are considered only its partial predicates. 'No matter how fully we may realize our own human natures by social discipline, there will always be a still higher order of nature which is not there, but which is desirable.'[12] In Frye, a traditional Christian problematic blends with an idealized Freudian duality of reality principle and pleasure principle. I shall comment on this further in the next section. For the moment, we need only observe that transcendent subjectivity occludes the real historical subjectivity of human praxis.

It is important to remember that 'subjectivity, . . . by its very essence, can only affirm, maintain and conserve its own immediate content. It can never create *by itself* the internal contradictions producing change.'[13] Frye's desire could not have become dissatisfied with its objects were it not for the production of new needs following satisfactions achieved in the labor process. Work is not simply the efficient agency of desire; desire itself is produced in the work process which is social man's metabolic interaction with nature, and produces both the human world of objects and the human nature of needs and desires (including their relative claims), in a dialectical spiral of reciprocity.[14] Ideologically, suppression of the emergence of qualitatively new aspects of human nature, or their subordination to a universal form of desire, precludes the supersession of alienation through the production of an anthropologically new future of genuinely new human forms, and capitulates to the prevailing material reality. Methodologically, this suppression locks art into the role of constructing the pure forms of desire 'clear of the bondage of history' (AC 347).

In fact, Frye shares the idealist orientation of symbolic form philosophy which sees man as an essentially symbolizing creature—an orientation built on a fetish of mental labor and particularly suitable to express the outlook of a new professional intelligentsia deeply involved in the system of neocapitalist production. In his view, desire is 'an impulse toward expression' (106), and the form of everything in human society and nature 'expresses an aspect of the human mind.'[15] As the outside world 'yields importance and priority to the inner world,' art, naturally, becomes the model of the creative power of man,[16] the 'matrix' of

111

the 'totality of imaginative power' in the mind. Literature, specifically, 'is the verbal part of the process of transforming the non-human world into something with a human shape and meaning, the process that we call culture or civilization.'[17]

The social significance of Frye's interpretation, as I shall note again in greater detail later, is a complete surrender to the established reality. Frye, like Althusser, claims that Marx's decisive eleventh thesis on Feuerbach is an epistemological manifesto, calling for 'a new state of mind,' which he interprets as an inward reference to creative vision in opposition to a rational study of a preconstituted material world. But even a creatively active consciousness is not a real substitute for the ontological activity of the totality of praxis. Frye's position can be seen as an ideological product of a culture of magical idealism where imagined satisfactions associated with given objects take the place of the social reorganization necessary to effect the genuine satisfaction of real needs. There is, for Frye, the world we live in and the world we want to live in (SS 17). Art, he claims, always gives us the latter, a vision of its images 'as permanent living forms outside time and space' (FS 85). Science gives us the former, and, as far as he is concerned, in studying literature as an autonomous part of reality, it is the task of scientific theory to establish the full context of the works of literature, relating an individual work to the whole of literature, culture, and civilization.

B The Critical Universe

Frye's search for 'a coherent and comprehensive theory of literature, logically and scientifically organized,' (AC 11) develops the scientistic attitude of the New Criticism; he makes it clear that a new scholarly discipline is in the process of paradigm formation. Anatomy is itself defined as 'a vision of the world in terms of a single intellectual pattern' (310), and Frye suggests that there is a finite number of valid critical methods which 'can all be contained in a single theory' (72). That, in the *Anatomy*, criticism is conceived as a science, systematic and progressive (7–8), while, in retrospect, the *Anatomy* is regarded as 'schematic' rather than primarily systematic,[18] makes no essential difference to the ideological drive toward rationalized integrity that characterizes this tradition.

Geoffrey Hartman's perspective on Frye suggests that 'the most serious claim he makes is the possibility of system.'[19] Certainly, the attempt to treat literature as a structured language, with priority of the whole over its parts, grasped through several phases of displacement or transformation, on the foundations of a synchronic methodology (that uses the notion of 'simultaneity' to freeze time-data in a spatial design)—all these being, we must recognize, the standard apparatus of modern structuralism—prepares for the stabilization and systematization of a formal discipline that is intended to be, in the prevailing positivist and scientistic conception, a workable schema to guide practical fieldwork, and 'not a view of the universe, whether true or fictional.'[20] Hartman is right, too, in arguing that a teachable system democratizes criticism, challenges the 'English mystique of English Studies,' and breaks the spell of the priest-interpreters.[21] I want only to add that the corollary is a rationalization of ideological heterogeneity and a more effective enforcement of the unifying scientistic ideology of domination. It is this specific feature of our period that we must perceive: that very *official* extension of democracy is at the same time an extension and deepening of the modes of oppression, in so far as it brings with it a broader participation in, and adherence to, the administration of a tendentially total domination, under an increasingly systematic and stabilized rationality.

This last point, of emancipation from mystique, holds further ambivalences whose source within the theory is in the intimate coexistence of scientific and non-scientific elements, or put more broadly, in that contradictory unity of rational and irrational elements that is repeatedly formed through the process of rationalization in each phase of the tradition. It has been noted, by poet-critics, that Frye's work in essential respects is mythic and poetic,[22] that is, that it is a mixed discourse; and that his diction propagates a religious mystique of literature,[23] and carries 'constant implication or intimation of the primordial, the more mysterious the better.'[24] Frye talks of 'the fertilizing of life by learning' (AC 25), but he revives archaic doctrines, such as Ptolemaic cosmology, four levels of existence, or the four elements and humors, and insists that these are eternal and ineluctable structures of symbolism, belonging, of necessity and forever, to both the poetic and the critical universes.

Thus earth, air, water, and fire are 'not the elements of nature,' and useless to chemistry, but they 'are still the four elements of imaginative experience, and always will be'. Likewise, the four humors are 'not the constituents of human temperament' and useless to medicine, yet remain 'the elements of imaginative perception.'[25] Indeed, he makes this claim for the 'whole

113

pseudo-scientific world of three spirits, four humours, five elements, seven planets, nine spheres, twelve zodiacal signs, and so on,' and, in general, for symmetrical cosmologies and systems of correspondences (161). The critical science becomes very obscure in the attempt to interpret literary works in terms of the ideas and conventions of their authors' times. Frye does this, in particular, with Dante, Shakespeare, Milton, Blake, and Yeats. It has been said of Frye's system that 'its prominent quality is its incorporation of idealistic, irrationalist, and obscurantist tendencies from the whole of Western tradition.'[26] A stress on the adjectives makes for a useful descriptive statement. But we can gain significant analytic insight only by placing the emphasis on the word 'incorporation.' For the specificity of the position is precisely that moments that express an alienation from the present in space and time and ideology are drawn into and contained within a scientistic system-building schematism.

We can note, too, in this complex, some parallels with French structuralism. On one hand, there is the question of isomorphism between object discourse and critical discourse; thus structural discourse on myths would be, for Lévi-Strauss, as it tends to be in Frye, mythomorphic. On the other, as Jacques Derrida demonstrates, there is the separation of *method* from *truth* in the exploitation of old concepts as analytical tools in handling the machinery to which they belong. That is, Lévi-Strauss, like Frye again and again, seeks 'to preserve as an instrument that whose truth-value he criticizes.'[27] But this radical distinction between methodological value and onto-epistemological non-value is a positivism in the face of its object and, ultimately, an abdication of the historical centeredness of the critic and hence a vitiation of criticism.

The same abdication is involved in Frye's insistence on a 'categorical,' value-free criticism which, perhaps needless to say, was a characteristic social-scientific aspiration of the period, and was still welcomed by Hartman in 1965 as another aspect of democratization. Frye recognizes that value judgments are class-determined, and argues that criticism 'obviously has to look at art from the standpoint of an ideally classless society' (AC 22). But, since Frye does not situate the theory from the point of view of *struggle* for a classless society, this standard does not have a base in the future as the goal of a process of human activity. Here, as in the case of his 'hypothetical' art, future-oriented imperatives are precluded as standards for criticism of the present. The position, in

Frye, simply elevates science above the levels of historical interests, and hence, in effect, means total capitulation to the established class relations.

If value judgments are not cognitively demonstrable but rather 'a Narcissus mirror of our own experience and social and moral prejudice' (SS 68), then, says Frye, academic criticism is systematic, 'categorical and descriptive: it tries to *identify* a writer's work,'[28] that is, to see it 'as an individual of a class,' to place it 'into its proper literary context.'[29] This criticism requires of the critic that he have experience of literature, not experience of life, and aims at structure not content.[30] Accordingly, the claim goes, criticism proper is archetypal criticism, which begins beyond New Critical commentary with the study of conventional recurrences, archetypes and genres. The methodological principle involved is the discovery of analogies of structure. This analogical formalization permits the freezing, under the fixed categories of scientistic criticism, of diverse phenomena of broad cultural fields, for example, literature and television, whose differences Frye excludes as being mainly in value (101).

There are two main points I want to indicate here. Firstly, that we cannot escape valuation, that the fact/value separation is untenable for a human life conceived as becoming. Facts are moments of a subject/object totality in motion and they are known only within this historical context; the ontological life processes are the source of value and these figure, ultimately, in the constitution of fact. But this point is perhaps by now becoming more or less accepted; many philosophers of science recognize that there is no neutral observation language and that scientific paradigms are normative as well as cognitive when they give form to scientific life in determining theory, methods, and standards together, as well as the criteria of legitimacy of both problems and solutions.[31] In this respect, the critic always faces the object in the light of his own history, and structures the object—never exhaustively—through the choice of what is essential in relation to his location in that history. We must remember Lucien Goldmann's warning that any pretension to non-ideological value-free social science is one of the gravest forms of dogmatism.[32] In the case of archetypal criticism, this means projection of a specific rationality into works of art as their inherent structure, followed by postulation of this as the basis of formalization.

The second point, beyond the intervention of genetic etiology into epistemological judgment, concerns the desirability of critical statement beyond description. If art has subversive, defetishizing capabilities, then it is the task of criticism to make this available on the conscious level. Criticism must confront and choose what is essential about art for our epoch in this sense, and translate into discursive language the generic hierarchy of values that can serve as a standard of critique against the fetishism of everyday life. It must find vital ways to speak for and to speak about the work of art; by contrast, the critical theories of neocapitalism are oriented only to consumption.

One last aspect of scientistic criticism needs to be examined here, the search for internal coherence that intervenes in the definition of the object of the science. Frye argues that literature cannot be taught, only criticism can; the former is the object, the latter the subject of study. He defends criticism against charges of parasitism, and seeks to establish criticism as an independent 'structure of thought and knowledge' (AC 11, 3, 5). As the first postulate of the coordinating principle of critical science, Frye posits 'the assumption of total coherence' (FI 9–10). Then he finds that 'criticism cannot be systematic unless there is a quality in literature which enables it to be so, an order of words corresponding to the order of nature in the natural sciences' (12). He presses this analogy to a comparison with Aristotle's *Physics* which he interprets to assert that

> physics *has* a universe. The systematic study of motion would be impossible unless all phenomena of motion could be related to unifying principles, and those in their turn to a total unifying principle of movement which is not itself merely another phenomenon of motion. (AC 126)

Like Frye's 'desire' that moves civilization, this 'total unifying principle of movement' is an idealist essence that takes the place of that uniform behavior of matter in all of human experience which has made possible the systematic study of motion. Human literary verbalizations are not comparably uniform: 'literature does not have a unifying and immutable structure because human beings produce it as an ideological form of their social experience which is constantly changing with history.'[33] We have seen before that scientism eliminates from attention the real ontology of its object; in Frye it makes impossible the real historical task of criticism. The reduction by analogy to the condition of natural phenomena locks art into permanence and blocks the critical translation of art from a form of aesthetic self-consciousness into a form of discursive consciousness that is relevant to and essential for the historical reality of the epoch.[34] In this way, a transhistorical fetish again triumphs over the concrete historical problematic. Complete surrender to the positivity of identifying fixed structures in a synchronic field means that critical theory, and, in its characterization, art, are not to be available as moments of human liberation.

C The Poetic Universe

Frye rejects 'chronology' as the organizing principle of literature and transforms Eliot's problematic of an ideal order of works into the assertion that 'literature is not a piled aggregate of "works," but an order of words' (AC 16–18), organized by recurring, that is, conventional, forms. The study of conventionality is to solve the problems of relating individual works to the intermediate groupings of genre, or to the whole of literature. Frye is interested in a poem 'as a unit of poetry' (96), concentrates on the connections of literary works through what they have in common on the level of form, and focusses on the 'archetypal' and 'anagogic' aspects of literature which reveal the relation between 'the order of nature as a whole' and 'a corresponding order of words' (96).

Raymond Williams has argued that criticism needs the concept of 'structure of feeling,' that is, a sense of concrete, historical-cultural density, to explore the relations between what is specific to the individual work and what is specific to higher level groupings such as genre.[35] Frye eliminates this entire dimension; the methodological choice of formal simultaneity, of transhistorical synchronic structure, lifts literature out of history, cuts the lifeline from experience to expression, and, as has been noted,[36] fosters critical systematizing by abolishing the problem of valuation in considering a unity of the whole of literature as a given of our literary experience.

Moreover, dissolution of the individual work in the perspective of universality impedes conceptualizing artistic catharsis, and eliminates the concrete social effect of art. It is, in fact, the incomparable formal perfection and self-enclosedness of each work (unlike the openness and interdependence of *scientific* theorems, which serve as Frye's models), its self-reliance in relation to other works, that permits the reality of the world created in each work to have experiential cogency, to enforce intensive participation by the recipients, and to effect the cathartic confrontation with the world of everyday experience.[37]

In its archetypal aspect, for Frye, literature is a 'mode of communication' structured by the units of communication, the 'typical or recurring' symbols, that is, the conventions that connect individual works and 'unify and integrate our literary experience' (AC 99). But literary experience as part of the continuum of life, of civilization, 'is still useful and functional' (115). To complete the analysis, Frye postulates an 'anagogic' aspect to literature, 'where it is disinterested and liberal' (115), a completely 'self-contained literary universe' (118). In this aspect, 'Nature is now inside the mind of an infinite man who builds his cities out of the Milky Way. This is not reality, but it is the conceivable or imaginative limit of desire, which is infinite, eternal, and hence apocalyptic' (119). We now have to deal with 'a universal man who is also a divine being, or a divine being conceived in anthropomorphic terms' (120). Thus, in Frye, the image of divinity is preserved in the deification of man. This hazard of transcendentalism haunts a humanism that has no perspective on the future for judging human activity.[38] Literature in this view exists 'in its own universe,' 'containing life and reality in a system of verbal relationships' (122). In the anagogic aspect, its organizing principle is not analogy but its ideological complement, identity, the unity of variety: 'everything is potentially identical with everything else' (124–5).

The position has at its center a significant ideological determination.

> The study of literature takes us toward seeing poetry as the imitation of infinite social action and infinite human thought, the mind of a man who is all men, the universal creative word which is all words. About this man and word we can, speaking as critics, say only one thing ontologically: we have no reason to suppose either that they exist or that they do not exist. (125)

Art and critical theory are here divorced not only from historical determinations in their origins and formation, but even from the realm of real historical existence altogether. An ontological agnosticism reduces both art and critical theory to purely epistemological status, without a real basis in the real life process of real human beings. Literature no longer has the ontological reference it had in Ransom and it no longer embodies a significance. Frye's very influential position holds that literary symbolism is not actual knowledge of some substance, but a mode of apprehension, a language (FI 218); not truth, but 'a means of expression' (236), that is, a system of signifiers.[39]

The symbolist aspects of this position are contained by the stress on conventionality. Archetypal criticism resolves the militant romantic opposition between desire and convention by casting the former irrevocably in the forms of the latter. If literature expresses the forms of desire, the principle of form is recurrent conventionality. According to this argument, just as science takes mathematical symbols for the only objectivity in the material world, so literary science takes archetypal symbols for the only objectivity in the literary world. Frye separates form and content radically. The poet gains impersonality (in an extension of T. S. Eliot's conception) through the myth or archetype, the 'separate form.'[40] It is said that the forms of literature come out of the structures of literature itself; the poet does not imitate 'life' but other poems; he always 'imposes the same kind of mythical form on his content, but makes different adaptations of it' (AC 63). 'Literature may have life, reality, experience, nature, imaginative truth, social conditions, or what you will for its *content*; but literature itself is not made out of these things. . . . Literature shapes itself, and is not shaped externally' (97). Form 'is a manifestation of the universal spirit of poetry' (98).

The point here is not only the suppression of content as a determination of literature, nor only the vacuousness of a conception of form as something that is desocialized and no longer regarded as the objectification of social experience and informing *telos*. Nor is it only that Frye, like structuralists in general, cannot explain formal development and transition, and, in fact, does not even try, his literary history being simply a cyclical image of transformations in the idea of the hero. What is most important is the technological picture of a form that is independent of all content, *but able to absorb all content*. This ideology of the recurrence and essential immutability of a universal rationality excludes all conflict, and precludes all qualitative change that depends on a gap between form and content; the theory provides no access to such conflict and change.

We meet the same ideological construction in the analysis of the function of art. For Ransom, art was hypothetical, but a primary imitation of particularity.[41] For Frye, it is also hypothetical, but a secondary imitation of thought and action, an imitation of universality without external model (FI 53), which may or may not have any kind of relation with the 'worlds of truth and fact' (AC 92–3). About the relation of this art to our everyday experience, Frye makes two seemingly contradictory statements. Firstly, he rejects the view that literature as a whole serves 'to illuminate something about life, or reality, or experience, or whatever we call the immediate world outside literature,' in other words, that it is 'a vast imaginative allegory, the end of which is a deeper understanding of the nonliterary center of experience.'[42] Secondly, he argues that literature 'creates an autonomous world that gives us an imaginative perspective on the actual one' (SS 298). At first sight, the two statements appear to be in opposition: it seems that literature both does and does not cast light on actual life.

The inconsistency, however, is only apparent, and a third statement of Frye's presents a resolution in terms that suggest that, although the imaginative construct throws no light on the actual workings of non-literary life, yet, in the light of the imaginative construct, we can recognize the inferior or illusory reality of non-literary experience. According to Frye, art guarantees 'a reality in our lives that is clear of the dissolving chaos of experience. We go out of the theatre into "real life" again, which we know now to be also an illusion because of a reality that we have glimpsed for an instant in the illusion of the play.'[43] Critical theory here capitulates totally to the prevailing material reality by abandoning it. Art becomes not an imaginative symbolic world that makes available a defetishized experience of our real world with the imperative to change our actual lives, but, instead, an alternative and superior reality that competes with and exposes (to no practical purpose) the inadequacy of actuality. Instead of the mimetic evocation of the essentials and potentials of our reality, art is said to offer a 'spectacular mimesis' that can look down on experience because of the presence of an ecstatic vision of innocence (AC 301).

For Frye, the key to this problem is in a conception of the archetypal function of literature as the visualization of the world of desire: 'not as an escape from "reality," but as the genuine form of the world that human life tries to imitate' (184). Art and material life, we are asked to remember, are both forms of expression of the transhistorical principle, 'desire;' but art, in its innocence of history, gives us the genuine form of desire, experience, its always inadequate corruptions. This, too, is why the arts, in Frye's view, do not evolve or improve: 'vision, being pure wish, can reach its conceivable limits at once' (FI 153).

We must notice that Frye is operating here a Freudian transformation of what was the Platonizing Renaissance version of the Christian duality consisting in two levels of nature, unfallen and fallen, with 'art being identical with nature at its higher level.'[44] Murray Krieger has located the model for Frye's account of creativity in Sidney's *Apology*, where our 'erected wit' is exempt from the fall and able to apprehend perfection, while our 'infected will' is subject to it and incapable of attaining perfection.[45] But where the Renaissance subordination of nature to human creativity was progressive, as the metabolism characterizing the always ineluctable relationship of mankind with nature was shifting toward social domination of the relationship on the basis of an expansion of human productive power, Frye's superordination of imaginative power over the material world leaves the latter unchanged. It is another form of the fact/value or is/ought separation. Abdicating from the actualization of value, it blocks the dialectics of qualitative change. And if the Renaissance did not yet have a future orientation, only an ideal 'ought' referring to its present,[46] the 'ought' in Frye's critical theory is an escape from and denial of the future, and a surrender to the present.

The stress on desire and wish suggests a Freudian problematic. Indeed, Freud exempts fantasy from control by the reality principle. Frye's 'desire' is the eternal and transhistorical id idealized and satisfied in the imaginative realm free from the historical ego. In the modern period, Freud's structure of the psyche has been repeatedly adopted, adapted, and used by anti-historical ideologies of permanence. The imagination, however, as Marcuse argues, is restrained by sense experience and reason, both products of class history, so that 'history enters into the projects of the imagination.'[47] But most important are the two key effects of Frye's contraposition of a pure, superior imaginative dream to an impure reality. On one hand, we find once more the abolition of *catharsis*, the shock to subjectivity in the confrontation of aesthetic immediacy with everyday immediacy, in favor of *ecstasis*, the vision of innocence accessible only symbolically. On the other hand, by corollary, we find that this symbolic ecstasy is substituted for the transformation of material reality, in such a way as to obscure the real historical possibility of realizing this ecstasy in the actual everyday life of real human beings. As it stands, literature remains a dream, indeed, 'two dreams, a wish-fulfilment dream and an anxiety dream, . . . focussed together, like a pair of glasses.'[48] Alvin C.

Kibel has noticed that this makes an unattractive program for culture if it has 'social issue by rigorously manipulating all expressions of desire and anxiety into a coordinated whole.'[49] In this respect, Frye's critical theory is precisely an ideological articulation of the manipulative culture of neocapitalism.

The Freudian view of literary functionality is paralleled here by a Freudian conception of literary structure. Myths or archetypes (equivalent terms, the former used to refer to narrative, to the recurrent and hence conventional image or image cluster as part of a total rhythm, the latter used to refer to meaning, to the image seen as part of a total pattern) are structural elements in literature 'because literature as a whole is a "displaced" mythology' (FI 1, 14–15), myth itself being the 'union of ritual and dream in a form of verbal communication' (AC 106), operating 'near or at the conceivable limits of desire' (136). In Frye's view, the structural principles of literature can be found in undisplaced form in the Greek and biblical mythologies, which is why literature revolves around certain classics.[50] Later, myth is displaced toward verisimilitude, that is, made plausible in several transformations that retain the basic structure (136–7). The archetype 'changes its context but not its essence' (SS 82).

There have been three main criticisms of this position, and I will add some of my own. Firstly, the explicit matrix of time. Frank Kermode has noted, with some validity in spite of a certain naive rationalism and historical relativism, that literature today has a different reality principle from myth, appropriate to *this* time, as myth was to another.[51] Others, including Wimsatt, have attributed the appeal of the position to its 'primitivist aura,'[52] something that we shall meet again in McLuhan. Although Frye distinguishes between the treatment of ritual in criticism and in anthropology (AC 109–10), and rejects the genetic stress on origins in general, 'primitive' remains an important category in his poetics as a synonym for formal, stylized, allusive, mythic poetry.[53] On the whole, the return to the mythical represents a nostalgic search for unity, a desire for essence, a striving for permanence[54]—all typical components of the modern tradition of critical theory.

Secondly, M. H. Abrams has argued that the analogical canon of Freudian displacement theory, that 'analogy justifies identification,' is the formula of archetypal reasoning, such that any complex work can be 'made to resemble almost any archetypal shape.'[55] He has noted as well that the methodology involves 'a steady regress to unity,' 'to one hypothetical *Urmythos*.'[56] I have suggested earlier the ideological function of analogy as the means to unity in the process of rationalization; it now seems worth adding two further features of Frye's system. On one hand, he contends, the basic principles for assimilating nature to human form in myth or poetry are 'the most primitive categories, the categories of analogy and identity, simile and metaphor, . . . essentially the categories of magic' (CP 289–90). On the other, all stories in literature are episodes of a central story, the Fall: 'this story of the loss and regaining of identity is . . . the framework of all literature.'[57] Identity, of course, is the goal of rationalization; it is supported and reinforced in Frye's work by three converging obsessions: the idealist-mystical obsession with subject/object identity, the Freudian obsession in the 1950s with ego problems, and the Canadian obsession with national identity, often as a cover for class and colonial oppression. (All these, naturally, have a certain social mandate.)

Thirdly, there has been widespread New Critical assertion that the use of typological materials has to be earned and comprehended through minute particularity.[58] As a set of empiricist arguments against structure, I think this New Critical campaign fails; Frye could always reply that he too wants his structures embedded, and that structure, in fact, means greater concreteness. None the less, I believe we can join the critique of Frye on this point, but from a different angle. For Frye's structural readings present only changing immobilities, not history; limited to a cross-section, they can give only a system of abstract possibility from which no concreteness can be disengaged. We need to redirect attention, however, not merely to extensive particular detail, but to the immanent intentionality within art of a class-related and species-related *telos* that articulates the minute particulars into the specific typologies of the literary form.

In general, what I want to stress is that, ideologically, Frye's theory is an expression of, and surrender to, immobility. Methodologically, displaced myth is a fixed principle that varies quantitatively; in other words, it admits change but not qualitative history. Conventions are naturally crucial in human life, but the real essence of humanity is expressed in the new. Today, especially, the struggle between old and new is decisive for our future, and Frye's theory has no place for the genuinely new—its center of gravity is deeply entrenched in recurrence. There is, of course, recurrence in real life, because mankind is transhistorical and labor is characteristic of all our specific and transient social systems in space

123

and time. More particularly, for the individual, everyday life is composed of a pattern of recurrence. But a point of view that makes a fetish of form also makes a *fetish* of the transhistorical recurrence, in abstraction from its socio-historical place. In this respect, we find, as we did with Ransom, that critical theory fails to supersede the point of view of everyday life. History, which for us now must mean future not only past, is precluded. Cycle takes its place, the temporal equivalent of Frye's spatial systematization; and the five modes of his literary history 'evidently go around in a circle' (AC 42). On the whole, the controlling ideas of the theory make supersession of the given actuality inaccessible. Archetypal criticism deforms the real human subject even within the poetic universe by denial of historical concreteness. In a static recurrence, 'men no longer have faces, only functions. History is senseless.'[59]

D The Verbal Universe

If the poetic universe is freed of all historical determinations with respect to origin and formation, this is Frye's means to a structural reintegration of the poetic universe within the web of social life, in a constitutive role as a primary instrument of 'mental production' (SS 16). On one hand, there is the poetic universe proper, the upper verbal world of imagination, the 'holiday or Sabbath world where we rest from belief' (CP 341); on the other, there is the lower verbal world of 'belief, concern, argument, and every form of verbal defence or aggression' (340). Together they make up the verbal universe which has a continuous structure in poetic myth. Before we can investigate this integration and arrive at Frye's notion of cultural revolution, we need to examine this second (lower) verbal world, and to trace a sequence of thought from it to notions of education, leisure, and the epistemological dialectic of appearance and reality. Frye's argumentation is laced with the Cold War polarities of open and closed societies, open and closed mythologies, and their correlations, as well as with analyses of the present epoch. There is no need here for a full and detailed examination of these; but in passing to the study of the general theoretical framework, I would observe that they serve primarily to disguise the absence of really open relations, genuine community, authentic individual autonomy, and equality of essential conditions and resources in the given society.[60]

Unlike disinterested literary mythology, says Frye, the social mythology of concern is an encyclopedic compendium of what most concerns a society to know in relation to the central question, 'what must we do to be saved?' (CP 277, 283). Its function is to cement social cohesion (341) and Frye permits the synonym of 'ideology' in 'most contexts' (305). We must observe that Frye considers the ideological impulse 'a central part of the religious impulse,' at least in the sense of '*religio*, of binding together a society with the acts and beliefs of a common concern' (MS 25; CP 308). Evidently, the whole tradition of modern critical theory assimilates culture to religion. At the same time, problems of social cohesion are central to the whole tradition. The Agrarian critique, Frye's concern mythology, and McLuhan's vision of a universal communion manifest in the global village are all uncritical explorations of aspects of this problematic. The historical difference is that, for the Agrarians, these cultural moments contradict the structural social development, for Frye, they are integrated as conditions and expressions of it, while for McLuhan, they are fully constitutive and determinant. In the immediate, the concern myth leads in Frye to the depreciation of social and national boundaries as he affirms, without historical mediation, that 'the only abiding loyalty is one to mankind as a whole' (MS 26).

Frye combines the moment of cohesion with an internal elite tendency, 'the myth of freedom,' which is the sole preserve of an educated minority and defends objectivity and tolerance (CP 278). In this argument, open societies like the North American require open mythologies; these are founded on a myth of freedom that embodies a spiritual authority of loyalty to scientific rationality. This is 'the permanent centre of real authority in a civilized community' (310). In no respect does this 'myth of freedom,' which here unites the scientistic with the religious, pose the real problematic of liberation. Instead, it recalls Arnold, who sought a center of authority in the influence of the 'best' individuals, a minority of class 'aliens' led by a 'humane spirit,'[61] or Karl Mannheim, who looked for social salvation to the minority social group of intellectuals.

All concern myths, says Frye, involve a notion of social contract and a Utopian notion of future ideal. Both are projections from the present—into the past and future, respectively, 'of a source of social authority that sits in the middle of our society, and which I shall call the educational contract' (334). The massive neocapitalist expansion and idolatry of education, the transformation of knowledge production into a key industry, have established the institution of education as an important ideological apparatus of the state—an ironic historical action in the Arnoldian problematic of authority. Arnold's class 'aliens' and the New Critical literary minority are now an ideologically aggrandized intellectual caste, while Arnold's (state) authority that was to be a vehicle to perfection continues to represent particular class interests. If Frye's philosophy of science takes criticism out of the hands of 'priest-interpreters,' as Geoffrey Hartman claimed, Frye's philosophy of education, in the meantime, locates the critics as new high priests, in the sense of guardians of the given order. It is the university which, for Frye, defines the community of spiritual authority. Ordinary society, he insists, is mere appearance, too transient to be real.

> Real society itself can only be the world revealed to us through the study of the arts and sciences, the total body of human achievement out of which the forces come that change ordinary society so rapidly. Of this world the universities are the social embodiment, and they represent . . . the only visible direction in which our higher loyalties and obligations can go. (SS 256)

It is important for us to understand this conception as deeply reified ideology cast in idealist form. What is true is that much of our humanity, developed over the course of history, exists today only outside individuals, in objectifications whose appropriation is blocked by the given mode of our social reality. The arts and sciences are among these objectifications. Moreover, the power of these objectifications is at present set against the human subjects, and determines the activities of ordinary life. But this is the reification that we must abolish, not entrench. Frye's position involves a double fetish. The emphasis on the 'achievement,' on the tradition that has been already accomplished, against the need and the power to transform the old, to create the new, is a fetish of transhistoricality that preserves the reification of the *constituted* culture against any creative historical activity that might defetishize the achievement in the rhythm of revolutionary praxis. And the fetish of *spiritual* objectifications, as if they composed the whole body of humanity, obscures the reification of other systems of objectifications, of the relations and institutions of material culture, all of which must be not only studied but defetishized in the struggle to end reification. We will gain contact with our real humanity, not through positive scholarship by itself, but through actively changing our relations to the world and to ourselves. An idealist depreciation of everyday life not only embodies a vicious contempt for the actual humanity and struggles of real people, but, methodologically, signals a failure to locate the daily praxis that sustains reification, and, consequently, represents a total capitulation to it as an eternal principle.

Frye's awareness of the new historical problem of leisure dovetails with his educational philosophy. Neocapitalist leisure, in fact, is socially manipulated to effect a dual reproduction of the person as a type of labor power shaped to the specific exigencies of neocapitalist production, and as a type of citizen shaped to the specific exigencies of the neocapitalist state. As long as our category is leisure (as in Frye) and not liberation of our productive powers and the world they create, we remain tied to this totalitarian cycle of reproduction. Guy Debord points out that 'none of the activity stolen within labor can be rediscovered in the submission to its result;'[62] that is, leisure is dependent on its source, the rationality of production. In Frye, the alienated alternation of work and leisure is reproduced in the categorical duality of 'economic structure' and 'leisure structure' of society; and education, whose discipline (in the sense of Edmund Burke and Hulme) is to raise us to the upper level of nature, becomes the content, the 'positive aspect' of this leisure structure (MC 88–90).

The whole issue is unfolded in the abstract matrix indicated above, where the ideally educated mind is apparently aware that mid-century bourgeois society is 'not the real form of human society, but the transient appearance of that society.'[63] We have both an actual life and an imaginative life; the latter is the source of 'the dignity and joy of life.'[64] Heaven and Hell, it seems, both *are* this world—as it *appears* to an awakened or repressed imagination (FS 83). It can be argued, by contrast, that a truly awakened social imagination would not be content to preserve the actuality of the world. Instead, it would see it as a contradictory man-made Hell with potentials for Heaven, and would mediate its material transformation into a Heaven. A humanism that depends on inwardness to control meaningless empirical experience capitulates to the given society and renounces its claims to humanism by effectively denying humanity to the vast majority of mankind.[65] Frye's rationalism ignores that there are humanly objective (object-mediated intersubjective) conditions of existence independent of the *individual* will, and, ultimately, his theories reinforce the passivity he deplores. But it is important to notice that what had been in the romantic commotion an ontological bifurcation of the historical praxis into ideal and material realms has now become an epistemological problematic on an integrated ontological basis.

Frye's notion is that our cultural environment, formed by the real human society of the arts and sciences, is 'the permanent model of civilization which our present society approximates.' And the educated man 'is the man who tries to live in his social environment according to the standards of his cultural environment.'[66] Of course, he stresses, we can never attain in social life the social ideal implied in culture (AC 348). At the same time, 'in a modern democracy, a citizen participates in society mainly through his imagination' (SS 104). Here Pater's goal of living as much as possible in an imaginatively constructed ideal, even amidst the debris of daily life,[67] joins Arnold's concerns with perfection and 'the best' in a new commotive specification. It is surely evident that this whole conception, of living in society according to the imagination, that is, according to what we desire, seeing what we want to see, is the ideological materialism of a magical spectacle, of living in manipulated imaginative hypostasis the dreams and needs that are denied genuine socially organized material satisfaction.

And here we may return to the structure of the verbal universe. For Frye, since paradise is not in the outward environment but in the mind, it is a vision evoked by words. As a perspective, this means that 'the only new worlds for man are those which the free and disciplined use of words can help to create.'[68] And 'every arrangement of words is a narrative, and so has a narrative shape, and a study of narrative shapes involves the study of literature' (CP 337). Myths of concern, specifically, as visions of society, 'have literary shapes, generally romantic and comic shapes' (336). For Frye, that means Freudian shapes, and, as we know from his fatalistic typological ideology, they involve 'a victory of the pleasure principle that Freud warns us not to look for in ordinary life.'[69] By being freed of all historical determinations, literature had been assigned a technological form in a self-contained poetic universe—that is, an independent, neutral form adaptable to all content. In consequence, precisely by virtue of that independence, literature can become an integrated structural principle of the entire verbal universe. 'Literature, conceived as a total structure, is not in itself a myth of concern: what it presents is the language of concern' (323).

In other words, in Frye's critical theory, literature becomes, like mathematics, 'substantially useful, and not just incidentally so' (AC

352). 'The verbal structures of psychology, anthropology, theology, history, law, and everything else built out of words have been informed or constructed by the same kind of myths and metaphors that we find, in their original hypothetical form, in literature' (352). If Eliot's ideal synchrony was elaborated and made concrete in the poetic universe, so is Richards' mythic epistemology in this. Myth, for Frye, is the 'source of the coherence' of social discourse, and 'literature, like mathematics, is a language, and a language in itself represents no truth, though it may provide the means for expressing any number of them. . . . The mathematical and the verbal universes are doubtless different ways of conceiving the same universe' (354).

This conception, which bears similarities with the language fetish of French structuralism, permits a new examination of criticism as the decisive agency of cultural revolution. Criticism, it is argued, has two aspects, 'one turned toward the structure of literature as a whole and one turned toward the other cultural phenomena that form its environment' (CP 275). In this latter respect, it has a central role in the study of the society's production and use of its myths (296), in the interpretation of all symbolic systems[70] in terms of poetic language, and in attaining knowledge of the language of concern and belief (337).

In the first aspect, the study of art, Frye argues that 'the contemporary development of the technical ability to study the arts . . . forms part of a cultural revolution' (AC 344). Frye adopts a crucial neocapitalist ideological position (surrendering permanently to alienation), that 'it is the consumer, not the producer, . . . who becomes humanised' (344). The consequence of this is that cultural production 'may be, like ritual, a half-involuntary imitation of organic rhythms or processes' while 'the response to culture is, like myth, a revolutionary act of consciousness.' Thus criticism, which can facilitate and intensify consumption, is part of a revolution in 'spiritual productive power' (344).

In the second aspect, the critical mission for Frye is even broader and more visionary. It is to supply the language to unify our experience on the level of the 'higher intellectual universe.' The social effect of critical activity is 'reforging the broken links between creation and knowledge, art and science, myth and concept' (AC 354). It is essential to recognize the total positivity of this program for cultural revolution. Oblivious to domination, exploitation, and struggle, to bureaucracy, power, hierarchy, property, the social division of labor, the political economy of the sign, surplus normatization, or revolutionary praxis, that is, to the social structures, social relations, and social collisions of real human history, Frye's conception remains within the existing structures of neocapitalism, and implies no more than, and no conflict with, actual developments in the integration of mental production and consumption. Ultimately, it poses, at the given level of social development, only the standard problematic of order and unity typical in the modern tradition of critical theory: the fusion of the dissociated moments of culture and sensibility.

E Conclusion

In general, Frye's archetypal orientation is an expression of deepening reification. It is a dehistoricization and desocialization of life, ontologically a despecification. Paradoxically, the search for literary identity which, contrary to Ransom, Frye defines as the class, not the unique, expresses a loss of identity, a loss of the specificity of personality in space and in time, which means a loss of the ability to define identity through transformative activity. Ultimately, this is not only a loss but a suppression of identity: a denial of the function of personality, of historical and cultural specificity. In fetishizing the reference to the *status quo ante*, Frye's theoretical position capitulates to the *status quo*. McLuhan moves on from there to embrace neocapitalist reification and to preach its dominant tendencies.

Freud, unlike Frye, was sharply critical of the repressive content of the cultural achievements that Frye accepts as the genuine forms of humanity. Frye's chief debt to Freud is the elimination of the future dimension. Yet Freud's important contribution was to have shown the concrete multiplicity of levels of signification. It is from this totality that Frye abstracts levels of permanence and universality in such a way that, in the end, he, and even more the epigones, systematize an unmediated simultaneity of abstract particularity and abstract generality. The result is especially congenial to both scientism and religion.

But the most decisive problem in the whole theory is formulating the relations between material life and imaginative life simply on an epistemological level. This problematic fails to locate culture as a whole way of life, and thus it does not provide theoretical space for moments in the formation of (rational and imaginative) consciousness within the process of the production and reproduction of everyday existence, at exploited work and at manipulated leisure. It involves no internal need to grasp objective mediations, and remains on a purely subjective (at best intersubjective) level. In consequence, praxis is unavailable to it, and reification is admitted as a level of nature. Therefore, when in our period technological progress realizes the imaginary, when the aesthetic merges with the political and the economic, [71] the theory can neither resist the change nor account for it, and necessarily yields to McLuhan's theory of a technology-dominated social-biological metabolism that permits virtually unlimited scope to reification on all levels and, by specifying myth and analogy as the fundamental epistemological and ontological structures, allows virtually unlimited rationalization.

PART IV

Marshall McLuhan
The Critical Theory of Counterrevolution

CHAPTER 10

Introduction to McLuhan

Marshall McLuhan, considered by some to be 'the most important thinker since Newton, Darwin, Freud, Einstein, and Pavlov,'[1] represents not only the most complete and most advanced development of the Richards–Eliot program, but also a qualitative departure from the tradition. The unity of these two aspects resides in an attempt at rationalizing the full range of human life, conceived as cultural phenomena, under a single set of categories derived essentially from the tradition but projected onto the whole of social life. McLuhan describes his own approach as 'systems development,' that is, 'a structural analysis . . . concerned with the inner dynamics of the form,'[2] with 'structure and configuration' (UM 28). As we shall see, his argument is that systems are fully determined according to the independent laws of the dominant technological environment and its relations with antecedent technologies.[3] McLuhan's critical theory, it will become apparent, is effectively cut off from its genuine ontological basis in a similar fashion to any other objectivistic rationalism. That is, by a deep and unbridgeable methodological abyss into which essential structural realities of socio-historical life —for example, any categories related to human self-determination —disappear without trace.

With McLuhan, critical theory acquires a new domain and a new attitude to the world. The relation to the dominant features of the social landscape is no longer oblique. Art is reintegrated with social life, and culture and civilization become inseparable. As it comes to embrace and express the neocapitalist integration directly, cultural ideology seizes the opportunity to emerge as a strategically central approach to totality. In his own language, McLuhan indicates a wide historical, structural, phenomenological, and ecological scope for his

135

reflections, and situates his analysis, in effect, in the problematic of the change from the stage of classical capitalism to the stage of neocapitalism.

> The stepping-up of speed from the mechanical to the instant electric form reverses explosion into implosion. In our present electric age the imploding or contracting energies of our world now clash with the old expansionist and traditional patterns of organization. (UM 47)

The 'essence of automation technology' is today restructuring the relations of production and association that were patterned by the 'essence of machine technology' (23). In consequence, he contends, the mediations of intermediate groupings are dissolved; social groups 'can no longer be *contained*' in limited association and yield to total reciprocal involvement of individuals with each other (20), in a social situation characterized by 'concern with effect rather than meaning' (39).

McLuhan's mature critical theory, I would argue, will best be understood as the bourgeois ideological form of the main tendencies characterizing the manipulative and hegemonic structural modifications of the post-war period. In this capacity, it has been able to become a powerful ideological construction.[4] One decisive side of this construction, we could say, is a historical problematic, involving the nature of the transition from one stage of capitalism to another. Another can be described as the ontological problematic of reification. Here, the central coordinating principle is McLuhan's extension theory, a theory of human objectification that postulates these objectifications, in effect, as eternally alienated and fetishized, with eternally ineluctable power over human beings. A third side is an epistemological problematic, structured around McLuhan's notion of technological alteration of the human sensorium, on one hand, and, on the other, his attempt to rationalize the symbolic field through an exegesis of the symbology of the world (in its actually given forms) by means of the symbolist technique of mythic and analogical parataxis (that is, juxtaposition without coordinating or subordinating connectives). In this opening overview, I wish to highlight certain general considerations about each of these main problematics, as well as about the overall methodology and implications of McLuhan's theoretical work.

In each of the above three interlocking areas, as we shall see, McLuhan assumes that the specific forms of neocapitalist alienation are the general forms of mankind. In so confounding them, he fails to perceive alternatives, and considers general developmental tendencies only within their specific given alienated forms. The concrete present is carried over into the future, while an abstract future is asserted as already present. All formulations retain as their basis the existing class-determined reality. His analysis is completely positive, in that it is completely uncritical, and has no place for contradictions or alternatives. It submits to the authority of 'total inclusiveness'— the total inclusiveness of everything that is given in neocapitalist development. And it accepts that authority as rational (cf. UM 30). The idolatry of neocapitalist rationality sinks the theory in the quicksand of immediacy, and the whole theory, much more so than Ransom's or Frye's, is stuck within the parameters of everyday life. McLuhanacy, as the present study will show, is the ideological face of the counterrevolutionary neocapitalist reification of the production and reproduction of everyday existence. This is the main source of its appeal, power, and barbarity.

With human life conceived as a formal, closed order, like a book, McLuhan's *découpage* uncovers communications technology as the strategic structural feature. 'Understanding media' will not only account for the socio-cultural totality, but help to integrate it. Elsewhere, Claude Lévi-Strauss has proposed the analysis of society via a theory of communication, and Raymond Williams has argued that, cutting across its economic and political dimensions, 'society is a form of communication, through which experience is described, shared, modified, and preserved.'[5] It is undoubtedly true that sociality is a fundamental feature of the human life process, a constitutive and indispensable aspect of the construction of consciousness and the perceptual world, of the appropriation of reality. But, for this discussion, it helps to bear in mind that the new and widespread theoretical attention to communication is itself an expression of and response to the novel and decisive importance of communication in contemporary social life. A primary characteristic of the neocapitalist transformation, consolidation and integration, in regard both to the essential new productive forces, such as electronics and computers, and to mass culture, is the production, movement, and appropriation of information. McLuhan's importance for bourgeois theory is that he is working at the center of this strategic problematic. But he abstracts from, and thus preserves, the existing class-determined historical embedment of communications, its forms, directions of development, and social use. The partial truths of his formulations serve as vaccinations against considering communications with a view to its real contemporary relevance and potential for making history.

Herbert I. Schiller, in an informative book, documents the way in which 'communications are being developed as the supporting instrumentation for the global enforcement of the status quo.'[6] In general, not only are communications systems in the United States structurally and organizationally hierarchical and manipulative extensions of power, but they extend that power to the domination of the communications environments of foreign countries and serve as the institutional basis for cultural imperialism.

To accept McLuhan's methodology, one has to forget the political, economic, military, and value dimensions of power, control, and class interest forming the communications matrix. In stressing that *in itself* technology is not neutral (for example, UM 26), he moves, not closer to, but further away from its *socio-historical* determinations; with respect to these latter, technology is presented as effectively neutral or indifferent. The paradox is the paradox of reification. The fetish of technology in itself, in its internal characteristics, suppresses the historical fact that it is not some technology in the abstract, but always an *established* technology that is not neutral, because of its determinate relations to 'the *quality* of human needs it is best suited to satisfy.'[7] But McLuhan does not consider communications primarily in terms of social relations among human beings, but in terms of relations between human beings and things, and among the things themselves. His version of critical theory renounces questions of human needs, interests, values, or goals. The type of technocratic ideology that he constructs totally excludes creative historical projects, praxis, or qualitative changes. The structural preclusion and the explicit rejection of a social ontology of alternatives make inconceivable the choices within which we could consciously make a genuinely new, liberated historical future.

McLuhan's general schema is a historical periodization, built on cultural transformations effected by changes in communications technology corresponding to sensory stress, and ordered in the 'hot-cool' binary typology. Roughly, the periodization yields the four successive stages of primitive, precapitalist, capitalist, and monopoly capitalist or neocapitalist societies: a cool, audile tribal culture, with an oral technology of speech, is followed by a hot, visual culture with the scribal technology of the phonetic alphabet, then a hotter visual culture with the mechanical technology of print, and finally, the coolest audile-tactile culture, with an electric technology of television and computer. The persistent issue is the rise and decline of visuality, which McLuhan associates with linear continuity, uniformity, abstraction, and individualization, in contrast to the instantaneous inclusiveness of simultaneous configuration associated with pre- and post-visual cultures. Within this context, McLuhan's use of his categories is vacillating and the periodization uncertain and contradictory. At times, the culture of the Middle Ages is selected as a balanced audile-tactile culture, and both the Greeks and Elizabethans are attributed a relatively balanced sensibility (GG 28, 59, 108, 111, 129). At other times, decisive moments of the reduction to the disapproved visual rationality are variously placed 3,000 years ago, 2,500 years ago, and in every century from the thirteenth to the seventeenth.[8]

It is difficult to see how a single-axis model of technological sensory extension could account by itself for the historical fluctuations and developments that disorganize the elegance of McLuhan's schematism; in any case, precision in this respect seems inessential for McLuhan. As in Frye's structuration of the literary field, so in McLuhan's structuration of the historical field, the cultural periodization is resolved in a mythic pattern of Fall and salvation. The full thrust of the theory is found in a tribalism-detribalization-retribalization triad. The two chief visual periods collapse into a single phase of literacy between phases of pre-literacy and post-literacy, and the strategic locus of the Fall shifts according to the exigencies of the argument. Both a historical regression and an eschatological anticipation of salvation in 'the final phase' (UM 19) are typical *leitmotifs* of the modern tradition of critical theory. McLuhan's matrix for these, in his interpretation of the modern modulations of the social-cultural order, is the dissolution of a mechanical Gutenberg Galaxy and its replacement by an organic Electric Age (GG 253). He argues that implosion and feedback displace explosion and linearity. Integration displaces fragmentation. In his view, this transition from a visual to an audile-tactile culture involves great tension. This sense of an 'ultimate conflict between sight and sound,' raising 'wars within and without us' (UM 19, 30), gives McLuhan's work a quality of historical specificity and urgency. But it is the anti-humanist dismissal of the whole of humanist history that gives it a special interest within the humanist tradition.

Reification, as we shall see, dominates the historical schema. The whole typology is founded on a semiotic whose cutting edge is comprised in the cybernetic formula, 'the medium is the message,' 'la formule même de l'aliénation dans la société technique.'[9] For McLuhan, technology is not merely the distinctive feature of every cultural formation; it is each specific technological environment that dominates the structures of both society and individual, and it is transformations in the former that effect inexorable changes in the latter. Social theory is thus reduced to technological ecology, and history is dissolved in an apparently spontaneous generation of technologies, and in a homeostatic interchange between (human) organism and (technological) environment.

The technocratic ideology can be related to the new electric ideologies of equilibrium that similarly postulate independently active objective systems as structural principles of the internal coherence of historical formations and render science and action anti-Promethean and stabilizing.[10] In contrast to the stress placed on continuity in evolutionist ideologies, the future for McLuhan is defined by discontinuity and a 'harmony' of discontinuous elements, that is, by stability.[11] All those concerned with problems of content or quality are ruthlessly labelled 'somnambulists,' or mechanical, linear, visually oriented survivals from a bygone epoch. Like the new eleatic ideologies, McLuhan's arguments abolish history both by structuring it without human perspective or meaning, and by claiming that electric media may 'conceivably usher in the millennium' (PI 158), that is, that the attainment of technological rationality is the end of history.[12] It has to be stressed that what is at issue here is not the elimination of change, but its control and stabilization.

McLuhan, of course, always insists that he has no commitment to his own theories, that they are explorative 'probes' that he is always ready to discard (PI 54). A thinker's right and responsibility to change his views according to criteria of intellectual and historical integrity is, naturally, incontrovertible. But it is time to note that McLuhan has not in fact changed his 'probes' for over a decade, and to emphasize their underlying unity: they combine to educate to submission. He likes to quote Carlyle's comment that Margaret Fuller had, indeed, better 'accept the universe' (PI 74). But, as it is not a question for him of resignation but one of acceptance, he claims that in principle no imperative of valuation is involved. Like Frye, he stresses the need for description to precede valuation (GG 7), and proposes a suspension of judgment (GG 276)—in practice, indefinitely—as the means to understanding the forces shaping our lives through arresting the action, as Poe's mariner did in studying the maelstrom.[13]

I do not wish to argue again the impossibility of escaping the choice and value dimensions of human life, owing to the specificities of historical becoming and social location;[14] I want only to draw attention again to the dogmatism implicit in the pretension to non-ideological social science. This is a compulsion to positivity which, in fact, blocks the possibility of understanding any alternative potentialities that supersede the given. Moreover, McLuhan's refusal to judge is not simply a voluntary, easily discarded pose. As a concretization of the bourgeois ideal of pure theory without presuppositions, McLuhan's stance of neutrality is a fully integral aspect of his determinist fetishism of technology. By denying that human action is itself responsible for the changes that our socio-cultural world is undergoing and will undergo, McLuhan necessarily denies that a critical attitude is morally significant or practically important.

What then is the purpose of 'understanding media,' whose urgency McLuhan always presses (GG 213; UM 20)? In *Understanding Media*, he writes: 'It is the theme of this book that not even the most lucid understanding of the peculiar force of a medium can head off the ordinary "closure" of the senses that causes us to conform to the pattern of experience presented' (286). Ultimately, the answer refers to survival strategy:

> It's inevitable that the worldpool of electronic information movement will toss us all about like corks on a stormy sea, but if we keep our cool during the descent into the maelstrom, studying the process as it happens to us and what we can do about it, we can come through. (PI 158)

We may even bring media into 'orderly service' (UM 21) according to their natural laws. In other words, cognition will abandon the task of mediating a qualitative control by humanity of the world in the transition from the present to the future. It will offer only the possibility of relatively painless and effective psychic and social adjustment to the changes in which we are caught up, and the possibility of effecting a certain orderly rationalization of independent forces. The measure of quantitative control accessible through understanding, however, in no way counteracts the fetish-like quality or determinist powers that technology assumes in McLuhan's theories. On the contrary, cognition as a whole has, in McLuhan, become the pivot of a technocratic ideology of reified rationalization.

According to McLuhan, 'we *live* mythically but continue to think fragmentarily and on single planes' (UM 39), in the forms of pre-electric linearity. This makes real causality inaccessible for us, since, as Hume showed, 'there is no principle of causality in a mere sequence' (UM 27). Fortunately, McLuhan says, with electric instantaneity, which ends sequence, 'the causes of things . . . emerge to awareness again' (27). In studying simultaneity, the mosaic approach, focussing on the internal relations of each problem in isolation, becomes 'the only relevant approach' (GG 42).[15]

Naturally, McLuhan himself attempts to offer us, in terms of these principles, the cognitive counterpart to our mythic lives, a mythic, integral understanding on multiple planes with no fixed point of view. I want to draw attention in this respect to the false etiology that emerges from this epistemological attitude. The mythic notion of technological causality is not explicative, but a demarcative invocation to coordinate the givenness of disparate detail.[16] Its essential determinations, in consequence, are purely ideological. The 'medium' functions in McLuhan's critical theory as an indeterminate symbol that collects and focusses in itself all the determinations of a social system of domination. At the same time, and of necessity, its image is unhistorical and depoliticized.

In this connection, it is appropriate to cite Roland Barthes' penetrating analysis:[17]

> *Myth is depoliticized speech.* One must naturally understand *political* in its deeper meaning, as describing the whole of human relations in their real, social structure, in their power of making the world; one must above all give an active value to the prefix *de-*: here it represents an operational movement, it permanently embodies a defaulting. . . . Myth does not deny things, on the contrary, its function is to talk about them; simply, it purifies them, it makes them innocent, it gives them a natural and eternal justification, it gives them a clarity which is not that of an explanation but that of a statement of fact. . . . In passing from history to nature, myth acts economically: it abolishes the complexity of human acts, it gives them the simplicity of essences, it does away with all dialectics, with any going back beyond what is immediately visible, it organizes a world which is without contradictions because it is without depth, a world wide open and wallowing in the evident, it establishes a blissful clarity: things appear to mean something by themselves.

This depoliticized mythic speech, in which things become signifiers, is the epistemic corollary in McLuhan's critical theory to the magical semiosis of control that has become a specificity of neocapitalist culture. This is its ideological face, no longer oblique as in Frye, or ambivalent as in Ransom. In McLuhan, myth and analogy are fundamental structures of consciousness, and the mosaic approach, in effect a development of the New Critical close reading, embracing its dogmatic realism, is the means to an exegesis of what is assumed to be an inherent intelligibility in things, an exegesis of the world as a book of symbols. A basis of positive facts is assumed without question. The spirit is to be read *in* the letter, not *into* it, and meaning is to be uncovered in facts rather than created. All things in the world are to be perceived in their metaphoric dimension, as a web of significance, not as a collection of phenomena. It is through this sort of approach, supposedly 'now widely accepted,' that McLuhan claims that 'we are moving very rapidly today to a grasp of scriptural, poetic and social communication which promises to take up all the wealth of patristic insight and to go far beyond it.'[18]

Myth and analogy in McLuhan's epistemology are opposed to logic and dialectic, and are said to produce a multi-level inclusive consciousness as opposed to the single-level awareness attributed to logic and dialectic. Mythic parataxis or analogical apposition, as cognitive techniques, involve a juxtaposition, without either coordinating or subordinating connectives, of 'widely diverse thoughts, feelings, and experience as facts of existence quite independent of logical coherence or conceptual unity.'[19] McLuhan holds that this technique of juxtaposition 'develops analogical tensions and proportions of metaphysical scope.'[20] His usage of the category here joins its traditional usage in theology, and opens the door to the displacement of attention from immanent connections (whether social, political, economic, or cultural) to transcendent unities formed outside human control. We may note that the universalized mythic comportment in McLuhan is simply the universalization of the positivist objectivistic attitude first analyzed by Husserl: of cognitions connected with and limited to the immediate pragmatism of particularist everyday life. The everyday 'facts of existence,' and the ready-made structures and transcendences facing the individual in everyday life, are then projected analogically (via the mediation of the extension theory) as the anthropomorphized picture of objectivity.[21] In consequence, the possibilities, goals, and meaning of human praxis are not only not given theoretical elaboration, but are precluded from critical theory. The supersession of alienation is made impossible *a priori.*

Barthes points out that in myth 'there is no regular ratio between the volume of the signified and that of the signifier.'[22] What this means for the present discussion is that McLuhan's mythic signifiers, such as the media, become focal points for virtually unlimited fields of significance; that is, they have virtually unlimited powers of rationalization, *ad libitum.*[23] But an over-use of analogical technique produces a static picture of actuality with no real bearing on, or discrimination of, alternatives for the future. It is claimed that reality becomes transparent and reveals its laws, if only its elements are juxtaposed for reciprocal illumination. But the world has significance for us only because it is shaped by associated labor, by the workings of human purpose. What is involved in understanding this significance cannot be reduced to a positivist or religious exegesis of some preconstituted plenum of juxtaposed or juxtaposable parts. This plenum, Maurice Merleau-Ponty has argued, 'opens up at the place where behaviour appears';[24] the issue is the constitution of our open history, which means the struggle within the realm of teleological human activity over the nature of our present and future lives, and envelops conflicting historical possibilities, intentionalities, and ideologies. As long as we are confronted with these conflicts, and not with 'the ultimate harmony of all being' in which McLuhan professes faith (UM 21), only an ideologue of neocapitalist integration would reduce the horizon of alternatives to the reified one-dimensionality of an exegetic revelation of the necessities of the given.

Frye's scientist-religious structures reduce the aesthetic ontology of possibility and choice to the mythic ontology of fate,[25] and, under the formula of assimilating the natural to human form, effectively bind the social forms to the model of natural order. Similarly, McLuhan's mythic constructions eliminate the living, praxis-based foundations of human history, and assume the dimensions of fate and natural law. For three reasons, this critical theory can be considered a counterrevolutionary ideology. Firstly, it shares with Comtean positivism and the original philosophies of counterrevolution sponsored by Bonald and DeMaistre, 'a repudiation of man's claim to alter and reorganize his social institutions in accordance with his rational will,' and the teaching that 'society possesses an immutable natural order to which man's will must submit.'[26] Technological fetishism preempts, in principle, the revolutionary undertaking. Secondly, the theory is laced with attitudes, perceptions, and propositions that link it with the general counterrevolutionary forces of our times.[27]

And thirdly, the theory is not merely a descriptive prophecy of the movement of dominant neocapitalist tendencies toward integration and one-dimensionality; it embraces them and polemicizes against alternatives.[28] Despite occasional ambivalences and disclaimers, to the effect that he is not taking sides, and neither endorsing nor prescribing the changes (GG 43; COB 64), the thrust of the argument, in three main respects, unequivocally favors the electric age with its simultaneity and inclusiveness. Firstly, there is a constant critique of literacy as partial, impoverished, illusory, and epistemologically and ontologically false. Secondly, there is the weight of continuity in the association of the features of the electric age with the favored side of correlated dichotomies from three decades of McLuhan's work: with encyclopedism, oral stress, multiplicity, discontinuity, making (versus matching), and so forth. Thirdly, there is the superiority of the electric age with regard to liturgical or dogmatic implications.[29]

Ultimately, as becomes apparent in studying McLuhan, the electric age is welcomed as the objective correlative of the ordered totality that is the fundamental programmatic end of the whole tradition. This tradition, that reduces human life to a striving for totality, reaches its climax in the McLuhanatic self-recognition in the totality of neocapitalism. The tradition's totality has become even more of a pseudo-totality, with the progressive expulsion of social liberation from the problematic. The re-engagement of cultural ideology with social life takes the form of a mimetic identification with the counterrevolutionary technocratic society. And the successful fulfillment of the tradition reveals its hollowness and appalling failure as a humanism. For, although McLuhan is prepared to pay it, the electric totality exacts a high price: it requires 'utter human docility' (UM 64).

CHAPTER 11

Three Phases of Development

A McLuhan in the Tradition

Critics of McLuhan have tended to discuss his work in terms of either continuities or discontinuities between his earlier and his later formulations. My own view is that the theory unfolds in three phases of development; and, more significantly, that these phases recapitulate the three stages in the development of the modern tradition of critical theory (with which they roughly coincide in chronology), and that they embody its ideological evolution from the tension of defensive reaction through the stasis of capitulation to the activism of counterrevolution. It is only in the form achieved in the third phase, with the articulation, for the first time, of the three essential interlocking moments of the theory as a whole—the uncompromising formalism, the extension theory, and the theory of sense ratios—that McLuhan's critical theory could become the dominant cultural ideology, representing a movement beyond Ransom and Frye, as well as beyond the corresponding first two phases of his own work. After some comparative remarks on McLuhan and the tradition as a whole, I shall look at each phase in McLuhan's own development.

McLuhan and the tradition illuminate each other. In both, the center of gravity of the critical attitude moves from subjectivity to objectivity, and elements subjectively desired in first stage problematics (for example, unified sensibility, harmonious balance of opposites, or organic, non-mechanical culture) appear objectively given in third stage problematics, but as purely involuntary developments, without their humanist value content. The general tendency is from a subjectivist challenge of the existing order to an objectivist acceptance of the authority of the given as the very condition of understanding and discourse. The ethical counterpart of this leads from moralism to legalism. The moralistic critique typical of the first stage, in both Ransom and McLuhan, counterposes to the world a model of (anti-dialectical, anti-mechanistic) interiority unavailable in material form and, accordingly, seeks to separate 'ought' and 'is,' value and fact, morality and cognition. This yields, in the second stage, to a transcendentalist capitulation to ongoing material processes and patterns in both Frye and McLuhan. Here, attention is directed to transhistorical forms (of 'language,' whether literary mythology or cultural technology) that occur in and are specified in time, yet that are free of the bondage of historical formation, even while they themselves *structure* historical forms. Accordingly, value and fact are, on one hand, demarcated even more explicitly, and, on the other, brought closer together on a common basis and referred to a common standard.

Finally, as we shall see, critical theory in the counterrevolutionary third stage of the tradition, embodied in McLuhan's fully matured theory, descends from transcendent transhistoricality to embrace the particular historical forms of contemporary social and cultural development as the full material incarnation of the model of interiority initially affirmed. All alternatives are neglected or rejected. In this thoroughgoing apologetic, there is thus no longer any realm of value that is not entirely reducible to established fact, that is, there is no basis for supersession of the given. It is claimed that salvation and value-realization *are* available, and are available *only*, in terms of the currently prevalent material tendencies. Value is dissolved without residue, therefore, into fact, and fact becomes its own value. An abstract moralism, despite a certain categorical continuity, turns into its opposite, a legalism that now not only poses all human relations as being between the particularized individual and the abstract generality of the world, but poses them exclusively from the point of view of the given structures and operative principles of the latter.[1] With the third phase of McLuhan, the tradition finds fulfillment in the technological and social developments that it had previously wished to resist. Its metaphysical posture now becomes the mature ideology of historically specific manipulated integration and ordered stability.[2]

From the start, McLuhan's theory always carries a drive toward the realization of its counterrevolutionary potential. In phases one and two, in spite of, respectively, moments of accommodation and collaboration with actuality, this drive is mitigated by controlling factors of style, emphasis, and point of view. In the first phase, the moralistic critique contains an external (if abstract) reference in its attack on a chaotic, disordered age considered to be marked by passivity and technological manipulation. In the second phase, the critique is suspended and chaos is arrested mentally by detached revaluation. McLuhan now studies popular culture in its own terms, rather than from a ground of literary culture as he and others had done earlier. Culture is redefined as a network of communication, and attention shifts from moral and intellectual content to form by itself. Consequently, a favorable view of the 'vulgar' is adopted. In this period, McLuhan develops the substance of his system, and already encourages accepting and understanding the changes happening subliminally, but he still tends to write from the point of view of literacy. The central articulation is dichotomous, visual versus oral, with the latter coming into dominance.

In the third phase, the suspended critique becomes a polemic directed inwards at literate visual bias. McLuhan shifts to writing from the oral point of view, and actively stimulates acquiescence to neocapitalist technological reification. A new unifying articulation emerges with the principle that the medium is the message/the massage/the mess age/the mass age. McLuhan changes from a type of cultural historian to a prophetic protagonist of an ineluctable psychic and social order: the contemporary electric counterrevolution against the revolution of literacy,

Perhaps the most interesting aspect of this development is that the means to this third stage in modern critical theory is the extension of the realm in which the traditional aesthetic categories are expected to operate. Within the context of a social transition with basic tendencies toward one-dimensional integration, McLuhan represents the counterrevolutionary pole of an aesthetic of social life, as Marcuse represents the revolutionary pole. The separation and tension between art and social life that has prevailed (with some difficulty in this century) since the romantic period is terminated. On one hand, art is redefined as feedback, a control loop by which we, information machines, can maintain and rectify our functioning. On the other hand, the aesthetic program is proclaimed realizable, and inexorably being realized, in and through technologically determined social and economic institutions. The problem of Eliot's dissociation of the sensibility is alleged to be finally solved. Electricity, it is said, heals 'the print-made split between head and heart' (GG 170); 'the machine had broken the senses apart, and circuitry does the reverse' (CA 196).

In general, as McLuhan employs the traditional corpus of critical theory as a novel means of social study, society becomes the content of aesthetics. A (Richardsian and Thomist) interest in psychic order converges with an interest in social order in the course of McLuhan's application of his understanding of symbolist landscaping aesthetics[3] to social analysis. The method he employs to analyze social phenomena is an objectivist, essentially New Critical (and scholastic) exegesis, incorporating myth in the fundamental role that it performs in tradition from Richards and Eliot to Ransom and Frye. According to principles acquired from the New Criticism, McLuhan cannot study the mind directly, only the objective data. For this purpose, his theory that technologies are extensions of the senses provides 'objective correlatives' of the senses that can be examined. These technologies, it can then be said, alter both the (Eliotic) sense ratios and the social landscape. They act, according to these modes of analysis, as formal zoning agencies, just as in the symbolist aesthetic the poem is considered a technical mode of zoning the mind without relying on the nature of the content. Allegedly it follows that to achieve the appropriate (Richardsian) psychic balance, we can control the psychic organization through the rationing of the new technological art forms. A (Richardsian-symbolist) stress on effect thus becomes in this usage an extended formula for manipulation: decide on the effect (for example, cooling down the South African tribes) and then, working backwards, build the cause (feed in television).

A certain continuity of categories in the tradition should not mislead us into neglecting that there are modulations in the ideological character of these categories. This shifts from an abstract negativity all the way to complete positivity. In McLuhan, much of the same aesthetic remains throughout the three phases. But what accounts for the shift in ideological character is precisely that this aesthetic moves out of its own sphere and projects its categories, proportioned with ideological coherence, into the social sphere, *to replace all ethical and historical categories*. In what follows, I will try to indicate the relevant elements of McLuhan's development.

B Phase One: 1936–51

This first period, which has the strong moralistic flavor of Agrarian religious metaphysics, and displays an acute distaste for social reality, prepares the program and the theoretical constituents for the later periods. In 1936, McLuhan praises G. K. Chesterton's efforts 'to re-establish agriculture and small property as the only free basis for a free culture.'[4] Later he identifies the 'same tendency' in electric and agrarian societies, both characterized by an absence of 'goals or objectives or specialized techniques of production' (WP 113). Both societies are conceived in relation to transcendent forces; at this stage McLuhan notes that agrarians are people who can '*feel* the ineluctable fatalities' (LC 188). What is later to become a pan-societal dichotomy in chronological time between mechanical and electric systems of objectification is, in this period, an intra-societal intellectual dichotomy embodied in geographical space and referred, in particular, to the South-North conflict. 'The most important intellectual fact about America,' writes McLuhan, is that, 'geographically separated for the first time in their age-old struggle, there exist, profoundly entrenched in this country, the two radically opposed intellectual traditions' at war since the Greeks (214). Both the 'Southern resistance to technology and industry' and the 'Northern passion for machinery and bureaucracy' are 'inherent in age-old but divergent intellectual traditions' (221, n. 2). The conflict here, in McLuhan's view, is between an encyclopedist oral tradition, comprised in the Ciceronian ideal of *doctus orator* and adopted by the South from 'the main current of European and Western culture' (199), and a specialist dialectical tradition that destroys the possibility of metaphysics (194) and founds Northern technology, considered, accordingly, to be 'built on the most destructive aberration of the Western mind—autonomous dialectics and ontological nominalism' (199).

Of course, McLuhan insists that 'the "cause of the South" is quite independent of geography' (199); the real issue is this 'ancient quarrel' that he discovers as the key to the conflicts of every age from Greece and Rome, through the Middle Ages and the Renaissance, to modern America. This dichotomy (like Ransom's) will remain, through all its transformations, the basis of McLuhan's formulations, and the oral principle will remain throughout the favored protagonist, until, finally, the electric age objectively resolves the dualism into a permanent, apocalyptic monism in which the specialist technological environment becomes simply the content of the new encyclopedist technological environment. As McLuhan, in this first phase, traces this duality through history in his doctoral dissertation[5] and a series of articles (185–234), history is reduced to a technical conflict within the trivium between grammar and dialectic. Since this problematic is

150

centered on the important moments of language and analogy, and since it has points of contact with the contemporary structuralist fetish of language, it is worth sketching very briefly.

The problematic is structured by the analogical logos doctrine, the view that the external world, society, the human mind, and, especially, human speech, are mirrors of the Logos (227), that is the universal reason, the life and order in everything (TN 15). In consequence, speech is the *differentia* between humans and animals (LC 227), and grammar, the keystone of patristic theology, is the reigning science, until it is displaced by dialectic for a period in the twelfth and thirteenth centuries and, again, until it is dethroned in the post-Renaissance world by mathematical Cartesian rationalism and the utilitarian logic of Ramistic nominalism (TN 1–2, 32).[6] The grammarian doctrine is that nature's secrets must be approached through language (208). Science and grammar are 'united by the concept of language as the expression and analogy of the Logos' (25), of language as a world in itself, analogous to the visible world of order (24). In this tradition, up to Francis Bacon, the world is viewed as a book whose lost language—lost to us with the Fall—is analogous to that of human speech: grammatical exegesis becomes the means to metaphysical knowledge (ix, 4). 'In our own time,' McLuhan states, 'the methods of anthropology and psychology have re-established grammar as, at least, a valid mode of science' (5). His own mythic-analogical exegetic methodology, with its emphasis on understanding the grammar of media languages as the key to our world, will be an application derived from this position. And finally, 'the business of art,' in this conception, is 'to recover the knowledge of that language [of nature] which men once held by nature' (4).

In a most important essay, McLuhan restates this problematic in relation to 'the chaos of our time,' and praises Chesterton for placing metaphysical intuition 'in the service of the search for moral and political order.'[7] McLuhan argues that the achievement of 'a high degree of abstract mechanical order' by means of Cartesian strategy has been accompanied by a developing 'moral, psychological, and political chaos.' The diversion from the task of ordering 'appetite and emotion' has placed a disproportionate burden on the artist, to whom has been left entirely the effort 'to introduce or to discover order in man's psychological life.'[8]

This Thomist–Richardsian problematic of psychological order is presented as a comprehensive program: we must face 'the problem of creating a practical moral and social order . . . and this necessarily means an action which co-operates in multiple ways with the numerous hopeful features of the contemporary world.'⁹ To accomplish this task (of adjustment not supersession, unity not freedom), we are urged to use such discoveries as Vico's method for finding psychological and moral unity in the practical order, based 'in his perception that the condition of man is never the same but his nature is unchanging.' We can 'perfect social order' on the basis of these principles of natural unity in changing conditions, and must 'train, simultaneously, esthetic and moral perceptions in acts of unified awareness and judgment' on the model of Eliot and F. R. Leavis' discoveries.¹⁰ This program is later considered realized once electric technology has been identified as a 'hopeful feature' of the objective world, and revealed as the principle of unification in the practical realm, bringing psychological and social order. If one seeks order with a belief that human nature never changes, only the conditions of human life do, then it becomes perversely comprehensible how one would be concerned only with the emergence of what seem to be ordered conditions, while being indifferent in value terms to the specific features of the emerging order.

In another important article from this period, we find further components of this problem complex and more light on 'the common human nature which persists intact beneath all the modes of mental hysteria rampant from Machiavelli and Calvin until our own day.'¹¹ Anticipating *The Mechanical Bride*, McLuhan investigates the advertising 'jungle of folklore' as a 'world of symbols, witticisms, and behaviour patterns,' which may be a cathartic 'interim strategy for maintaining hope, tolerance, and good-humour in an irrational world,' and which comprises 'a common experience and a common language for a country whose sectional differences and technological specialisms might easily develop into anarchy.'¹² At the same time, he condemns market research as an aspect of social engineering (which, of course, he later embraces), and as the centralized exploitation of desires for super-profits. He insists, however, that this activity does no more than provide our world with 'a spectacular externalized paradigm of its own inner drives'; and, equally significantly, that 'creative political activity today, therefore, consists in rational contemplation of these paradigms.'¹³

McLuhan's attitude here to manipulated consumption is important because he clearly realizes that the laws of association which sell junk presented in desirable contexts are drawn into 'campaigns of systematic sophistry and hallucination.' But for him this does not make the state of affairs worse; he does not see manipulation of needs as falsification of real needs, as formation and deformation of consciousness and culture in the interests of power and profit. He insists only that we are no better than the society in which we are manipulated, that the advertisements contain nothing 'which has not been deeply wished by the population for a long time.'[14] The fault is in ourselves, in our appetites and fantasies, and the goal, as in Ransom and Frye, is 'moral and intellectual regeneration which we have always known must precede any sort of genuine improvement.'[15]

In consequence, an active perspective essential for change, namely, that interiority and exteriority must change together, and a recognition that alienation is based in real objective social relations of oppression, are lost. McLuhan's program is passive, contemplative, and individual-oriented. It requires no 'social machinery,' and offers, in fact, no hope for 'genuine improvement.' It is simply a form of education: 'to contemplate the products of our own appetites rather than to anathematize the people who are keen enough to exploit them.'[16] Indeed, advertising, in McLuhan's view, in parading for our daily contemplation 'the luxuriant and prurient chaos of human passions,' may make the recovery of rational detachment possible. What is needed to unite the energy of advertising and the Jeffersonian political tradition, is 'a frank educational program based on the curriculum provided by the ad.-men.'[17]

We must note that McLuhan's agrarianism of the 1940s has, in general, nowhere near the critical negativity of Ransom's in the 1930s, and we need only to recall Ransom's explicit rejection of the soft educational solution. McLuhan's program—contemplate, don't anathematize—with its fact-value separation, its contempt for the oppressed, and its belief in a kind of original sin of universal affective degeneracy, vitiates any considerations of power and makes impossible any understanding of real freedom. Indeed, prolonged uncritical contemplation of manipulation, with an attitude of scorn toward the manipulated, ultimately undermines and displaces any notions of power and freedom altogether. It is in this context that we can understand *The Mechanical Bride* as the extension of the article I have been discussing, and as the last moment of moralization.

In the first phase, as in the later two, technology is central to McLuhan. But in this period he persistently attacks 'the technological bias of the age'[18] which he considers 'the negation of the human person' (LC 186). In the *Bride*, this emphasis continues. He attacks 'inhuman specialism' (MB 50) and technology as 'an abstract tyrant' that ravages the psyche (33). Like F. R. Leavis, he seeks to offer a 'conscious scrutiny' of 'the huge technical panorama' (4). Agrarian and distributist themes combine (for example, 21–2) to provide an acute critique of some aspects of social life. McLuhan observes the passivity of the majority and the power of the minority, and repeats the Ransomian critique of dependence on machines and machine products. 'It would,' he notes, 'require an exceptional degree of awareness and an especial heroism of effort to be anything but supine consumers of processed goods' (21).

In later periods, there will be no place or need for this heroism that McLuhan does not really expect from people in any case. Objective tendencies will bring about participation, and awareness will be required only for effective adjustment to the given processing. In the *Bride*, however, the steps toward solution come through a homeostatic repulsion from extremity, which operates automatically in all of McLuhan's cybernetic constructions, and which he later calls 'reversal of the overheated medium' (UM 45). An aware minority simply detaches itself from 'the dream-locked majority' as passivity grows extreme. McLuhan is satisfied to claim that 'much can be done to foster this state of awareness, even though little can be done directly to change the policies of those in control today of the media of communication' (MB 22).

Thus McLuhan's discussions of mechanical culture as a means of domination are very ambivalent. He recognizes that the mechanization of the human personality is related to questions of economic control. He is aware of the 'psychological misery of millions' who cannot keep up financially with the advertised consumer image for their social group (115). He refuses only 'to talk of freedom but never of power' (134). In the later periods, McLuhan stops talking of both; here power is left unchallenged while a place for freedom is found *within* the realm of power. While later he urges surrender, it is important that here he still urges us to 'resist the mechanism of mass delirium and collective irrationalism,' the agencies of 'education, production, distribution, entertainment, and advertisement' (144), the mass culture aiming 'to manipulate, exploit, control' our minds (v). But the stress is on inner resistance only, and freedom becomes a question of understanding: 'freedom, like taste, is an activity of perception and judgment' (22). There is no unbridgeable clash between this Eliotic–Leavisite delimitation of freedom and the later McLuhanatic glorification of 'utter human docility' (UM 64).

The story of the modern tradition of critical theory is the story of the passage over that bridge.

One last aspect of the *Bride* must be mentioned. Although the book still involves a critique of the external landscape, and has neither the characteristic oral/visual structure of the later periods nor the explicit unifying principle of total formalism found in the third phase, it does include numerous elements that recur later, such as the emphasis on discontinuity and on the world as a 'single city,' in the context of the 'new insights into the universal fabric' produced by the new physics (3, 10). But most important, perhaps, is a methodological principle. McLuhan makes the Richardsian point that aesthetic criticism is trained to discover the means to artistic unity of effect, argues that the Western world has developed such a unity, and suggests that aesthetic criticism could be a 'citadel of inclusive awareness' in regard to the state. The application of 'the method of art analysis to the critical evaluation of society' (vi), I have argued, is fundamental to McLuhan, and it has been a most appealing, influential, and significant aspect of his work. We must remember, however, that in the later periods the value is found in the given facts themselves, and the 'evaluation' of society is not critical.

The last aspect of this first phase to which I want to draw attention is the analysis of symbolist aesthetics that provides for McLuhan a series of technical principles through which to control his social analysis in subsequent phases. I have already discussed the most relevant aspects in this area and will be very brief here. McLuhan's interest in this aesthetic realm is, typically, in its technology. He claims that the symbolists made a metaphysical breakthrough in discovering a quality of intelligibility in things;[19] for them, the artist becomes 'an impersonal agent, humble before the law of things, as well as before his own artistic activity as revealer.'[20] Their technique of paratactic juxtaposition[21] is thus the means to an interior landscape that is the analogy of the signatures of things. What I want to stress is that, once this aesthetic is projected onto society in phase two and, especially, phase three, it presupposes there a universal rationality that marks all things. By the very nature of the methodology, society is stabilized as the fixed mirror of a transcendent principle which, for McLuhan, is technology—a kind of essence behind a multitude of phenomena. This universalization of technological rationality, of course, is the technocratic ideology of our times.

The poetic process for McLuhan, as for Richards, is continuous with ordinary cognition; it is the retracing and hence epiphanizing of the stages of ordinary apprehension. The aesthetic moment of arrested cognition is analyzed into equivalent fragments (fission) and then, by the suggestions of analogy (not contiguity as in ordinary cognition), it is reconstructed (fusion). Learning and creation are united in an affair of zoning (LC 164–6). This position becomes the basis for McLuhan's subjectivist notions of time and space. By corollary, the assertion of analogy between interiority and exteriority serves to paralyze efforts to alter the given objectivity.

Two further consequences of the projection of this aesthetic into social analysis are significant. Firstly, if the aesthetic fission dissolves everything into fragments of equal significance, the proportioned structures and relations of alienation become invisible, and the aesthetic fusion (by juxtaposition) is limited to a reconstruction or manipulation of the given alienation—it can neither see the nature of alienation nor grasp liberating potentialities. This is evident in McLuhan's own analyses, which touch upon a great range of phenomena, often in novel combinations, but always preserve them in their alienated forms. Secondly, this conception, like the structuralist conceptions analyzed by Henri Lefebvre,[22] brackets the richness of human praxis and history, and reduces intellect and intelligibility to a function of analytic separation of wholes into elements and their reconstruction: breakdown and creation of forms, classification and combination. This is a technological view of operational efficiency appropriate to the cybernetic formulations of games theory, decision theory, information theory, and communications theory.

C Phase Two: 1952–8

The dominant feature of McLuhan's second phase is the journal *Explorations*, founded on a Ford Foundation grant in 1953, which became the vehicle for spreading his ideas to people unhappy with specialized academicism. The *Explorations* manifesto, envisaging an interdisciplinary investigation cutting across the humanities and social sciences,[23] caused much intellectual excitement, and gained an early base for the McLuhan success story that did not effectively unfold until the 1960s. This second phase begins more or less in 1952 when McLuhan rejects the high-culture Victorianism that 'everything connected with industry, commerce, sport, and popular entertainment is merely vulgar,'[24] in favor of a universalization in which culture is defined as a communication network with which all objects and activities have some kind of relation so that 'there are no non-cultural areas' in society.[25] By shifting attention to form, he perceives the formal continuity of cultural expression in a multiplicity of fields.[26] (From this step of perceiving the universality of capitalist *forms*, in the next period McLuhan is to move to the complete and counterrevolutionary suppression of all possible liberating *content*.) He determines to study cultural forms in their own terms and to carry out his own cognitive program. Communications media come to be depicted as 'both form and vehicle of the flux of human cultures,' unique art forms that alter human sensibility (LC 7). The new media, he states, are 'serious culture.'[27]

McLuhan argues that the artist was always a magician; while primitive art sought to control the external world, modern art seeks to control the mind. Modern science merges the two, and applies techniques developed to control the external world to controlling the mind: magical 'mass media' invade the mind and society with patterned information (LC 84–5). In terms of his conception of media, McLuhan extends his analyses of symbolism, and conceives new media as art, the popular press, for example, as 'static landscape,' that is, spatial manipulation of mental states (21, 10). Perhaps most important in this context is the analysis of advertisements as 'the main channel of intellectual and artistic effort in the modern world,'[28] 'a form of magic which have come to dominate a new civilization,' using 'all the techniques of symbolist art' to create a promised land of dreams in which people can live through 'communal participation' in the 'totemistic institutions' such as national brand commodities like Coca-Cola.[29]

McLuhan is aware of the vast economic role of advertising[30] in producing a mass market for mass production, but his more important insight is the recognition that mass media do not only sell products but form a magical culture. This should make possible a historical location of the erosion of class lines in the production of a consumer culture and the production and control of the individual as a consumer with manipulated and standard experiences and expectations. Instead, by limiting the analysis to aesthetic categories, McLuhan allows these forms a permanent aesthetic closure that falsely separates them from their role and origin in oppression. Walter Benjamin has argued that mechanically reproduced art is, in any case, susceptible to independent existence freed from its source. As criteria of authenticity become meaningless, art exists in its immediacy as political practice.[31] But McLuhan does not treat this political-ideological practice; at most he offers a resistance to advertising magic through 'paying conscious attention to it.'[32] This position fails to penetrate beyond the immediacy of the situation and capitulates to the social and economic institutions that produce it.

In general, during this second phase, McLuhan attributes independent powers of determination to the new media he investigates. They all appear to be 'art forms that have the power of imposing, like poetry, their own assumptions.'[33] Comparably to Frye, he insists that 'technological art takes the whole earth and its population as its material, not as its form.' Indeed, these new media are not ways of relating us to the real world: 'they *are* the real world, and they reshape what remains of the old world at will' (EC 182). He notes: 'It has long been a truism that changes in material culture cause shifts in the patterns of the entire culture.'[34] At the same time, paralleling Frye's formulations in regard to literature, McLuhan argues that the new media are 'new languages with new and unique powers of expression' (EC 2).

Jonathan Miller[35] and James W. Carey[36] have both tried to bring McLuhan in general into some relation with the Harold Innis hypothesis that communications technology is determinant in socio-cultural disposition and with the Sapir–Whorf hypothesis that, since language is the means to the appropriation of reality, its specific grammar is determinant in the structuration of reality. McLuhan himself has suggested that *The Gutenberg Galaxy* may be viewed as a footnote to Innis.[37] I would argue that, to the extent that it is useful to locate McLuhan in relation to Innis and Sapir–Whorf, it is to this second phase that the comparisons properly belong, not to the third.

It is important to observe that two pillars of McLuhan's mature system, the extension theory and the theory of sensory organization, are not articulated until the third phase; that is, that the *differentia* of the theory, which specifies McLuhan beyond Sapir-Whorf and especially beyond Innis in ways that make assimilation difficult and forced, is not yet present in phase two. Here, as in Innis, the emphasis is on social and psychological change without the mediation of the reified sense-extension ecology. At the same time, in *Explorations*, McLuhan and other contributors frequently discuss different codifications of reality, and McLuhan has made it clear, as I have been showing, that he considers media to be artistic languages that impose their own assumptions, which *are* the forms of our reality. This second phase, in other words, is already marked by a fetishization of technological language, but it must be distinguished from the third stage where specific new forms of articulation embody a different ideological attitude.

Finally, we may note here, in contrast to the first phase, that technology is now differentiated into old and new, visual and oral. Indeed, McLuhan criticizes the *Bride* for defending book culture against the ascendant technology.[38] This redefined bifurcation, transforming what had been a quarrel in space between North and South, or in principle between dialectic and grammar, or in economics between technological and agrarian, into a temporal conflict of old and new, accomplishes a strategic about-turn. McLuhan can still retain the *structures* of his analysis, and continue to oppose oral culture to mechanical technology, but now in terms of the superiority and priority of a future about to be realized on the basis of a non-mechanical technology against the immediate mechanical past. In other words, without much alteration, he can now capitulate in full to objectively given tendencies, that is, he can collaborate with neocapitalism.

McLuhan now comes to oppose new media to traditional educational texts (EC 1), acoustic space and time to visual space and time, and encyclopedic oral culture to specialist print culture (125, 128–9, 134, 127). He also finds a new historical location for his basic methodological principle: 'Analogical proportion is a basic aspect of auditory space and of oral culture. It is the oral equivalent of the golden section in architecture and design.'[39] The starting point for him now is 'the drive of the past century towards the dominance of the auditory and oral as the ruling dynamic in Western experience';[40] 'oral means "total" primarily, "spoken" accidentally.'[41] Evidently we find ourselves more and more deeply in the problematic of totalitarian order. The oral revolution brings 'new insistence on long-term goals and on social security and equilibrium,' on decorum, harmony, and teamwork.[42] This is neocapitalist stabilization, and McLuhan's attitude to it is that approval or disapproval is a terribly dangerous preparation for a cultural strategy and we must rather look at the situation 'on its own terms.'[43]

Looking 'on its own terms,' we find:[44]

Always the key to oral culture, primitive or model 1957, is the stress on participation, on creative passivity. It is the twentieth-century consumer attitude which has given such great retrospective stress to Keats' 'negative capability' and to T. S. Eliot's 'catalyst' concept of creativity.

159

'Creative passivity,' we must recognize, is Orwellian Newspeak. In the third phase, this term is suppressed, while the term that stood in apposition to it, the mystical 'participation,' replaces it to become a keyword. But the substance is unchanged. This is the vicious ideology of consumerism that robs human beings of their fundamental ontological dimension as producers of themselves and of the whole world. The productive power, which in this society is alienated, literally sold and bought as a commodity, would in this view be forever lost to the producer; a fraction of its energy is returned to the consumer so that he may frenetically take part in his own permanent alienation and enslavement. This profound collaboration with the system expresses deepening reification and stands on the brink of excluding the subject of social history altogether.

D Phase Three: 1959-

In 1951, McLuhan saw his task as the 'enlightenment' (MB v), and in the 1954 *Counterblast*, as the 'reorientation,' of technological man. In the 1969 *Counterblast*, McLuhan quotes the opening passage from 1954, deletes the last paragraph that presents his work mystagogically, as demystification or revelation, and substitutes a paragraph that presents his work behaviorally, as 'Pavlovian conditioning.' This behaviorism represents the change to a counterrevolutionary phase that excludes all dimensions of value or content or purposive social activity. In 1959, McLuhan introduces the formula 'the medium is the message,' in a fairly cautious statement that 'primarily the social action of these forms is their meaning in the long run.'[45] He insists that both the message and the effect of media is in their form and not in their content, and always subliminal.[46] This form is both linguistic and mythic, and, in addition, media are mythopoeic.[47] A year later 'The Medium Is the Message' becomes the title of an article[48] and increasing stress is placed on subliminality. In the same year, the general emphasis is on languages permeating our experience. In a series of articles during the next two years, the automatism of the technological fetish is specified and intensified. Finally, in 1962, *The Gutenberg Galaxy* offers the fully mature theory, including, for the first time, the essential ontological-epistemological moments of the extension theory and the theory of sensory rationalization. These, together with the formalist formula of meaning ('the medium is the message,' later, 'massage'), guarantee a reified whole that is coherent and complete, and able to control and coordinate all disparate social data on the basis of an all-encompassing technological determinism. History is stabilized for technological manipulation, and art itself becomes a cybernetic control device. I have suggested 1959 for the opening date of this third phase only because of the first appearance of the essential 'medium is the message' formulation; this stage could be taken to begin in 1962 with *The Gutenberg Galaxy* where its essential determinations are for the first time synthesized. In what follows, I shall examine some of the key moments of this mature theory.

CHAPTER 12

Technocratic Ideology of One-Dimensionality

A Technological Fetishism

Contingent content and system, we have seen repeatedly, are antagonists. The emergence of a unifying articulation in the 'medium is the message' formula necessarily entails the suppression of content. This objective is relentlessly pursued by McLuhan, from the beginning of the 1960s, when the 'content concept' is defined as a 'crippling' literate cultural attitude[1] that testifies to 'insufficient structural analysis,'[2] to the end of the decade, when content is considered to be of 'about as much importance as the stenciling on the casing of an atom bomb' (PI 56). Indeed, content, McLuhan says, is an 'illusion' that 'derives from one medium being "within" or simultaneous with another' (CB 24). Form relates only to form; 'the "content" of any medium is always another medium' (UM 23). Such a conception moves beyond Frye, where form, though separated from content, is yet the form of a content which it absorbs and to which it adapts. This formal closure in McLuhan's theory seems to be an unmistakable ideological indication of a growing tendency to one-dimensionality in an increasingly total consumer culture. As Jean Baudrillard notes:[3]

> Bref il se constitue un univers multiple de media homogènes les uns aux autres en tant que tels, se signifiant l'un l'autre et renvoyant les uns aux autres—contenu réciproque l'un de l'autre: à la limite c'est bien là leur message—message totalitaire d'une société de consommation. . . . Pourtant ce procès technologique délivre bien une certaine sorte de message, très impératif: message de consommation du message, de spectacularisation, d'autonomisation et de mise en valeur de l'information *comme*

marchandise, d'exaltation du contenu en tant que signe (en ce sens, la publicité est le médium contemporain par excellence).

In short, there comes into being a manifold universe of media that are homogeneous in their capacity as media and which mutually signify each other and refer back to each other. Each one is reciprocally the content of another; indeed, this ultimately is their message—the totalitarian message of a consumer society.
. . . This technological complex, nevertheless, does convey a certain kind of imperious message: message of consumption of the message, of spectacularization, of autonomization and valorization of information *as a commodity*, of glorification of the content treated as sign. (In this regard, advertising is the contemporary medium par excellence.)

McLuhan develops the other side of this ideology in a determinist fetishism of technology; 'macroscopically, the content fades and the medium itself looms large' (CB 22). Comparing his formula to Richards' 'meaning of meaning,' McLuhan argues that 'the medium is the message' simply restates that 'meaning' is 'not statement so much as the simultaneous interaction of many things'; media are complex sets of events that work us over and change us.[4] Indeed, far beyond anything that Richards explicitly conceived, but within the same positivist line of ontological passivity, McLuhan goes on to present technology as not only 'message' but 'massage,' and as not only causing social and psychological change, but as the only cause of change. On one hand: 'All media work us over completely. They are so pervasive in their personal, political, economic, aesthetic, psychological, moral, ethical, and social consequences that they leave no part of us untouched, unaffected, unaltered. The medium is the massage' (MM 26). On the other: 'All social changes are the effect of new technologies (self-amputations of our own being) on the order of our sensory lives' (WP 5). I shall return to the sensory extension part of this last statement in the next section; for now I want only to observe that McLuhan shares B. F. Skinner's emphasis on conditioning and determinism (177–8) and seeks to trace etiology to the independent powers of technological environments.

One immediate consequence of this fetish, we must note, is the effective legitimation of war. Technological innovations are said to alter our images of ourselves and of the world: 'wars necessarily result as misbegotten efforts to recover the old images' (5). The obsession with identity we saw earlier in the tradition gains new application:

McLuhan accounts for both the origins and the persistence of war 'as the quest for that identity that is always threatened by technological innovations' (116) and specifies that this quest, manifested in 'violence in its many forms,' is always 'involuntary' (123). I cannot emphasize too strongly the counterrevolutionary character of the ideology in evidence here, in this ugly deduction of involuntary and necessary war. Within the theoretical space of an ideology that posits a self-contained technological rationality as the prime and inexorable cause, beyond the reach of human will and practice, we must note that there are no categories for resistance or opposition to the effects of that rationality, in this case, the atrocities of imperialist class violence.[5]

B Cybernetic Reification: Idealist Materialism

In order to ensure that there are no loopholes in the network of technological determination, McLuhan provides for the formalist 'medium is the message' an ecological basis, comprising a direct cybernetic relation between the individual organism and the technological environment. The conception of sensory extension is the center of the whole theory. It is an ideological construction whose standpoint is that of social integration, harmony, and equilibrium. It works to preclude conscious, purposive revolutionary change by considering psychic and social order through the paradigm of biological homeostasis. Human objectifications, the products of work activity, called 'extensions' by McLuhan, are in his view strategies of the organism 'to exert staying power, constancy, equilibrium, and *homeostasis*.' 'All organizations, but especially biological ones,' he claims, 'struggle to remain constant in their inner condition amidst the variations of outer shock and change. The man-made social environment as an extension of man's physical body is no exception' (UM 98). Media, defined broadly as 'any technology whatever that creates extensions of the human body and senses' (PI 56), are considered to 'constitute a world of biochemical interactions that must ever seek new equilibrium as new extensions occur' (UM 181). These media perpetually modify people 'physiologically' (55) as they alter human sense ratios, the internal analogue of technological rationality. In other words, cultural ecology has its base and strategic level of significance, not in a historical dialectic, but in physiology (GG 35), so that 'the medium is the message,' McLuhan's communications theory, is ultimately revealed as the expression of an infrahistorical semiology.

Essentially, the extension theory relies on biological theories of discomfort evolved out of research into stress by medical scientists such as Hans Selye. According to such argument, to counteract irritation it cannot avoid, the body resorts to a strategy of self-amputation (extension). In the physical stress of super-stimulation of various kinds, the central nervous system acts to protect itself by this strategy of the isolation of the offending organ, sense, or function. The acceleration of the pace of life stimulates further innovation; irritation invites counterirritation which, in turn, amplifies human functions and causes a pain that must be anaesthetized 'through numbness or blocking of perception.' For McLuhan, 'the principle of self-amputation as an immediate relief of strain on the central nervous system' is a satisfactory account of 'the origin of the media of communication from speech to computer' (UM 52). The endless cycle of irritation-counterirritation is the action-reaction rhythm of the 'systole-diastole movement' (CA 46) that McLuhan projects as the form of motion of cultural history, which he casts as a simple cybernetic system with an automatic control loop that effects transition at the point of saturation. Of course, a theory of history as a theory of disease makes irresistible an eschatological impulse to health. For McLuhan, the apocalyptic promise of the electric age represents a break with this cyclical dynamism—a break achieved in the stabilization of equilibrium.

I shall return to this in the next section. For the moment, I want to draw attention to the perceptual numbness, explained as a self-protective mechanism, that is said to accompany in this cycle the technological extension of a sense as a response to specialized irritation. McLuhan notes that we fail to recognize ourselves in the technologies that dominate us, and argues that the technological environment is invisible to our 'automatically' displaced perceptions (UM 55) so that we live our relations with our extensions in the form of the Narcissus myth. He stresses the need to reject 'the Narcissus attitude of regarding the extensions of our own bodies as really *out there* and really independent of us' (73). Media systems are 'pseudo-events of our own manufacture, since they stem from man's own psyche' (CA 57). It is important to take note of this idealist aspect (often misinterpreted as a genuine humanism in McLuhan) at the heart of the extension theory. We shall see later that it is an essential moment of one-dimensional reification.

For McLuhan, psychic rationalization recapitulates technological rationalization: 'any extension of the sensorium by technological dilation has a quite appreciable effect in setting up new ratios or proportions among all the senses' (GG 35). As a result, 'the psychic and social impact' of new technological environments reverses the 'characteristic psychic and social consequences' of the old (WP 82). The point is that the message of media, that which produces these personal and social consequences, consists of 'the change of scale or pace or pattern' introduced into our lives (UM 23–4) by the incessant action of these media on the sensorium (WP 136). It is on this level of mediation, namely, the technological alteration of sense ratios or patterns of perception, 'steadily and without resistance' (UM 33), that the transcendent etiology of cultural ecology is fundamentally asserted. 'When these ratios change, men change' (MM 41).[6]

Norbert Wiener described a human being as a 'special sort of machine';[7] and the President of the International Association of Cybernetics defined the science Wiener founded as 'the science of robots.'[8] McLuhan's own definitions move into the realm of this development.

> Man is not only a robot in his private reflexes but in his civilized behavior and in all his responses to the extensions of his body, which we call technology. The extensions of man with their ensuing environments, it's now fairly clear, are the principal area of manifestation of the evolutionary process. (WP 19)

In this perspective, we are stripped completely of mediations, complexity, and the ability to control ourselves and our world. The reified circle is closed with this theoretical dethronement of the historical human subject who might have created a new world and a new human nature. The transformative praxis that initiates history has no further realm of activity. We are said to relate to the technologies we embrace as 'servomechanisms.' 'We must, to use them at all, serve these objects, these extensions of ourselves, as gods or minor religions' (UM 55). We must serve them with 'servomechanistic fidelity' (64).

The passivity that has been a key feature of the tradition since Richards, here becomes manic. The human world of meaning and project, of ontological creativity, is suppressed, and, as things are animated, humanity is deanimated, reduced to a mere means of reproduction of objective forms.

Man becomes, as it were, the sex organs of the machine world, as the bee of the plant world, enabling it to fecundate and to evolve ever new forms. The machine world reciprocates man's love by expediting his wishes and desires, namely, in providing him with wealth. (56)

Particularist satisfactions pay for the subservience of creativity to generalized reification. Domination as a social category, we might note, is absent from the theory; it enters only obliquely as technological domination.

McLuhan is quick to explore the technocratic implications of this massive passivity. We are unable to resist the qualitative impact of technology on our senses, and the technological system is not susceptible to an assertion of *qualitative* human priorities. Only technocratic manipulation within the given framework remains for us as servomechanisms. 'In the future, the only effective media controls must take the thermostatic form of quantitative rationing' (267). In such a reduction of the horizons of human will and practice to *quantitative* rationing of media, there is no question of challenging the autonomous fetishized powers that technology exerts over us. It becomes a question rather of harnessing its powers of 'massage' to the conscious manipulation of the sensory lives of whole populations and cultures in order to 'improve and stabilize their emotional climate,' on the (neocapitalist) model, McLuhan says, of maintaining 'equilibrium among the world's competing economies' (PI 72).[9] McLuhan's vision of a computer-orchestrated interplay of all media is set against a background of a socio-cultural tendency toward total one-dimensional integration. Evidently, he speaks from the point of view of power and identification with the established system. In this context, the assertion that 'the human nervous system itself can be reprogramed biologically as readily as any radio network can alter its fare,'[10] must be recognized as a high point of counterrevolutionary ambition.

I want now to locate McLuhan's theory as the specific technocratic cultural ideology of neocapitalist one-dimensionality. The extension theory as a whole, we should note at once, is once again a projection from aesthetics into social analysis, a projection of anthropomorphism. In fact, it is only in the realm of art that an actually disanthropomorphized capitalist technology, which, in real life, is increasingly distinct from anthropological attributes, can be reanthropomorphized on the basis of an identity of subject and object, and raised, according to the specificities of art, to the higher level of generic immediacy.[11] In other words, the nature of art permits an immediately sensible humanization of technology. Outside the aesthetic sphere, however, on the level of theory, a similar subject-object identity is untenable. An anthropomorphic theory, which considers technology to be an immediate human extension, fails to provide a genuine theoretical elaboration of the relations between a historical society and its technology, and, specifically, fails to take note of the reified nature of those relations in the present society.

The significance of this point, indeed, of the whole problematic, to an analysis of McLuhan cannot be overstressed. In relation to the contemporary alienation of human powers, the anthropomorphism of McLuhan's extension theory (claiming immediate identity between humans and human objectifications) is a false and deceptive reappropriation of those powers by mere assertion, that is, by finding what 'ought to be' in what actually 'is,' or by projecting what actually 'is' as what 'ought to be'—in any case, by valorizing the *actually established* facts and relations. He accepts the *fact* of reification, the social rule of technology and technological rationality, but legitimates it by suppressing the *consciousness* of alienation, in insisting that technologies and their alien rule *are* really ourselves, and in denying that objectified praxis *has* really *been alienated* from us. In this way, the *real* problem of the reappropriation of our creative human powers, of our humanity—for mankind as a whole, management over its own life processes; for each individual, a full and free share in the abundance of human products and capacities—is abolished, obliterated, by sleight of hand. McLuhan's position in this respect is the inverse of Hegel's. Both identify alienation and objectification with one another but, where Hegel sees all objectification as alienated, McLuhan dissolves all real alienation in the permanent principle of objectification (extension). The Utopistic energies with which McLuhan pinpoints actual tendencies of our present and perhaps future lives, consequently, are always sustained—without challenge and without any other available recourse—within the framework of ongoing social domination. It is not that McLuhan's theory is too radical in its scope and sweep as regards human life; it is not radical enough. With the technological base and the cultural transformations that are now plausibly within our reach, our human possibilities for a free, rich, and actively self-enhancing and self-developing, ecologically sound human community are absolutely mind-blowing; yet in McLuhan there is no hint of this. He permits no theoretical space for dispute or alternatives, and none at all for self-conscious historical subjectivity, free of fetishes. The supersession of alienation and domination is not only *not* envisioned by McLuhan (at this late stage of the critical twilight within 'the humanist tradition'); it is methodologically *precluded* by the terms of the categorical articulation.

However, we must press this analysis deeper to find the commotive specificity of reified ideology, and to resolve some apparent ambiguities. Some interpretations of McLuhan will stress the technological focus, and classify the theory as materialist; others will stress the psychic sensory focus, and consider it idealist. McLuhan's technological determinism has been viewed by some as *simply* an anti-humanist surrender to transcendence. By contrast, it has also been argued that his notion that technologies are extensions of ourselves, *are* ourselves, or, more strongly, that the psyche is the real locus of social and cultural momentum, and technologies are not really *out there* independently, is a humanist affirmation of the anthropocentric immanence of social life. All these arguments have been put by critics, but they are all one-sided and inadequate formulations. Rather, the specific unity of the theory resides exactly in the integration of all these aspects. Like the social features it expresses, McLuhan's critical theory is an idealist materialism, a humanist anti-humanism, an immanent transcendentalism.[12]

Le positivisme technocratique n'est qu'un humanisme en creux.
Il n'y a pas de politique, parce qu'il n'y a que de la technique;
il n'y a pas de technique, parce qu'il n'y a que de l'homme.
L'homme ou la technique, c'est la même chose.

Ce dualisme moniste (l'homme se heurte aux choses, mais tout se passe toujours bien, parce que l'homme est une chose, ou les choses sont humaines; selon le technocratisme, l'humanité ne résout que des tâches qu'elle ne se propose pas) s'affirme donc comme un dualisme pour aussitôt se résoudre en monisme. Le dualisme ne réside qu'à la surface du langage technocratique, dans ses affirmations les plus béates. Le monisme, c'est ce *système organique*, qui prétend épuiser tout le réel, et qui exprime les vues du technocratisme sur la société, l'entreprise, etc.

Technocratic positivism is merely a hollow humanism. There is no politics, since there is only technique; there is no technique, since there is only man. Man or technique: the same thing.

Man clashes with objects, but everything always works out because man too is an object, or objects too are human; according to the technocratic view, mankind can only resolve tasks that it does not set for itself. This monistic dualism thus asserts itself as dualism only to resolve itself immediately into monism. The dualism exists only at the surface of technocratic language—in its most complacent affirmations. The monism is this *organic system* at such which claims to exhaust the totality of the real and which expresses the technocratic view of society, of business, etc.

More rapidly, with infinitely greater confidence, and at a much deeper level than was the case with Ransom, McLuhan's dualism dissolves into a systematic monism. His anthropomorphism cannot be resolved into either subjective idealism or mechanical materialism. *The assertion of identity between subject and object, between human beings and the forces that dominate them, is the precise ideological form of one-dimensional reification.* As Marcuse has argued, once people identify themselves with what is imposed on them, alienation 'has become entirely objective; the subject which is alienated is swallowed up by its alienated existence. There is only one dimension, and it is everywhere and in all forms.'[13] McLuhan's sensory extension and message theory finds its adequate location as the technocratic ideological mimesis of this new order of reification; it presumes and promotes, moreover, the continuing assent of human beings to the humanly created forces which at present dominate them.

C Stabilized History: the Apocalypse of Global Stasis

Mimetic identification with the existing modes of domination is proposed as the legitimate form of the contemporary electric age. McLuhan urges that we must become fully involved with our new technological environment: 'we must maximize rather than minimize the various features of our new media' (CB 133). What is said to have happened is that mechanical culture, having reached its full potential, its point of saturation, has reversed its characteristics. Civilization, the product of literacy, 'dissolves with the electronic revolution' and we rediscover 'a tribal, integral awareness that manifests itself in a complete shift in our sensory lives' (WP 97, 24–5). Like the 'all-at-once' simultaneity of Eliot's 'tradition' ('in fact,' says McLuhan, 'a report of an immediate and present reality' (VP 257)), the new world, owing to the instantaneous speed of information movement, is a simultaneous, non-linear, all-at-once world where individuals are deeply involved in one another (VP 251).

The binding of the vision to the cybernetic mode of ordered information reduces *historical process* (known to McLuhan only as formal sequence in duration, as structurally recurrent environmental series) to *technical processing*, that is, to pattern recognition. And pattern recognition is considered 'post-historical,' since both the whole present and the entire past—that is, the totality of human reality in space and time—are 'simultaneously present' (CB 131). This is an ideology of an eternal present, which reduces society into technology, and not only leaves the existing forms of power unchallenged but also leaves the given modes of existence untested by needs, values, or interests. It is a technocratic ideology that presumes a society essentially free of conflicts, a manipulable totality given as an axiom and inaccessible to theoretical and practical social criticism.[14] It is immediate and inclusive only because the cybernetic semiotic of the medium as message is hollow and empty of genuine humanity; because, as has been noted, 'mere noise permits of no articulated interactions,'[15] or, put differently, because all articulations are flattened out within the one-dimensional universality of the given structure of rationality.

McLuhan finds a solution in this electric world to all the key problems of his early concerns. Television, considered an iconic two-dimensional mosaic of tactile values rather than a picture, exercising its effect through physiological completion of the dots of electronic scansion (PI 61), is said to reassemble ('in sensorial terms') what was split apart by the media of literacy (CB 131) and to heal the dissociated sensibility. Computer-orchestration is viewed as bringing psychic communal integration (PI 72) and making possible a programmed unification of existence. Meanwhile, automation is regarded as embodying 'the ultimate extension of the electro-magnetic form to the organization of production' (GG 130). The tribal condition, it is argued, 'has already overtaken private enterprise, as individual businesses form into massive conglomerates' (CA 13), at the same time that 'big business itself' is a leader in reversing centralizing strategies in favor of 'the new drive for decentralism and pluralism' (GG 230).

McLuhan, here as elsewhere, is emphasizing an integration of particularities, on the cybernetic and information theory model of analysis and combination, extended fragmentation and extended integration. This is the form of neocapitalist social culture which both particularizes (atomizes) and generalizes (standardizes) the ego-centered individual on the grounds of the overall priority of the whole. In relation to economic power, McLuhan now obfuscates the question of centralization that had still been visible in the *Mechanical Bride*. He ignores the fact that decentralization on one level means, not the abolition or democratization, but the re-formation, of power and control on higher levels of centralization.

Involvement, mystical participation, is a central category for McLuhan, and it continues to mean the ontological passivity that it expressed in phase two. 'The involvement in role creates the image that is collective process' (CB 138); goals disappear with mechanical culture, to be replaced by 'knowing one's place': the 'total involvement in role' (137). While eliminating the teleological aspect from everyday life, McLuhan also eliminates it on the level of social action. The stability of an achieved corporate society of tribal loyalties becomes the focus of attention. McLuhan is entranced by the social cohesion of the tribe, and by the allegedly richer and more complex inner life of oral people in pre-literate tribal societies than of people in literate Western civilization (PI 59; UM 59). This allegation is false, and denies the historical development of interiority, whose richness is a matter of the totality of its potential relations on the basis of needs, abilities, capacities, and powers that evolve socially in time. To the extent that it contains an element of truth, it relates to a gap that McLuhan does not ever face: the gap in our time between individual and social development, that is, between individual impoverishment and growing social abundance. But its chief interest here for us lies in the demonstration that the face of the never-ending all-at-once present is turned away from the future toward the distant past. The 'noble savage' fiction preserved in the Catholic tradition, the neocapitalist impulse to arrest history, and the structural dynamics of McLuhan's own theory, all combine in the idolatry of the primitive, as ideological reinforcement—or mythic parallel, as Eliot and McLuhan would say—for the dominant articulations of the present.

'The twentieth century, the age of electric information, instant retrieval and total involvement,' McLuhan finds, 'is a new tribal time' (COB 7). And what distinguishes a tribal society is that it has 'the means of stability far beyond anything possible to a visual or civilized and fragmented world' (WP 23). What had been an ideological 'ought' earlier in the tradition and then an ideological practice, a persistent program but always only a program, is now claimed to be a material reality in the process of unfolding. 'A new stasis is in prospect,' the end of the irritation-counterirritation cycle (UM 68). 'Electricity has brought back the cool, mosaic world of implosion, equilibrium, and stasis' (257). The controlling image of this apocalypse is the 'global village,' which is the effect of the electric extension of the central nervous system (CB 40): the image of harmonized discontinuity, of decentralization and interdependence, described, in contrast to dynamic Western civilization, as 'static and iconic or inclusive' (UM 50). The characteristic features of this new society are spelled out explicitly: 'We become reactionaries. Involvement that goes with our instant technologies transforms the most "socially conscious" people into conservatives' (46). And further:

> The world tribe will be essentially conservative, it's true, like all iconic and inclusive societies; a mythic environment lives beyond time and space and thus generates little radical social change. All technology becomes part of a shared ritual that the tribe desperately tries to keep stabilized and permanent. (PI 70)

A point needs to be clarified here. Obviously, it is not space and time in the sense of objects and events that this ideology seeks to abolish; that would obliterate life and there would be no need for the theory. The important point is the stabilization that is announced; its opponent is not time and change but the history that strives to explode the existing stable forms, to revolutionize change, to break with recurrence in creating the new, the qualitatively different future. McLuhan's position was already presented in the first issue of *Explorations*:[16]

> History has been abolished by our new media. If prehistoric man is simply preliterate man living in a timeless world of seasonal recurrence, may not post-historic man find himself in a similar situation? May not the upshot of our technology be the awakening from the historically conditioned nightmare of the past into a timeless present? Historic man may turn out to have been literate man. An episode.

The same point is clarified later. In McLuhan's view, writing, the 'visualization of the acoustic,' sets up 'a cultural disequilibrium of great violence.' He suggests:

> The dynamism of the Western world may well proceed from the dynamics of that disequilibrium. If so, our present stage of media

development suggests the possibility of a new equilibrium. Our craving today for balance and an end of ever-accelerating change, may quite possibly point to the possibility thereof. (CB 131)

The end of dynamism is the end of the historical episode. McLuhan's most significant statement in this respect, by its historical reference, is a precise clarification of this issue. Moving beyond his usual periodization, McLuhan notes that 'circuitry is the end of the neolithic age' (33). Electric culture, like paleolithic culture, is 'zero gradient,' total environment, versus the 'single gradient' neolithic cultures 'moving toward specific ends and destinies': 'Today, in the age of electric circuitry, when information retrieval can be both instant and total, the intervening ages of specialism between us and Paleolithic Man the Hunter seem quaint and odd' (VP 7).

Such arrogant renunciation of the whole of human history (as 'quaint and odd') is staggering. But it is crucial to understand what is being rejected. The specialism-totality axis confuses the issue. The problems of human existence are not resolved in a vague search for totality, the modern tradition of critical theory notwithstanding. It is important to examine the ontological dimensions of human praxis. The hunters, of course, had, within their static societies, a mobile everyday practice, oriented to their reproduction. It is not operational practice or mobility that McLuhan rejects. What characterizes the neolithic period, by contrast, in addition to the social division of labor, is (for the first time) an active productive praxis that transforms both mankind and nature. The neolithic revolution is a fantastically significant revolution in human history: an ontological trans-formation. With agriculture (15,000 B.C.) and domestication of animals (10,000 B.C.), means of subsistence are for the first time *produced actively* under direct human design and control, as opposed to the *passivity* of hunting, fishing, fruit gathering. Humanity begins to produce its own resources, to create the new.[17] In other words, historical praxis is the characteristic feature of this period. It is this praxis, the mode of associated historical being, the indispensable means to the future, to the creation of human destinies, that appears to McLuhan as a quaint relic. Technocracy streamlines, controls, stabilizes change and positive practice; it seeks to preclude the means to a new world and to occlude historical subjectivity. McLuhanacy is ontological counterrevolution.

D Mind and Art: the Control Tower

The road through praxis to the unity of humanity involves concrete struggle. Technocracy prefers to eliminate praxis and to depend only on technology and the psyche. For McLuhan, the global village implies global consciousness; the computer is to achieve psychic communal integration (PI 72) beyond the 'divisive Tower of Babel' of linguistic social discourse (UM 83–4).

> The computer, in short, promises by technology a Pentecostal condition of universal understanding and unity. The next logical step would seem to be, not to translate, but to by-pass languages in favor of a general cosmic consciousness which might be very like the collective unconscious dreamt of by Bergson.

From this condition (by itself, somehow magically), McLuhan expects 'a perpetuity of collective harmony and peace' (84). This is the epistemological aspect of the static global apocalypse:[18]

> the final phase of the extensions of man—the technological simulation of consciousness, when the creative process of knowing will be collectively and corporately extended to the whole of human society, much as we have already extended our senses and our nerves by the various media. (19)

It is important to understand the onto-epistemological unity of McLuhan's theory. He argues:

> Perhaps the most precious possession of man is his abiding awareness of the analogy of proper proportionality, the key to all metaphysical insight and perhaps the very condition of consciousness itself. This analogical awareness is constituted of a perpetual play of ratios among ratios. . . . This lively awareness of the most exquisite delicacy depends upon there being no connection whatever between the components. If A were linked to B, or C to D, mere logic would take the place of analogical perception. Thus one of the penalties paid for literacy and a high visual culture is a strong tendency to encounter all things through a rigorous story line, as it were. Paradoxically, connected spaces and situations exclude participation whereas discontinuity affords room for involvement. (VP 240).

This view expresses the epistemological vanity of a consciousness that locates itself, as it were, *hors de combat*. Only the point of view of a passive spectator can so atomize and disconnect human reality. We know that, historically, it is the technocratic cybernetic comportment that depends on such analysis and juxtaposition; that is, this view is the basis for manipulation and control. Methodologically, a one-sided fetish of discontinuity suppresses—in the theory as in the social practice—the ontological, epistemological, and ethical connections and continuities of historical totalization. In consequence, within McLuhan, it is the adequate theoretical attitude for a repudiation of history.

McLuhan's 'paradox' above, regarding participation and involvement, we recognize as the ideological version of a historical inversion. As the ontological passivity of consumerism (or, put differently, the attempt to reconstitute the active moments of social ontology on ideological/epistemological grounds) is socially sanctified uncritically with the ethos of activity, so cultural ideology, in Frye, in McLuhan, and in structuralism generally, disguises the element of passivity inherent in its categorical framework through the use of active terms. That is, the manipulation of language abuses and corrupts certain active terms captured as ideological prisoners of war. In McLuhan, 'participation' and 'involvement' become the operative slogans for an essentially uncritical and *contemplative* attitude that is active only in its capacity as a mode of appropriation with respect to a system of signs.

Epistemologically, the position is resumed as 'making not matching.' 'Matching presumes to refer to outer fact; making captures inner fact' (VP 165). McLuhan replaces representational 'matching' mimesis with 'magical' mimesis seen as 'the technique of continuous parallel that Eliot indicates as the essential myth-making form of mimesis' (CA 147). This mythic, hendiadys doubleness—having evolved through the tradition—is asserted as 'essential to the very structure of consciousness' (99). In this 'making' epistemology, words, for post-literates as for pre-literates, are magical evocations of things. They do not refer to something: 'they are the thing itself' (CB 91, 112). For McLuhan, as we recall, the inner construction is an analogue of the order of being, rather than a cognitive complex produced to guide everyday success in, and overall transformation of, the ongoing processes of reality. Epistemological rationality thus reproduces ontological rationality (conceived metaphysically). This magical mimesis, as it happens, expresses a truth of neocapitalist culture; McLuhan's theory is the uncritical bourgeois ideological form of the magical semiosis of a 'society of the spectacle.'[19] This epistemology of 'the word made flesh' is both subjectivist (in its hypothesis of a creative consciousness, of 'making') and objectivist (in its hypothesis that the image *is* the thing, owing to the analogy between the order of the mind and the order of being). In this sense it reproduces the same contradictory subject-object unity that characterizes the extension theory,[20] and expresses the same mimetic identification with the established reified forms.

The complementarity of McLuhan's epistemological and onto-historical positions is focussed through the mediation of the tribalist ideology. Tribal life for McLuhan 'is the richest and most highly developed expression of human consciousness' (PI 68). Under conditions of electric retribalization, the capturing of inner fact in the magical mimesis becomes a welcome retrogression into the heart of tribal darkness, into what Joseph Conrad termed 'the Africa within' (70). The epistemological specificity of McLuhan's multi-leveled awareness is now revealed as 'the tribal inertia of multi-consciousness' which takes the place of the 'mobile individual consciousness of the print-oriented man' (CA 6). The mind becomes as limited as the whole culture.

I have indicated the importance for every stage of the modern tradition of psychoanalytic formulations that permit the obfuscation of history and the displacement of attention from historical possibilities that could be seized for making a qualitatively better world. McLuhan insists that 'we are now compelled . . . to take this inner trip and encounter the self in its primal inner state.'[21] The regression to the tribe in the historical sphere finds its epistemological parallel in the psychoanalytic regression. Moreover, in this counterrevolutionary stage of the tradition, this level of interiority becomes materially ontologized in social being. In the electric age:[22]

> speedup of information-movement has the effect of putting the whole human Unconscious outside us as environment—and thereby creating what appears in every way to be a crazy world. The Unconscious is a world where everything happens at once, without any connections, without any reasons at all. We're making the outside world just as crazy and mixed-up as our own Unconscious has always been.

It is in this context that we can understand the function of art according to McLuhan's theory. McLuhan argues that perception is partial, a kind of remembering; but sensation is always 100 per cent and its after-image is locked into the subconscious. 'Only the artist has the power to elevate it to the conscious life. Our response to experience is typically so inadequate and confused that without the artistic confrontation of the unconscious image the human condition becomes confused indeed' (VP 5).

This conception recalls Ransom's search for the fullness of sensation; but in McLuhan's system the artist is particularly well placed for the cognition of the whole of reality. McLuhan argues that 'media effects are new environments as imperceptible as water to a fish, subliminal for the most part' (CB 22); they are imperceptible because they are extensions of 'the archetypal forms of the unconscious' (31). Since interiority is the analogue of exteriority, a primary function of art is 'to make tangible and to subject to scrutiny the nameless psychic dimensions of new experience' (VP 28). The cognitive role attributed to art in the tradition is emphasized. As much as science, it is 'a laboratory means of investigation' (CA 143). It is also more: if anti-environments are necessary to make environments visible, artists create anti-environments 'as a means of perception and adjustment' (COB 192). This notion of art as an experimental laboratory has emerged and will continue (in artistic and academic circles) to flourish as one of McLuhan's most appealing formulations, because of its promise that the aesthetic realm may provide new and valuable (even indispensable) means for understanding the complexities of our world and for orienting ourselves. But this cognitive potential ascribed to art (expanding the New Critical position) is, in McLuhan, strictly and always subordinated to the ascribed social function of art, which is to guide our adaptation to the actual forms of life that allegedly prevail beyond qualitative human control.

The point here is that the cathartic role of art remains suppressed, but precisely through its cognition of reified reality in its immediacy, art re-acquires a social function. 'Social navigation and survival,' McLuhan argues, depend on recognition of the processes of the technological environments that determine our lives (7); the artist 'alone can see the present clearly enough to navigate' (16). Art, with respect to environmental change, is an 'early warning system,' a 'radar feedback' whose purpose is 'not to enable us to change but rather to maintain an even course' (UM xi), that is, to ensure stability by rationalizing our new position through feeding back our new image. The Eliot–Leavis program helps us to adjust; 'art as anti-environment becomes more than ever a means of training perception and judgement' (ix). 'Human history is a record of "taking it on the chin"'; what the artist can do in relation to the 'coming violence' to our psyches from the technological counterirritants is to 'show us how to "ride with the punch," instead of "taking it on the chin"' (71).

McLuhan's view of art is a technocratic reduction of aesthetics to the pragmatic modalities of the everyday response. Artistic cognition, like everything else in McLuhan, is frozen in immediacy as a means to social and psychic stability. His speculations, whose pedigree he traces from Ezra Pound, Wyndham Lewis, and the tradition under consideration, indicate the vast distance that has been covered between the romantic negation and the contemporary counter-revolution:

> If men were able to be convinced that art is precise advance knowledge of how to cope with the psychic and social consequences of the next technology, would they all become artists? Or would they begin a careful translation of new art forms into social navigation charts? I am curious to know what would happen if art were suddenly seen for what it is, namely, exact information of how to rearrange one's psyche in order to anticipate the next blow from our own extended faculties. (71)

Arnoldian criticism is lost beyond recall in this position. The function of art is no longer to defetishize the fetishized stabilities of human life. McLuhan's artist, instead, perpetuates the fetishized appearance of society and offers ways to identify with them. Indeed: 'To prevent undue wreckage in society, the artist tends now to move from the ivory tower to the control tower of society' (70). In other words, the expectation of salvation from art characteristic of the tradition here advances to a crucial concretization. Art becomes a strategically decisive cybernetic control device for human navigation, a thermostat for stable auto-regulation. The historical reversal involved in this type of movement from 'ivory tower' to 'control tower' embodies the counterrevolutionary technocratic termination of the romantic problematic, in an ideological form that is appropriate to the commotive relocation of culture within the historical totality of neocapitalist society.

CHAPTER 13

Conclusion to McLuhan

A Secular Religion

The prominent ideological pillar of McLuhan's theory is, of course, the fetish of technology, the reduction of the totality of a structured social formation to a technological environment that is postulated, not as a moment of, but as the exhaustive determinant of the life activity of a society. This substitution of a type of ecological theory for social theory is not only a vulgar reduction of a complex reality to the transparent simplicity of a single social factor, but also a reified projection of history as a lawful natural order. If human objectifications are autonomously animated, humanity becomes inanimate; if 'electric information systems are live environments in the full organic sense' (WP 36), then mankind is no longer the subject of history. The animation of technology, the reification of social relations, means necessarily that human beings take on the properties of things, of robots dominated by environmental forces, which, at best, may be differentially programmed.

Thus, the theory conceals the fact that it is people who dominate other people through objective mediations in a structured system of domination. McLuhan makes inaccessible the recognition that alienated human beings remain human beings, producers even of our own reification (where, today, objectifications actually are determinant). It is not that we are transformed into passive things but that we are living humanly the condition of things. 'Man in a period of exploitation *is at once both* the product of his own product and a historical agent who can under no circumstances be taken as a product.'[1] As we have seen, the key to this contradiction, the movement of historical praxis, is suppressed in McLuhan's theory.

Methodologically, McLuhan abstracts one moment from a

complex of objectifications produced by a specific historical praxis, and assumes its etiological primacy. The shared characteristics of moments of a determinate historical totality serve to permit the pseudo-causality thus generated (through a mythic rationalization of a broad range of phenomena by means of a technique of homologous juxtaposition) to effect a deceptive cogency. Marx, who, in McLuhan's view, 'never studied or understood causality' (CB 57), remaining unaware of 'the means of communication as the constitutive social factor' and failing to notice 'that English and American industry were merely projections of print technology,'[2] in fact tried to understand capitalism in terms of a tendency toward universal development of the social productive forces within a context of a specified field of social relations, and showed that the feudal system 'foundered on urban industry, trade, modern agriculture (even as a result of individual inventions like gunpowder and the printing-press).'[3] For McLuhan by contrast, linear typography alone was responsible for ending the feudal 'extension of the stirrup' (UM 163) and for the rise of such phenomena, *inter alia*, as:

> nationalism, the Reformation, the assembly line and its offspring, the Industrial Revolution, the whole concept of causality, Cartesian and Newtonian concepts of the universe, perspective in art, narrative chronology in literature and a psychological mode of introspection or inner direction that greatly intensified the tendencies toward individualism and specialization engendered 2000 years before by phonetic literacy. (PI 60)

It is much easier to coordinate and control multiplicity by superficial reduction than to explain concrete development. As a general point, we may note that McLuhan never properly situates or specifies phenomena in their complex interrelations and dynamics. He does not account for development, fluctuation, difference, or function. His theory relies on analysis of structure; but the rigid association of given structures and given technologies is very tenuous (even in its own terms) on empirical grounds. Real history tends to escape the system at both ends: some events reproduce a given structure without the intervention of the specified technology, while other events, within the field of a given technology, fail to show the required structure.[4] And, on methodological grounds, if technology is seen in principle as directly or indirectly determining the society, rather than as a means for the development of the decisive social productive forces—that is, people with all their abilities and power—then the uneven rhythm and the direction of its own development are unexplained. *Technologism*, or reified object-determination, I want to emphasize, is the bourgeois ideological vision of neocapitalist *technocracy*, which is a social determination. And to profess faith, as McLuhan does (with great popularity), in a technological solution of our problems is, to quote István Mészáros, worse than belief in witchcraft, 'for it tendentiously ignores the devastating social embeddedness of present-day science and technology.'[5]

In his critique of Bukharin, Lukács notes that technology is a significant moment of the forces of human development but 'neither simply identical with them nor . . . the final or absolute moment of the changes in these forces,'[6] and stresses the historical and methodological primacy of the socio-economic structure over technology.[7] McLuhan, by contrast, abstracts technology from the social production and reproduction of human life and asserts its autonomy; it becomes a transcendent force in human life. It is this transcendence to which I want to draw attention here, for in McLuhan's theory, technologism effectively becomes a secular religion.

The traditional religious foliage merely masks (while reinforcing) this real religious core of the theory. In 1953, calling for a 'Thomistic theory of social communication,' McLuhan describes modern media as 'superhuman' and 'almost angelic in their speed and scope.'[8] In 1957, he remarks that electronic culture is transforming Christian ritual; 'we are returning to collective liturgical participation.'[9] In 1962, he rejects Mircea Eliade's identification of religion with irrationality by refusing the limitation of rationality to what he interprets as linear, sequential, visual rationality.

Since Richards, the apology for religion had taken the defensive route of eliminating doctrine and postulating religion as a type of symbolic response that does not challenge, and hence need not be destroyed by, the prevailing rationality. Now, McLuhan identifies the form of the religious response as the central rationality of the electric world (GG 71, 69). We have seen that for him, under electric conditions, the mystical body of Christ is a technological fact (PI 72). In general, 'the new city is one that demands a mystical participation in the whole enterprise,'[10] a 'religious study' rather than a debunking of myths (70), and the shifting of our values 'into the spiritual domain.'[11] The global stasis he fabricates is highly susceptible to religious exegesis; and the polemical edge of McLuhan's work, in any case, is always directed against materialism. He is sufficiently aware of his own parameters that his prophecy associates the two on the basis of his general pendulum theory of transformation:[12]

> I think we're heading into a profoundly religious age. . . . I think that human affairs proceed by a sort of *reductio ad absurdum* and in reaching this *reductio ad absurdum* in order that the opposite proposition begin to be attractive. There are very clear indications of this, all round, including evil, this sort of business, of these drugs and things, which in my opinion are very degraded.

As Guy Debord notes: 'Spectacular technology has not dissipated the religious clouds where men had placed their own powers detached from themselves; it has only tied them to an earthly base.'[13] Technological transcendence, the technocratic myth that abstracts from real history and from the totality of our social possibilities, is a secular religion that ties the life of the particularized individual to his personal transcendent fate in the world. Under all the spiritualism, this is the real structure of McLuhan's religion. I have argued repeatedly that McLuhan's religious-magical attitude adopts the structures of everyday thought. It should be noted that the religious need itself is a problem of everyday practicality and flows from the absence of possibilities for a satisfying and meaningful life. Lukács has specified the *differentia* of religion as the invocation of transcendent power to solve the everyday contradiction between self-interest and generic values, between human particularization and its supersession in higher level objectifications.[14] In McLuhan, all such conflicts between the particular and the generic, between the individual and the social, that is, between immediacy and the forms, structures, and modes of ethics, politics, art, and science, are finally resolved in the apocalypse of a one-dimensional electric integration beyond value and purpose. In other words, the elevation above particularity is not through immanent, consciously applied human strengths and abilities, but through the grace of subliminal technological effect.[15]

To situate technologism further, we can recognize it as the effective religious ideology of our age that replaces the traditional other-worldly religious ontology. Technocratic manipulation today is progressively taking over, as Ágnes Heller has observed, all the bad functions of religion without taking over its valuable functions. It substitutes new myths for old ones, assimilates the private sphere to the social, inhibits individual ethical autonomy in questions of world view and politics, and forms dispositions and ideologies that promote what exists without in any respect challenging it. Above all, it feeds particularization and particularized motivations, but reinforces (and tolerates) the development of only those faculties and aptitudes that serve the goals of given forms of organization. And today, as Heller has also noted, none of this has any longer any historical justification. Over the centuries, religion set generic values against particularized demands with some justice; today the conditions exist for the formation of free social individuals, for the abolition of the gap between generic and individual development. In the contemporary period, there may still occur technocratic-religious suppression of certain particularized inclinations (in the interest of particularization as a whole) but this no longer bears generic values, and in no way represents generic development.[16] This is a most important point to emphasize. McLuhan's own technologism is the affirmation of the 'liturgical and corporate' against 'self-assertion' (VP 61). But as a dominant ideological form of technocratic manipulation, it is an alienated secular religion which, far from expressing the cause of humanity, is a profoundly anti-humanist obstacle to it.

B Appeal and Significance

McLuhan's technocratic-religious eschatology of mimetic identification with the existing system and its tendencies has naturally made him very popular in certain sectors of society. The Lintas chain of advertising agencies published a long tribute to McLuhan, welcoming what they saw as his optimism about the human condition and his refusal to judge it. They noted, too, that he had become 'a cult figure in America and particularly on Madison Avenue.'[17] McLuhan has collected substantial fees for talking to executives of Bell Telephone, IBM, Container Corporation of America, and General Motors. Donald F. Theall has observed that McLuhan's sense of the corporate 'may even have made the executive suite as attractive a base of operations for him as the throne room had been for the early humanists.'[18] Not only has McLuhan advised the Canadian government, he has also conferred with that of the United States. In his own book, McLuhan reprints a *Washington Post* cartoon depicting the US State Department consulting him about their difficulty communicating with North Vietnam (COB 265). His media exposure has been unprecedented for a scholar. According to

Newsweek, he has had an office at Time Inc. and an arrangement to write articles for *Look*. His face has appeared on the covers of *Newsweek* and *Saturday Review* and many times on television. His own articles have appeared not only in scores of scholarly journals but also in mass circulation magazines such as *Look*, *Vogue*, and *Family Circle*. Material about him has reached vast and varied audiences through such further organs as *Fortune, Life, Esquire, Playboy, National Review, New Yorker, New York Times Magazine, National Catholic Reporter*, and *Popular Photography*.[19] He has made radio and television programs, a record, and films; he has published over a hundred articles and over a dozen books. In the early years of his rise to public attention, Toronto newspaper coverage alone of McLuhan jumped from 4½ column inches in 1961 to 1,223 column inches in 1964.[20] *Understanding Media* has sold well over 100,000 copies.[21]

Earlier, I discussed the institutional basis for the entrenchment of New Critical ideology; it is clear that McLuhan has extended, not only the domain of cultural ideology, but also the nature of its institutional support. McLuhanacy has been itself a socio-cultural phenomenon that could fruitfully be studied seriously and at length. Even inside the academies, directly or indirectly, McLuhan has been becoming an influential cultural ideologue; outside, the media which he has embraced have embraced him. His orientation in every respect has been to the continuity of the system; at the same time, he has sustained a pose of rebellion that has captured for him an audience among the mystified libertarians and the conservative *avant-garde*. Kingsley Widmer found his influence among anarchists;[22] and people like John Cage, the composer, have claimed to be influenced by and grateful to McLuhan at every moment in time.[23] Sociologically, the leading categories of his supporters have been the vertically concentrated but horizontally widespread categories prominent in technocratic society: 'they include high-school and primary school teachers, painters, sculptors, architects, engineers, turned-on businessmen, advertising agents, museum curators, film makers, television producers, public relations men, newspaper reporters, poets and hippies.'[24] Through these people, his influence has been great; newspapers have routinely referred to him as 'communications prophet' or 'media guru' without quotation marks; and *mcluhanisme* has become a common noun in the French language, signifying mixed-media cultural forms.

The major opposition to McLuhan has so far come from an

anachronistic group of high-brow academics who defend, against the concentration on mass culture, the values and 'content' retained from a bygone historical problematic. They remain occupied in the defense of sublimated culture in a period of repressive desublimation. (At least McLuhan, the ideologue of the latter, has contemporary historical relevance.) Beyond that group, McLuhan's aphoristic provocations, with their mystagogic overtones, are designed, not only to impress with profundity and urgency, but to offer something to everyone, and thus, in effect, to avoid challenging the prevailing rationality in any respect. This is the appeal of pluralistic consensus, within which McLuhan plays the roles of legitimator, dream peddler, pardoner, rebel, and theoretical guru.[25] These roles seem to permit discontinuous response; thus many young people may be attracted by McLuhan's argument that traditional education is reactionary (PI 62), while neglecting or not caring that he rejects both sexual enjoyment without reproduction and homosexuality as 'jaded,' and forecasts a tight moral institutional decorum for the retribalized society (65).[26] It is this discontinuity that tends to lead even some of the harshest critics to applaud McLuhan's 'insights' in isolation. Of course, these insights cannot be the real basis for a defense of his work, just as it is no defense of saturation bombing that it occasionally hits even a 'military' target. Against such pick-and-choose elementalism, I would argue that once these isolated insights, like technical military successes, are situated in the overall patterns to which they contribute, and by which their function is shaped and distorted, they can be seen as moments of a counterrevolutionary totality.

Ideology, in general, is a structuring of reality from the standpoint of a specific historical interest. Bourgeois ideology imposes the interests of domination both on the objective features of reality and on popular aspirations. In McLuhan, a desire for synthesis is merged with the cybernetic drive to program the world; a perception of the massive technocratic manipulation and administration of needs is perverted into a biological extension theory that reinforces technological reification. The hope for a new future is subsumed in an automatic technological apocalypse; the transcendent necessity projected into history absolves inactivity and emancipates us from responsibility for the world or for altering its quality. If history is governed by unconscious determinations of technological-sensory rationality, then humanization is not realizable by conscious social praxis. The need for solidarity is corrupted in the prophecy of corporatism: the response to the loneliness of manipulated particularization is a fetish of communication. At the same time, we have seen, the theory is the ideological form of objective tendencies toward corporate integration and stabilization. In effect, it serves to control people's needs and desires on the grounds of the given order. The structure of McLuhan's theory duplicates the structure of the consumer situation in which people, who are denied the satisfaction of their deepest needs for a meaningful life at the present level of historical possibility, are encouraged to find themselves in things, in beer, or detergents, or cars, or televisions, that is, things that become effectively their extensions.

This is the fundamental locus of McLuhan's appeal and significance. Today, technology circumscribes our culture and projects a 'world';[27] it is far from neutral, being a moment of the historical undertaking of spectacular society which helps to constitute it. People subject to technocratic domination experience real impotence in the face of technological forces. McLuhan's theory speaks to this condition. On one hand, 'the medium is the message' formula coordinates a broad argument that technology is not neutral. On the other, the theory leads out of the historical totality into the self-sufficiency of the technological world that is said to determine the culture. Since the specific character of the technology is not regarded as socio-historical, adaptation to it, not social transformation of it to suit human needs, is the only option. In other words, the theory both expresses (and legitimates) the sense of impotence, and presents, conceptually and exhortatively, the same response that people in their everyday lives are making to this impotence. That is, it presents the attempt to assimilate and identify oneself with the transcendent forces, and hence to cooperate with these forces in breaking down one's own resistance. Thus McLuhanatic ideology—and I have noted various aspects of this before—is the theoretical face of the tendentially one-dimensional reification of neocapitalist everyday life. Its adequacy to the structures and projects of a period, and its capacity to mediate a pragmatic everyday assimilation to the established social forms, have been the source of its ideological power and the primary ground of its appeal.

This is likewise the significance of McLuhan's theory. McLuhan has been perhaps the major bourgeois ideologue of one-dimensional society. He comprehended its essential aspects—of course, from the point of view of its perpetuation—when competing cultural theories did not, and he assumed the mantle of prophet. Where Herbert

Marcuse fulfilled the role of a prophet of revolution, of the destruction of one-dimensionality, McLuhan fulfilled, correspondingly, the role of an apologist of counterrevolution, of the permanent stabilization of one-dimensionality. It must be emphasized that for us, one-dimensional integration is not, as for McLuhan, the inescapable shape of a timeless present that is now in the process of formation; it has been a dominant tendency of the neocapitalist social formation, neither permanent nor necessarily successful—and, at present, it is losing ground to other tendencies within the overall context of a potentially evermore totally administered society. Indeed, there *are* other tendencies and possibilities, and I would argue that it is our task to seek to strengthen the tendencies, and realize the possibilities, of liberation from one-dimensionality, that is, to join in the concrete struggle against it, and indeed, to effect a libertarian supersession of administered society altogether.

In this context, it may be well to take note of the critical custom to praise McLuhan for being the first to make us aware of the effect on our lives of the modes of communication. The point that needs to be made is that, while directing attention to an important problem, McLuhan has simultaneously blocked access to it. This is why methodological critique of McLuhan is so important, in order to clear the way to discovering the questions that need urgent answers.

Fortune magazine once noted: 'Control communication and you control.' I commented earlier on the commotive emergence of communication in a prominent social role; this observation about control brings to our attention again the fact that communication cannot be separated from the matrix of power in which it is embedded. Modern mass communications, for example, transmit only standardized messages directed simultaneously at a multiplicity of isolated people. Moreover, the material transmitted, embodying the needs, interests, values, and goals of relations of domination, displaces the knowledge of the oppressed that had stemmed from -and had mediated their own needs and practices.[28] We obviously have to recognize the aspects of social conflict involved here in the creation of the conditions for manipulation. If we do so, we have then to repudiate the efforts of technocratic ideology to reconcile antagonisms and to *assume* a homogeneous society upon the foundations of real, continuing class division and a multiplicity of social antagonism; further, we have to resist as well any efforts actually to *construct* a pervasive homogeneity in place of the creativity and heterogeneity that are among the post-domination potentialities of free social individuals in decentralized human communities.

The same power relations are manifest today, on the formal level, in the confinement of communications within a hierarchical consumption model. In principle, a receiver is also a transmitter. If, today, it remains a means of consumption, then it embodies a class-enforced limitation of the potentialities that communications media would realize as universal means of exchange in a society of genuinely democratized information movement (which presupposes democratized ownership, power, management, control, and reciprocity). To talk of communications, then, must mean to talk of a concrete, effective community, and to pose an authentic libertarian socialization of the means of communication. And we must note with Enzensberger that the real political core of the media problematic involves the mobilization of the masses for social control by the self-organization of individuals at present isolated from the social learning and production process.[29]

With the neocapitalist evolution in the mode of production, the appropriation of knowledge becomes a decisive feature. In consequence, it becomes today, more than ever, essential to discuss communications within the problematic of liberation and praxis. It is widely recognized that today we are on the threshold of another industrial revolution that holds absolutely immense possibilities, subject, of course, to the alternatives of history. A single laser beam, for example, could provide enough communications channels for everyone in the world to converse in pairs.[30] Meanwhile, in Vietnam, lasers have been used to guide pilots in pin-point bomb attacks. In general, we may be able to dispose of unprecedented possible energy sources; even the very first step of what this could mean is that a high living standard for everyone in the world is, in principle, easily (and without social or ecological damage) within reach.[31] The question of whether all the world's just needs and creative desires are satisfied, as we embark on undreamt of imaginative adventures, or whether humanity wallows in barbarism or is even physically destroyed, is a question of the social and cultural organization of our historical-technological possibilities. In contrast to McLuhan, we may insist that reified passivity is not necessary to technology, and that a genuinely new period in human history has not yet begun, but begins only with a qualitative break in the continuity of capital and, more broadly, of domination.

PART V

General Conclusion
Struggle

CHAPTER 14

Politics of Cultural Ideology

A Problematic of Positivity

I have been examining decisive moments in the evolution of modern North American critical theory in order to disengage some dominant features of the transformations in the ideological field. It is in this context that I have tried to formulate the questions that found and give sense to a writer's responses, and that I have argued the constitutive character of historical location and orientation. The point has not been to show the derivation of ideology from social existence, but rather to demonstrate relative adequation of ideology with the dominant social project, and hence its effectiveness and popularity. It has been neither possible, nor really necessary, to be exhaustive in breadth; strategic moments provide adequate access to the main lines structuring the whole. I have been shaping (totalizing) the material from the standpoint of a future to be made against the present that is given. I believe such a perspective is a necessary condition of any theoretical construction that is to be relevant to the deepest truth of the reality of our time: the need for fundamental qualitative change.

What becomes evident is that the modern tradition has been evolving as a type of aesthetics with no real capacity for critique. It has developed to an ideological position as the counterrevolutionary form appropriate to the governing technocratic design of neocapitalist society. An initial philosophy of what 'ought to be' has collapsed into a dialectic of actuality/potentiality confined to the realm and to the existing dynamics of what actually 'is.' Critical theory expresses the modern disaffection for reality, but progressively incorporates and assimilates it within the categories of the prevailing social rationality. This endows it with a double power of appeal, and the expanding scope of the theory, corresponding to the expanding role of cultural appropriation in the neocapitalist mode of the production and reproduction of social life, gives it authority as a major ideology. At the same time, the increasingly structural insensitivity of the theory to the inhumanity of the dominant social practice reveals the bankruptcy of this type of humanism. Indeed, with McLuhan, a fetish of technology, abstracted from all other aspects of social possibilities, grows into a technocratic secular religion that specifically obstructs man's potential to be a self-conscious historical subject, by finding a material ground for such obstruction in what are said to be objective tendencies of actual historical development.

It is in this context that the basic structure of modern critical theory is constructed as virtually a social-scientific paradigm that syncretizes the traditionally separated realms of precision and of imagination, and perhaps strategically prefigures transformations in other social sciences. Cynthia Russett notes and regards with optimism the appearance (even in a periodical dedicated to scientific rigor, such as *Behavioral Science*), of what she argues is an increasingly representative contemporary 'plea for a "bilingual" social science, one which will employ "both logical or mathematical exactness and mythological imagination." ' [1] The investigation in the present study should illuminate this development and make clear that this new methodological alliance, based on the structural evolution of social life, finds its historical location as the commotive strategy for ever more systematic rationalization of content that always threatens to escape and explode formal, totalitarian organization.

The prominent aspects of the paradigm—contemplative attitude, depersonalized mythopoeic epistemological ontology, formal synchronization, and an analytic technology of analogical juxtaposition, metaphoric identification, and ambiguity or structural discontinuity—all serve to compose a rationalized field. Raymond Williams expresses the conviction that 'the most penetrating analysis would always be of forms' which, being transindividual, can be 'related to a real social history.' [2] Ironically, the problem about the limitless formalization in the modern critical tradition is precisely that it cuts forms off from their ontological basis in the processes of real social history by projecting achieved wholes (art object, order of words, or technological environment) removed from such processes. A corollary is a systematic displacement of the subject/object dialectic into an appearance/ reality problematic of signification that brackets questions of praxis. This tendency has a complement in an attitude of passivity which, from Richards to McLuhan, in expanding contexts, looks to a manipulative harmonization of the psychic and cultural fields.

The scientistic and ideological imperatives of coherence mean for the tradition a questioning of all forms of objectivity in relation to a *telos* of harmonic integration. That is, the central problematic of the tradition is structured by questions of unity and equilibrium, of order and stability. From the beginning, but increasingly systematically, the tradition embraces the 'whole,' and structures a totality without struggle and historical movement, that is, without the conditions necessary for the development of the historical subject. It manufactures, in this way, what Karel Kosik calls the false totality of structuralism, in which reality is grasped only in the form of achieved fact, and not subjectively as objectifying human praxis.[3] The transition from the romantic stress on creative production to the modern stress on 'creative' consumption, first concretized in the New Critical fetish of the object, is complete in McLuhan; the real human subject disappears.

The above point has deserved emphasis, because it is essential to understand that the fundamental axis for the movement of the tradition is the praxis/structure axis. A reified notion of a given structured order appears already in Eliot, and the emphasis in the tradition shifts increasingly away from praxis determinations to structured system determinations. The moment of praxis is free, if circumscribed by the enduring forms of objectification; the tradition suppresses this moment of freedom in an evolving philosophy of determinism. Perspective on the future is dissolved in reified everyday immediacy. If the function of genuine art is to defetishize, it can be argued that the program of modern critical theory is refetishization.

It seems important to extend this critique to contemporary structuralism, in general. Structuralism is not a neutral methodology intelligible *in vacuo*; it represents a motion in theory away from living praxis.[4] In the 1960s, structuralism emerged as a philosophy of scientific cognition, rapidly becoming a major antagonist of dialectical humanism, the Marxist philosophy of liberation. Some variants explicitly profess an anti-humanism, and suppress the categories of alienation and praxis, of historical subjectivity. The French versions, in particular, recapitulate the Comtean obsession with invariances and stabilities, in the context of the worst excesses of dogmatic rationalism. Meaning becomes limited to the most superficial levels of signification; what moves us and sustains us, it is claimed, is *system*: we are merely bearers of its determinations. It is forgotten that these structures and systems are not dead things, but all the products and forms of human activity, living complexes of human relations and objective mediations which support much human aspiration and intention and are every minute sustained in their human meaning by human consensus. Attention is shifted away from the ways in which human beings have altered and do alter and may yet alter their objectifications; in consequence, structuralism finds nothing to investigate but order, the codes of order, reflections upon order, and the experience of order.[5] The problematic creates its own methodological solution of rigorous scientistic exegesis, realist *lecture*, made possible by the suppression of the limits of formalization. Such scientism denies that objectivity is always none other than the *struggle* for *human* objectivity, and thus collapses into the positivity of neocapitalist integration. As Lefebvre has noted, structuralism is the project of structuring the existing society and stabilizing or immobilizing it within these given structures; everything is defined and fixed.[6]

In this sense, structuralism can be interpreted as an epistemological strategy of technocratic rule. Placing himself methodologically at the vantage point of a transcendent observer, the structuralist scientist claims cognitively a privileged power that the technocrat exercises in social practice. For this kind of theoretical consciousness, the world appears given to us not as the ground of historical praxis and the field of goals, needs, and efforts, but as an object of knowledge, a system of formal signs. It renounces the projects around which society is built, and sees everything, from literature to social relations, from spiritual objectifications to the work process, as forms of signification. Structuralism either studies these signs as synchronic constituted sign systems or, diachronically, seeks to study the production of signs, that is, to provide an epistemological critique of these sign systems by dissolving them in the process of signification. But, in both cases, the reduction of ontology to epistemology prevails, in harmony with a general tendency in advanced Western societies for the production and consumption of information to assume major importance. As mass-manufactured significations and images come to dominate the field of attention, define the experience of reality, and mediate human relations, epistemological concerns come to take on ever more social and theoretical standing.

The tendency of the neocapitalist program to make reality for masses of people increasingly an object of consumption and contemplation has been observed by Guy Debord who, in drawing for us a map of what he calls our 'society of the spectacle,' points to 'the uninterrupted conversation which the present order maintains about itself, its laudatory monologue.'[7] Structuralism uncritically accepts the parameters of this monologue, which it proposes to analyze and organize; it does not seek to mediate the supersession of these parameters by theorizing an active, value-based response in line with real human possibilities. In effect, the structuralist semiotic is revealed as the theoretical complement to the neocapitalist cultural semiosis of never-ending signifying practice; it is a positivism that accepts this semiosis as the eternal ontology of social being.

It is a consequence of this position, too, that structuralism, especially following Lacan, eternalizes the elimination of the subject from the center. The off-center subject is a historical, not a categorical problem, and becomes categorically decisive only for an epistemological fetishism. What is true is that history has never been made, decisions never taken, upon a basis of 100 per cent knowledge of totality in all its subjective and objective complexity, and, today, our present is even more conjectural. But, as Lukács points out, on the ontological level we must act without waiting for complete knowledge; we must try to find our way out of a forest where we have got lost before someone brings us a full map of the region.[8] Structuralists use this fact, of our inadequate consciousness of operative levels of determination, to eliminate the subject. The point that must be made is that the subject, today displaced from the center by the reification of social relations, can in fact be centered: not the epistemological subject of structuralism, but the ontological subject of historical praxis. What structuralism denies, in effect, is the ability of human beings to achieve a conscious relation to themselves, to each other, and to objectifications; its ideological leanings tend to cancel history and to assume, as it were, the permanence of reification and domination.

B Problematic of Supersession

The increasing stress on integration, order, and system, I have been arguing, is the ideological form of a feature of the social structure. In the United States, this integration involved the incorporation of labor in the counterrevolutionary pluralism of the New Deal;[9] the state became, at least *de jure* through such legislation as the Wagner Act or National Labor Relations Act, guarantor of certain essential labor rights and mediator between labor and capital (of course, in the ultimate service of relations of domination and the general class interests of capital as a whole). By 1950, politically tamed by a bureaucratic CIO, and paralyzed by the 1947 Taft Hartley Act, the 1948 McCarran Act, the red scare, the 1949–50 depression, and the effective self-destruction of the CIO through the expulsion of its radical unions,[10] a sector of the working class was safely contained within the social equilibrium. Indeed, the post-Second-World-War social situation is properly characterized as a period of class compromise guaranteed not only by the instrumentalization of economics to ensure that the internal opposition provided by the traditional working class is integrated into the system as a much-needed regulatory mechanism, but also by the massive intervention of proliferating state apparatuses into all aspects of everyday life, and by the unprecedented growth of a culture industry designed to stabilize and exploit the contradictions of subjectivity displaced from the productive sphere to the cultural dimension, the sphere of consumption, and the production and reproduction of social, personal, and spiritual life as a whole.

In a study of the evolution of bourgeois theory during this specific period, the focus has necessarily been on the ideology of integration, of one-dimensional harmony. But it should by no means be assumed that there are no continuing and new contradictions; on the contrary, the United States—a model of advanced capitalist formations—is a profoundly contradictory society and its rationality attempts to organize staggering irrationalities. Manipulation and coercion constitute the indivisible unity of the social system, affecting its structure and daily life. Technocratic manipulation is complemented by structural and casual violence peculiar to the social formation, in its productive structuration, its many forms of private and public armies, and its internal and external colonies, and this coercion generates perpetual conflicts. Economic insecurity, debts, terrible working conditions, political uncertainty, and cultural confusion affect almost everyone in the society, and remain a source of disaffection. In this regard, I think it is too easy to exaggerate the satisfaction of even particularized needs in the society. In any case, the question of the extent to which the system does in fact deliver the goods to satisfy needs involves the determination of the historical level of needs, a uniquely difficult problem in a social formation which depends structurally on the control and administration of escalating needs and expectations necessary for consumerism.

The late 1960s have indicated the explosive potential of the profound crisis of the quality of life through the social action of three especially militant sectors, blacks, women, and youth. The point I am making, in general, is that the extent to which the social integration and the one-dimensional pressures can succeed is an open issue. Already in the face of deteriorating political and economic conditions, these are losing ground to countervailing tendencies, including the growing militancy of an expanded base of opposition. But even if militant sectors should become for a time politically exhausted or docile, and even if the new scarcities were to recur only as periodic aberrations readily manipulable for the consolidation of social control, one-dimensionality still may have been only a passing stage characteristic of the transition from entrepreneurial to monopoly capitalism. In a maturing, ever more totally administered society, whose system of meanings and social value is capable of absorbing and instrumentalizing all contraries, critical opposition, negativity, or creative subjectivity become less threats to than urgent requirements of the system itself, necessary to its continuing functioning. This is the most profound and paradoxical of neocapitalist contradictions: to guarantee its continuing viability and to ensure its permanent renewal, the system of universal domination needs to foster and generate teleological human activity, projects, initiatives, and symbolic adventures; at the same time, to achieve its chief goal of retaining the existing relations of domination, it must at all costs delimit and cripple and contain the subjectivity it calls into being. In so far as the precarious health of this manipulative corporate reality depends on regular shots in the arm from artificially created free spaces, the system of domination remains balanced on a tightrope stretched between the functioning subjectivity essential for social survival and development and the society of free subjects that such subjectivity prefigures and whose authentic realization would mean the end of the structures of domination.

In this context, the logic of neocapitalism thrives on the birth of radical needs and desires and the elaboration of radical alternatives, confident of its monumental systematic capacities to instrumentalize these in its own service. It is equally possible, of course, that the empirical proportions of this contradiction may change, and that its dynamic may yet fully challenge and explode the existing power relations. Already some sociologists suggest that the recent growth in the spheres of rational public discourse, providing a springboard, specifically, for the possibilities of a challenge by technicians to the bureaucratic irrationalities of economics and politics, and by intellectuals in the cultural apparatus to the manipulations of the consciousness industry, may signal a thrust within present society favorable to human emancipation.[11] However overly optimistic this important analysis may be as a specific assessment of changes in the realm of language and ideology, and in its methodological identification of the ontogenesis of rational discourse with the fate of humanity, I do not think it is necessary to believe that people are infinitely malleable to manipulation. We know, moreover, from the heroic struggles of the people of Vietnam, that coercion too can be resisted and defeated. The mimetic identification with domination, which has been frequently mentioned, is not, I think, a straightforward positive identification indicating positive satisfaction. It involves self-repression, for survival in a system of appalling barbarity where no accessible alternatives seem immediately conceivable. It involves defeatism as much as satisfaction, and that could be a pivot in the contradictory popular consciousness on which may turn the future of the society according to the relative success or failure of revolutionizing forces in the struggle to defetishize consciousness and mediate the practical transformation of human relations.

Of particular interest for us here is the question of intellectual work in this context. In the recent period, mental labor has been considerably expanded in volume and significance, and it has been brought into the frame of the capitalist labor process in both industry and the institutional structures of ideology, such as the state bureaucracies, the educational system, and the media. This development produces a rich contradiction between the position of the intelligentsia as an ideological agency of hegemonic domination, and their situation as oppressed, alienated labor. As mental activity takes on the characteristics of capitalist work, the age-old social division between physical and mental activity is structurally terminated. This is of decisive importance for the self-recognition of the dominated in the image of genuine universality. If this division can also be politically terminated, if amidst a growth of the public sphere the technical, scientific, and cultural intelligentsia, and within it the groupings of intellectuals who, by nature of their work, have full access to rational political discourse within the entire symbolic spectrum, can transcend their functional subjectivity[12] toward a self-consciously radical and Utopian social consciousness embodying a projected society of free subjects, then the intelligentsia can make an immense contribution to social revolution. The social and cultural revolution whose aim is to leap beyond domination is unique in having to be a conscious revolution aimed at realizing the historical possibilities of generic development; it is only in this context that mental labor, specifically, theoretical work, can and must assume a substantial importance beyond the elitist megalomania of careerist bourgeois intellectualism.

The cause of humanity cannot bypass class struggle. Intellectuals who wish to assert it must engage in this struggle in their capacity as intellectuals; that is, their work must strive for an objectivity (consensus) with its value base in an alternative future. With respect to the aesthetic-cultural problematic specifically, the intellectual can seek to rethematize the interpenetration of Eros and civilization, to carry the claims of desire and happiness, of the erotic and the pleasurable, of the body and the spirit, of the sensuous and the concrete, onto the social terrain, and to resist the authoritarian instrumentalization of aesthetic and Utopian imagination. In this context, it may be possible to find the dynamic synthesis of fragmented fields and to reunite aesthetic and social consciousness, to link the aesthetic response with the problems of social liberation, to unite 'all power to the imagination' with 'all power to the people.' This means rejecting all reductions of one principle to another as well as relating all social forms—aesthetic, economic, or other—to that historical praxis which forms the present, and to that needed to create the new. It also means recognizing, as Merleau-Ponty said, that there is no inevitability of realizing a final synthesis; we cannot even affirm *a priori* the possibility of integral man.[13] This is not a problem of knowledge or psychotherapy but of historical possibility and activity; of value and material commitment to its realization. But it can be posed properly only in a concrete context of struggle against the neocapitalist blockages to all-round development of free individuality and community.

In any case, art cannot solve the subject/object problem for us. What art does is to question the extent to which our world is human, and tailored to our humanity.[14] Criticism must make this question

201

conscious as art makes it sensible. If bourgeois literary theory refetishizes, if its work is counterinsurgency in aesthetics and hence in society, then the task of critical theory is to preserve the subversive/Utopian features of art, to bring them to consciousness in a historical translation appropriate to our own needs and in a form suitable to guide a subversive/Utopian practice. Moreover, in the informational context of modern society, criticism has access and strategic relevance to a vastly expanded domain of signs. Aesthetic criticism is uniquely equipped to carry its methods and concerns to every realm of symbolic space and to fulfill its mature historical mission, in the name of emancipation, by engaging all the proliferating forms of social narrative and imagery with a view to superseding the codes of domination.

This, in general, is the task of all intellectual work: to articulate the possibilities of supersession and to illuminate and condemn domination in the given. We do not have to use such categories as 'necessity' with transcendent meaning. Rather, contradictory historical possibilities are available to immanent choice, and theory has to supply the meaning of the choices we face, that is, the meaning of history. What is methodologically crucial is to avoid what Adorno calls 'topological thinking,' that is, mechanical categorization that 'knows the place of every phenomenon and the essence of none' and makes the world ready for domination. We must beware of alienated cognition that transforms 'all observation of capitalism as a system itself into a system.'[15]

This methodological point, as always, is most important; it is part of the necessary transformation of the intellectual means of production (hardware and software), designed to effect, through relevant improvement, the alienation of the apparatus from the ruling class in favor of revolutionary struggle. Walter Benjamin has argued this very effectively, showing that the simple transmission of the preconstituted bourgeois apparatus of production can lead to the assimilation of left-wing themes without endangering the apparatus of the class that possesses it. Insidiously, if the intellectual fails to transform the language, forms, and techniques of the apparatus, he remains in reciprocal solidarity with the privileged class culture.[16]

Ultimately, of course, no intellectual work can *of itself* solve materially the historical subject/object problems, and the mystique of the intellectual should always be challenged. 'For the revolutionary struggle does not take place between capitalism and the intellect, but between capitalism and the proletariat.'[17] From this may devolve a methodological imperative for a broad cultural practice to deny the existing order and prefiguratively embody the new. Lefebvre has argued (as has Marcuse) that the objective insertion of dialectical thought into the current period means insisting on negativity and its rights against the prevailing forms of thought that stress equilibrium, structure, self-regulation, and positive constants. In the commotion, negation is a creative principle.[18] Under the pressures of the drive toward one-dimensionality (as an inaccessible limit), of the total organization of society and culture, as well as under the crisis of the disintegration of one-dimensionality, the counterculture and the forms of struggle must be both negative and self-confidently Utopian. This needs to be a structured, not a one-sided, negativity, a negativity that contains the Utopian *within* it, realized in the *mode* and *orientation* of struggle. This both leaves the future open to something new while refusing the established present, and begins to realize the future in the practices and values of the Utopian present. The position implies both a popular revolution and the revolutionary transformation of everyday life—in accord with the recognition that we choose our future as we live our present. The project, as activity of struggle, is Utopian negativity, while the project as lived praxis, as our chosen mode of self-creation and orientation in the process, constitutes the Utopian positive. This latter must work within the heart of our negativity; it must *be* the heart of our negativity.

Intellectual work remains of crucial importance for us within this frame of reference. But what kind? I can touch only on the most immediate context of the question, on the chief novelty of our current situation: the great orientational challenge that stretches before us. The conservative cultural apparatus that had for so long linked the institutions of family, work, church, school, army, government, and sex has not been able to stand up against the pressures of the social crisis in the 1960s, and has irreparably cracked. Obedience, loyalties, allegiances, legitimations, and responsibilities have been disintegrating; the deepest layers of internalized domination have been eroding away on both unconscious and conscious levels. The growing struggle against work both on and off the shop floor, as well as in the family where women have been refusing the work assigned them in the sexual division of labor, and the spreading culture of insubordination everywhere, highlight a vast process of de-institutionalization.

With the continuing collapse of established frames of reference, newly emerging forms of personal or communal integrity are having to share the social and cultural space with forms of anomie, panic, or exhaustion. At the same time, the potentialities of our new and conceivable technologies make of the most Utopian post-scarcity dreams the most realistic human possibilities—subject only to our social and cultural imaginations and abilities. By contrast, the manipulation of an economic crisis for rationalization and social control threatens to impose upon us the unspeakable fraud of mere survival structures.

In such a context, the stakes are not only to avoid the perverted human catastrophe that lurks within the established forms, but to realize the vast promises that the efforts of countless generations have at last opened up for the development of mankind and of each and every individual. In such a context there can be no more important social task than the ideological work of seeking, and helping others to seek and find, a clear, rich, and effectively liberating orientation.

On one hand, there is indispensable intellectual work to be done in *the indicative mode*: the work of criticism and negation, of rejecting, denying, subverting all established forms of domination, and exploring and articulating all available options and potentialities in present forms for strategically effective, emancipating action. This is the basis, the *sine qua non*, of orientation—its bread and butter. But it is not enough. Especially not today when we are in urgent need of goals and values capable of guiding us to the fullest and freest ensemble of our future possibilities. There is, on the other hand, therefore, the equally indispensable (and enormously neglected) intellectual work of creating in *the subjunctive mode*: the work of values, ideals, and longings, of hypotheses and fantasies, of shaping, forming, developing a new vision of, not only what can be done now, but what ought to come about. This is the work of *orientation proper*—its spirit, flesh and color. This is the work of evolving a new way of seeing and feeling the future and our relation to it, and hence of perceiving and relating to the present. The tension between immediate activity and the subjunctive rational imagination —a tension that has all but collapsed in the past few years with disastrous results—needs to be stretched as far as the wealth and sensitivity of our minds can take it in expanding real human possibilities. No liberation can come from negation alone. Our minds and spirits must learn to see and find, and learn to need and desire, the forms of freedom: we must learn to experience and understand and change our world from within the claims and possibilities of human destiny as well as from within the subverting practices and opportunities of the given social formation. Then intellectual work will be situated as a moment of the theoretico-practical power of definition: the creation/appropriation of the world and the control/management of its phenomena according to the language of revolutionary emancipation. Then intellectual work will be part of affirming, preparing, and realizing an ontological leap to liberation.

And here we can see a last clarification. In regard to the project of supersession, the historical location of the intellectual is, *mutatis mutandis*, exactly the same as that of everyone in the society: to borrow a phrase, he is either part of the processes of the problem or part of the processes of the solution (although, of course, never in a final or terminal sense). Likewise, his mission and responsibility, his challenge and opportunity, evidently, are the same as everyone else's: to take an active part, with all his powers, in the historical transition from problem toward solution.

Appendices

Appendices

APPENDIX A

'How to Criticise a Poem'

(in the manner of certain contemporary critics[1])
THEODORE SPENCER

1

I propose to examine the following poem:

> Thirty days hath September,
> April, June and November:
> All the rest have thirty-one,
> Excepting February alone,
> Which has only eight and a score
> Till leap-year gives it one day more.

2

The previous critics who have studied this poem, Coleridge among them, have failed to explain what we may describe as its fundamental *dynamic*. This I now propose to do. The first thing to observe is the order in which the names (or verbal constructs) of the months are presented. According to the prose meaning—what I shall henceforth call the prose-*demand*—'September' should not precede, it should follow 'April,' as a glance at the calendar will show. Indeed 'September' should follow not only 'April,' it should also follow 'June' if the prose-demand is to be properly satisfied. The prose order of the first two lines should therefore read: 'Thirty days hath April, June, September and November.' That is the only sequence consonant with prose logic.

3

Why then, we ask ourselves, did the poet violate what educated readers know to be the facts? Was he ignorant of the calendar, believing that September preceded April in the progress of the seasons? It is difficult to imagine that such was the case. We must find another explanation. It is here that the principle of dynamic analysis comes to our aid.

4

Dynamic analysis proves that the most successful poetry achieves its effect by producing an *expectation* in the reader's mind before his sensibility is fully prepared to receive the full impact of the poem. The reader makes a *proto-response* which preconditions him to the total response toward which his fully equilibrized organs of apperception subconsciously tend. It is this proto-response which the poet has here so sensitively manipulated. The ordinary reader, trained only to prose-demands, expects the usual order of the months. But the poet's sensibility knows that poetic truth is more immediately effective than the truth of literal chronology. He does not *state* the inevitable sequence; he *prepares* us for it. In his profound analysis of the two varieties of mensual time, he puts the *gentlest* month first. (Notice how the harsh sound of 'pt' in 'September' is softened by the 'e' sound on either side of it.) It is the month in which vegetation first begins to fade, but which does not as yet give us a sense of tragic fatality.

5

Hence the poet prepares us, dynamically, for what is to follow. By beginning his list of the months *in medias res*, he is enabled to return later to the beginning of the series of contrasts which is the subject of his poem. The analogy to the 'Oedipus Rex' of Euripides and the 'Iliad' of Dante at once becomes clear. Recent criticism has only too often failed to observe that these works also illustrate the dynamic method by beginning in the middle of things. It is a striking fact, hitherto (I believe) unnoticed, that a Latin poem called the 'Aeneid' does much the same thing. We expect the author of that poem to begin with the departure of his hero from Troy, just as we expect the author of our poem to begin with 'April.' But in neither case is our expectation fulfilled. Cato, the author of the 'Aeneid,' creates dynamic suspense by beginning with Aeneas in Carthage; our anonymous poet treats his readers' sensibilities in a similar fashion by beginning with 'September,' and then *going back* to 'April' and 'June.'

6

But the sensibility of the poet does not stop at this point. Having described what is true of *four* months, he disposes of *seven* more with masterly economy. In a series of pungent constructs his sensibility sums up their inexorable limitations: they *All* (the capitalization should be noted) 'have thirty-one.' The poet's sensibility communicates a feeling to the sensibility of the reader so that the sensibility of both, with reference to their previous but independent sensibilities, is fused into that momentary communion of sensibility which is the final sensibility that poetry can give both to the sensibility of the poet and the sensibility of the reader. The texture and structure of the poem have erupted into a major reaction. The ambiguity of equilibrium is achieved.

7

Against these two groups of spatial, temporal and numerical measurements—one consisting of four months, the other of seven—the tragic individual, the sole exception, 'February,' is dramatically placed. February is 'alone,' is cut off from communion with his fellows. The tragic note is struck the moment 'February' is mentioned. For the initial sound of the word 'excepting' is 'X,' and as that sound strikes the sensibility of the reader's ear a number of associations subconsciously accumulate. We think of the spot, the murderous and lonely spot, which 'X' has so frequently marked; we remember the examinations of our childhood where the wrong answers were implacably signalled with 'X'; we think of ex-kings and exile, of lonely crossroads and executions, of the inexorable anonymity of those who cannot sign their names. . . .

8

And yet the poet gives us one ray of hope, though it eventually proves to be illusory. The lonely 'February' (notice how the 'alone' in line four is echoed by the 'only' in line five), the solitary and maladjusted individual who is obviously the hero and crucial figure of the poem, is not condemned to the routine which his fellows, in their different ways, must forever obey. Like Hamlet, he has a capacity for change. He is a symbol of individualism, and the rhythm of the lines which are devoted to him signalize a gaiety, however desperate, which immediately wins our sympathy and reverberates profoundly in our sensibility.

9

But (and this is the illusion to which I have previously referred) in spite of all his variety, his capacity for change, 'February' cannot quite accomplish (and in this his tragedy consists) the *quantitative* value of the society in which circumstances have put him. No matter how often he may alternate from twenty-eight to twenty-nine (the poet, with his exquisite sensibility, does not actually *mention* those humiliating numbers), he can never achieve the bourgeois, if anonymous, security of 'thirty-one,' nor equal the more modest and aristocratic assurance of 'thirty.' Decade after decade, century after century, millennium after millennium, he is eternally frustrated. The only symbol of change in a changeless society, he is continually beaten down. Once every four years he tries to rise, to achieve the high, if delusive, level of his dreams. But he fails. He is always one day short, and the three years before the recurrence of his next effort are a sad interval in which the remembrance of previous disappointment melts into the futility of hope, only to sink back once more into the frustration of despair. Like Tantalus he is forever stretched upon a wheel.

10

So far I have been concerned chiefly with the dynamic *analysis* of the poem. Further study should reveal the *synthesis* which can be made on the basis of the analysis which my thesis has tentatively attempted to bring to an emphasis. This, perhaps, the reader with a proper sensibility can achieve for himself.

Notes Toward a Critique of McLuhan's Polemic against Vision [1]

In affirming that electric culture is characterized by synesthesia, simultaneity, and unified perception, McLuhan mercilessly and tirelessly attacks what he regards as the dissociated sensibility of visual-gradient culture. What follows below is a brief sketch of his position. He says:

> Any culture is an order of sensory preferences, and in the tribal world, the senses of touch, taste, hearing and smell were developed, for very practical reasons, to a much higher level than the strictly visual. Into this world, the phonetic alphabet fell like a bombshell, installing sight at the head of the hierarchy of senses. Literacy propelled man from the tribe, gave him an eye for an ear and replaced his integral in-depth communal interplay with visual linear values and fragmented consciousness. As an intensification and amplification of the visual function, the phonetic alphabet diminished the role of the senses of hearing and touch and taste and smell, permeating the discontinuous culture of tribal man and translating its organic harmony and complex synaesthesia into the uniform, connected and visual mode that we still consider the norm of 'rational' existence. The whole man became fragmented man; the alphabet shattered the charmed circle and resonating magic of the tribal world, exploding man into an agglomeration of specialized and psychically impoverished 'individuals,' or units, functioning in a world of linear time and Euclidean space. (PI 59)

If the phonetic alphabet fell like a bombshell on tribal man, 'the printing press hit him like a 100-megaton H-bomb,' and assured the eye 'a position of total dominance in man's sensorium.' Today, electric media, especially television, have put an end to 3,000 years of visual supremacy (Pl 60).

A full discussion of the relation of media and the senses remains an important task, as yet barely begun. Here, I offer only some brief considerations toward a critique of McLuhan's anti-vision polemic.

1. Not only is the vision-tactility opposition phony, but the hand and sight, combined in the work process and tool formation, were both crucial variables of human evolution from the pre-human. By minimizing the role of vision before the alphabet, McLuhan makes his own claim that man is a 'tool-making animal' (GG 4) unintelligible. According to Gordon Childe, binocular vision gives us solid, stereoscopic, three-dimensional images whose association with sensations of touch and muscular activity makes possible the accurate assessment of distance and depth. Otherwise, toolmaking would be impossible. 'It is the perfectly adjusted, but sub-conscious, co-operation of hand and eye that allows man to make tools from the roughest eolith to the most sensitive seismograph.'[2]

2. Vision is refined in the division of labor of the senses in the work process, and the eye assumes tactile perceptions to liberate the hand for work. The eye learns to sense in the visual field characteristic signs that would, without mediation, have fallen outside its domain, that is, such properties as weight, texture, and so forth; these become essential constituents of visual apprehension. With respect to this historical development, sight and touch are inseparable. McLuhan's construction of a totally purified visuality, not only abstracted from but opposed to tactility, is a fiction that abrogates history.[3]

3. McLuhan's sensory categories are static natural archetypes, transhistorical essences, that absorb and stabilize dynamic socio-economic relations. His schematic discussions of alterations of sense ratios are not a recognition of the historical development of the senses but manipulative transformations of fixed categories. Instead, the real changes are not on the proposed level of physiological rationalization; they are social and oriented to the adequate appropriation of our reality at the determinate level of productive power, and to our self-humanization. Marx said that the formation of the senses was 'a labor of the entire history of the world down to the present.'[4] This represents, on one hand, an elaboration of human senses to correspond to the wealth of the world, and, on the other, making our senses human, that is, bringing them into

relation with the transhistorical human essence (existing, of course, only in history and totalized in relation to a specific historical location). The character of our perceptual patterns is not a problematic of physiological dilation by technology, but of social-conceptual mediation directed by received knowledge, including language in particular.[5] A crucial consequence is that vision is not in itself mechanical, but is today alienated, as are consciousness and perception in general. McLuhan takes the specific form for the general. Hence, he can only counterpose *alienated* sensory modalities, and can neither locate modern capitalist sensory impoverishment, nor pose, not just forms of rationalization, but the liberation of the sensorium and of sensuality.

4. McLuhan's use of his sensory categories is metaphoric, mythic rather than explicative. Thus he can say that the press mosaic, though it is seen, has an auditory structure, and that television, although seen and heard, is tactile. This is confusing but not inadmissible: we must simply understand, on the whole, something like linearity by visuality, and simultaneity by auditivity or tactility. But we need to be especially sensitive, in consequence, to the ideological moments in his sensory preferences. In terms of his own definitions, the more purposive sense, vision, is rejected in favor of the receptivity of hearing and the inclusiveness of touch. Praxis, in effect, is exchanged for totalitarian passivity.

Notes

Preface

1 I am not using the term 'critical theory' in order to associate the modern theorists with the Kantian philosophical tradition, although significant points of contact with Kantianism and, especially, neo-Kantianism do exist; nor in order to link them with the 'critical theory' of the Frankfurt School of Marxism. The aim of this usage is to avoid the narrow conceptual limitations of the alternative terms 'literary theory' or 'literary criticism' and to encompass the broader matrix of attention that was established through efforts from within the realm of literary studies to apprehend and assimilate—the forms of this assimilation being the subject matter of this study—categories of culture that have been emerging from the transformation of capitalism in this century and imposing their presence. (Northrop Frye, himself, uses the term 'critical theory.')

2 'Moment' is a dialectical term for a part of a totality. It has substance and exercises leverage on the totality and on other moments of the totality. It is determined by, and in turn determines, the totality and its other moments.

3 The notion of 'adequation' is used in order to provide a non-reductive historical dimension for the examination of *ideology*. We need to put aside transcendent illusions of having access to a Truth against which the accuracy or degree of mystification of an ideology can be measured, and to stop viewing ideologies as deformed reactions to Reality. If ideologies are not symmetrical to their objects, but particularize, structure, totalize, and give meaning to phenomena, then a number of ideologies, all valid within certain limits, can coexist and enter into conflict. It is possible to understand them as appropriating the culture of an epoch from the point of view of a determinate social teleology, but in relation to the whole of society with all its divisions and conflicts, and the whole of civilization and history. To inquire into ideologies does not mean to ask how exhaustively they apprehend, or how correctly they characterize, their objects, how 'true' they are. It means to investigate how 'adequately' they mediate between the present and the future, that is,

216

how adequately and fully they articulate and organize an intentionality immanent within and characteristic of a determinate social project. Thus, the problem of ideology has its ground not in epistemology, but in social ontology, and investigation into ideology—whether concerned with categorical continuity, structure, development, proportioning, or homology, or with sociological points of reference—will assume that ideology does not 'reflect' or 'correspond' to Reality but constitutes a sphere of historical activity. The notion of ideology as 'false consciousness' should properly be reserved for characterizing ideological formulations that have no bearing on any objective possibilities.

4   See Preface, n.3.

5   See Martin Sklar's stimulating discussion, 'On the Proletarian Revolution and the End of Political-Economic Society.' *Radical America*, III (May–June 1969), 8–12.

6   For an original and important elaboration of this problematic, the best source is the series of studies by Jean Baudrillard, including *Le Système des objets* (Paris, 1968); *La Société de consommation* (Paris, 1970); *Pour une critique de l'économie politique du signe* (Paris, 1972); and *Le Miroir de la production* (Paris, 1973). This last is available in English as *The Mirror of Production*, trans. and intro. Mark Poster (St Louis, 1975).

7   'Culture' and 'civilization' are two antagonistic terms of early nineteenth-century diction which identify a cleavage in the historical practice of the age. This cleavage took shape in the form of a split between the spheres of material production and reproduction of life, empirical 'civilization,' and the sphere of 'culture,' of the valuable objectifications and abilities that were dispensable in relation to the former. Romantic cultural theory opposes the two categories; modern theory reintegrates them under the extended categories of neocapitalist production relations.

8   I have adopted the terms 'negativity' and 'positivity' from Herbert Marcuse's usage. The former indicates criticism of the latter, which in turn represents the self-confirming empirical actuality of the prevailing order of domination.

9   In order to avoid misunderstandings, I should emphasize that it is not my intention to use these categories either in the manner of polemic or of incantation. They are meant to serve a precise analytic function and to situate the theories (in their capacities as concrete mediations) in relation to each other and in relation to ongoing social projects. I try to show extensively the ways in which Ransom's position is defensive and ambiguously backward-looking; the entire thrust of the section on Frye is to draw attention to the categorical surrender embedded in the structural politics of his theoretical formulations; and the 'counter-revolutionary' character of McLuhan's outlook is explicitly defined (pp. 144ff.) and argued both generally and specifically throughout.

Chapter 1 Nineteenth-century problematics

1   A 'problematic' is a social, ideological, or theoretical framework

within which complexes of problems are structured and single problems
acquire density, meaning and significance.

2   Cited in Arnold Hauser, *The Social History of Art*, trans., in
collaboration with the author, Stanley Godman (New York, 1951), III,
p. 208.

3   Ibid., p. 209.

4   *William Morris: Romantic to Revolutionary* (London, 1955), p. 28.

5   Ibid., p. 47.

6   Ibid., p. 104.

7   *One-Dimensional Man: Studies in the Ideology of Advanced
Industrial Society* (Boston, 1966), p. 60.

8   *Culture and Society, 1780–1950,* 2nd ed. (Harmondsworth, 1963), pp.
60, 63.

9   Hauser, III, p. 170.

10   For a brilliant and provocative discussion of the dialectics of social
spheres, see Karel Kosik, *La Dialectique du concret*, trans. Roger
Dangeville (Paris, 1970), pp. 75–103; and *Dialektik des Konkreten*,
trans. Marianne Hoffmann (Frankfurt-am-Main, 1967), pp. 104–49.

11   See above, pp. xix ff.

12   See citation from Herbert Marcuse above, p. 6.

13   'Culture and Anarchy,' in *Poetry and Criticism of Matthew Arnold*,
ed. A. Dwight Culler (Boston, 1961), pp. 409–13.

14   *Negations: Essays in Critical Theory*, trans. Jeremy J. Shapiro
(Boston, 1969), p. 95.

15   Arnold, p. 412.

16   Ibid., p. 411.

17   Ibid.

18   Ibid., pp. 410–11.

19   This whole problematic later becomes decisive in Frye.

20   Arnold, p. 412.

21   Ibid., p. 423. 'The idea which culture sets before us of perfection,—an
increased spiritual activity, having for its characters increased
sweetness, increased light, increased life, increased sympathy,—is an
idea which the new democracy needs far more than the idea of the
blessedness of the franchise, or the wonderfulness of its own industrial
performances.' Of course, the criticism of sentimentality is just, but in
the context scarcely decisive.

22   *Negations*, p. 98.

23   *William Morris: Romantic to Revolutionary*, pp. 283–4.

24   Arnold, p. 426.

25   Ibid., p. 452.

26   Ibid.

27   Arnold (p. 428) is not unaware that he is open to criticism:

It is said that a man with my theories of sweetness and light is full of
antipathy against the rougher or coarser movements going on around
him, that he will not lend a hand to the humble operation of
uprooting evil by their means, and that therefore the believers in
action grow impatient with him. But what if rough and coarse action,
ill-calculated action, action with insufficient light, is, and has for a

long time been, our bane? What if our urgent want now is, not to act
at any price, but rather to lay in a stock of light for our difficulties? In
that case, to refuse to lend a hand to the rougher and coarser
movements going on round us, to make the primary need, both for
oneself and others, to consist in enlightening ourselves and qualifying
ourselves to act less at random, is surely the best and in real truth the
most practical line our endeavours can take.

This in 1869. A different view, from a radically different class position,
is implied of 'our urgent want' by the formation in London in 1864 of the
International Workingmen's Association, the First International, and
the publication in 1867 of *Capital*.

28   'The Study of Poetry,' *Poetry and Criticism of Matthew Arnold*,
       p. 306.
29   Ibid., p. 307.
30   'The Function of Criticism at the Present Time,' *Poetry and Criticism
       of Matthew Arnold*, p. 245.
31   *The Renaissance: Studies in Art and Poetry*, 5th ed. (London,
       1912), p. 252. See also p. 249, and *passim*, especially 'Sandro Botticelli,'
       'Leonardo da Vinci,' and 'Winckelmann.'
32   Ibid., p. 250.
33   Ibid., p. 249.
34   William Joseph Rooney, 'The Problem of "Poetry and Belief" in
       Contemporary Criticism' (diss., The Catholic University of America,
       1949), p. 139.
35   I shall comment on this in much greater detail in another section.
36   *Marius the Epicurean: His Sensations and Ideas* (London, 1891),
       p. 117.
37   Ibid., pp. 38–9.
38   The whole of this position involves a shift of focus from Arnold. Frye is
       the specific unity of Arnold's theory of 'the best' in a classless culture
       of class aliens as the source of spiritual authority and Pater's view of
       education as the means to living in the material world by the standard
       of the ideal. Of course, the problems are posed on a different historical
       level at a different level of confidence.
39   Human activity is activity through objects. Human subjectivity is
       objectified in praxis. 'Generic objectifications' are historically created
       products (objects, institutions, methods, abilities) of human activity,
       grasped categorically at the level of the human species, of
       genus man. I am using these categories as developed by the Lukács
       School in Budapest in the works of Lukács, Ágnes Heller, Mihály Vajda,
       György Márkus, Ferenc Fehér and others, and as defined by Heller
       (*A mindennapi élet* [*Everyday Life*], Budapest: Akadémiai Kiadó,
       1970, pp. 183–9). These objectifications are systems of reference
       which embody typological variations of human genus being and have to
       be appropriated (internalized) by individuals. Such objectifications can
       be *appropriated* by everyone relatively equally. However, there are two
       kinds of generic objectifications: differential ability to *form* them
       distinguishes 'for-itself' generic objectifications from 'in-itself' generic
       objectifications. Heller argues (p. 184) that without the latter society

cannot exist, that the sphere of in-itself generic objectifications, consisting of three organic moments of work activity, viz., instruments and products, customs and conventions, and language, is both the result of human activity and its condition of possibility. Both phylogenetically and ontogenetically, becoming human begins with the appropriation of this sphere through activity. The sphere of in-itself generic objectifications constitutes the starting point of everyday life and, as well, the starting point of all culture. For-itself generic objectifications, on the other hand, are '*ontologically secondary*' (p. 187), in that societies can exist without art or science, ethics or religion. These objectifications depend on a conscious, value-based relationship to our humanity; they can function only through conscious human intentionality directed toward them and cannot come into being at all without '*conscious relations to genus being*' (p. 188). For-itself generic objectifications represent human development not purely objectively but permeated with intentionality directed toward genus being, imbued with a concern for the destiny of mankind. They are forms of the consciousness or self-consciousness of mankind, and embody human freedom at a determinate historical level. These objectifications are not mere fictions but realities, objectifications of man's rule over human and non-human nature. To the extent that they have a strictly independent development, governed by an internal logic, it is secondary. Their essence is to respond to, or at least bring to generic consciousness, the questions posed by current social development. In this respect they have as their basis, but transfigure, the in-itself generic (p. 188). (Translations from the Hungarian, here and elsewhere, are mine.)

40 · With the neocapitalist blending of different social and cultural spheres, in part through the strategic agency of mass communications, the commodity form becomes the universal common denominator bearing the rationality of the existing social reality into all areas of life. The result is the contemporary 'society of the spectacle,' for which Guy Debord has provided a stimulating and provocative analysis. This is a society lived as 'a social relation among people mediated by images,' as people's experience of reality comes increasingly from contemplation and consumption rather than from active creation. 'The present phase of total occupation of social life by the accumulated results of the economy,' writes Debord, 'leads to a generalized sliding of *having* into *appearing*, from which all actual "having" must draw its immediate prestige and its ultimate function. At the same time all individual reality has become social, directly dependent on social force, shaped by it.' (*Society of the Spectacle, Radical America*, IV, no. 5, 1970, paras 4, 17.) Under the pure regard of the spectator, the object of consumption generates much of social life and social value as if these were its inherent quality. The soft drink that makes one feel the community of a generation, the beer that means life can be pleasant, the cosmetics that bring romance and happiness, the big cars that guarantee social respect—by a mechanism of magical association, all these intrinsically link the consumption of individual goods with human desires to which they lack genuine reference, that is, with real desires that might find real

satisfaction in a different social, economic, and cultural organization. Yet the magical inducements of the spectacle do deliver to the spectator some magical satisfactions that offer to validate personal fantasy, and the consumer in a consumer culture may live this magical life in place of the one he cannot have under the class-determined categories of the system. As Raymond Williams notes ('The Magic System,' *New Left Review*, 4, July–August 1960, p. 29): 'People will indeed look twice at you, upgrade you, respond to your displayed signals, if you have made the right purchases within a system of meanings to which you are all trained.' In this way, the society of the spectacle tends to become theatre, appearances tend to become reality, and significations come to dominate forms of activity. Consequently, in this world of magical reification, problems of social ontology tend to be displaced by problems of epistemology. In looking ahead to the discussions to come, I want to suggest that this problematic is the source of all the modern formalist and structuralist reductions of human reality to signification, of the contemporary fetish of language, and of the overemphasis on epistemology in the growing tendency to restrict the subject/object problematic to the appearance/essence problem (which becomes so docile that it can be safely handled 'systematically' and 'scientifically').

41 See, for example, Villiers de l'Isle-Adam's *Axel*, posthumously published in 1890, trans. Marilyn Gaddis Rose (Dublin, 1970), pp. 169–70. Preparing to drink poison, Axel says:

The future? . . . Sara, have faith in my words: we have just exhausted it. What would all those realities be tomorrow in comparison with the mirages we have just lived through? . . . The quality of our hope forbids the earth to us now. What can we ask of this wretched star, where our melancholy lingers, but pale reflections of such moments of dream? . . . If we accepted life now, we should commit a sacrilege against ourselves. As for living? our servants will do that for us.

42 Hauser, *Social History of Art*, IV, p. 201.
43 György Lukács, in a discussion of philistinism (*Writer and Critic and Other Essays*, ed. and trans. Arthur Kahn, London, 1970, p. 15), protests against the redefinition of the category to mean merely 'a stupid response to genuine art.' He argues that in the Enlightenment, evidenced by the creative struggles of Diderot, Rousseau, Lessing, and Goethe, what had been considered philistinism was 'resignation before degrading circumstances.' Later, at a point in the bifurcation of culture and civilization, the 'resignation to degrading circumstances implicit in the aesthetic pseudo-protest came to be glorified, and philistinism was transformed into a limited concept.' And he insists, quite accurately, that 'mere aesthetic scoffing at philistinism results in its perpetuation both in the ironist and in the object of his irony.'
44 'The Decay of Lying' in *The Works of Oscar Wilde* (London, 1963), pp. 842–3.
45 *Culture and Society*, pp. 173–5.
46 See above, pp. 9 ff.
47 Cf. Stéphane Mallarmé, in defining art as an aristocratic mystery ('Art for All,' *Mallarmé: Selected Prose Poems, Essays, Letters*, trans.

and intro. Bradford Cook, Baltimore, 1956, p. 12): 'But does this mob understand you now that it has *bought* you because you were cheap?'

48 Cf. Arnold, 'The Function of Criticism,' *Poetry and Criticism*, p. 239: 'Now, in literature, —. . . the elements with which the creative power works are ideas . . . current at the time.'

49 *One-Dimensional Man*, p. 68.

50 Cf. Arthur Rimbaud's letter to Paul Demeny, 15 May 1871 (*Complete Works, Selected Letters*, trans., intro., and notes by Wallace Fowlie, Chicago, 1966, p. 309): 'A language has to be found.' Also Mallarmé ('Crises in Poetry,' *Mallarmé: Selected Prose Poems, Essays, and Letters*, p. 40): 'Speech is no more than a commercial approach to reality. In literature, allusion is sufficient: essences are distilled and then embodied in Idea.'

51 By the term 'transcendence' I mean independence or abstraction from human praxis. Whether this occurs at the subject pole or at the object pole is not directly relevant.

52 *Complete Works, Selected Letters*, p. 307. Modified translation.

Chapter 2 Foundations of modern critical theory

1 It should not be thought that the real point of interest is the traditional liberal-conservative opposition. The focus of attention is the emergence of the new anti-liberal ideology of corporate liberalism, the unity of particularity and general order. In this respect, if the history of nineteenth-century thought is the degeneration of critical liberalism, the history of twentieth-century thought is the development of uncritical corporate liberalism and its rise to dominance.

2 Hulme once told a friend: 'I am more than a conservative; I am a reactionary.' Cited in the editor's introduction to Hulme's *Further Speculations*, ed. Sam Hynes (Minneapolis, 1955), p. xxx.

3 'Romanticism and Classicism,' *Speculations: Essays on Humanism and the Philosophy of Art*, ed. Herbert Read, 2nd ed. (London, 1936), p. 113.

4 A superficial and limited awareness of this is offered in Robert Wooster Stallman, 'The New Critics,' *Critiques and Essays in Criticism 1920–1948: Representing the Achievement of Modern British and American Critics* (New York, 1949), p. 493: 'Hulme defined the mood and perspective of our age; and this is his importance, almost exclusively.'

5 'Romanticism and Classicism,' *Speculations: Essays on Humanism and the Philosophy of Art*, p. 133.

6 Ibid., p. 126.

7 Ibid., pp. 132–3. See also 'Bergson's Theory of Art,' *Speculations*, p. 160.

8 Ibid., p. 117.

9 (London, 1961).

10 For example, the professions of classicism of Hulme, Eliot and Ransom.

11 William K. Wimsatt, Jr, and Cleanth Brooks, *Literary Criticism: A Short History* (London, 1970), I, p. 134.

12   I offer the category 'commotion,' in its various grammatical
     forms, as an alternative to 'conjuncture' whose use is fashionable
     in structuralist diction. 'Conjuncture' is a synchronic denotation of a
     given balance of forces in a given moment of time and freezes history as
     a field within which forces can be stabilized for 'scientific' analysis, or
     as a diachronic quantity which can be grafted mechanically *post festum*.
     'Commotion' denotes a moment of historical totalization defined by a
     specific relation of the transhistorical (objectified praxis) and the
     historical (objectifying praxis), a moment of the dialectical unity of
     continuity and discontinuity. It carries notions of form, structure,
     function, and development within a view of history as a dimension of
     human activity. 'Commotion' replaces the abstract positivist juncture of
     forces and relations with the location of concrete potentialities in the
     motion of interdeterminations of human activity and its products, and
     leaves room for the revolutionary praxis of a historical subject who is
     self-constituting through his objectifications. It is an ontological
     category that permits the abolition of alienation, not an epistemological
     category that reinforces it. If the term 'commotion' seems to carry some
     connotations of disorder that we find inappropriate, that is merely an
     indication of how much ideologies of rationalized order and stability
     have come to prevail.

13   Reification, as developed and used by Lukács, has connotations of
     alienation, rationalization, atomization, and deactivization. In a
     society whose main metabolism flows from the commodity structure,
     'reification' denotes the tendency of the social world to take on the form
     of a frozen 'second nature' governed by natural laws. Human products
     become a system of objective, independent things (commodities) with
     autonomous laws that rule over the people who labor to produce and
     maintain them. People, in turn, become (ontologically) deactivized, and
     estranged from their own powers as well as from their products. To
     employ the distinctions formulated by Andrew Arato ('Lukács' Theory of
     Reification,' *Telos*, no. 11, Spring 1972, p. 33 n. 33): 'Objectification is
     the active formation of objects, and intersubjective (species) methods
     and capabilities. Alienation is the separation of individuals from the
     objective creations—from "themselves"—and reification is the form of
     this separation (second nature) in the world of commodities.' An
     objectivistic (reified) consciousness—which accepts that we are not
     subjects in our world—corresponds to this 'second nature' of
     appearances that are the phenomena of reification in the world of
     commodity exchange, and even embraces the illusion that these
     immediate appearances (the forms of existence in which human activity
     under capitalism is manifested) are permanent and unchangeable. In such
     a naturalized dialectic, people encounter society, practically and
     intellectually, on the level of immediacy. The problem of mediation,
     therefore, becomes central to the problem of abolishing reification.

14   Theodor W. Adorno, *Prisms*, trans. Samuel and Shierry Weber
     (London, 1967), p. 34.

15   T. S. Eliot, 'Tradition and the Individual Talent,' *Selected Essays*
     (London, 1951), p. 22.

16 *The Well Wrought Urn: Studies in the Structure of Poetry* (London, 1968), p. 60. Cf. Allen Tate (*Essays of Four Decades*, London, 1970, p. xi), who records that after *Practical Criticism* in 1929, 'one had to read poetry with all the brains one had and with one's arms and legs, as well as what may be inside the rib cage.'

17 'T. S. Eliot on Criticism,' *The Saturday Review of Literature*, X (24 March 1934), 574.

18 'The Frontiers of Criticism,' *On Poetry and Poets* (London, 1957), p. 113.

19 *Coleridge on Imagination*, 3rd ed. (London, 1962), p. 231.

20 *The Philosophy of Rhetoric* (New York, 1965), p. 131.

21 'Ulysses, Order, and Myth,' 1923, reprinted as 'Myth and Literary Classicism,' *The Modern Tradition: Backgrounds of Modern Literature*, ed. Richard Ellmann and Charles Feidelson, Jr (New York, 1965), p. 681.

22 *Philosophy of Rhetoric*, p. 134.

23 *Coleridge on Imagination*, p. 228.

24 Ibid., p. 172.

25 Ibid., p. 227.

26 *The New Apologists for Poetry* (Minneapolis, 1956), pp. 124–5.

27 Such a subject/object dualism stands in the way of understanding that the 'autonomous,' formal perfection (aesthetic closure) of the world of the art object is precisely the *means* of evoking an experiential effect and, through the power of the medium, of enforcing the cathartic reception (internalization) of a new 'world.' Lukács deals with this problem in depth in the great aesthetic work of his late period (*Az esztétikum sajátossága* [*The Specificity of the Aesthetic*], trans. from the German into Hungarian by István Eörsi, 2 vols, Budapest, 1965; hereafter cited as *Aesthetics*, with all translations into English being mine). In Lukács's analysis, everyday life is heterogeneous and lived pragmatically by particularized beings who take their own selves as the starting point for viewing and manipulating the world. To the extent that they are also generic (*human*) beings—they work, speak, etc.—they are generic beings without self-consciousness. But it is possible for people, by creating or internalizing *objectifications*, to rise consciously to the (generic) level of humanity. If a single task concentrates (homogenizes) all of one's human powers and capacities (otherwise diversely at work in the heterogeneous everyday world), then, in this process, the heterogeneity of the world is suspended and particularity dissolves in the generic. (The concrete content of the generic, always historically specific to a given period, is made up of the social imperatives, customs, and morals of the society and of the communities in it that carry the essence of human development.) Art, which operates through a homogeneous medium (visual, linguistic, etc.), is one form of objectification through which this process of elevation to the generic level can take place. The possibilities are by no means exclusive to the realm of aesthetics (ethical, scientific, or political concentrations, too, can bring all human powers into a unified focus), but *homogenization*, Lukács stresses, is the only means of reaching the generic level.

Art, the argument goes, is—in each work—both the *memory of mankind* (concentrating in itself an essential step of human historical development) and the (always *sensible*) *self-consciousness of humanity* (blending acutely concentrated subjectivity and objectivity, and expressing in the substance of the art *object* the substance of the generic essence within the *subject*). In experiencing the work of art, the person who receives it, like the one who created it, 'suspends' everyday life and rises to the level of humanity as a whole. This breaks through his fetishized world picture. The generic value hierarchy (organized from the point of view of human development and destiny) that is embodied in the formally closed 'world' of art collides with the fetishes of the everyday world. A question is posed as to how human is the world (of the work and of the receiver's daily life)? This elicits a shock (which Lukács calls *catharsis*, generalizing that category beyond its classical restriction to tragedy), and demands of the individual: change your life. In this way, Lukács shows, aesthetics and ethics meet, and precisely from the specific formal objectivity (aesthetic integrity) of the work does the (defetishizing) social function of art flow. (For a fuller elucidation, see the ever-rich text of the *Aesthetics*; also Ágnes Heller's review, 'Lukács's Aesthetics,' *The New Hungarian Quarterly*, VII (Winter 1966), 84–94, which the description above largely follows.)

If, by contrast, the art object is separated from the (creating or receiving) subject, and the fundamental links binding them together in a significant human process are broken, then, as in modern critical theory, both the object pole and the subject pole (of the suppressed relationship) suffer distortion. And, by excluding from *aesthetic* consideration the cathartic critique of the humanity of our everyday world, critical theory embraces the fetish of immediacy.

28   *The Use of Poetry and the Use of Criticism: Studies in the Relation of Criticism to Poetry in England*, 2nd ed. (London, 1964), p. 111.

29   *Aesthetics*, I, p. 646. I am using the category of immediacy here as an ontological-historical category, rather than a psychological category (that might imply simply underdeveloped awareness or knowledge). 'Immediacy' refers to the 'second nature' of immediate 'appearances,' and indicates the failure (or refusal) to move past these phenomena of reification (see n. 13 above) to the potentialities of the substratum of historical activity ('essence') of which they are the given forms of manifestation. The level of immediacy is the level where the given forms of life are accepted 'in themselves.' For an aesthetic embodiment of the conscious subscription to dehumanization, see Eliot's play *The Cocktail Party*.

30   'The Function of Criticism,' *Selected Essays*, p. 34.

31   'Tradition and the Individual Talent,' ibid., p. 17.

32   Ibid., p. 20.

33   See n. 27 above. This part of the process is what the Kantians develop in a formalist, contemplative way as 'disinterest.'

34   See, for example, I, pp. 488, 491, 600–1, 608, 615, 749.

35   *Aesthetics*, I, p. 732. It is important to distinguish this position from even the best of structuralisms, such as Lucien Goldmann's, which are

happy to eliminate the individual personality. It may be added that both the individual and generic moments of art, and the specific form of their relation, involve a class-determined historical reality.

36   *Selected Essays*, p. 19.
37   *The Interior Landscape: The Literary Criticism of Marshall McLuhan, 1943–1962*, ed. Eugene McNamara (New York, 1969), p. 164.
38   *Selected Essays*, p. 15.
39   See Stanley Edgar Hyman, *The Armed Vision: A Study in the Methods of Modern Literary Criticism*, rev. ed., abr. by the author (New York, 1955), p. 62.
40   *Selected Essays*, p. 22.
41   Ibid., pp. 14–15.
42   'Milton II,' *On Poetry and Poets*, pp. 152–3.
43   'Milton I,' ibid., p. 143.
44   We can accept Ransom's position that 'philosophy as a part of the critical discipline' has its real origins with Richards after Coleridge ('The Concrete Universal: Observations on the Understanding of Poetry,' *The Kenyon Review*, XVII (Summer 1955), 384), but must specify it. Richards' contribution is limited to a type of value theory, epistemology, and philosophy of language and meaning. There is, for example, no social ontology, philosophy of history, or philosophy of everyday life, branches of philosophy that are essential to a critical and effective humanism.
45   *Poetries and Sciences—A Reissue of Science and Poetry with Commentary* (London, 1970), pp. 55–6.
46   Cf. Richards, *Principles of Literary Criticism* (London, 1960), p. 84, for the position that only *how* things behave is meaningful.
47   *Poetries and Sciences*, p. 54.
48   It is easy to see why Richards could be so readily adopted into the pragmatist philosophical field of the United States.
49   This whole problem is deeply interrelated with the naturalistic, contemplative attitude of scientific objectivism in social study (scientism). Scientistic attitudes (structuring social science on the model of the natural sciences) reduce mankind to an object of science and, by confounding people and things, reinforce that reified inversion of the subject/object relationship in which people are ruled by the products they have created. Positivism is the culmination of tendencies reducing, not only nature, but also society to abstractions interrelated by independent laws that can be manipulated for technical successes. The entire question of constituting a society of subjects in conscious relation to each other and to their objectifications becomes tendentially inaccessible. Science, then, which was to take part in terminating the objectively given transcendence (pre-constituted world of ready-made objects, institutions, language, interrelations, etc.) that surrounds particular man in everyday life, effectively ends up elevating transcendence (pre-given forms, laws, relations) into its own view of reality. Although in many respects its structure is significantly different, in certain decisive respects science has thus failed to grow out of and to move beyond the objectivistic, pragmatic structure of everyday, fetishistic, individual thought. (For

interesting critical discussion of the crisis of science in this general vein, see: Edmund Husserl, *The Crisis of European Sciences and Transcendental Phenomenology*, trans. David Carr, Evanston, Ill., 1970; Mihály Vajda, *Zárójelbe tett tudomány: a husserli fenomenológia tudományfelfogásának bírálatához* [*Science in Brackets: Toward a Critique of the Conception of Science in Husserlian Phenomenology*], Budapest, 1968; and Paul Piccone, 'Towards a Socio-historical Interpretation of the Scientific Revolution,' *Telos*, no. 1 (Spring 1968), 16–26; and 'Reading the *Crisis*,' *Telos*, no. 8 (Summer 1971), 121–9.)

50 *Poetries and Sciences*, p. 54.
51 György Lukács, 'The Dialectic of Labor: Beyond Causality and Teleology,' trans. Adolph W. Gucinski, *Telos*, no. 6 (Fall 1970), 165.
52 *Poetries and Sciences*, p. 55.
53 Ibid., p. 60.
54 Ibid., p. 61. Richards, in his 1970 Commentary (p. 92), remarks in relation to this point: 'I do not think that any who have been noting the recrudescence and the return of violence and ruthlessness in so many parts of what was called "the civilized world" will consider these dreary surmises to have been exaggeration.'
55 This is one of Richards' legacies to the modern tradition. In the context of a generalized language fetish, the tradition, of course, has not overcome the weaknesses of such a miscategorization.
56 *Poetries and Sciences*, p. 60, n. 1.
57 John Holloway, 'The Critical Intimidation,' *The Hudson Review*, V (Winter 1953), 476. In this article, Holloway, in a useful if limited critique that moves on a very different axis from mine, comes perhaps closest of modern scholars to seeing the paradoxical subordination of art to the categories of science, even in the process of differentiation. But Holloway does not discuss either the alienation or the specific *telos* of either art or science.
58 Richards, in his 1970 defense (*Poetries and Sciences*, p. 91), justly answers the first question in the negative and the second in the affirmative.
59 Ibid., p. 60.
60 *The Armed Vision*, p. 312. See also p. 17. It is worth noting that Hyman traces this principle of 'continuity' to C. S. Peirce and John Dewey, the philosophers of United States pragmatism.
61 *Poetries and Sciences*, p. 78.
62 Ibid., p. 61.
63 Ibid., p. 78.
64 Cf. Raymond Williams, *Culture and Society 1780–1950*, 2nd ed. (Harmondsworth, 1963), p. 245.
65 *Poetries and Sciences*, p. 38.
66 Ibid., p. 39.
67 Ibid., p. 36.
68 See *Principles of Literary Criticism*, p. 251: 'The equilibrium of opposed impulses, which we suspect to be the ground-plan of the most valuable aesthetic responses, brings into play far more of our personality than is possible in experiences of a more defined emotion.'

69 Cf. ibid., p. 288: 'Value . . . is a quantitative matter. . . . the best life is
that in which as much as possible of our possible personality is
engaged. And of two personalities that one is the better in which
there is more which can be engaged without confusion.' The critical
moments involved in the full development of personality are here
subordinated to the capitalist principles of quantitative rationalization.

70 *Poetries and Sciences*, pp. 33–4.

71 *Language, Thought and Comprehension: A Case Study of the
Writings of I. A. Richards* (London, 1965), p. 106. Cf. *Coleridge on
Imagination*, p. 175.

72 *Poetries and Sciences*, p. 57.

73 *Principles of Literary Criticism*, p. 181.

74 Ibid., p. 184.

75 Ibid., p. 61.

76 Ibid., p. 233.

77 Ibid., p. 237. We should note that, using Arnold's concept of stock
notions, Richards poses the problem of mass culture as the fixation of bad
attitudes, a degeneration of response (ibid., p. 203). He also raises the
question of information overload (*Practical Criticism: A Study of
Literary Judgment*, London, 1964, pp. 320–1). In both cases, he
counterposes poetic ordering as the valuable remedy. That he raised the
question of mass culture for the tradition is a historical event; that his
attitude is critical is significant. Mass culture does not receive its
adequate neocapitalist formulation until McLuhan.

78 *Culture and Society*, p. 245.

79 This new unity is preserved in Richards' later reformulations
in terms of the aeolian harp.

80 Richards warns (*Principles of Literary Criticism*, p. 70) that the
satisfaction of an impulse is not identical with the quality of a pleasure.
This has no bearing on my argument. I am not trying to reduce
Richards to a hedonist. Nor was the romantic tradition opposed to
pleasure. It was opposed to the utilitarian fixation in immediacy.

81 *Coleridge on Imagination*, p. 228.

82 Ibid., pp. 212, 231.

83 Ibid., p. 183.

84 Ibid., pp. 171, 172, 175.

85 Ibid., p. 228.

86 Ibid., pp. 163–4.

87 Ibid., p. 163.

88 Ibid.

89 Cf. Agnes Heller, *A reneszánsz ember* [*Renaissance Man*] (Budapest,
1967), pp. 153–4.

90 Hotopf, pp. 19, 336.

91 *Principles of Literary Criticism*, p. 25.

92 Ibid., p. 26.

93 Ibid., p. 25.

94 *Practical Criticism*, p. 11.

95 C. K. Ogden and I. A. Richards, *The Meaning of Meaning: A
Study of the Influence of Language upon Thought and of the Science of*

Symbolism, 10th ed. (London, 1949), p. 262.
96   *Practical Criticism*, p. 341.
97   Ibid., pp. 334–5.
98   Ibid., p. 334.
99   Ibid., p. 337.
100 'The Frontiers of Criticism,' *On Poetry and Poets*, pp. 104–5.
101 *The Philosophy of Rhetoric*, p. 92.
102 *Practical Criticism*, p. 223.
103 *Coleridge on Imagination*, p. 91. Cf. William Empson, *Seven Types of Ambiguity* (Harmondsworth, 1961), pp. 236–7, for an analysis of the newspaper headline 'Italian Assassin Bomb Plot Disaster.'
104 *Coleridge on Imagination*, p. 230.
105 Ibid., p. 231.
106 I am indebted to Brian Turner ('Sociological Functionalism,' unpub. typescript) whose stimulating work on functionalism suggested to me these similarities in the specific features and internal development of two different social-scientific paradigms.

Chapter 3 Paradigm in motion

1   Art and religion have a point of contact in their common anthropomorphism: both present reality in human form. But they are radically opposed ontologically. The conditions of existence of religion reside in transcendent teleology; of art, in the dissolution of all moments of transcendence in human life as being fetishes of objective human relations. Religion seeks to refer transcendent teleological determinations back to the individual life of the particularized ego. Art has precisely the opposite task of 'making sensible the man-created meaning of human life' (*Aesthetics*, II, p. 771) through which a person is lifted out of everday particularity and may appropriate the self-consciousness of the human genus as ruler of destiny. (Lukács discusses in detail the centuries-long struggle of art against religion in the last chapter of the *Aesthetics*, II, pp. 627–811. Of course, we should take care to remember that, over long periods, religion too has been a vehicle for generic values. Moreover, the religious longing embodies a Utopian sense, which, like the orientation to transcendence, can imply (as does art) a criticism and rejection of the world as being incomplete and humanly inadequate. This aspect is most comprehensively developed in the work of Ernst Bloch.)
2   Cf. Raymond Williams, *Orwell* (London, 1971), p. 30.

Chapter 4 Introduction to John Crowe Ransom

1   Murray Krieger, *The New Apologists for Poetry* (Minneapolis, 1956), p. 4n., records the earlier usages of F. Brunetière, 1906; J. E. Spingarn, 1910; Ludwig Lewisohn, 1919; and Edwin Berry Burgum, 1930.
2   H. J. Muller, 'The New Criticism in Poetry,' *The Southern Review*, VI (Spring 1941), 812.
3   Krieger, pp. 5–6.

4 Richard Foster, *The New Romantics: A Reappraisal of the New Criticism* (Bloomington, 1962), pp. 23, 210.

5 For 'commotive' to replace 'conjunctural,' see chapter 2, n. 12.

6 Ransom is usually placed 'at the head of the . . . movement' (C. Hugh Holman, 'The Defense of Art: Criticism since 1930,' in *The Development of American Literary Criticism*, ed. Floyd Stovall, Chapel Hill, 1955, p. 232). William Elton, who, in thirty-five pages in three issues of *Poetry* magazine undertook to list and define the technical language of the New Criticism, explaining more than one hundred of the basic terms, calls Ransom the 'Apostle' to Richards' 'Father' ('A Glossary of the New Criticism,' *Poetry: A Magazine of Verse*, LXXIII, December 1948, 153). John L. Stewart, a specialist in the New Critics, compares him to 'Moses leading us through the deserts to the promised land of poetry' (D. David Long and Michael R. Burr, eds, *John Crowe Ransom, Gentleman, Teacher, Poet, Editor Founder of the Kenyon Review: A Tribute from the Community of Letters*, a supplement to vol. LXXXX, no. 7, *The Kenyon Collegian*, Gambier, 1964, p. 9). Allen Tate writes that some of his own essays were 'scholia' on Ransom's (*Essays of Four Decades*, London, 1970, p. xi), and that 'every page' of his essays bears the traces of Ransom's work (*A Tribute . . .*, p. 18). And Cleanth Brooks claims to have become 'a hero-worshipper' at Vanderbilt College in Nashville, studying under Ransom (ibid., p. 27). The tributes are perhaps exaggerated, but they leave no room to dispute Ransom's powerful influence.

7 Op. cit., p. 137.

8 *Marx's Theory of Alienation* (London, 1970), p. 70.

9 The contradictory attitude to reality, the need for integration as well as the resistance to it, is expressed, for example, in the New Critical obsession with irony.

10 Bernard Smith, *Forces in American Criticism: A Study in the History of American Literary Thought* (New York, 1939), p. 347, observes justly: 'It is one of the critical jokes of all time that these men should have bestowed upon themselves the title "New Humanists." ' In fact, the present study is in many respects a documentation of the bankruptcy of modern bourgeois humanism. For useful descriptive material on the intellectual antecedents of and background to the New Criticism, in addition to Smith, see also: Stovall, ed., *Development of American Literary Criticism* (Chapel Hill, 1955); Walter Sutton, *Modern American Criticism* (Engelwood Cliffs, 1963); and Frederick J. Hoffman, *The Twenties: American Writing in the Postwar Decade*, rev. ed. (New York, 1962).

11 Smith, p. 373.

12 'Proletarian Literature: A Political Autopsy,' *The Southern Review*, IV (Winter 1939), 627.

13 Allen Tate, who retained his (reactionary) critique of capitalism longer than Ransom, recorded this situation in an editorial ('The State of Letters,' *The Sewanee Review*, LII, October 1944, 611):

I allude to the once powerful school of Marxist critics, whose disappearance ought to be celebrated in a *ballade* constructed on the *ubi sunt* formula: *Mais ou sont les Marxistes d'antan?* Having done much to disorganize an entire generation, which might otherwise have been prepared to carry American literature through the apathetic crisis of the war, the Stalinist wing of this school is now talking very much like Mr. De Voto about democracy and nationalism, the wonderful union of which will probably become the religion of the next age.

14 I am not trying to lay the entire blame for the rise of New Criticism on the Marxist movement. In fact, I have been arguing that the establishment of New Critical ideology is primarily a function of its adequacy to the historical changes of the period. But what I *am* also arguing, is that the left must accept some responsibility for the fact that, through the concrete struggles of the day, these ideologies, and the corresponding social projects, could be asserted and made to prevail. If the left does not accept some responsibility for major strategic defeats, it will never learn from the historical experience of its limitations and errors.

15 *New Apologists for Poetry*, p. 189.

16 *New Romantics*, p. 3.

17 See chapters 1 and 2 above, especially pp. 18–19.

18 Krieger, p. 189; Foster, pp. 33–4. It is worth noting that far too much of the evidence Foster cites to sustain his position is drawn from statements made by the critics in periods well past their peak influence.

19 See above, pp. 7–8.

20 It should be noted that the negative aspects of initial neoromantic elements in Ransom are weak from the start. There are three moments that are relevant to the general considerations. Firstly, Ransom is already far removed from English romanticism in both time and space. Secondly, romanticism in the United States was more docile and far less hostile to conventional values; in general, a more limited and more idealist movement, even in its protests. Thirdly, romanticism was stifled and deformed by the codes and operative imperatives of the South; the requirements of social cohesion in a slave society were not compatible with a dynamic and creative critical movement. (For material on U.S. romantic critical theory, see Bernard Smith, 'The Criticism of Romance,' pp. 63–133.)

21 Foster, p. 138.

22 'John Crowe Ransom: A Study in Irony,' *The Virginia Quarterly Review*, XI (January 1935), 111. Cf. Cleanth Brooks, *Modern Poetry and the Tradition* (Chapel Hill, 1965), p. 88: 'To an astonishing degree, the problems which engage Ransom's attention turn out to be aspects of one situation: that of man's divided sensibility.'

23 *The Burden of Time: the Fugitives and Agrarians . . .* (Princeton, 1965), p. 261.

Chapter 5 Fugitive and post-Fugitive

1 See Louise Cowan, *The Fugitive Group: A Literary History* (Baton Rouge, La., 1959), p. 5.

2   Ibid., p. xv; John M. Bradbury, *The Fugitives: A Critical Account* (Chapel Hill, 1958), p. 3.
3   Cited in John L. Stewart, *The Burden of Time*, p. 25.
4   W. Y. Elliott, in a letter from Oxford to the other Fugitives, 11 October 1923. Cited in Stewart, p. 36.
5   Allen Tate, 'For John Ransom at Seventy-Five,' *Shenandoah*, XIV (Spring 1963), 8.
6   Cleanth Brooks, 'The Doric Delicacy,' *The Sewanee Review*, LVI (July 1948), 415. Cf. Randall Jarrell, 'John Ransom's Poetry,' *The Sewanee Review*, LVI (July 1948), 388, and F. O. Matthiessen, 'Primarily Language,' *The Sewanee Review*, LVI (July 1948), 401.
7   Stewart, p. 84.
8   John Crowe Ransom, *Selected Poems*, 3rd ed., rev. and enlarg. (London, 1970), pp. 61–2. Hereafter cited in the text as (SP).
9   F. O. Matthiessen, 'American Poetry, 1920–40,' *The Sewanee Review*, LV (January 1947), 40.
10   Robert Penn Warren, 'John Crowe Ransom,' 102–3.
11   Originally in *The Literary Review*, III (14 July 1923); reprinted in *Modern Essays* (second series), ed. Christopher Morley (New York, 1924), pp. 349–50.
12   Ibid., p. 351.
13   I hesitate to use the category of 'partisanship' because of the sense that has been imposed on it by Stalinist deformations of Marxist theory that attempted to enforce the assimilation of both artistic and theoretical production to the politics of state power. I merely wish, in using it, to take note that all ideological production totalizes its object in terms of a determinate historical location, situated within a class structure and in relation with the determinate motions of class struggle and generic development.
14   See *The Calendar of Modern Letters*, I (August 1925), 462.
15   Ibid.
16   Ibid., 463.
17   *The Theory of the Novel: A Historico-philosophical Essay on the Forms of Great Epic Literature*, trans. Anna Bostock (London, 1971), p. 90.
18   John Crowe Ransom, letter to Tate, 20 February 1927. Cited in Cowan, p. 237.
19   John Crowe Ransom, letter to Tate, 5 September 1926. Cited in Cowan, pp. 232–3.
20   Cited in Stewart, p. 266.
21   Ibid., p. 267.
22   John Crowe Ransom, letter to Tate, 3 and 13 April 1927. Cited in Stewart, p. 342.
23   Cited in Cowan, p. 211.
24   Ibid., p. 212.
25   Cf. Walter Benjamin, *Illuminations*, ed. Hannah Arendt, trans. Harry Zohn (New York, 1968), p. 257.
26   *The Wretched of the Earth*, trans. Constance Farrington (Harmondsworth, 1967), p. 180.

27 See Harold M. Baron, 'The Demand for Black Labor: Historical
    Notes on the Political Economy of Racism,' *Radical America*, V
    (March–April 1971), 3 and passim. Also, see Robert S. Starobin,
    'Racism and the American Experience,' *Radical America*, V
    (March–April 1971), 3 and *passim*. Also, see Robert S. Starobin,
    Black Liberation,' *Radical America*, II (July–August 1968), 1–13;
    Robert S. Starobin and Dale Tomich, 'Black Liberation Historiography,'
    Radical America, II (September–October 1968), 24–8; Richard O. Boyer
    and Herbert M. Morais, *Labor's Untold Story*, 3rd ed. (New York,
    1971), *passim*. For more detailed material, see the work of Eugene D.
    Genovese, *The Political Economy of Slavery: Studies in the Economy
    and Society of the Slave South* (New York, 1966); *The World the
    Slaveholders Made: Two Essays in Interpretation* (New York, 1969); and
    *In Red and Black: Marxian Explorations in Southern and
    Afro-American History* (New York, 1971). Also, George Rawick, *The
    American Slave: A Composite Autobiography*, vol. I, *From Sundown
    to Sunup: The Making of the Black Community* (Westport, Conn.,
    1972). The slave narratives in vols 2–19 of *The American Slave: A
    Composite Autobiography* provide invaluable source material. See also
    George Washington Carleton's *The Suppressed Book About Slavery*
    (New York, 1864), prepared in 1857 as part of the abolitionist
    campaign to discredit the slave system, first published in 1864, and
    reprinted in 1968. And Harold D. Woodman, ed., *Slavery and the
    Southern Economy: Sources and Readings* (New York, 1966). For a
    comparative perspective, see some of the essays in Laura Foner and
    Eugene D. Genovese, eds, *Slavery in the New World: A Reader in
    Comparative History* (Englewood Cliffs, N.J., 1969).

28 Ransom wrote ('The Aesthetic of Regionalism,' *The American
    Review*, II, January 1934, 303): 'The peculiar institution of slavery set
    this general area [the South] apart from the rest of the world, gave a
    spiritual continuity to its many regions, and strengthened them under the
    reinforcement of "sectionalism". . . .' And further (p. 308): 'The darkey
    is one of the bonds that make a South out of all the Southern regions.
    Another is the climate.' Cf. Tate (*Stonewall Jackson, The Good
    Soldier*, New York, 1928, p. 39): 'The institution of slavery was a
    positive good only in the sense that Calhoun had argued that it was:
    it had become a necessary element in a stable society. He had argued
    justly that only in a society of fixed classes can men be free.' And, in his
    other biography, of the president of the Confederacy (*Jefferson Davis:
    His Rise and Fall*, New York, 1929, p. 87), Tate specified his preference
    for 'class rule and religion *versus* democracy and science.' The
    contemporary political context should be noted as well. Since its
    revival in Atlanta, Georgia, in 1915, the Ku Klux Klan was rapidly
    expanding. By 1924, that is, about the period when the Fugitives
    began to develop social consciousness, Klan membership was at four and
    a half million at a membership cost of ten dollars (*Labor's Untold
    Story*, p. 34; Stewart, p. 108, gives a figure of six million), and
    constituted a powerful formation against change, so that Ransom and
    others were not alone. The Klan elected politicians to all levels from

mayor to governor to Congress, and dominated the politics and governments of seven states. (By the 1930s when the Agrarians launched full steam ahead into their program, the Klan had declined.) Andrew Lytle, one of the Agrarians, wrote yet another biography (*Bedford Forrest and his Critter Company*, New York, 1931) about the Confederate cavalry commander who later became the Grand Commander of the Ku Klux Klan. The book is an unreserved endorsement of Klan activities. And the following is the perspective in 1930 of another Agrarian, Frank Lawrence Owsley ('The Irrepressible Conflict,' in *I'll Take My Stand: The South and the Agrarian Tradition*, by Twelve Southerners, New York, 1930, p. 62): 'for ten years [after 1865] the South, already ruined by the loss of nearly $2,000,000,000 invested in slaves, with its land worthless, its cattle and stock gone, its houses burned, was turned over to the three millions of former slaves, some of whom could still remember the taste of human flesh and the bulk of them hardly three generations removed from cannibalism. These half-savage blacks were armed.'

29   Letter to Tate, March 1927. Cited in Cowan, p. 214.
30   3 and 13 April 1927. Cited in Stewart, p. 342.

Chapter 6 Agrarianism

1   *God Without Thunder: An Unorthodox Defence of Orthodoxy* (London, 1931), p. xii. Hereafter cited in the text as (GWT).
2   *Mythologies*, trans. Annette Lavers (London, 1972), p. 146.
3   See Herbert Marcuse, *Negations: Essays in Critical Theory* (Boston, 1969), pp. 21–2.
4   Cf. Tate in 1930 ('Religion and the Old South,' *Essays of Four Decades*, London, 1970, p. 570): 'For the social structure depends on the economic structure, and economic conviction is still, in spite of the beliefs of economists from Adam Smith to Marx, the secular image of religion.'
5   'Flux and Blur in Contemporary Art,' *The Sewanee Review*, XXXVII (July 1929), 361.
6   See chapter 3, n. 1.
7   *History and Class Consciousness: Studies in Marxist Dialectics*, trans. Rodney Livingstone (London, 1971), p. 88. See also Karl Marx, *Capital: A Critical Analysis of Capitalist Production*, trans. Samuel Moore and Edward Aveling, ed. Frederick Engels (Moscow, 1965), I, pp. 374–6, 423–4, 460.
8   Karl Marx, *Grundrisse: Foundations of the Critique of Political Economy (Rough Draft)*, trans. Martin Nicolaus (Harmondsworth, 1973), p. 163. All further references are to this edition.
9   Ibid., p. 700.
10   Ibid., pp. 461, 455.
11   Ibid., pp. 409–10.
12   Ibid., p. 693.
13   Ibid., p. 706.

14 Ibid., p. 832.
15 John Crowe Ransom, 'Classical and Romantic,' *The Saturday Review of Literature*, VI (14 September 1929), 127.
16 Ibid.
17 Ibid.
18 Ibid., 125.
19 Ibid., 127.
20 Ibid.
21 *History and Class Consciousness*, p. 136.
22 Cf. Alfred Schmidt, *The Concept of Nature in Marx* (London, 1971), pp. 168, 169, 174; *Capital*, I, pp. 181, 508; *Grundrisse*, pp. 488–9.
23 The Distributists, especially Hilaire Belloc and G. K. Chesterton, were most significantly active in the first two decades of the twentieth century. They opposed capitalism and expected it to disappear. They urged the Distributist or Proprietary State, the generalization of ownership in the means of production. Like the Agrarians, they blended religious and philosophical ideas with their economic ideas. The Distributist influence reached Tate through Eliot. For a discussion of Distributists, see Seward Collins, 'Editorial Notes: Belloc and the Distributists,' *The American Review*, II (November 1933), 122–8.
24 See Seward Collins, 'Editorial Notes,' *The American Review*, I, (April 1933), 122–7. Collins, the editor, raised sympathetically in this first issue the question of fascist political changes and of the relative worth of democratic institutions. Also, he wrote, 'The Fascist economics, in particular, . . . are badly in need of sympathetic exposition' (p. 127).
25 John Crowe Ransom, 'The South—Old or New?,' *The Sewanee Review*, XXXVI (April 1928), 140. Reproduced as 'Reconstructed But Unregenerate' in *I'll Take My Stand* (New York, 1930).
26 'Reconstructed But Unregenerate,' *I'll Take My Stand*, p. 12. My italics. Italicized words not in the 1928 version; added in 1930.
27 'The South—Old or New?,' 139.
28 'The Bankruptcy of Southern Culture,' *Scribner's Magazine*, XCIX (May 1936), 296.
29 'A Liberal Looks at Tradition,' *The Virginia Quarterly Review*, XII (January 1936), 70.
30 Ransom writes ('Reconstructed But Unregenerate,' *I'll Take My Stand*, p. 14): 'Slavery was a feature monstrous enough in theory, but, more often than not, humane in practice.' Such racist mystifications of the Southern past even today find their casual echoes (see Frank Kermode, 'Old Orders Changing,' *Encounter*, XV, August 1960, 73): 'The Negro . . . was not—effectively at any rate—exploited (all parties, including Mr. Tate's Agrarians, seem to be agreed that the slave system was extremely, perhaps disastrously, wasteful).'
31 'The South—Old or New?,' 147.
32 Cited in John L. Stewart, *The Burden of Time* (Princeton, 1965), pp. 148–9.
33 ' "I'll Take My Stand": A History,' *The American Review*, V (Summer 1935), 313.

34 Cf. Ernest Mandel, *Marxist Economic Theory*, trans. Brian Pearce (London, 1968), I, pp. 288–92: Mandel shows that capitalist property-relations do not necessarily coincide in agriculture with capitalist production-relations, that the former come first and may oppose the latter for a long time.
35 Davidson, 306–7.
36 Ibid., 315.
37 Allen Tate's satiric article ('The Problem of the Unemployed: A Modest Proposal,' *The American Review*, I, May 1933, 129–49), modeled on Swift, poses the alternatives most sharply. The narrator compares three possible solutions for the problem of unemployment, of which two, Communism and Agrarianism (Property System) are, he says, 'totally subversive of the American system' (134). If unemployment continues or increases, the argument goes, there will be a revolution; Communists will redistribute the products of production and 'by eliminating the price-system and the creation of surplus value for the five percent of the population who own the means of production, they will put everyone to work like robots . . .' (134–5). Agrarians, by contrast, are totally irresponsible, fail to differentiate Capitalism from Communism, and argue 'that under either system the labour is slave labour' (136). They are blind to the 'great discovery of our age that man is chiefly a consumer' (137); and they proclaim the collapse of civilization unless we return to small property, 'as if civilization did not begin with the American system!' (137). The third solution, the one he goes on to propose, is 'merely one of readjustment,' 'in the spirit of American progress' (134), and 'absolutely necessary' (132) to save the American system. It involves killing 25 million people, the 8 million unemployed workers and their families, their lives not worth living anyway without work and consumption of machine produced goods (149). He suggests lethal gas but is content to leave the method to the specialists, noting that the bodies can be made valuable use of as raw materials—carbon, potassium, etc. (147–8). Hitler's 'final solution,' real life, not satire, points up the tragic historical irony of this chilling value rejection of the American system in a thinly veiled satiric anticipation of horror unless Agrarianism (or some such alternative to the American way of life) comes to prevail.
38 'The Hind Tit,' *I'll Take My Stand*, p. 203.
39 'Introduction: A Statement of Principles' [unsigned], *I'll Take My Stand*, pp. xiii–xiv.
40 Ibid., pp. xiv–xv.
41 Ibid., p. xx.
42 'Hearts and Heads,' *The American Review*, II (March 1934), 566–7.
43 'Introduction,' *I'll Take My Stand*, p. xvii.
44 'Hearts and Heads,' 566.
45 'Introduction,' *I'll Take My Stand*, p. xvii.
46 'The State and Land,' *The New Republic*, LXX (17 February 1932), 8.
47 Ibid., 9.
48 'Happy Farmers,' *The American Review*, I (October 1933), 530.
49 'Hearts and Heads,' 570; 'The South Is a Bulwark,' *Scribner's*

Magazine, XCIX (May 1936), 300. The position is linked to the call for 'moral, social, and economic autonomy' for the South in the 'Introduction,' *I'll Take My Stand*, p. x.

50   It should be noted that Ransom's concerns had a real basis in the terrible plight of farmers after the First World War and in the inhuman conditions of existence of U.S. agricultural workers. The overproduction of agricultural goods has been a fact since the last quarter of the nineteenth century, and between 1929 and 1934 a million farmers lost their property through foreclosure. (Richard O. Boyer and Herbert M. Morais, *Labor's Untold Story*, New York, 1971, p. 260.) In fact, the world agricultural crisis stretched back into the boom period. Between 1925 and 1934 Agricultural Malthusianism triumphed in the bourgeois world as 'a permanent psychosis of agricultural overproduction.' (Mandel, *Marxist Economic Theory*, I, p. 295. Mandel notes that bonuses were given for not cultivating land, for not growing certain crops; 'Eight million head of cattle were slaughtered in the U.S.A. in 1934. The area planted with cotton was reduced by nearly a half in that country—from 17.3 million hectares, on the average, between 1923 and 1929, to 9.8 million in 1938.') It is with this ideology for restricting production that Ransom's work is linked. It distorts completely the existing relations and possibilities. It advocates a type of asceticism which, whether it comes from the right or from the left, is always an ideology of inhumanity. And it renounces the great historical feature of capital, that is, the production of surplus labor beyond the minimum required for the immediate maintenance of life, the production of surplus labor that is 'superfluous labour from the standpoint of mere use value, mere subsistence' (*Grundrisse*, p. 325). Raising the production and reproduction of social existence beyond the subsistence level is the decisive historical contribution of capitalism. In abrogating this development by turning to the forms of the past, Ransom locks his position into an ineffectual individualism and absorbs complicity in the evils he condemns. As Marx said (*Grundrisse*, p. 162):

> In earlier stages of development, the single individual seems to be developed more fully, because he has not yet worked out his relationships in their fullness, or erected them as independent social powers and relations opposite himself. It is as ridiculous to yearn for a return to that original fullness as it is to believe that with this complete emptiness history has come to a standstill.

In other words, a critical comportment that is oriented to the past is contradictory and self-destructive. The reactionary critique remains abstract and unrealized. The methodological key to this problem is that the features of the present that must be the targets of a profound and inexorable critique reveal their full nature and importance, not when compared with a past period of history, but only when measured against the future, that is, against the concrete potentialities of the present.

51   See Ransom, 'Introduction,' *I'll Take My Stand*, p. xiv; 'Reconstructed But Unregenerate,' *I'll Take My Stand*, p. 23; 'Hearts and Heads,' 567; 'The Aesthetic of Regionalism,' 305.

52   At the same time that he criticized the slavishness of mechanized labor,

Ransom railed against the partisans of labor and attacked Communist sentimentality about the workers whom he saw as essentially simple, herdlike, and unintelligent. ('What Does the South Want?' *The Virginia Quarterly Review*, XII, April 1936, 190–3.) That is no more than could be expected from a position arguing not the recuperation but the renunciation of human productive forces, of work as man's world- and self-creating activity. W. T. Couch noted in 1937, in regard to a recently enacted Mississippi law that aimed to balance industry and agriculture, that the laws contained absolutely no protection for labor with respect to the kind of job, the hours of work, the conditions of labor, or the wages. Fairly typically, the Agrarian opposition to human exploitation seemed not to find its way into the laws in the form of labor protection. ('The Agrarian Romance,' *The South Atlantic Quarterly*, XXXVI, October 1937, 421.)

53 Couch, 'The Agrarian Romance,' 429. While Ransom wrote that the condition of black and white tenant farmers was the 'most urgent of all our permanent economic problems' and referred to the Agrarian solution ('Sociology and the Black Belt,' *The American Review*, IV, December 1934, 153–4), black and white sharecroppers were coming together in the Sharecroppers' Union and following the Populist advice to 'raise less corn and more hell!' (see Boyer and Morais, *Labor's Untold Story*, p. 264). While Edmund Wilson wrote that 'to this day, the relations in the South between the landowning gentry and the Negroes are more intimate and, in a sense, more human than the relations between the mill-owner and the workers in his factory' ('Tennessee Agrarians,' *The New Republic*, LXVII, 29 July 1931, 281), the same issue of the journal reported the murder of black people in Tallapoosa County, Alabama, for meeting in the Sharecroppers' Union to protest the Scottsboro case and to press demands upon the landowners ('The Week,' *The New Republic*, LXVII, 29 July 1931, 272). And the same isssue also carried an International Labor Defense report that Tallapoosa County landlords were paying men fifty cents, and women and children twenty-five cents, a day for work in the fields, and had refused to supply food for the six weeks from 1 July to 15 August (ibid., 270–1).

54 See the very interesting article by Mark D. Naison, 'The Southern Tenant Farmers' Union and the CIO,' *Radical America*, II (September–October 1968), 36–56. Naison analyzes aspects of the suffering and struggles for liberation among the eight million sharecroppers and tenant farmers on Southern cotton plantations during the depression. The New Deal's liberal Agricultural Adjustment Act (part of the Agricultural Malthusian program to which Ransom's ideology is linked), in the planters' interest, only intensified the crisis of the tenant. In 1934, in the cotton belt of Arkansas, the STFU was forced to attack the New Deal's cotton program, which reduced acreage to raise prices and led to labor reductions and evictions. The interracial union's activities were at first paternalistic socialist-reformist, exposing injustice through the courts, speaking tours, books, and pamphlets in order to appeal to conscience. Rapidly, under pressure of the

enthusiastic response to the union's organizing campaigns, the emphasis shifted from legal and educational work to mass action. At mass meetings, croppers demanded the seizure of plantations; by the beginning of 1935, membership exceeded 10,000 in eighty local units. When planters moved to arrest black organizers, mobs of white sharecroppers sometimes arrived to liberate them from jail. The union emerged as a 'total institution,' absorbing the entire life process of its members. It organized against school boards, relief agencies, courts, health programs, and police forces, as well as planters, to attack all aspects of the dehumanized cropper life. The first strike in 1935, after a war of nerves and much bloodshed, was effective. Then organization spread to Oklahoma, Missouri, Tennessee, and Mississippi, and the press began to report the terror that greeted sharecropper protest. Membership by the end of 1935 was 25,000. New Deal response, for example the appropriation of $50 million per year to place impoverished tenants on subsistence farms, 'was only a quixotic diversion in a sector of the economy where large-scale units alone could be profitable' (42). The union had to gain functional control of the plantation system; to transform U.S. politics, it sought the alliance of the newly vitalized wing of the labor movement, the CIO. The rest of the story is incredibly depressing and consists of the destruction of the radical STFU by the CIO and the Communist Party following a non-political and bureaucratic strategy of unionization designed to rationalize the capitalist economy. By 1939 the STFU was effectively dead in any radical capacity.

55 'Reconstructed But Unregenerate,' *I'll Take My Stand*, pp. 26–7.

56 In *The World's Body* (New York, 1938), p. 140, hereafter cited in the text as (WB), Ransom specifies the ontologically secondary character of religion, now considered to be effectively a parasite: 'Religion depends for its ontological validity upon a literary understanding, and that is why it is frequently misunderstood.' Ransom contends (p. 43) that 'religion is an institution existing for the sake of its ritual,' and thus provides a popular theorization for the modern phenomenon of religionists who disclaim any adherence to religious doctrine yet discover themselves inescapably attached to religious liturgy, that is, to a form of disciplined, preconstituted communality. The phenomenon has its roots in the modern transformations of the social metabolism in a corporatist direction.

57 *The Fugitives: A Critical Account* (Chapel Hill, 1958), p. 114.

58 Contemporary structuralism, in this regard, can be seen as a dogmatic ultra-rationalism that suppresses the contingent ontological field for which it substitutes a fully rationalizable epistemological field. It is upon this latter that it performs its systematic formalizations. It is to date the most precise theoretical incarnation of manipulative neocapitalist rationalization.

59 *History and Class Consciousness*, p. 120.

60 See *The Crisis of European Sciences* (Evanston, Ill., 1970).

61 It is worth noting, as has been argued (see Mihály Vajda, 'Marxism, Existentialism, Phenomenology: A Dialogue,' *Telos*, no. 7, Spring 1971,

10–13), that Husserl's brilliant achievement none the less deals
only with fetishistic consciousness and not with alienation and
reification, the actual rule of man-made objectifications over man.
Thus he, like Ransom, tends to consider the objectivistic attitude of
science and of everyday thinking as a cause of human crisis, and is
unable to explain why such false rationalism prevails.

62   *Essays of Four Decades*, p. 157.
63   In this context, it is important to be aware of New Critical sexism.
In a study of a literary ideology as powerful and widespread as the
New Criticism, it is important to relate its position to the key U.S.
ideological structures of sexism, racism, and chauvinism. The racism has
been fully evident through the examination of Agrarian writings.
National chauvinism is powerful enough to emerge in Ransom, in spite of
sectional allegiances and a posture of internal polarization, as soon as
it can come to a question of comparing the United States to any
other country. He advocates converting foreign war credits into a vast
educational fund for those U.S. nationals to study abroad who will use
their opportunities 'wisely and patriotically' ('Shall We Complete the
Trade?' *The Sewanee Review*, XLI, April 1933, 187); he proposes the
erection of a new capital city that is defined as 'larger, more modern,
and more beautiful than any city on earth' ('A Capital for the New
Deal,' *The American Review*, II, December 1933, 136); he considers
that the United States is better able than any other human society
'to afford the luxury of freedom' ('The South Is a Bulwark,' 301); and
what he wants to achieve with the whole Agrarian program is 'farmers
with more room, and more heart, than most of the farmers of the
world' ('Happy Farmers,' 531). All three ideologies fit easily into a
binary typology appropriate to Ransom's dualism, but perhaps the
masculine-feminine duality does so most conveniently. It is to be noted
that it occupies an important place in Ransom's work. Sexist concepts
structure several of the essays, and sexist ideology becomes a reliable
vehicle for Ransom's reactionary philosophical dualism. To return to the
question of intellectuality, Ransom explains, in an extraordinary essay
entitled 'The Poet As Woman' (WB 76–110), that, in comparison to men,
women are 'indifferent to intellectuality' (78). Indeed, Edna St Vincent
Millay's limitation is 'her lack of intellectual interest. It is that which
the male reader misses in her poetry, even though he may acknowledge
the authenticity of the interest which is there. I used a conventional
symbol, which I hope was not objectionable, when I phrased this lack of
hers: deficiency in masculinity' (98). Intellect is clearly identified,
a priori, as masculine; even empirical evidence cannot challenge this
'conventional' formulation. If some male poets are not intellectual, they
yield to 'feminine exercise;' if some women poets are intellectual, they
have some masculine characteristics. On one hand, the sexist categories
are used structurally; on the other, they are sexually identified:
women 'are not strict enough and expert enough to manage forms'
(103); and no 'obligation can lie upon the male adult requiring him
to assist at this sort of thing' (104). The view of femininity as an absence, a
lack, a deficiency, as in Freud, is not only vicious, but indicates an

area of the generally reactionary Freudian intervention in modern
critical theory. Two more examples from Ransom: in 'The South—Old
or New?', 140–2, Progress and Service are the masculine and feminine
forms of materialistic ambition: mastery and seduction respectively;
and in 'Flux and Blur in Contemporary Art,' 365, a listing of formless
and meaningless works of art is described as 'feminine rather than
masculine.' Tate, somewhat kinder to Emily Dickinson than Ransom to
Millay, probes 'her intellectual deficiency' (*Essays of Four Decades*,
p. 291); decides 'she cannot reason at all. She can only see' (289). His
essay on his friend ('Hart Crane: The Poet as Hero,' *Essays*, pp. 324–8)
is a sexist discourse on homosexuality and the 'victims' of homosexual
'neurosis' (325). And elsewhere (*Essays*, p. 555) Tate says, without any
self-consciousness: 'The woman in Mr. Eliot's poem *The Waste Land* is, I
believe, the symbol of man at the present time.' As early as 1925, in
The Fugitive, Robert Penn Warren criticizes Joseph Anslander's
poetry for emotionality, lack of 'cerebration,' 'feminine exaggeration'
(cited in Cowan, *The Fugitive Group*, p. 190). Later, Warren and
another Fugitive, Alfred Starr, dispute whether women are the highest
form of 'amusement' (Starr) or 'bemusement' (Warren) (*Fugitives'
Reunion: Conversations at Vanderbilt, May 3–5, 1956*, ed. Rob Roy
Purdy (Nashville, 1959), p. 69). And a last quotation from a major
critic outside the present group (F. O. Matthiessen, 'American Poetry,
1920–40,' *The Sewanee Review*, LV, January 1947, 50), in regard to
Marianne Moore: 'She is feminine in a very rewarding sense, in
that she makes no effort to be major.' The ideology runs wide and deep,
and is surprisingly explicit in this tradition.
64 *Selections from the Prison Notebooks*, ed. and trans. Quentin Hoare
and Geoffrey Nowell Smith (London, 1971), p. 445.
65 See Lukács, *Aesthetics*, II, p. 592. Cf. *Aesthetics*, II, pp. 563–626;
History and Class Consciousness, p. 234.
66 Visibility in painting is a homogeneous medium that concentrates *all*
aspects of life into itself. It is an error to mistake this, as Ransom appears
to do, for a *limited* field of sensory appropriation.
67 *Aesthetics*, I, p. 471.
68 Cf. *Aesthetics*, I, pp. 470–3.
69 Ibid., II, p. 368.
70 Cf. W. K. Wimsatt, *Hateful Contraries: Studies in Literature and
Criticism* (Lexington, 1966), p. 76: 'My own view is that it is impossible
for literary theory to make anything of *any* effective version of
katharsis, but that the theory itself is a harmless enough psychiatric
appendage to Aristotle's actual literary theory. We can take it or leave it.'
71 Cf. Christopher Caudwell's 'mirror revolutionaries,' *Illusion and
Reality: A Study of the Sources of Poetry* (New York, 1937), p. 90.
72 For brief discussions of Kantian 'disinterestedness,' see Lukács,
Aesthetics, I, pp. 270, 750–1.
73 'The Making of a Modern: The Poetry of George Marion O'Donnell,'
The Southern Review, I (Spring 1936), 872.
74 *Eros and Civilization: A Philosophical Inquiry into Freud* (New York,
1955), p. 18.

75 'The Making of a Modern,' 872.
76 John L. Stewart, *John Crowe Ransom*, University of Minnesota, Pamphlets on American Writers, no. 18 (Minneapolis, 1962), p. 44; John M. Bradbury, *The Fugitives: A Critical Account*, p. 130.
77 *Modern Poetry and the Tradition* (Chapel Hill, 1965), pp. 11–12.
78 'Hypothetical' later becomes a basic category in Northrop Frye's theory.
79 *History and Class Consciousness*, p. 139.

Chapter 7 New Criticism

1 'In Amicitia,' *The Sewanee Review*, LXVII (October 1959), 534, 536.
2 *The Fugitive Group: A Literary History* (Baton Rouge, La., 1959), p. xix.
3 Cf. Thomas S. Kuhn, *The Structure of Scientific Revolutions* (Chicago, 1962), pp. 64–5.
4 'The Irish, The Gaelic, The Byzantine,' *The Southern Review*, VII (Winter 1942), 541.
5 *The New Criticism* (Norfolk, Conn., 1941), p. 216. Hereafter cited in the text as (NC).
6 'Criticism as Pure Speculation,' *The Intent of the Critic*, ed. Donald A. Stauffer (Princeton, 1941), pp. 101–2.
7 'Ubiquitous Moralists,' *The Kenyon Review*, III (Winter 1941), 95.
8 'The Teaching of Poetry,' *The Kenyon Review*, I (Winter 1939), 81.
9 'Mr. Tate and the Professors,' *The Kenyon Review*, II (Summer 1940), 349–50.
10 'Strategy for English Studies,' *The Southern Review*, VI (Autumn 1940), 235, 226–7.
11 'Poets and Flatworms,' *The Kenyon Review*, XIV (Winter 1952), 159.
12 *The Kenyon Review* was discontinued in 1970.
13 The sessions of the Kenyon School of English in the late 1940s brought together a glittering list of critics. The following is a list, from an advertisement at the beginning of vol. XI (1949) of *The Kenyon Review*, of the fellows for the Second Session from 23 June to 6 August 1949. Senior Fellows: F. O. Matthiessen, John Crowe Ransom, Lionel Trilling. Fellows: Eric Bentley, Richard Blackmur, Cleanth Brooks, Kenneth Burke, Richard Chase, William Empson, Alfred Kazin, L. C. Knights, Robert Lowell, Philip Rahv, Herbert Read, Philip Blair Rice, Mark Schorer, Allen Tate, Austin Warren, Robert Penn Warren, Rene Wellek, Basil Willey, Yvor Winters, Morton Dauwen Zabel.
14 With Robert Penn Warren, *Understanding Poetry: An Anthology for College Students* (New York, 1938); and *Understanding Fiction* (New York, 1943). With Robert Heilman, *Understanding Drama* (New York, 1948). Brooks also put together, with Warren, two textbooks of rhetoric in 1949 and 1950. Ransom also published two textbooks: *Topics for Freshman Writing* (New York, 1935), and *A College Primer of Writing* (New York, 1943). And, in addition to their own poetry and prose, the New Critics published dozens of anthologies of poetry, fiction, and essays.

15   *A College Primer of Writing*, p. iv.

16   'Criticism as Pure Speculation,' p. 103.

17   'The Inorganic Muses,' *The Kenyon Review*, V (Spring 1943), 284.

18   Ibid., 291.

19   'Short Notice: The Rebirth of Liberal Education by Fred B. Millett,' *The Kenyon Review*, VIII (Winter 1946), 176.

20   'The Inorganic Muses,' 293.

21   'The Present Function of Criticism,' *Essays of Four Decades* (London, 1970), p. 199.

22   'Art Needs a Little Separating,' *The Kenyon Review*, VI (Winter 1944), 118.

23   Cited in Stewart, *The Burden of Time* (Princeton, 1965), p. 309.

24   'A Mirror for Artists,' *I'll Take My Stand* (New York, 1930), p. 50.

25   'Introduction: A Statement of Principles,' *I'll Take My Stand*, pp. xv–xvi.

26   'On the "Brooks–MacLeish Thesis,"' *Partisan Review*, IX (January–February 1942), 40–1.

27   'Art and the Human Economy,' *The Kenyon Review*, VII (Autumn 1945), 683–8, especially 685–6.

28   Ibid., 687.

29   See above, pp. 6–7.

30   By contrast, Donald Davidson (*Fugitives' Reunion*, ed. Rob Roy Purdy, Nashville, 1959, p. 181) recalls that the Agrarians defended and sought an order of life where politics, economics, and poetry were not separated; the modern 'separation of them into specialities' is what destroys poetry.

31   Ihab H. Hassan, 'Criticism as Mimesis,' *The South Atlantic Quarterly*, LV (October 1956), 475.

32   See William Elton, 'A Glossary of the New Criticism,' *Poetry*, LXXIII (December 1948), 153–62; LXXIII (January 1949), 232–45; and LXXIII (February 1949), 296–307.

33   Lukács, *History and Class Consciousness* (London, 1971), p. 104.

34   Yvor Winters attacks the consequences in terms of his doctrine of the fallacy of expressive form (*In Defense of Reason*, Denver, 1947, pp. 536–7). John Stewart, in his own admission repeatedly confused by the point, argues that the poem is a statement 'about,' not 'like,' its subject (*John Crowe Ransom*, Minneapolis, 1962, p. 45). And Francis X. Roellinger, Jr, who holds the neoscholastic anti-cognitive doctrine that the end of poetry is joy in encountering a perfect object, and is thus even less susceptible than Ransom to a view that the joy in art is the joy of experiencing a defetishized human world, rejects the hypothesis of harmony between poetic strategy and the constitution of the world ('Two Theories of Poetry as Knowledge,' *The Southern Review*, VII, Spring 1942, 705, 700).

35   'Flux and Blur in Contemporary Art,' 363.

36   'Humanism at Chicago,' *The Kenyon Review*, XIV (Autumn 1952), 658. Also in *Poems and Essays* (New York, 1955), p. 100.

37   'Poetry: I. The Formal Analysis,' *The Kenyon Review*, IX (Summer 1947), 436.

38 'Criticism as Pure Speculation,' p. 109.
39 Ibid., p. 110.
40 'Artists, Soldiers, Positivists,' *The Kenyon Review*, VI (Spring 1944), 279.
41 See, for example, Stallman, *Critiques and Essays in Criticism* (New York, 1949), p. 500 n. 6. See also R. S. Crane's criticism (*The Language of Criticism and the Structure of Poetry*, Toronto, 1953, p. 22), often adopted by other critics, to the effect that much of what Ransom considers texture would become part of structure if he made his paraphrase of the argument 'more precise,' that is, more qualified. Ransom's rebuttal to a similar point by Wimsatt serves to answer, on the level on which the dispute was pressed, both critics ('The Concrete Universal: Observations on the Understanding of Poetry,' *The Kenyon Review*, XVI, Autumn 1954, 557): Ransom argues that of course the concrete detail will not appear partly extraneous to the concept or universal 'if we won't let it; that is if we keep qualifying the concept . . . by every bit of the poem's concreteness, for then it becomes tautological to say that all the detail qualifies the concept. . . .' He had in mind the practical, 'efficient sort' of concept, 'which is taken with the minimum of qualifiers when we define it or use it.'
42 It should be noted, as well, that the multiplicity of Ransom's rational structures operating relatively independently and linked only tangentially by the contingencies which exceed them, is itself a relativistic anticipation of structuralist positions. See 'Acceptance Speech: The National Book Award for Poetry, March 10, 1964,' *The Sewanee Review*, LXXII (July 1964), 549.
43 'Poetry: I. The Formal Analysis,' 442.
44 'The Bases of Criticism,' *The Sewanee Review*, XLII (October 1944), 559, 562.
45 'Poetry: I. The Formal Analysis,' 442.
46 'The Bases of Criticism,' 563.
47 *The Well Wrought Urn: Studies in the Structure of Poetry* (London, 1968), pp. 168–9. See also pp. 58, 162–3, 166.
48 In Frye, and even more in McLuhan, the use of such notions as analogy, myth, juxtaposition (parataxis) without logical connection, and simultaneity, makes possible the rationalization of a significantly expanded range of phenomena, far beyond that which is accessible to a linear logic.
49 Ibid., p. 170.
50 See the 'Introduction' to Ransom's edition of *Selected Poems of Thomas Hardy* (New York, 1961), pp. xix, xxiv.
51 *The Well Wrought Urn*, p. 171.
52 'The Bases of Criticism,' 563.
53 'The Poems of T. S. Eliot: A Perspective,' *New Republic*, CXXVII (8 December 1952), 17.
54 'Poetry: I. The Formal Analysis,' 438.
55 'The Shores of Criticism,' *Partisan Review*, XX (January–February 1953), 109. (Reprinted in *Poems and Essays*, p. 104.)
56 Ibid., 111 (or p. 108).

57 'The Strange Music of English Verse,' *The Kenyon Review*, XVIII (Summer 1956), 465.

58 'Symbolism: American Style,' *New Republic*, CXXIX (2 November 1953), 20.

59 'Poetry: II, The Final Cause,' *The Kenyon Review*, IX (Autumn 1947), 640–58.

60 'The Concrete Universal: Observations on the Understanding of Poetry,' *The Kenyon Review* XVI (Autumn 1954), 554–64, and XVII (Summer 1955), 383–407. The first essay casts the poem as a triple icon in the figure of head, heart, and feet. The second essay is also in *Poems and Essays*, pp. 159–85.

61 'Why Critics Don't Go Mad,' *Poems and Essays*, p. 157.

62 'Humanism at Chicago,' 657–9. Also *Poems and Essays*, pp. 99–101.

Chapter 8 Conclusion to Ransom

1 'Acceptance Speech,' *The Sewanee Review*, LXXII (July 1964), 550.

2 'The Idea of a Literary Anthropologist . . .' *The Kenyon Review*, XXI (Winter 1959), 135, 137.

3 Ibid., 140. Cf. Ransom at the *Fugitives' Reunion* (ed. Rob Roy Purdy, Nashville, 1959, p. 193) in 1956: 'And I must confess that I think it's very healthy that we are starting all over here in this country with a kind of culture which is based on mass consumption.'

4 'William Wordsworth: Notes toward an Understanding of Poetry,' *The Kenyon Review*, XII (Summer 1950), 509–10.

5 'New Poets and Old Muses,' in *American Poetry at Mid-Century*, by John Crowe Ransom, Delmore Schwartz and John Hall Wheelock. Lectures Presented Under the Auspices of the Gertrude Clarke Whittall Poetry and Literature Fund (Washington: Reference Dept, Library of Congress, 1958), p. 11.

6 'Alienation a Century Ago,' *The Kenyon Review*, XV (Spring 1953), 336.

7 'Art and the Human Economy,' *The Kenyon Review*, VII (Autumn 1945), 685–6.

8 *Fugitives' Reunion*, p. 193.

9 'The Communities of Letters,' *Poems and Essays* (New York, 1955), pp. 116–17.

10 Lukács, *History and Class Consciousness* (London, 1971), p. 202.

11 John Holloway, 'The Critical Intimidation,' *The Hudson Review*, (Winter 1953), 487–8.

12 Already during the Fugitive period, Stanley Johnson, one of the group, in his novel (*Professor*, New York, 1925) offered an incredibly obscure modernist poem about coffee, 'Ebullient Bean,' for analysis, and burlesqued the Fugitive methods of close textual reading. See Cowan, *The Fugitive Group* (Baton Rouge, La., 1959), pp. 194–6. But the best critique I have seen of the subjectivism of New Critical close reading, one which I include as Appendix A with great delight, is Theodore Spencer's brilliant parody of an analysis of the poem 'Thirty Days

Hath September': 'How to Criticize a Poem (In the Manner of Certain Contemporary Critics),' *The New Republic*, CIX (6 December 1943), 816, 818.
13   Cf. 'The First *Telos* International Conference: "The New Marxism"—Waterloo, Ontario, October 8–11, 1970,' *Telos*, no. 6 (Fall 1970), 314.

Chapter 9   Mythological structuralism

1   'Ghostlier Demarcations,' *Northrop Frye in Modern Criticism: Selected Papers from the English Institute*, ed. Murray Krieger (New York, 1966), p. 109.
2   'Utopian History and the *Anatomy of Criticism*,' ibid., p. 32.
3   'Reflections in a Mirror,' ibid., p. 133.
4   Murray Krieger, 'Northrop Frye and Contemporary Criticism: Ariel and the Spirit of Gravity,' ibid., p. 1.
5   'The Encyclopaedic, Two Kinds of,' *Poetry*, XCI (February 1958), 328.
6   It is worth observing that Frye, and later McLuhan, both Canadians, are, like Ransom the Southerner, major 'outsiders' in the history of cultural ideology (see above, p. 44).
7   'The Critical Path: An Essay on the Social Context of Literary Criticism,' *Daedalus, Journal of the American Academy of Arts and Sciences*, XCIX (Spring 1970), 268. Hereafter cited in the text as (CP).
8   *Anatomy of Criticism: Four Essays* (Princeton, 1957), p. 342. Hereafter cited in the text as (AC).
9   *Fables of Identity: Studies in Poetic Mythology* (New York, 1963), p. 127. Hereafter cited in the text as (FI).
10   'The Road of Excess,' *Myth and Symbol: Critical Approaches and Applications*, ed. Bernice Slote (Lincoln, Nebraska, 1963), p. 17.
11   Northrop Frye, ed., *Selected Poetry and Prose of William Blake*, by William Blake (New York, 1953), p. xxv.
12   Northrop Frye, 'Nature and Nothing,' *Essays on Shakespeare*, ed. Gerald W. Chapman (Princeton, 1965), p. 48.
13   Tran Duc Thao, 'The Rational Kernel in the Hegelian Dialectic,' *Telos*, no. 6 (Fall 1970), 124 (italics added).
14   For important and exhilarating explorations in the dialectic of need and desire, and for discussions of the contemporary shift in the center of gravity of this thoroughly *historical* dialectic from need to desire, from the claims of political economy to the claims of new human possibilities, pleasures, and fulfillments, and for the implications of this commotive shift for *revolution*, see Murray Bookchin, *Post-Scarcity Anarchism* (Berkeley, 1971), especially 'Desire and Need,' pp. 271–86.
15   Northrop Frye, *Fearful Symmetry: A Study of William Blake* (Princeton, 1969), p. 123. Hereafter cited in the text as (FS).
16   Northrop Frye, *The Stubborn Structure: Essays on Criticism and Society* (London, 1970), pp. 206–7. Hereafter cited in the text as (SS).
17   Northrop Frye, 'The Rising of the Moon: A Study of *A Vision*,' *An Honoured Guest: New Essays on W. B. Yeats*, ed. Denis Donoghue and J. R. Mulryne (London, 1965), p. 8.

18   Frye, 'Reflections in a Mirror,' p. 136.
19   'Ghostlier Demarcations,' p. 110.
20   Frye, 'Reflections in a Mirror,' p. 137.
21   Hartman, pp. 110–11, 114, 115.
22   Robin Skelton, 'The House that Frye Built,' *Canadian Literature*, no. 24 (Spring 1965), 63; A. J. M. Smith, 'The Critic's Task: Frye's Latest Work,' *Canadian Literature*, no. 20 (Spring 1964), 6; John Holloway, 'The Critical Zodiac of Northrop Frye,' *The Colours of Clarity: Essays on Contemporary Literature and Education* (London, 1964), p. 153.
23   Walter Sutton, *Modern American Criticism* (Englewood Cliffs, N.J., 1963), p. 183.
24   W. K. Wimsatt, 'Northrop Frye: Criticism as Myth,' *Northrop Frye in Modern Criticism*, p. 98.
25   Northrop Frye, 'Preface,' *The Psychoanalysis of Fire*, by Gaston Bachelard, trans. Alan C. M. Ross (London, 1964), vii.
26   Pauline Kogan, *Northrop Frye: The High Priest of Clerical Obscurantism*, Literature and Ideology Monographs, no. 1 (Montreal, 1969), p. 56.
27   'Structure, Sign, and Play in the Discourse of the Human Sciences,' *The Languages of Criticism and the Sciences of Man: The Structuralist Controversy*, ed. Richard Macksey and Eugenio Donato (Baltimore, 1970), pp. 255, 257.
28   Northrop Frye, 'Literary Criticism,' *The Aims and Methods of Scholarship in Modern Languages and Literatures*, ed. James Thorpe (New York, 1963), p. 61.
29   Ibid., p. 66.
30   Ibid., pp. 63, 68.
31   See Thomas S. Kuhn, *The Structure of Scientific Revolutions* (Chicago, 1962), p. 108.
32   'Structuralisme, marxisme, existentialisme,' *L'Homme et la société*, no. 2 (October–December 1966), 110.
33   Kogan, p. 13.
34   Cf. Lukács, *Aesthetics*, II, p. 145.
35   *Drama from Ibsen to Brecht* (London, 1968), pp. 17–18.
36   Alvin C. Kibel, 'Academic Circles,' *The Kenyon Review*, XXVI (Spring 1964), 422.
37   In this general area is the real basis for the widespread criticism of Frye by defenders of 'minute particularity,' who sense that the autonomy of each work is being violated, although, it must be stressed, the issue ought to be one of intensive totality, not of the extensive totality sought by empiricist critical apprehension.
38   In general, Frye explicitly acknowledges the connections between anagogy and religion (for example AC 120–2). But his general attitude had already been proclaimed a decade before, in the affirmation of a 'structure which will make room for humane values and established religion and not scare the pants off the middle-class reader' ('Toynbee and Spengler,' *The Canadian Forum*, August 1947, 111).

39   Henri Lefebvre has repeatedly argued that since the early part of this century—roughly, since the early preparatory stages of neocapitalism—there has taken place, under the pressure of science, technology, and social changes, a decline of referentials, a destruction of systems of reference to perceptible reality (involving the disappearance of perspectival space from painting and the tonal system from music), and with this, an uncoupling of signifier and signified within the sign. (*Everyday Life in the Modern World*, trans. Sacha Rabinovitch, London, 1971, pp. 112–13, 118–19; *Au-de là du structuralisme*, Paris, 1971, pp. 247–8.) We should understand this rupture of denotation and connotation as a necessary mechanism of manipulative capitalism in its drive for the complete rationalization of a one-dimensional totality. Earlier, Mallarmé and the Symbolists had tried to divorce signifiers from signifieds, meaning from what was meant, in a desperate and abstract protest against the social dehumanization of language and in the search for innocence. When neocapitalism makes the process systematic, the innocence of signifiers is only a transitional step to their greater corruption. In principle, signifiers are freed for a rich expanded field of significances; in practice the associations are provided, sanctioned, and institutionally enforced on the grounds of the existing reality. In principle, signifiers and signifieds can be recoupled *ad libitum*; in practice, all recoupling is formed and controlled by the rule of the commotive categories, and all signifiers articulate the system itself. Frye's view of literature represents the abject surrender of critical theory to this process of rationalization.

40   'Phalanx of Particulars,' *The Hudson Review*, IV (Winter 1952), 631.

41   *The World's Body* (New York, 1938), p. 132.

42   *A Natural Perspective: the Development of Shakespearean Comedy and Romance* (New York, 1965), p. 2.

43   'Nature and Nothing,' p. 58. All three statements date from 1965.

44   Ibid.

45   'Northrop Frye and Contemporary Criticism,' p. 16. Naturally, Frye himself recognizes this distinction in Sidney between 'the golden world of poetry and the brazen world of nature' (CP 340).

46   See Ágnes Heller, *A reneszánsz ember* (Budapest, 1967), p. 151.

47   *An Essay on Liberation* (London, 1969), p. 29.

48   Northrop Frye, *The Educated Imagination* (Toronto, 1963), p. 43.

49   'The Imagination Goes to College,' *Partisan Review*, XXXII (Summer 1965), 466.

50   Northrop Frye, 'The Developing Imagination,' *Learning in Language and Literature* (Cambridge, Mass., 1963), pp. 44–5, 41.

51   'Frye Reconsidered,' *Continuities* (London, 1968), p. 120.

52   'Northrop Frye: Criticism as Myth,' p. 97.

53   See 'Preface to an Uncollected Anthology,' *Studia Varia . . .*, ed. E. G. D. Murray (Toronto, 1957), p. 33; 'Poetry,' *University of Toronto Quarterly*, XXV (April 1956), 291. In a decade of doing the annual review of poetry for the 'Letters in Canada' section of the *University of Toronto Quarterly*, Frye reported and/or shaped and

influenced a growing tendency among Canadian poets toward a 'steadily more professional . . . emphasis on the formal elements of poetry, on myth, metaphor, symbol, image, even metrics' ('Poetry,' *University of Toronto Quarterly*, XXVII, July 1958, 438).

54   Cf. Ernst Fischer, *The Necessity of Art: A Marxist Approach*, trans. Anna Bostock (Harmondsworth, 1963), p. 166.

55   [Review of *The Anatomy of Criticism*,] *University of Toronto Quarterly*, XXVIII (January 1959), 194–5.

56   Ibid., 195–6.

57   *The Educated Imagination*, pp. 20–1.

58   See, for example, John Casey, *The Language of Criticism* (London, 1966), pp. 145–6, 150.

59   Ágnes Heller, 'Shakespeare and History,' *New Left Review*, no. 32 (July–August 1965), 19.

60   For a discussion of open and closed society, see, *inter alia*, Stanley Ryerson, *The Open Society: Paradox and Challenge* (New York, 1965). Frye's discussions of the present are almost unrelieved apologetics, some aspects of which ought to be recorded. He argues 'the decline of confidence in progress' (*The Modern Century*, Toronto, 1967, p. 65; hereafter cited in the text as (MC)) as part of his systematized bulwark against the qualitatively new; 'the only conceivable goal is greater stability' (MC 33). Democracy, in fact, is a 'genuinely revolutionary society, neither about to be revolutionized nor trying to retain its present structure, but mature enough to provide for both change and stability' (SS 60). Indeed, revolution 'can now, in our society, only be associated with some kind of centralized action, usually by the government' (MC 91). He explicitly rejects social revolution as producing a worse situation than the present class inequality ('The Knowledge of Good and Evil,' *The Morality of Scholarship*, ed. Max Black, Ithaca, 1967, p. 12; hereafter cited in the text as (MS)); as it happens, contemporary American social mythology, he claims, is 'an unusually benevolent and well-intentioned one' (MS 17). The test is its realization in practice, and the practice for which Frye and the social mythology provide justification is perhaps the most appalling in human history. He recognizes the alienation of youth, but explicitly rejects imperialist war, exploitation, competition, and racism as possible causes, in favor of 'such factors as noise, pollution and overcrowding' (CP 311–12). Moreover, he says, 'a great deal of youthful spontaneous idealism is obviously being exploited by leaders who do not share it' (318). On the whole, Frye's social analysis is a reductive psychologism that operates in a domesticated Freudian frame. Today there are no tyrants to hate, 'no one essentially different from ourselves' (SS 6); parasite and host are both passive, tyranny 'a projection of . . . pusillanimity' (FS 57). No social action 'such as expropriating a propertied class, would end alienation in the modern world'; 'alienation becomes psychological' (MC 24); the tyrant is part of 'our own death-wish' (25). Frye specifies social Freudianism as the 'democratic counterpart of Marxism' (SS 293); for him, the twentieth-century proletariat is Freudian not Marxist and the issue is the liberation

of the sexual instinct, associated with the creative process, from the repressive anxiety structure of society (CP 304; MC 79; MS 15). Frye simply raises the bankrupt slogan, borrowed from the US Declaration of Independence, of 'life, freedom, and happiness' (MS 15), while his psychologism dismisses, *ex cathedra*, every real social demand. For example, the struggle of Quebec people for liberation from Canadian colonial and class oppression is described as the 'compulsion' of 'neurotic social groups' (MC 44). Finally, in establishing the ironic vision (taken over from the New Criticism), with 'its features of anguish, nausea, and absurdity' (MS 23) as the predominant poetic and social mythology of our day, marking 'the ascendence of a technological society' (SS 53), Frye legitimates the sense of powerlessness in the face of these categories.

61 See above, p. 11.
62 *Society of the Spectacle*, *Radical America*, IV, no. 5, 1970, par. 27.
63 'The Developing Imagination,' p. 56.
64 Northrop Frye, *The Well-Tempered Critic* (Bloomington, 1963), pp. 154–6.
65 Cf. Lukács, *History and Class Consciousness* (London, 1971), p. 191.
66 'The Developing Imagination,' p. 57.
67 See above, pp. 13–14.
68 *The Well-Tempered Critic*, p. 51.
69 *A Natural Perspective: the Development of Shakespearean Comedy and Romance* (New York, 1965), pp. 75–6.
70 This does not apply only to verbal systems. Frye frequently reduces social action to anti-historical mythological form as symbolic drama. Literary criticism, it is claimed, can help to recognize symbolic patterns. Thus People's Park in Berkeley, for example, can be comprehended through the pastoral mode, the principle of the demonic, and the archetypes of the murder of Abel and the expulsion from Eden (CP 336).
71 Cf. Marcuse, *One-Dimensional Man* (Boston, 1964), pp. 247–9.

Chapter 10 Introduction to McLuhan

1 Tribute from the *New York Herald Tribune*, cited on the outside cover of Marshall McLuhan, *Understanding Media: The Extensions of Man* (New York, 1964). Hereafter cited in the text as (UM). This kind of tribute was the typical response to McLuhan from the middle to the late 1960s.
2 Marshall McLuhan and Gerald E. Stearn, 'A Dialogue,' *McLuhan: Hot and Cool . . .*, ed. Gerald E. Stearn (New York, 1967), p. 288.
3 In Frye's social theory, the present system is kept 'open' by the 'myth of freedom' and by the innocence of literary mythology in internal tension within the verbal universe with the uncritical beliefs of hegemonic social mythology. This principle of tension is eliminated by McLuhan. In his view, the electric age moves us into the closed world of 'a new tribal encyclopedia of auditory incantation' ('Introduction,' *The Bias of Communication*, by Harold A. Innis,

Toronto, 1964, p. xi). Science and art are attributed a role mainly in facilitating our adjustment to this world, and do not point beyond it. In other words, they are servants of the closure of the system as a whole. See also the discussion by McLuhan (*The Gutenberg Galaxy: The Making of Typographic Man*, Toronto 1962, pp. 7–8; hereafter cited in the text as (GG)) of open and closed societies, the former based on visual, the latter on auditory technologies.

4   It is appropriate to mention here that McLuhan is a professed Thomist and his work is always susceptible to religious exegesis. Ong is, of course, right that, without making explicit the dogmatic or liturgical implications, McLuhan 'leaves open a hundred doors . . . into every area of Catholic life.' (Walter J. Ong, S.J., 'A Modern Sensibility,' *McLuhan: Hot and Cool*, p. 98). But what has invariably been neglected by McLuhan's critics, whether approving a 'Catholic renascence' (Rudolph E. Morris, review of McLuhan, *McLuhan: Hot and Cool*, p. 90), or criticizing the 'arch-conservative' rehabilitation of Catholic medieval thought (Gerald Taafe, 'Marshall McLuhan— Electronic Medievalist,' *Parallel*, I, July–August 1966, 15, 17), is the material basis for a renewal of Catholic ideology. Just as Protestantism could emerge as the religious form of classical capitalist accumulation, so today it is the development of neocapitalism that is ideologically favorable to corporatist and ritualistic religions and that provides a basis to account for the adequacy of McLuhan's theory as a chief contemporary cultural ideology.

5   *Communications*, rev. ed. (Harmondsworth, 1966), p. 18.

6   *Mass Communications and American Empire* (New York, 1970), p. 76. Defense Department statements to the United States Congress make clear that ' ''the military services are using electronics and the radio spectrum as an integral part of the weapons system. . . . People are paid to invent new ways of using electronics in this way'' ' (ibid., p. 67). Meanwhile, there are one billion illiterates in over a hundred countries. According to the UNESCO Director General, two-thirds of this adult illiteracy could be overcome in a ten-year project costing 200 million dollars a year, that is, 'ten percent of *one year's* budget allocation for U.S. military communications spending' (p. 76). On the international level, communications systems simply reproduce and entrench existing imperialist power relations. With respect to the consortium (Intelsat) formed by nineteen countries on a share basis in 1964 to own and control space communications, involving sixty-four countries by 1970, it is explicitly specified that, regardless of the volume of new membership, 'the United States share cannot fall below 50.6 percent' (p. 136). At the same time, U.S. media are involved in over a hundred countries (pp. 80–2).

7   Mészáros, *Marx's Theory of Alienation* (London, 1970), p. 247.

8   See, for example, McLuhan and Quentin Fiore, *The Medium is the Massage* (New York, 1967), pp. 20, 44, 57, 61; *War and Peace in the Global Village* (New York, 1968), p. 163; McLuhan with Wilfred Watson, *From Cliché to Archetype* (New York, 1970), p. 5. Hereafter cited in the text, respectively, as (MM), (WP), and (CA).

9   Jean Baudrillard, 'Marshall McLuhan: *Understanding Media*,'
     L'Homme et la société, no. 5 (July–September 1967), 230.
10   See Henri Lefebvre, 'Claude Lévi-Strauss et le nouvel éléatisme,'
     Au delà structuralisme (Paris, 1971), p. 271.
11   'Playboy Interview: Marshall McLuhan . . .,' *Playboy* (March
     1969), 70. Hereafter cited in the text as (PI).
12   Cf. Lefebvre, p. 273.
13   *The Mechanical Bride: Folklore of Industrial Man* (New York,
     1951), p. 5. Hereafter cited in the text as (MB). Cf. (GG 77); (MM 150).
     With respect to the maelstrom, to view social reality on the model of
     natural laws is to view social reality through a reified objectivistic
     attitude. Understanding on that model can be the means only to
     submission, not to qualitative change.
14   See above, p. 115.
15   I. A. Richards, *The Philosophy of Rhetoric* (New York, 1965), pp. 56,
     69, rejects the mosaic manipulation of fixed pieces. The harmonic
     stability in McLuhan, based on a mosaic of discontinuities, indicates
     the movement in the tradition.
16   Cf. Claude Lévi-Strauss, *The Savage Mind* (Chicago, 1966),
     pp. 230–1.
17   *Mythologies* (London, 1972), p. 143.
18   See McLuhan's review of Rosemond Tuve's *A Reading of George
     Herbert*: 'Symbolist Communication,' *Thought*, XXVIII (Autumn
     1953), 456–7.
19   'T. S. Eliot,' *Renascence*, III (Autumn 1950), 44. See also McLuhan's
     essays from 1950 and 1951, especially those concerned with the
     'interior landscape' (discontinuous juxtaposition), in *The Interior
     Landscape: The Literary Criticism of Marshall McLuhan, 1943–1962*,
     ed. Eugene McNamara (New York, 1969), particularly pp. 55, 79,
     141, 144, 158, 159, 165–6. Hereafter cited in the text as (LC). See also
     'Joyce, Aquinas, and the Poetic Process,' *Renascence*, IV (Autumn
     1951), 9, 11.
20   'A Survey of Joyce Criticism,' *Renascence*, IV (Autumn 1951), 13.
21   Cf. Mihály Vajda, *Zárójelbe tett tudomány* (Budapest, 1968), pp.
     76–8.
22   *Mythologies*, p. 120.
23   This includes, now transposed to the socio-cultural realm as a
     whole, with greater scope and power, the unification of opposites found
     in New Critical irony.
24   *The Structure of Behaviour*, trans. Alden L. Fisher (London, 1965),
     p. 125.
25   For a discussion of simple fate-stories (myth) versus complex
     choice-stories (plot), see G. S. Fraser, 'Mythmanship,' *The New York
     Review of Books*, I (6 February 1964), 18.
26   Herbert Marcuse, *Reason and Revolution: Hegel and the Rise of Social
     Theory*, 3rd ed. (Boston, 1960), pp. 344–5.
27   Under this heading, most important are the strivings for order and
     equilibrium through official power. McLuhan proposes programming
     whole cultures 'to keep their emotional climate stable in the same way

that we have begun to know something about maintaining equilibrium in the commercial economies of the world.' Thus, perhaps soon, 'we can program twenty more hours of TV in South Africa next week to cool down the tribal temperature raised by radio last week' (UM 41). He is personally eager to get involved in media manipulation of minds and senses to effect behavior therapy; his services have been offered to the Trudeau government, and accepted, on a voluntary, unpaid basis. He told Trudeau that 'he felt that if the government would accept his advice on communications, U.S. trends to violence could be headed off in this country.' (See W. A. Wilson, 'Marshall McLuhan to Advise Trudeau,' *Montreal Star*, 22 October 1968, 55). We might in this context note, too, some of McLuhan's more outrageous statements. People involved in collectivist politics are described as 'puny subliminal automatons aping the patterns of the prevailing electric pressures' (UM 275). Racism: 'Since black is not a color but an interval, may this not be the ultimate secret of Negro mastery of rhythm?' (*Culture Is Our Business*, New York, 1970, p. 226; hereafter cited in the text as (COB)). Racist imperialism: Reading print drains off energy; this is 'the simple reason' why Africans acquiring literacy take to wearing European clothes (WP 159). Also, the North Koreans who captured the U.S. spy ship *Pueblo*, are repeatedly called 'a band of illiterate yokels' (*Counterblast*, London, 1970, p. 74, hereafter cited in the text as (CB); (COB 148, 266)).

28   We should note in particular the anti-Communist, and anti-literacy statements. There are many statements such as 'Marx never studied or understood causality' (CB 57), but we are not interested here in McLuhan's private prejudices. What is more relevant is the social reference. In McLuhan's view, the point of reversal in service environments, the point where corporate services, such as postal routes, transport, telephone, etc., which become available to workers, can no longer be bought for private exclusive use by the owners of private wealth, is 'the invisible moment of change from individualism to communism. It had occurred in England by 1830 at the latest—well before Marx' (COB 322). 'The Marxists spent their lives trying to promote a theory after the reality had been achieved. What they called the class struggle was a spectre of the old feudalism in their rear-view mirror' (CB 140). 'By now Communism is something that lies more than a century behind us, and we are deep into the new age of tribal involvement' (WP 5). And McLuhan does not neglect to 'BLESS the practical communism and cosmic conformity achieved by American MASS-PRODUCTION' (*Counterblast*, Toronto, 1954, p. 7). As regards literacy, its epistemology of matching, which inspires 'a direct correspondence between the input and the experience,' that is, its science and rationality, is false (WP 141), 'a diminution of ontological awareness, or an impoverishment of Being' (GG 52). Perspective, a moment of literacy, brings 'much loss of sensory life' (McLuhan and Harley Parker, *Through the Vanishing Point: Space in Poetry and Painting*, New York, 1968, p. 73; hereafter cited in the text as (VP)). On one hand, single plane awareness is 'totally alien to the nature of

language and of consciousness' (GG 244); on the other, 'all language and experience was, and had always been, this simultaneous and many-layered thing' (CB 83). In general, when the alternatives are described as the distorting hypertrophy of a single sense and the more complete awareness of the 'full interplay of all the senses at once' (GG 52), it is difficult to see how McLuhan is avoiding taking sides, or, rather, how the reader could.

29 McLuhan argues that in electric culture 'we are returning to collective liturgical participation' ('Verbi-Voco-Visual,' *Explorations: Studies in Culture and Communications*, no. 8, October 1957, item 17); that 'the Christian concept of the mystical body—all men as members of the body of Christ—this becomes technologically a fact under electronic conditions' (*McLuhan: Hot and Cool*, p. 261); 'and Christ, after all, is the ultimate extension of man' (PI 72). Explicitly, in fact, McLuhan professes distaste for the process of change while welcoming its results (158).

Chapter 11 Three phases of development

1 In this discussion of the North American tradition, a point must be made about Richards. On one hand, Richards' bias is on the individual side; a theory of interests poses the relation between particular and general from the point of view of the former. On the other, the stress on the organization of particulars, that is, on order and equilibrium, anticipates even the moments of integration and adjustment in the third stage of the tradition. Richards still opposes mass culture, yet points toward its glorification; the development beyond Richards in the tradition is not strictly linear, and in many respects Richards seems to reach beyond his own time. To locate Richards' theory in relation to the North American tradition, which it helped to found and whose development in many respects it comprehends, I want to draw attention to a historical consideration. By the 1920s, notably after the defeat of the 1926 General Strike, the English system was capable of structurally integrating the working class in a way that the United States was not to be until Roosevelt and Truman, nor Canada until the latter years of Mackenzie King. Thus, Richardsian ideology could anticipate North American developments. As England was left behind in technological and social development, it is comprehensible that Richardsian ideology would find a more congenial home in the developing North American tradition.

2 Ágnes Heller uncovers a comparable three-stage dialectic in the development of Plato's system in the context of the decline of the *polis*. She shows his movement from the rebellion of honest moralistic outrage against the corruptions of his age, to an acceptance of transcendence, and from there to a position of apology for the society and of ethical conformism. This motion was inevitable, she argues, since Plato tried to oppose his age with the ideas of a *polis* that was incapable of reversing its disintegration through internal self-renewal. His decay into an apologist signals not his purely personal shipwreck but the fact that the *polis* order is irreversibly gone

(*Az aristotelési etika és az antik ethos* [*Aristotelian Ethics and the Ethos of Antiquity*], Budapest, 1966, especially pp. 127–8). This is the general structure we find in Ransom, in McLuhan, and in the tradition as a whole. What this means in terms of the present discussion is that to oppose to the world a purely moralistic nostalgia for an irrecoverable past leads inexorably to an accommodation with the given facticity of the present. The forms and relations of the present can be opposed effectively only by new forms and new relations. Specifically, in our age, neither precapitalist nor classical capitalist fcrms are recoverable, and effective opposition to neocapitalism means seeking to supersede capitalism altogether through a realization of the real potentialities existing today (and creatable tomorrow) for a higher historical rationality.

3   See chapter 10, n. 19.
4   'G. K. Chesterton: A Practical Mystic,' *The Dalhousie Review*, XV (1936), 457.
5   'The Place of Thomas Nashe in the Learning of His Time' (diss., Cambridge University, April 1943). Hereafter cited in the text as (TN).
6   This is a parallel of Ransom's analyses of scientific-utilitarian positivism. I must insist, however, against all the modern forms of language fetish, that the notion of linguistic *differentia* makes sense only in the context of the work process, of a praxis ontology, both genetically and structurally. The neglect of praxis distorts McLuhan's reading of intellectual history. He fails to understand the historical location of Socratic and Sophist positions in relation to a disintegrating *polis*, just as in the Renaissance he fails to distinguish More and Erasmus, although they were historical opposites: the latter objectively compromised, incapable of either posing or understanding the new problems of his age, the former, a clear-sighted martyr (Cf. Ágnes Heller, *Az aristotelési etika*, *passim*; *A reneszánsz ember*, Budapest, 1967, pp. 28–9).
7   'Introduction,' *Paradox in Chesterton*, by Hugh Kenner (London, 1948), pp. xi–xii.
8   Ibid., pp. xv–xvi.
9   Ibid., p. xvii.
10 Ibid., pp. xvii–xviii.
11 'American Advertising,' *Horizon*, XCIII (October 1947), 134.
12 Ibid., 132–3.
13 Ibid., 135.
14 Ibid., 141.
15 Ibid., 135.
16 Ibid.
17 Ibid., 141.
18 'Mr. Connolly and Mr. Hook,' *The Sewanee Review*, LV (January 1947), 171.
19 'T. S. Eliot,' *Renascence*, III (Autumn 1950), 45.
20 'Joyce, Aquinas, and the Poetic Process,' *Renascence*, IV (Autumn 1951), 5.
21 Cf. Richards, *Principles of Literary Criticism* (London, 1960), p. 241:

'The lunatic will beat any of us at combining odd ideas'; Frye: 'the poet shares with the lunatic and the lover' the categories of analogy and identity ('The Critical Path,' pp. 289–90). This is another instance of the changing notions of rationality that I have been tracing through the tradition. In this regard, we should also note the French structuralist interest in madness.

22 See *Au-delà du structuralisme* (Paris, 1971), pp. 202–3.

23 *Explorations: Studies in Culture and Communication*, no. 1 (December 1953), 3.

24 'Defrosting Canadian Culture,' *American Mercury*, LXXIV (March 1952), 96.

25 'Technology and Political Change,' *International Journal*, VII (Summer 1952), 191.

26 Ibid., 192.

27 'Sight, Sound and the Fury,' *The Commonweal*, LX (9 April 1954), 7.

28 'The Age of Advertising,' *The Commonweal*, LVIII (11 September 1953), 556.

29 Ibid., 555.

30 Paul A. Baran and Paul M. Sweezy, in *Monopoly Capital: An Essay on the American Economic and Social Order* (New York, 1966), p. 115, say that 'in its impact on the economy,' the sales effort 'is outranked only by militarism.'

31 *Illuminations*, ed. Hannah Arendt, trans. Harry Zohn (New York, 1968), p. 226. Cf. Stuart B. Ewen, 'Advertising as Social Production,' *Radical America*, III (May–June 1969), 43, who stresses that the advertising industry obfuscates the complicity of the art forms it produces.

32 'The Age of Advertising,' 556.

33 'Media Log' in Edmund Carpenter and Marshall McLuhan, eds, *Explorations in Communication: An Anthology* (Boston, 1966), p. 182. Hereafter cited in the text as (EC).

34 'Sight, Sound and the Fury,' *The Commonweal*, LX (9 April 1954), 8.

35 *McLuhan* (London, 1971), pp. 88–91.

36 'Harold Adams Innis and Marshall McLuhan,' *McLuhan: Pro and Con*, ed. Raymond Rosenthal (Baltimore, 1969), pp. 281–2.

37 'Introduction,' *The Bias of Communication* by Harold A. Innis (Toronto, 1964), p. ix.

38 'Sight, Sound and the Fury,' 11. See also a later critique of the *Bridge*, 'Myth and Mass Media,' *Daedalus*, LXXXVIII (Spring 1959), 346.

39 'Verbi-Voco-Visual,' *Explorations*, no. 8, item 8.

40 Ibid., item 16.

41 Ibid., item 1.

42 Ibid., item 15.

43 Ibid., item 24.

44 Ibid., item 17.

45 'Myth and Mass Media,' *Daedalus*, LXXXVIII (Spring 1959), 340.

46 Ibid., 342.

47 Ibid., 339–40, 344–5.

48 *Forum* (University of Houston), III (Summer 1960). The phrase also appears in 'Around the World, Around the Clock,' *Renascence*, XII (Summer 1960), 205.

Chapter 12 Technocratic ideology of one-dimensionality

1 'Around the World, Around the Clock', *Renascence*, XII (Summer 1960), 205.
2 'Effects of the Improvements of Communication Media,' *The Journal of Economic History*, XX (December 1960), 572.
3 'Compte Rendu de Marshall MacLuhan [*sic*]: *Understanding Media— The Extensions of Man,' L'Homme et la société*, no. 5 (July–September 1967), 230.
4 'The All-at-Once World of Marshall McLuhan,' *Vogue*, CXXIII (August 1966), 72.
5 Naturally, at the same time that the theory legitimates imperialist war, it strips revolutionary action of its meaning, purpose, and value— of its historical rationality.
6 McLuhan concretizes this perspective on sensory extension chiefly in his pervasive polemic against vision as the dominant sensory modality of a mechanical, specialist, visual-gradient culture of dissociated sensibility, in contrast with the synesthesia of a primitive or electric, zero-gradient culture of simultaneity and unified perception. For notes toward a critique of McLuhan's anti-vision polemic, see Appendix B.
7 *The Human Use of Human Beings: Cybernetics and Society*, 2nd ed. (London, 1954), p. 79.
8 G. R. Boulanger, 'Prologue: What Is Cybernetics?' *Survey of Cybernetics: A Tribute to Dr. Norbert Wiener* (London, 1969), p. 4.
9 It is worth noting that in 1965 McLuhan announced that he was engaged in trying to measure the sensory thresholds of the Toronto population, with the intention of preparing quantitative data for the computer ('Address at Vision 65,' *The American Scholar*, XXXV (Spring 1966), 202).
10 'Notes on Burroughs,' *The Nation*, CXCIX (28 December 1964), 517.
11 Cf. Heller, *A mindennapi élet* (Budapest, 1970), p. 243.
12 XXX, 'L'idéologie technocratique et le teilhardisme,' *Les Temps Modernes*, XX (August 1966), 293.
13 *One-Dimensional Man* (Boston, 1964), p. 11.
14 Cf. two aspects of modern bourgeois ideology as political justification: 'modernization,' discussed by Raymond Williams (ed., *May Day Manifesto 1968*, Harmondsworth, 1968, p. 45), and 'universalism,' discussed by Herbert Marcuse (*Negations*, Boston, 1969, p. 7). McLuhan's constructions comprehend both.
15 Hans Magnus Enzensberger, 'Constituents of a Theory of the Media,' *New Left Review*, no. 64 (November–December 1970), 36.
16 'Culture without Literacy,' *Explorations: Studies in Culture and Communication*, no. 1 (December 1953), 119.
17 See Mandel, *Marxist Economic Theory* (London, 1968), 1, pp. 28–9.

18 It may be worth noting that this position is comparable to Teilhard de Chardin's metaphysics promising a terminal phase of evolutionary integration where the unification of all human cultures into a single world culture is paralleled in interiority by the psychic concentration of the 'noosphere' into the Omega point of Hyperpersonal Consciousness.

19 See chapter 1, n. 40.

20 See above, pp. 167–70.

21 'Love,' *Saturday Night*, LXXXII (February 1967), 27.

22 Ibid., 25.

Chapter 13 Conclusion to McLuhan

1 Jean-Paul Sartre, *Search for a Method*, trans. Hazel E. Barnes (New York, 1967), p. 124.

2 'Verbi-Voco-Visual,' *Explorations: Studies in Culture and Communication*, no. 8 (October 1957), item 2.

3 Marx, *Grundrisse* (Harmondsworth, 1973), p. 540.

4 For useful material in this respect, see, for example: Sidney Finkelstein, *Sense and Nonsense of McLuhan* (New York, 1968), pp. 15–18, 23, 26; E. H. Gombrich, *The Story of Art* (London, 1961), pp. 164, 410; Hauser, *The Social History of Art* (New York, 1951), II, pp. 11–14, 32–6, 115–16; Kathleen Gough, 'Implications of Literacy in Traditional China and India,' *Literacy in Traditional Societies*, ed. Jack Goody (Cambridge, 1968), pp. 70–84; S. H. Steinberg, *Five Hundred Years of Printing*, 2nd ed. (Harmondsworth, 1961), pp. 25, 117, 166; Samuel Lilley, *Men, Machines and History* . . . , 2nd ed. (New York, 1966), *passim*.

5 *The Necessity of Social Control* (London, 1971), p. 23.

6 'N. Bukharin: Historical Materialism,' trans. Ben Brewster, *Political Writings, 1919–1929: The Question of Parliamentarianism and Other Essays*, ed. Rodney Livingstone (London, 1972), p. 136.

7 Ibid., p. 139.

8 'Maritain on Art,' *Renascence*, VI (Autumn 1953), 44.

9 'Verbi-Voco-Visual,' item 17.

10 'Love,' *Saturday Night*, LXXXII (February 1967), p. 28.

11 Ibid.

12 From the transcript of *The Way It Is* broadcast over CBLT-TV, Toronto 1968, published as 'Mailer, McLuhan and Muggeridge: On Obscenity,' *The Realist*, no. 83 (October 1968), 12.

13 *Society of the Spectacle, Radical America*, IV, no. 5, 1970, par. 20.

14 *Aesthetics*, II, p. 510.

15 Asked why media effect is primarily subliminal, McLuhan replied: '*Grace* is subliminal.' Cited by Christopher Ricks, 'McLuhanism,' *McLuhan: Pro and Con*, ed. Raymond Rosenthal (Baltimore, 1969), p. 103.

16 See Heller, *A mindennapi élet* (Budapest, 1970), pp. 161–2.

17 Barry Day, *The Message of Marshall McLuhan*, 3rd ed. (London, 1967), pp. 1–2.

18 *The Medium is the Rear View Mirror: Understanding McLuhan* (Montreal, 1971), p. 93.

19 For additional items, see Harry H. Crosby and George R. Bond, *The McLuhan Explosion: A Casebook on Marshall McLuhan and 'Understanding Media'* (New York, 1968), p. 5.

20 See Arnold Rockman, 'McLuhanism: The Natural History of an Intellectual Fashion,' *Encounter*, XXXI (November 1968), 31–3.

21 It would be unreasonable to expect public interest in McLuhan to continue at such a level, and indeed, the McLuhan fashion is already on the wane and seems somewhat dated. But it is not at all necessary to my argument that McLuhan's popularity should go on increasing, or even remain at its peak. The point is that, for a period, McLuhan achieved a degree of exposure, and a measure of popular attention and following, that were unprecedented for an academic, and certainly unusual for a professor coming out of a tradition of literary theory. This sociological side to the reception of McLuhan's work adds interest (and urgency) to an inquiry (such as the present study) into the character of his theory, and the nature of the relation between the categorical framework of the cultural ideology he advanced and the dominant historical tendencies of the period. I have argued that McLuhan's version of critical theory is the adequate (technocratic) ideological form of a specific phase of one-dimensional reification. This means neither that the ideological field is stable nor that McLuhan is the final development in critical theory. He does represent essential tendencies whose influence continues to spread through our cultural institutions, as it continues to spread through the society as a whole. But if McLuhan's immediate or direct impact is at present on the wane, it is fair to say that the tendencies of neocapitalist one-dimensionality have also been suffering a setback since the late 1960s. A social crisis has erupted in the last ten years that has now deepened into an economic and political crisis as well, while the base of opposition has been expanding. The system has been losing legitimacy, conflict has reappeared, and a nearly-suppressed historical subject and historical praxis have been experiencing a slow but important renaissance. There are indications, moreover, that the system itself may both need and be ready for strategies other than one-dimensionality for its continuing viability.

22 'McLuhanism: A Libertarian View,' *Anarchy*, X (September 1970), 283.

23 Cited in Rockman, 29.

24 Ibid., 28.

25 For a discussion of these roles, see Rockman, *passim*.

26 He writes: 'marriage and family will become inviolate institutions, and infidelity and divorce will constitute serious violations of the social bond, not a private deviation, but a collective insult and loss of face to the entire tribe' (PI 65).

27 Marcuse, *One-Dimensional Man* (Boston, 1964), p. 154.

28 Cf. Heller, *A mindennapi élet*, p. 258.

29 'Constituents of a Theory of the Media,' *New Left Review*, no. 64 (November–December 1970), 23, 26.
30 Lilley, *Men, Machines and History* (New York, 1966), p. 311.
31 Stanley Ryerson, *The Open Society* (New York, 1965), pp. 66–8. For further possibilities of the new industrial revolution, see also Mandel, *Marxist Economic Theory* (London, 1968), II, pp. 605ff. For perhaps the best discussion on this subject, uniting the best elements of the Marxian tradition, the anarchist tradition, and the tradition of thought that includes Lewis Mumford and Buckminster Fuller, see 'Towards a Liberatory Technology' in Bookchin's *Post-Scarcity Anarchism* (Berkeley, 1971), pp. 85–139.

Chapter 14 Politics of cultural ideology

1 *The Concept of Equilibrium in American Social Thought* (New Haven, 1966), p. 178. The citation is from Kurt Back, 'The Game and the Myth as Two Languages of Social Science,' *Behavioral Science,* VIII (1963), 70.
2 'Literature and Sociology: In Memory of Lucien Goldmann,' *New Left Review*, no. 67 (May–June 1971), 15.
3 *La Dialectique du concret* (Paris, 1970), pp. 42–3; and *Dialektik des Konkreten*, pp. 57–8.
4 It should go without saying that the issue is not the use of the category 'structure,' an essential category of analysis. What is at issue is rather an ideological-methodological fetish.
5 See Michel Foucault, *The Order of Things: An Archaeology of the Human Sciences* (London, 1970), pp. xx–xxi. Sartre is right ('Replies to Structuralism: An Interview with Jean-Paul Sartre,' *Telos*, no. 9, Fall 1971, 110) that Foucault's study is not an archaeology retracing the development of objectified praxis, but a geology presenting a series of successive immobile strata: a denial of history.
6 *Au-delà du structuralisme* (Paris, 1971), p. 369.
7 *Society of the Spectacle*, *Radical America*, IV, no. 5, 1970, par. 24.
8 *Éntretiens avec Georg Lukács*, by Wolfgang Abendroth, Hans Heinz Holz, Leo Kofler, Theo Pinkus, trans. Marcel Ollivier (Paris, 1969), p. 120.
9 The fascist structural tendencies were also contained (limited) by the same historical solution.
10 In Canada, where there were linkages between a social-democratic political party and social-democratic unionists, the expulsion of Communists was even more rapid and vicious.
11 Alvin Gouldner, *The Dialectic of Ideology and Technology: The Origins, Grammar and Future of Ideology* (New York, 1976). For a valuable critical discussion that takes issue with Gouldner's optimistic outlook regarding the technical and cultural intelligentsia, see Paul Piccone, 'Review of Gouldner's *The Dialectic of Ideology and Technology*,' unpub. typescript.
12 Martin J. Sklar, 'On the Proletarian Revolution and the End of Political-Economic Society,' *Radical America*, III (May–June 1964), 34.

13 *Sens et non-sens*, 3rd ed. (Paris, 1948), p. 141.
14 *Aesthetics*, I, p. 220.
15 *Prisms* (London, 1967), pp. 33, 236.
16 'The Author as Producer,' trans. John Heckman, *New Left Review*, no. 62 (July–August 1970), 96, 90.
17 Ibid. Although this formulation embodies a limited sociology that is now obsolete, it none the less accurately seeks to indicate that the struggle of social forces is not restricted to the dimension of ideology. Indeed, such struggle needs to encompass all levels and aspects of social life.
18 See *Au-delà du structuralisme* (Paris, 1971), pp. 254–5.

Appendix A Theodore Spencer, 'How to Criticize a Poem'

1 *The New Republic*, CIX (6 December 1943), 816, 818. See chapter 8, n. 12.

Appendix B Notes toward a critique of McLuhan's polemic against vision

1 See chapter 12, n. 6.
2 *Man Makes Himself*, 3rd ed. (London, 1956), p. 26.
3 For a discussion, in relation to this sensory division of labor, of a somewhat different but comparable idealist purification of vision, by Konrad Fiedler, see Lukács, *Aesthetics*, I, pp. 191–2, 211.
4 *Economic and Philosophic Manuscripts of 1844*, ed. Dirk J. Struik, trans. Martin Milligan (New York, 1964), p. 141.
5 See Heller, *A mindennapi élet* (Budapest, 1970), p. 265; György Márkus, *Marxizmus és 'antropológia': az emberi lényeg fogalma Marx filozófiájában* [*Marxism and 'Anthropology': The Concept of Human Essence in Marx's Philosophy*], 2nd ed. (Budapest, 1971), pp. 50–2.

Selected Bibliography

This selected bibliography is organized in the following way:
A Primary Sources (chronological organization by year, alphabetical within the year):
    i John Crowe Ransom
   ii Northrop Frye
  iii Marshall McLuhan
B Secondary Sources (alphabetical organization). Under this heading, I have included consulted material related directly or indirectly to Ransom, Frye, or McLuhan, or to their problematics; material from within the same tradition; and material of general informational, philosophical, or methodological relevance to the discussion.

The more common periodicals are abbreviated as follows:

AR	The American Review
HR	The Hudson Review
KR	The Kenyon Review
NLR	New Left Review
NR	(The) New Republic
Ren	Renascence
SeR	The Sewanee Review
SR	The Southern Review
TLS	The Times Literary Supplement
UTQ	University of Toronto Quarterly

A Primary Sources

i John Crowe Ransom
1922   'Editorial.' The Fugitive, I (October 1922), 66–8.
1923   'Waste Lands.' The Literary Review, III (14 July 1923), 825–6. Reprinted in Modern Essays (second series), ed. Christopher Morley. New York, 1924, pp. 345–59.
1924   'Freud and Literature.' The Saturday Review of Literature, I (4 October 1924), 161–2.

1925   'A Man Without a Country.' *SeR*, XXXIII (July 1925), 301–7.
       'Thoughts on the Poetic Discontent.' *The Fugitive*, IV (June 1925),
       63–4. Reprinted in *The Calendar of Modern Letters*, I (August
       1925), 461–3.
1927   'The ABC of Aesthetics.' *NR*, LIII (14 December 1927), 104.
1928   'The South—Old or New?' *SeR*, XXXVI (April 1928), 139–47.
1929   'Classical and Romantic.' *The Saturday Review of Literature*, VI
       (14 September 1929), 125–7.
       'Flux and Blur in Contemporary Art.' *SeR*, XXXVII (July 1929),
       353–66.
       'The South Defends Its Heritage.' *Harper's*, CLIX (June 1929),
       108–18.
1930   *God Without Thunder: An Unorthodox Defence of Orthodoxy.*
       London, 1931. First published New York, 1930.
       'Introduction: A Statement of Principles' (unsigned). *I'll Take My
       Stand: The South and the Agrarian Tradition*, by Twelve
       Southerners. New York, 1930, pp. ix–xx.
       'Reconstructed But Unregenerate.' *I'll Take My Stand*, pp. 1–
       27.
1932   'Land! An Answer to the Unemployment Problem.' *Harper's*,
       CLXV (July 1932), 216–24.
       'The State and the Land.' *NR*, LXX (17 February 1932), 8–10.
1933   'A Capital for the New Deal.' *AR*, II (December 1933), 129–42.
       'Happy Farmers.' *AR*, I (October 1933), 513–35.
       'Shall We Complete the Trade?' *SeR*, XLI (April 1933), 182–90.
1934   'The Aesthetic of Regionalism.' *AR*, II (January 1934), 290–310.
       'Hearts and Heads.' *AR*, II (March 1934), 554–71.
       'Sociology and the Black Belt.' *AR*, IV (December 1934), 147–54.
       'T. S. Eliot on Criticism.' *The Saturday Review of Literature*, X
       (24 March 1934), 574.
1935   'Modern with the Southern Accent.' *The Virginia Quarterly Review*,
       XI (April 1935), 184–200.
       'Poetic Strategy.' *The Saturday Review of Literature*, XII (27
       July 1935), 6.
       'Thomism and Esthetic Experience.' *The Saturday Review of
       Literature*, XII (31 August 1935), 17.
       Topics for Freshman Writing. New York, 1935.
1936   'Autumn of Poetry.' *SR*, I (Winter 1936), 609–23.
       'Characters and Character: A Note on Fiction.' *AR*, VI (January
       1936), 271–88.
       'The Content of the Novel: Notes Toward a Critique of Fiction.' *AR*,
       VII (Summer 1936), 301–18.
       'Fiction Harvest.' *SR*, II (Autumn 1936), 399–418.
       'Gestures of Dissent.' *The Yale Review*, XXVI (September 1936),
       181–3.
       'The Making of a Modern: The Poetry of George Marion
       O'Donnell.' *SR*, I (Spring 1936), 864–74.
       'The South Is a Bulwark.' *Scribner's Magazine*, XCIX (May 1936),
       299–303.

'What Does the South Want?' *The Virginia Quarterly Review*, XII (April 1936), 180–94. Reprinted in *Who Owns America?*, ed. H. Agar and Allen Tate, Boston, 1936, pp. 178–93.

1938 'Mr. Empson's Muddles.' *SR*, IV (Autumn 1938), 322–39.
The World's Body. New York, 1938. Reprints fifteen essays published between 1933 and 1938 inclusive.

1939 'The Aesthetic of Finnegans Wake.' *KR*, I (Autumn 1939), 424–8.
'The Arts and the Philosophers.' *KR*, I (Spring 1939), 194–9.
'One Thousand Sonnets.' *KR*, I (Spring 1939), 229–31.
'The Teaching of Poetry.' *KR*, I (Winter 1939), 81–3.
'Was Shakespeare A Philosopher?' *KR*, I (Winter 1939), 75–80.
'Yeats and His Symbols.' *KR*, I (Summer 1939), 309–22.

1940 'André Malraux' Novels.' *KR*, II (Winter 1940), 93.
'Apologia for Modernism.' *KR*, II (Spring 1940), 247–51.
'Concerning the Symposium.' *KR*, II (Autumn 1940), 476–7.
'Honey and Gall.' *SR*, VI (Summer 1940), 2–19.
'Mr. Tate and the Professors.' *KR*, II (Summer 1940), 348–50.
'Old Age of a Poet.' *KR*, II (Summer 1940), 345–7.
'The Pragmatics of Art.' *KR*, II (Winter 1940), 76–87.
'Strategy for English Studies.' *SR*, VI (Autumn 1940), 226–35.

1941 'The Aesthetics of Music.' *KR*, III (Autumn 1941), 494–7.
'Constellation of Five Young Poets.' *KR*, III (Summer 1941), 377–80.
'Criticism as Pure Speculation.' *The Intent of the Critic*, ed. Donald A. Stauffer. Princeton, 1941, pp. 89–124.
'Indefatigable Tommy.' *KR*, III (Autumn 1941), 519–20.
'Moholy-Nagy's New Arts.' *KR*, III (Summer 1941), 372–4.
'Muses and Amazons.' *KR*, III (Spring 1941), 240–2.
The New Criticism. Norfolk, Conn., 1941.
'Ubiquitous Moralists.' *KR*, III (Winter 1941), 95–100.
'The Younger Poets.' *KR*, III (Autumn 1941), 491–4.

1942 'An Address to Kenneth Burke.' *KR*, IV (Spring 1942), 219–37.
'Bright Disorder.' *KR*, IV (Autumn 1942), 430–2.
'The Irish, The Gaelic, The Byzantine.' *SR*, VII (Winter 1942), 517–46.
'Mr. Russell and Mr. Schorer.' *KR*, IV (Autumn 1942), 406–7.
'On the Brooks–MacLeish Thesis.' *Partisan Review*, IX (January–February 1942), 40–1.
'War and Publication.' *KR*, IV (Spring 1942), 217–18.
'We Resume.' *KR*, IV (Autumn 1942), 405–6.

1943 *A College Primer of Writing*. New York, 1943.
'E. M. Forster.' *KR*, V (Autumn 1943), 618–23.
'The Inorganic Muses.' *KR*, V (Spring 1943), 278–300.
'Positive and Near-Positive Aesthetics.' *KR*, V (Summer 1943), 443–7.

1944 'Artists, Soldiers, Positivists.' *KR*, VI (Spring 1944), 276–81.
'Art Needs a Little Separating.' *KR*, VI (Winter 1944), 114–22.
'The Bases of Criticism.' *SeR*, XLII (October 1944), 556–71.
'The Essays of Horace Gregory.' *KR*, VI (Summer 1944), 469–73.

1945   'Art and the Human Economy.' *KR*, VII (Autumn 1945),
        683–8.
        'Art Worries the Naturalists.' *KR*,VII (Spring 1945), 282–99.
        'Beating the Naturalists with the Stick of Drama.' *KR*, VII
        (Summer 1945), 515–20.
        'Brief Comment: Cannery Row by John Steinbeck.' *KR*, VII
        (Summer 1945), 526–7.
        'Brief Comment: Mission of the University by José Ortega y
        Gasset.' *KR*, VII (Summer 1945), 524–5.
        'Brief Comment: The Power House by Alex Comfort.' *KR*, VII
        (Summer 1945), 522–3.
        'The Severity of Mr. Savage.' *KR*, VII (Winter 1945), 114–17.
1946   'Brief Notices: 27 Wagons Full of Cotton and Other One Act
        Plays by Tennessee Williams.' *KR*, VIII (Spring 1946), 344–5.
        'Brief Notices: William Ernest Henley: A Study in the "Counter-
        Decadence" of the 'Nineties by Jerome Hamilton Buckley.' *KR*,
        VIII (Spring 1946), 338–9.
        'Delta Fiction.' *KR*, VIII (Summer 1946), 503–7.
        'Descartes's Angels.' *SeR*, LIV (January 1946), 153–6.
        'Short Notice: Memoirs of a Shy Pornographer by Kenneth
        Patchen.' *KR*, VIII (Winter 1946), 171.
        'Short Notice: The Rebirth of Liberal Education by Fred B.
        Millett.' *KR*, VIII (Winter 1946), 176–7.
        'These Little Magazines.' *The American Scholar*, XV (Autumn
        1946), 550–1.
1947   'On Shakespeare's Language.' *SeR*, LV (April 1947), 181–98.
        'Poetry: I. The Formal Analysis.' *KR*, IX (Summer 1947),
        436–56.
        'Poetry: II, The Final Cause.' *KR*, IX (Autumn 1947), 640–58.
1948   'The Literary Criticism of Aristotle.' *KR*, X (Summer 1948),
        382–402. Also in *Lectures in Criticism: The Johns Hopkins
        University*, ed. Huntington Cairns. New York, 1949, pp. 15–42.
        'The New Criticism.' *KR*, X (Autumn 1948), 682–8.
1950   'The Understanding of Fiction.' *KR*, XII (Spring 1950), 189–218.
        'William Wordsworth: Notes toward an Understanding of Poetry.'
        KR, XII (Summer 1950), 498–519.
1951   'Introduction.' *The Kenyon Critics: Studies in Modern Literature
        from The Kenyon Review*, ed. John Crowe Ransom. Cleveland,
        1951, pp. vii–x.
        'The Poetry of 1900–1950.' *KR*, XIII (Summer 1951), 445–54.
1952   'An Age of Criticism.' *NR*, CXXVI (31 March 1952), 18–19.
        'The Art of Prose.' *NR*, CXXVII (6 October 1952), 17–18.
        'Hardy—Old Poet.' *NR*, CXXVI (12 May 1952), 16, 30–1.
        'Humanism at Chicago.' *KR*, XIV (Autumn 1952), 647–59.
        'The Poems of T. S. Eliot: A Perspective.' *NR*, CXXVII (8
        December 1952), 16–17.
        'Poets and Flatworms.' *KR*, XIV (Winter 1952), 157–62.
1953   'Alienation a Century Ago.' *KR*, XV (Spring 1953), 335–6.
        'Empirics in Politics.' *KR*, XV (Autumn 1953), 648–50, 652–4.

'Reply by the Author' in 'Communications.' *KR*, XV (Spring 1953), 301–4.

'Responsible Criticism.' *SeR*, LXI (April 1953), 300–3.

'The Shores of Criticism.' *Partisan Review*, XX (January–February 1953), 108–11.

'Symbolism: American Style.' *NR*, CXXIX (2 November 1953), 18–20.

1954 'The Concrete Universal: Observations on the Understanding of Poetry.' *KR*, XVI (Autumn 1954), 554–64.

1955 'The Concrete Universal: Observations on the Understanding of Poetry.' *KR*, XVII (Summer 1955), 383–407.

'On Shakespeare's Language' in 'Communications.' *SeR*, LV (July 1955), 536–7.

Poems and Essays. New York, 1955. Contains forty-four poems, and eight essays published between 1947 and 1955 inclusive, some of them revised.

1956 'The Strange Music of English Verse.' *KR*, XVIII (Summer 1956), 460–77.

1958 'New Poets and Old Muses.' *American Poetry at Mid-Century*, by John Crowe Ransom, Delmore Schwartz and John Hall Wheelock. Lectures Presented Under the Auspices of the Gertrude Clarke Whittall Poetry and Literature Fund. Washington: Reference Dept, Library of Congress, 1958, pp. 1–14.

1959 'The Idea of a Literary Anthropologist and What He Might Say Of the Paradise Lost of Milton.' *KR*, XXI (Winter 1959), 121–40.

'In Amicitia.' *SeR*, LXVII (October 1959), 528–39.

1961 'Introduction.' *Selected Poems of Thomas Hardy*, by Thomas Hardy; ed. John Crowe Ransom. New York, 1961, pp. ix–xxxiii.

1962 'The Most Southern Poet.' *SeR*, LXX (April 1962), 202–7.

1963 ' "Prelude to an Evening": A Poem Revised and Explicated.' *KR*, XXV (Winter 1963), 70–80.

1964 'Acceptance Speech: The National Book Award for Poetry, March 10, 1964.' *SeR*, LXXII (July 1964), 548–50.

'On Theodore Roethke's "In a Dark Time." ' *The Contemporary Poet as Artist and Critic: Eight Symposia*, ed. Anthony Ostroff. Boston, 1964, pp. 26–35.

'The Planetary Poet.' *KR*, XXVI (Winter 1964), 233–64.

1966 'Gerontion.' *SeR*, LXXIV (April 1966), 389–414.

1970 *Selected Poems*, 3rd ed., rev. and enlarg. London, 1970.

ii Northrop Frye

1947 *Fearful Symmetry: A Study of William Blake*. Princeton, 1947. Reprinted with new preface. Princeton, 1969.

[Review of Alfred Kazin's *The Portable Blake*.] *UTQ*, XVII (October 1947), 107.

'Toynbee and Spengler.' *The Canadian Forum*, August 1947, 111–13.

1951 'Notes on Several Occasions.' *HR*, III (Winter 1951), 611–19.

'Poetry.' *UTQ*, XX (April 1951), 257–62.

'Poetry and Design in William Blake.' *The Journal of Aesthetics and Art Criticism*, X (September 1951), 35–42.

'The Young Boswell.' *HR*, IV (Spring 1951), 143–6.

1952   Ed. and intro. *Across My Path*, by Pelham Edgar. Toronto, 1952. 'Editor's Introduction,' pp. vii–xi.

'Phalanx of Particulars.' *HR*, IV (Winter 1952), 627–31.

'Poetry.' *UTQ*, XXI (April 1952), 252–8.

1953   'Long Sequacious Notes.' *HR*, V (Winter 1953), 603–8.

'Poetry.' *UTQ*, XXII (April 1953), 269–80.

Ed. and intro. *Selected Poetry and Prose of William Blake*, by William Blake. New York, 1953. 'Introduction,' pp. xiii–xxviii.

1954   'Content with the Form.' *UTQ*, XXIV (October 1954), 92–7.

'Poetry.' *UTQ*, XXIII (April 1954), 253–63.

1955   'English Canadian Literature, 1929–1954.' *Books Abroad*, XXIX (Summer 1955), 270–4.

'Poetry.' *UTQ*, XXIV (April 1955), 247–56.

1956   'Graves, Gods and Scholars.' *HR*, IX (Summer 1956), 298–302.

Ed. and intro. *I Brought the Ages Home*, by C. T. Currelly. Toronto, 1956. 'Introduction,' pp. vii–x.

'An Indispensable Book.' *The Virginia Quarterly Review*, XXXII (Spring 1956), 310–15.

'Poetry.' *UTQ*, XXV (April 1956), 290–304.

1957   *Anatomy of Criticism: Four Essays*. Princeton, 1957. Reprints in revised coherent form of material published between 1942 and 1955 inclusive.

'Neo-Classical Agony.' *HR*, X (Winter 1957), 592–8.

'Notes for a Commentary on *Milton*.' *The Divine Vision: Studies in the Poetry and Art of William Blake*, ed. Vivian de Sola Pinto. London, 1957, pp. 97–137.

'Poetry.' *UTQ*, XXVI (April 1957), 296–311.

'Poetry of the Tout Ensemble.' *HR*, X (Spring 1957), 122–5.

'Preface to an Uncollected Anthology.' *Studia Varia: Royal Society of Canada Literary and Scientific Papers/Société Royale du Canada: Etudes littéraires et scientifiques*, ed. E. G. D. Murray. Toronto, 1957, pp. 21–36.

[Review of books by W. B. Stanford and Cleanth Brooks.] *Comparative Literature*, IX (Spring 1957), 180–2.

Ed. and intro. *Sound and Poetry*. New York, 1957. 'Introduction: Lexis and Melos,' pp. ix–xxvii.

1958   'Poetry.' *The Arts in Canada*, ed. Malcolm Ross. Toronto, 1958, pp. 84–90.

'Poetry.' *UTQ*, XXVII (July 1958), 434–50.

'The Study of English in Canada.' *The Dalhousie Review*, XXXVIII (Spring 1958), 1–7. C.U.T.E. address, June 1957.

1959   'Interior Monologue of M. Teste.' *HR*, XII (Spring 1959), 124–9.

'Poetry.' *UTQ*, XXVIII (July 1959), 345–65.

Ed. and intro. *The Tempest*, by William Shakespeare. Baltimore, 1959. 'Introduction,' pp. 15–26.

'World Enough Without Time.' *HR*, XII (Autumn 1959), 423–31.

1960 'Introduction.' *The Stepsure Letters*, by Thomas McCulloch. N.p., 1960, pp. iii–ix.
'The Nightmare Life in Death.' *HR*, XIII (Autumn 1960), 442–9.
'Poetry.' *UTQ*, XXIX (July 1960), 440–60.

1961 'Blake's Treatment of the Archetype.' *Discussions of William Blake*, ed. John E. Grant. Boston, 1961, pp. 6–16. Reprinted, with slight alterations, from *English Institute Essays: 1950*, ed. Alan S. Downer. New York, 1951, pp. 170–96.
'The Critical Discipline' in *Canadian Universities Today/Les Universités canadiennes aujourd'hui*, ed. George Stanley and Guy Sylvestre. Toronto, 1961.

1962 Ed. and intro. *The Collected Poems of E. J. Pratt*, by E. J. Pratt; 2nd ed. Toronto, 1962. 'Preface,' p. xii. 'Introduction,' pp. xiii–xxviii.

1963 'The Developing Imagination.' *Learning in Language and Literature*. Cambridge, Mass., 1963, pp. 29–58.
The Educated Imagination. Toronto, 1963.
Fables of Identity: Studies in Poetic Mythology. New York, 1963. Reprints sixteen essays published between 1947 and 1962 inclusive.
'Literary Criticism.' *The Aims and Methods of Scholarship in Modern Languages and Literatures*, ed. James Thorpe. New York, 1963, pp. 57–69.
'The Road of Excess.' *Myth and Symbol: Critical Approaches and Applications*, ed. Bernice Slote. Lincoln, Nebraska, 1963, pp. 3–20. Later reprinted in *The Stubborn Structure*.
Romanticism Reconsidered, ed. New York, 1963. 'Foreword,' pp. v–ix.
T. S. Eliot. Edinburgh and London, 1963.
The Well-Tempered Critic. Bloomington, 1963.

1964 'Preface.' *The Psychoanalysis of Fire*, by Gaston Bachelard; trans. Alan C. M. Ross. London, 1964, pp. v–viii.
'Response to *Arion* Questionnaire: The Classics and the Man of Letters.' *Arion*, III (Winter 1964), 49–52.

1965 'Allegory.' *Encyclopaedia of Poetry and Poetics*, ed. Alex Preminger. Princeton, 1965, pp. 12–15.
A Natural Perspective: the Development of Shakespearean Comedy and Romance. New York, 1965.
'Nature and Nothing.' *Essays on Shakespeare*, ed. Gerald W. Chapman. Princeton, 1965, pp. 35–58.
'The Rising of the Moon: A Study of *A Vision*.' *An Honoured Guest: New Essays on W. B. Yeats*, ed. Denis Donoghue and J. R. Mulryne. London, 1965, pp. 8–33.
'Verse and Prose.' *Encyclopaedia of Poetry and Poetics*, ed. Alex Preminger. Princeton, 1965, pp. 885–90.

1966 Ed. and intro. *Blake: A Collection of Critical Essays*. Englewood Cliffs, N.J., 1966. 'Introduction,' pp. 1–7.
'Blake's Introduction to Experience.' *Blake: A Collection of Critical Essays*, pp. 23–31.

Five Essays on Milton's Epics. London, 1966.

'Letter to the English Institute: 1965.' *Northrop Frye in Modern Criticism: Selected Papers from the English Institute*, ed. Murray Krieger. New York, 1966, pp. 27–30.

'Reflections in a Mirror.' *Northrop Frye in Modern Criticism*, pp. 133–46.

'William Blake.' *The English Romantic Poets and Essayists: A Review of Research and Criticism*, ed. Carolyn Washburn Houtchens and Lawrence Huston Houtchens, rev. ed. New York, 1966, pp. 1–35.

1967　*Fools of Time: Studies in Shakespearean Tragedy*. Toronto, 1967.

'The Knowledge of Good and Evil.' *The Morality of Scholarship*, ed. Max Black. Ithaca, 1967, pp. 1–28. Later reprinted in *The Stubborn Structure*.

The Modern Century. Toronto, 1967.

1968　*A Study of English Romanticism*. New York, 1968.

1970　'The Critical Path: An Essay on the Social Context of Literary Criticism.' *Daedalus*, XCIX (Spring 1970), 268–342.

The Stubborn Structure: Essays on Criticism and Society. London, 1970. Reprints sixteen essays published between 1963 and 1969 incl.

iii Marshall McLuhan

1936　'G. K. Chesterton: A Practical Mystic.' *The Dalhousie Review*, XV (1936).

1943　'Herbert's "Virtue." ' *The Explicator*, II (October 1943), item 4.

'The Place of Thomas Nashe in the Learning of His Time.' Diss., Cambridge University, April 1943.

1944　'Eliot's "The Hippopotamus." ' *The Explicator*, II (May 1944), item 50.

'Kipling and Forster.' *SeR*, LII (July 1944), 332–43.

'Poetic vs. Rhetorical Exegesis: The Case for Leavis Against Richards and Empson.' *SeR*, LII (April 1944), 266–76.

1945　'The New York Wits.' *KR*, VII (Winter 1945), 12–28.

1946　'Footprints in the Sands of Time.' *SeR*, LIV (October 1946), 617–34.

1947　'American Advertising.' *Horizon*, XCIII (October 1947), 132–41.

'Inside Blake and Hollywood.' *SeR*, LV (October 1947), 710–15.

'Mr. Connolly and Mr. Hook.' *SeR*, LV (January 1947), 167–72.

1948　'Henry IV, A Mirror for Magistrates.' *UTQ*, XVII (January 1948), 152–60.

'Introduction.' *Paradox in Chesterton*, by Hugh Kenner. London, 1948, pp. xi–xxii.

1950　'Collected Poems by Roy Campbell.' *Ren*, III (August 1950), 101–3.

'T. S. Eliot.' *Ren*, III (Autumn 1950), 43–8.

1951　'Joyce, Aquinas, and the Poetic Process.' *Ren*, IV (Autumn 1951), 3–11.

The Mechanical Bride: Folklore of Industrial Man. New York, 1951; London, 1967.

'Poetry and Opinion, Examination of Ezra Pound and Letters of Pound.' *Ren*, III (Spring 1951), 200–2.

'A Survey of Joyce Criticism.' *Ren*, IV (Autumn 1951), 12–18.

1952 'Defrosting Canadian Culture.' *American Mercury*, LXXIV (March 1952), 91–7.

'Technology and Political Change.' *International Journal*, VII (Summer 1952), 189–95.

1953 'The Age of Advertising.' *The Commonweal*, LVIII (11 September 1953), 555–7.

'Culture without Literacy.' *Explorations: Studies in Culture and Communication*, no. 1 (December 1953), 117–27.

'Maritain on Art.' *Ren*, VI (Autumn 1953), 40–4.

'Symbolist Communication.' *Thought*, XXVIII (Autumn 1953), 456–8.

1954 *Counterblast*. Toronto, 1954.

'Media as Art Forms.' *Explorations: Studies in Culture and Communication*, no. 2 (April 1954), 6–13.

'Poetry and Society.' *Poetry*, LXXXIV (May 1954), 93–5.

'Sight, Sound and the Fury.' *The Commonweal*, LX (9 April 1954), 7–11.

1955 'The ABCED-minded.' *Explorations: Studies in Culture and Communication*, no. 5 (June 1955), 12–18.

'Nihilism Exposed.' *Ren*, VIII (Winter 1955), 97–9.

'Paganism on Tip-toe.' *Ren*, VII (Spring 1955), 158.

1956 'Music and Silence.' *Ren*, VIII (Spring 1956), 152–3.

Ed. and intro. *Selected Poetry*, by Alfred Lord Tennyson. New York, 1956. 'Introduction,' pp. v–xxiv.

'Stylistic.' *Ren*, IX (Winter 1956), 99–100.

1957 'The Subliminal Projection Project.' *The Canadian Forum*, XXXVII (December 1957), 196–7.

'Third Program in the Human Age.' *Explorations: Studies in Culture and Communication*, no. 8 (October 1957), 16–18.

'Verbi-Voco-Visual.' *Explorations: Studies in Culture and Communications*, no. 8 (October 1957).

1958 'Classic Treatment.' *Ren*, X (Winter 1958), 102–3.

'Compliment Accepted.' *Ren*, X (Winter 1958), 106–8.

'One Wheel, All Square.' *Ren*, X (Summer 1958), 196–200.

1959 'Joyce or no Joyce.' *Ren*, XII (Autumn 1959), 53–4.

'Myth and Mass Media.' *Daedalus*, LXXXVIII (Spring 1959), 339–48.

'Virgil, Yeats, and 13000 Friends.' *Ren*, XI (Winter 1959), 94–5.

'Yeats and Zane Grey.' *Ren*, XI (Spring 1959), 166–8.

1960 'Another Eliot Party.' *Ren*, XII (Spring 1960), 156–7.

'Around the World, Around the Clock.' *Ren*, XII (Summer 1960), 204–5.

'A Critical Discipline.' *Ren*, XII (Winter 1960), 93–5.

'Effects of the Improvements of Communication Media.' *The Journal of Economic History*, XX (December 1960), 566–75.

'Flirting with Shadows.' *Ren*, XII (Summer 1960), 212–14.

'Joyce as Critic.' *Ren*, XII (Summer 1960), 202–3.

'The Medium Is the Message.' *Forum* (University of Houston), Ill. (Summer 1960), 19–24.

'Melodic and Scribal.' *Ren*, XIII (Autumn 1960), 51.

'The Personal Approach.' *Ren*, XIII (Autumn 1960), 42–3.

Report on Project in Understanding New Media. 1960.

'Romanticism Reviewed.' *Ren*, XII (Summer 1960), 207–9.

1961   'The Electric Culture.' *Ren*, XIII (Summer 1961), 219–20.

'Producers and Consumers.' *Ren*, XIII (Summer 1961), 217–19.

1962   *The Gutenberg Galaxy: The Making of Typographic Man.* [Toronto,] 1962; London, 1962.

'Prospect of America.' *UTQ*, XXXII (October 1962), 107–8.

1964   'Introduction,' *The Bias of Communication*, by Harold A. Innis. [Toronto,] 1964, pp. vii–xvi.

'Murder by Television.' *The Canadian Forum*, XLIII (January 1964), 222–3.

'Notes on Burroughs.' *The Nation*, CXCIX (28 December 1964), 517–19.

Understanding Media: The Extensions of Man. New York and London, 1964.

1966   'Address at Vision 65.' *The American Scholar*, XXXV (Spring 1966), 196–205.

'The All-at-Once World of Marshall McLuhan.' *Vogue*, CXXIII (August 1966), 70–3, 111.

Explorations in Communication: An Anthology, ed. with Edmund Carpenter. Boston, 1966. Reprints, *inter alia*, five McLuhan essays from *Explorations*.

1967   'A Dialogue: Q. & A.' *McLuhan: Hot and Cool: A Primer for the Understanding of & a Critical Symposium with a Rebuttal by McLuhan*, ed. Gerald E. Stearn. New York, 1967, pp. 260–92.

'Love.' *Saturday Night*, LXXXII (February 1967), 25–8.

The Medium Is the Massage, with Quentin Fiore. New York, 1967.

'The Memory Theatre.' *Encounter*, XXVIII (March 1967), 61–6.

1968   'Mailer, McLuhan and Muggeridge: On Obscenity.' *The Realist*, no. 83 (October 1968), 5–12. Transcript of *The Way It Is* broadcast over CBLT-TV, Toronto, 1968.

Through the Vanishing Point: Space in Poetry and Painting, with Harley Parker. New York, 1968.

War and Peace in the Global Village, with Quentin Fiore. New York, 1968.

1969   *The Interior Landscape: The Literary Criticism of Marshall McLuhan, 1943–1962*, ed. Eugene McNamara. New York, 1969.

'Playboy Interview: Marshall McLuhan, A Candid Conversation with the High Priest of Popcult and Metaphysician of Media.' *Playboy*, March 1969, 53–74, 158.

1970   *Counterblast.* London, 1970.

Culture Is Our Business. New York, 1970.

From Cliché to Archetype, with Wilfred Watson. New York, 1970.

1971   *Voices of Literature: Sounds, Masks, Roles*, with R. J. Schoeck.
        New York, 1971.
1972   *Take Today: The Executive As Dropout*, with Barrington Nevitt.
        New York, 1972.

B Secondary Sources

ABDEL-MALEK, ANOUAR. 'Vers une sociologie comparative des
        idéologies.' *L'Homme et la société*, no. 7 (January–March 1968),
        115–30.
ABEL, DARREL. 'Intellectual Criticism.' *The American Scholar*, XII
        (Autumn 1943), 414–28.
ABRAMS, M. H. 'The Newer Criticism: A Prisoner of Logical Positivism?'
        KR, XVII (Winter 1955), 139–43.
—— [Review of Frye's *Anatomy*.]*UTQ*, XXVIII (January 1959), 190–6.
ADAMS, HAZARD. 'Criticism: Whence and Whither?' *The American
        Scholar*, XXVIII (Spring 1959), 226–38.
—— [Review of Frye's *Anatomy*.]*The Journal of Aesthetics and Art
        Criticism*, XVI (June 1958), 533–4.
ADAMS, ROBERT MARTIN. 'Dreadful Symmetry.' *HR*, X (Winter
        1957–8), 614–19.
ADORNO, THEODOR W. 'On Popular Music.' *Studies in Philosophy
        and Social Science*, published by the Institute of Social Research,
        Vol. IX. New York, 1941, pp. 17–48.
—— *Prisms*, trans. Samuel and Shierry Weber. London, 1967.
—— 'A Social Critique of Radio Music.' *KR*, VII **(Spring 1945), 208–17.**
—— 'Theses Upon Art and Religion Today.' *KR*, VII (Autumn 1945),
        677–82.
ALLEN, GAY WILSON, and CLARK, HARRY HAYDEN, eds.
        Literary Criticism: Pope to Croce. Detroit, 1962.
ALTHUSSER, LOUIS. *For Marx*, trans. Ben Brewster. London, 1969.
—— *Lénine et la philosophie*. Paris, 1969.
—— *et al. Lire Le Capital*. 2 vols. Paris, 1965.
—— and BALIBAR, ETIENNE. *Reading Capital*, rev. and abr.;
        trans. Ben Brewster. London, 1970.
AMES, VAN METER. 'Art and Science.' *KR*, VI (Winter 1944), 101–13.
—— 'Expression and Aesthetic Expression.' *The Journal of Aesthetics
        and Art Criticism*, VI (December 1947), 172–9.
ANDERSON, G. L. [Review of Frye's *Anatomy*.] *Seventeenth-Century
        News*, LVI (Summer 1958), 17–18.
ANDERSON, PERRY. 'Components of the National Culture.' *NLR*, no.
        50 (July–August 1968), 3–57.
ARNOLD, MATTHEW. *Poetry and Criticism of Matthew Arnold*, ed. A.
        Dwight Culler. Boston, 1961.
AUERBACH, ERICH. *Mimesis: The Representation of Reality in
        Western Literature*, trans. Willard R. Trask. Princeton, 1953.
BAKER, JOSEPH E. 'The Philosopher and the "New Critic."' *SeR*, L
        (April 1942), 167–71.
BARAN, PAUL A., and SWEEZY, PAUL M. *Monopoly Capital: An*

Essay on the American Economic and Social Order. New York, 1966.

BARON, HAROLD M. 'The Demand for Black Labor: Historical Notes on the Political Economy of Racism.' *Radical America*, V (March–April 1971), 1–46.

BARRY, JACKSON B. 'Form or Formula: Comic Structure in Northrop Frye and Suzanne Langer.' *Educational Theatre Journal*, XVI (December 1964), 333–40.

BARTHES, ROLAND. *Elements of Semiology*, trans. Annette Lavers and Colin Smith. London, 1967.

—— *Mythologies*, selected and trans. Annette Lavers. London, 1972.

—— *Writing Degree Zero*, trans. Annette Lavers and Colin Smith. London, 1967.

BASALDELLA, MIRKO. 'Visual Considerations.' *Education of Vision*, ed. György Kepes. New York, 1965, pp. 175–83.

BAUDRILLARD, JEAN. 'Compte Rendu de Marshall MacLuhan [*sic*]: *Understanding Media—The Extensions of Man.*' *L'Homme et la société*, no. 5 (July–September 1967), 227–30.

—— *Le Miroir de la production.* Paris, 1973.

—— *The Mirror of Production*, trans. and intro. Mark Poster. St Louis, 1975.

—— *Pour une critique de l'économie politique du signe.* Paris, 1972.

—— *La Société de consommation.* Paris, 1970.

—— *Le Système des objects.* Paris, 1968.

BAXANDALL, LEE. '*"New Criticism" und die Entwicklung bürgerlicher Literaturwissenschaft* by Robert Weimann.' *Science and Society*, XXIX (Summer 1965), 346–9.

BEATTY, RICHMOND C. 'On Shakespeare's Language' in 'Communications.' *SeR*, LV (July 1947), 536. Ransom's reply, 536–7.

BENJAMIN, WALTER. 'The Author as Producer,' trans. John Heckmann, *NLR*, no. 62 (July–August 1970), 83–96.

—— *Illuminations*, ed. Hannah Arendt; trans. Harry Zohn. New York, 1968.

BENZIGER, JAMES. 'Organic Unity: Leibniz to Coleridge.' *PMLA*, LXVI (March 1951), 24–48.

BERGER, JOHN. *Art and Revolution: Ernst Neizvestny and the Role of the Artist in the U.S.S.R.* Harmondsworth, 1969.

BERGSON, HENRI. *An Introduction to Metaphysics*, trans. T. E. Hulme. London, 1913.

BIRNBAUM, NORMAN. 'Classes sociales dans la société industrielle.' *L'Homme et la société*, no. 5 (July–September 1967), 69–87.

BLACKMUR, RICHARD P. 'Parody and Critique: Notes on Thomas Mann's *Doctor Faustus.*' *The Kenyon Critics: Studies in Modern Literature from The Kenyon Review*, ed. John Crowe Ransom. Cleveland, 1951, pp. 182–200.

—— 'San Giovanni in Venere: Allen Tate as Man of Letters.' *SeR*, LXVII (October 1959), 614–31.

BLISSETT, WILLIAM. [Review of Frye's books.] *UTQ*, XXXIII (July 1964), 401–8.

BLOOM, HAROLD. *Blake's Apocalypse: A Study in Poetic Argument*. London, 1963.
—— 'A New Poetics.' *The Yale Review*, XLVII (Autumn 1957), 130–3.
—— *Shelley's Mythmaking*. New Haven, 1959.
—— *The Visionary Company: A Reading of English Romantic Poetry*. London, 1961.
BODKIN, MAUD. *Archetypal Patterns in Poetry: Psychological Studies of Imagination*. London, 1963. First published 1934.
BOOKCHIN, MURRAY. *Post-Scarcity Anarchism*. Berkeley, 1971.
BOOTH, WAYNE C. *The Rhetoric of Fiction*. Chicago, 1961.
—— 'The Use of Criticism in the Teaching of Literature.' *College English*, XXVII (October 1965), 1–13.
BOURDIN, ALAIN. *MacLuhan* [sic]: *Communication, technologie et société*. Paris, 1970.
BOYER, RICHARD O., and MORAIS, HERBERT M. *Labor's Untold Story*, 3rd ed. New York, 1971.
BRADBURY, JOHN M. *The Fugitives: A Critical Account*. Chapel Hill, 1958.
BROOKS, CLEANTH. 'The Christianity of Modernism.' *AR*, VI (February 1936), 435–46.
—— 'The Doric Delicacy.' *SeR*, LVI (July 1948), 402–15.
—— 'Homage to John Crowe Ransom.' *Shenandoah*, XIV (Spring 1963), 50.
—— *Modern Poetry and the Tradition*. Chapel Hill, 1965.
—— 'The New Criticism: A Brief for the Defense.' *The American Scholar*, XIII (Summer 1944), 285–95.
—— 'The Poet's Fancy.' *NR*, LXXXV (13 November 1935), 26–7.
—— *The Well Wrought Urn: Studies in the Structure of Poetry*. London, 1968.
—— and HEILMAN, ROBERT B., eds. *Understanding Drama: Twelve Plays*. New York, 1948.
—— and WARREN, ROBERT PENN. *Modern Rhetoric* (*Shorter Edition*). New York, 1961.
—— and WARREN, ROBERT PENN, eds. *Understanding Fiction*. New York, 1943.
—— and WARREN, ROBERT PENN, eds. *Understanding Poetry: An Anthology for College Students*. New York, 1938.
BROUSSEAU, JEAN-PAUL. 'McLuhan et "mcluhanisme."' *La Presse*, 20 June 1970, 28.
BROWER, REUBEN A. 'Myth Making.' *Partisan Review*, XXXIII (Winter 1966), 132–6.
BUFFINGTON, ROBERT. *The Equilibrist: A Study of John Crowe Ransom's Poems, 1916–1963*. Nashville, 1967.
BUHLE, PAUL. 'New Perspectives on American Radicalism.' *Radical America*, II (July–August 1968), 46–58.
BURKE, KENNETH. 'The Encyclopaedic, Two Kinds Of.' *Poetry*, XCI (February 1958), 320–8.
—— *The Philosophy of Literary Form: Studies in Symbolic Action*, rev., abr. ed. New York, 1957.

CABRAL, AMILCAR. *Revolution in Guinea: An African People's Struggle*. London, 1969.

CALVERTON, V. F. 'The Bankruptcy of Southern Culture.' *Scribner's Magazine*, XCIX (May 1936), 294–8.

CAMPBELL, H. M. 'John Crowe Ransom . . .' *Southwest Review*, XXIV (July 1939), 476–89.

CANBY, HENRY SEIDEL. 'A Prospectus for Criticism.' *The Saturday Review of Literature*, XVIII (21 May 1938), 8–9.

CAREY, JAMES W. 'Harold Adams Innis and Marshall McLuhan.' *McLuhan: Pro and Con,* ed. Raymond Rosenthal. Baltimore, 1969, pp. 270–308.

CARLETON, GEORGE WASHINGTON. *The Suppressed Book About Slavery*. New York, 1968. First published New York, 1864.

CARRUTH, HAYDEN. 'People in a Myth.' *HR*, XVIII (Winter 1965–6), 607–12.

CARSON, ROBERT B. 'Youthful Labor Surplus in Disaccumulationist Capitalism.' *Socialist Revolution*, no. 9 (May–June 1972), 15–44.

'Cartographers of the Mind.' *TLS*, 23 April 1970, 451.

CASEY, JOHN. *The Language of Criticism*. London, 1966.

CASTORIADIS, CORNELIUS. *L'Institution imaginaire de la société*. Paris, 1975.

CAUDWELL, CHRISTOPHER. *Illusion and Reality: A Study of the Sources of Poetry*. London and New York, 1937.

CHENEY, SHELDON. *A World History of Art*. New York, 1937.

CHILDE, V. GORDON. *Man Makes Himself*, 3rd ed. London, 1956.

CLARK, AXTON. 'Poetry Without Purpose.' *NR*, LXXIX (20 June 1934), 148–50.

COLLINS, SEWARD. 'Editorial Notes.' *AR*, I (April 1933), 122–7.

CORNFORTH, MAURICE. *Marxism and the Linguistic Philosophy*. London, 1965.

COUCH, W. T. 'The Agrarian Romance.' *The South Atlantic Quarterly*, XXXVI (October 1937), 419–30.

COWAN, LOUISE. *The Fugitive Group: A Literary History*. Baton Rouge, La, 1959.

CRANE, R. S. *The Languages of Criticism and the Structure of Poetry*. Toronto, 1953.

CROSBY, HARRY H., and BOND, GEORGE R., eds. *The McLuhan Explosion: A Casebook on Marshall McLuhan and 'Understanding Media.'* New York, 1968.

DAICHES, DAVID. [Review of Frye's *Anatomy*.] *Modern Philology*, LVI (August 1958), 69–72.

DAVIDSON, DONALD. '"I'll Take My Stand": A History.' *AR*, V (Summer 1935), 301–21.

—— 'Lines Written for Allen Tate on his Sixtieth Anniversary.' *SeR*, LXVII (October 1959), 540–1.

—— 'A Mirror for Artists.' *I'll Take My Stand: The South and the Agrarian Tradition*, by Twelve Southerners. New York, 1930, pp. 28–60.

DAVIES, HUNTER. 'Joker or Genius . . . or Both.' *The Sunday Times*, 13 August 1967, 17.

DAY, BARRY. *The Message of Marshall McLuhan*, 3rd ed. London, 1967.

DEBORD, GUY. *Society of the Spectacle. Radical America*, IV, no. 5 (1970).

DERRIDA, JACQUES. 'Structure, Sign, and Play in the Discourse of the Human Sciences.' *The Languages of Criticism and the Sciences of Man: The Structuralist Controversy*, ed. Richard Macksey and Eugenio Donato. Baltimore, 1970, pp. 247–65.

DEWEY, JOHN. 'Anti-Naturalism in Extremis.' *Partisan Review*, X (January–February 1943), 24–39.

DONOGHUE, DENIS. 'The Well-Tempered Klavier.' *HR*, XVII (Spring 1964), 138–42.

DUDEK, LOUIS. 'McLuhanism in a Nutshell—The Dangers of a Theory.' *Montreal Gazette*, 8 April 1967, 28.

DUFFY, DENNIS. *Marshall McLuhan*. Toronto, 1969.

ELIOT, T. S. 'Myth and Literary Classicism.' *The Modern Tradition: Backgrounds of Modern Literature*, ed. Richard Ellmann and Charles Feidelson, Jr. New York, 1965, pp. 679–81. With a 1964 comment by Eliot, reproduces 'Ulysses, Order, and Myth.' *The Dial*, LXXV (1923), 480–3.

—— *Notes towards the Definition of Culture*, 2nd ed. London, 1962.

—— *On Poetry and Poets*. London, 1957.

—— *Selected Essays*. London, 1951. Reprints essays published between 1917 and 1936.

—— *To Criticize the Critic and Other Writings*. London, 1965.

—— *The Use of Poetry and the Use of Criticism: Studies in the Relation of Criticism to Poetry in England*. 2nd ed. London, 1964.

ELLIOTT, GEORGE P. 'Variations on a Theme by Frye.' *HR*, XVI (Autumn 1963), 467–70.

ELLMANN, RICHARD, and FEIDELSON, CHARLES, JR, eds. *The Modern Tradition: Backgrounds of Modern Literature*. New York, 1965.

ELLUL, JACQUES. *The Technological Society*, trans. John Wilkinson; intro. Robert K. Merton. New York, 1964.

ELTON, WILLIAM. 'A Glossary of the New Criticism.' *Poetry*, LXXIII (December 1948), 153–62; LXXIII (January 1949), 232–45; LXXIII (February 1949), 296–307.

EMPSON, WILLIAM. *Seven Types of Ambiguity*. Harmondsworth, 1961. First published 1930.

ENZENSBERGER, HANS MAGNUS. 'Constituents of a Theory of the Media.' *NLR*, no. 64 (November–December 1970), 13–36.

ERDMAN, DAVID V. 'Blake: The Historical Approach.' *Discussions of William Blake*, ed. John E. Grant. Boston, 1961, pp. 17–27. Reprinted from *English Institute Essays: 1950*, ed. Alan S. Downer, New York, 1951, pp. 197–223.

EWEN, STUART B. 'Advertising as Social Production.' *Radical America*, III (May–June 1969), 42–56.

FANON, FRANTZ. *Black Skin White Masks*, trans. Charles Lam
    Markmann. London, 1970.
—— *A Dying Colonialism*, trans. Haakon Chevalier. Harmondsworth,
    1970.
—— *Toward the African Revolution*, trans. Haakon Chevalier.
    Harmondsworth, 1970.
—— *The Wretched of the Earth*, trans. Constance Farrington; preface
    by Jean-Paul Sartre. Harmondsworth, 1967.
FARRELL, JAMES T. 'The Ground of Criticism.' *The Saturday
    Review of Literature*, III (2 July 1927), 939, 942.
FEDERICI, SILVIA. 'VietCong Philosophy: Tran Duc Thao.' *Telos*,
    no. 6 (Fall 1970), 104–17.
FEKETE, JOHN. 'Colonisation/Decolonisation: The Class Struggle
    1600–1968.' *The Struggle for Quebec*, by John Fekete, Victor
    Rabinovitch, and Bonnie Campbell. *Spokesman* pamphlet no. 13,
    published by The Bertrand Russell Peace Foundation. Nottingham,
    October 1970, pp. 1–18.
—— John Crowe Ransom, Northrop Frye, and Marshall McLuhan: A
    Theoretical Critique of some Aspects of North American Critical
    Theory. Diss., University of Cambridge, November 1972.
FEYERABEND, PAUL K. 'Linguistic Arguments and Scientific Method.'
    Telos, no. 3 (Spring 1969), 43–63.
FIEDLER, LESLIE A. 'Archetype and Signature: A Study of the
    Relationship between Biography and Poetry.' *SeR*, LX (April 1960).
—— 'In the Beginning Was the Word: *Logos* or *Mythos*.' *SeR*, LXIII
    (July 1955), 405–20.
FINKELSTEIN, SIDNEY. *Sense and Nonsense of McLuhan*. New York,
    1968.
FISCHER, ERNST. *Art Against Ideology*, trans. Anna Bostock. London,
    1969.
—— *The Necessity of Art: A Marxist Approach*, trans. Anna Bostock.
    Harmondsworth, 1963.
FISHER, PETER F. *The Valley of Vision: Blake as Prophet and
    Revolutionary*, ed. Northrop Frye. Toronto, 1961.
FLETCHER, ANGUS. *Allegory: The Theory of a Symbolic Mode*. Ithaca,
    N.Y., 1964.
—— 'Utopian History and the *Anatomy of Criticism*.' *Northrop Frye in
    Modern Criticism: Selected Papers from the English Institute*, ed.
    Murray Krieger. New York, 1966, pp. 31–73.
FOERSTER, HEINZ VON. 'From Stimulus to Symbol: The Economy of
    Biological Computation.' *Sign, Image, Symbol*, ed. György
    Kepes. New York, 1966, pp. 42–61.
FOGARASI, ADALBERT. 'The Tasks of the Communist Press,' trans.
    Paul Breines. *Radical America*, III (May–June 1969), 68–75.
FOGLE, RICHARD H. 'Romantic Bards and Metaphysical Reviewers.'
    ELH: A Journal of English Literary History, XII (September 1945),
    221–50.
FOSTER, RICHARD. *The New Romantics: A Reappraisal of the New
    Criticism*. Bloomington, 1962.

FOUCAULT, MICHEL. *The Order of Things: An Archaeology of the Human Sciences*. London, 1970.

FRASER, G. S. 'Mythmanship.' *The New York Review of Books*, I (6 February 1964), 18–19.

FRIEDMAN, MELVIN. [Review of Frye's *Anatomy*.] *Books Abroad*, XXXII (Autumn 1958), 451–2.

FROMM, ERICH. *The Crisis of Psychoanalysis*. New York, 1970.

GABEL, JOSEPH. 'La Fausse Conscience.' *L'Homme et la société*, no. 3 (January–March 1967), 157–68.

GENOVESE, EUGENE D. *In Red and Black: Marxian Explorations in Southern and Afro-American History*. New York, 1971.

—— *The Political Economy of Slavery: Studies in the Economy and Society of the Slave South*. New York, 1966.

—— *The World the Slaveholders Made: Two Essays in Interpretation*. New York, 1969.

GERAS, NORMAN. 'Essence and Appearance: Aspects of Fetishism in Marx's *Capital*.' *NLR*, no. 65 (January–February 1971), 69–85.

GILBERT, ALLAN H. *Literary Criticism: Plato to Dryden*. Detroit, 1962.

GILSON, ETIENNE. *Elements of Christian Philosophy*. New York, 1960.

GLUCKSMANN, ANDRÉ. 'A Ventriloquist Structuralism.' *NLR*, no. 72 (March–April 1972), 68–92.

GLUCKSMANN, MIRIAM. 'Lucien Goldmann: Humanist or Marxist?' *NLR*, no. 56 (July–August 1969), 49–68.

GODELIER, MAURICE. 'Myth and History.' *NLR*, no. 69 (September–October 1971), 93–112.

GOLDIN, HYMAN H. 'The Television Overlords.' *Atlantic*, July 1969, 87–9.

GOLDMANN, LUCIEN. *The Hidden God: A Study of Tragic Vision in The 'Pensées' of Pascal and the Tragedies of Racine*, trans. Philip Thody. London, 1964.

—— *The Human Sciences and Philosophy*, trans. Hayden V. White and Robert Anchor. London, 1969.

—— *Immanuel Kant*, trans. Robert Black. London, 1971.

—— *Marxisme et sciences humaines*. Paris, 1970.

—— *Pour une sociologie du roman*. Paris, 1964.

—— *Recherches dialectiques*. Paris, 1959.

—— 'Structuralisme, marxisme, existentialisme.' *L'Homme et la société*, no. 2 (October–December 1966), 105–24.

GOMBRICH, E. H. *The Story of Art*. London, 1961.

GOMME, ANDOR. *Attitudes to Criticism*. Carbondale and Edwardsville, Ill., 1966.

GOODY, JACK, and WATT, IAN. 'The Consequences of Literacy.' *Literacy in Traditional Societies*, ed. Jack Goody. Cambridge, 1968, pp. 27–68.

GORZ, ANDRÉ. *Strategy for Labor: A Radical Proposal*, trans. Martin A. Nicolaus and Victoria Ortiz. Boston, 1967.

GOUGH, KATHLEEN. 'Implications of Literacy in Traditional China and India.' *Literacy in Traditional Societies*, ed. Jack Goody. Cambridge, 1968, pp. 70–84.

GOULDNER, ALVIN. *The Dialectic of Ideology and Technology: The Origins, Grammar and Future of Ideology.* New York, 1976.

GRAMSCI, ANTONIO. *Selections from the Prison Notebooks*, ed. and trans. Quentin Hoare and Geoffrey Nowell Smith, London, 1971.

HALLIE, PHILIP P. 'The Master Builder.' *Partisan Review*, XXXI (Fall 1964), 650–8.

HANDY, WILLIAM J. *Kant and the Southern New Critics.* Austin, 1963.

HARDISON, O. B., JR, ed. *English Literary Criticism: The Renaissance.* New York, 1963.

—— , ed. *Modern Continental Literary Criticism.* New York, 1962.

HARMAR-BROWN, FRANCIS. 'A Cool View of Marshall McLuhan.' *The Advertising Quarterly*, no. 12 (Summer 1967), 17–22.

HARTMAN, GEOFFREY. 'Ghostlier Demarcations.' *Northrop Frye in Modern Criticism: Selected Papers from the English Institute*, ed. Murray Krieger. New York, 1966, pp. 109–31.

HASSAN, IHAB H. 'Criticism as Mimesis.' *The South Atlantic Quarterly*, LV (October 1956), 473–86.

HAUSER, ARNOLD. *The Social History of Art*, trans. Stanley Godman. 4 vols. London and New York, 1951.

HEATH, STEPHEN, MACCABE, COLIN and PRENDERGAST, CHRISTOPER, eds. *Signs of the Times: Introductory Readings in Textual Semiotics.* [Cambridge, 1971.]

HECHT, ANTHONY. 'A Few Green Leaves.' *SeR*, LXVII (October 1959), 568–71.

HEILMAN, ROBERT B. 'The Southern Temper.' *South: Modern Southern Literature in its Cultural Setting*, ed. Louis D. Rubin, Jr, and Robert D. Jacobs. Garden City, N.Y., 1961, pp. 48–59.

HEISENBERG, WERNER. *Physics and Philosophy: The Revolution in Modern Science.* New York, 1958.

HELLER, ÁGNES. *Az aristotelési etika és az antik ethos* [*Aristotelian Ethics and the Ethos of Antiquity*]. Budapest, 1966.

—— 'Lukács's Aesthetics.' *The New Hungarian Quarterly*, VII (Winter 1966), 84–94.

—— 'The Marxist Theory of Revolution and the Revolution of Everyday Life.' *Telos*, no. 6 (Fall 1970), 212–23.

—— *A mindennapi élet* [*Everyday Life*]. Budapest, 1970.

—— *A reneszánsz ember* [*Renaissance Man*]. Budapest, 1967.

—— 'Shakespeare and History.' *NLR*, no. 32 (July–August 1965), 16–23.

HEMPEL, CARL G. 'The Logic of Functional Analysis.' *Readings in the Philosophy of the Social Sciences*, ed. May Brodbeck. New York, 1968, pp. 179–210.

HEMPHILL, GEORGE. *Allen Tate.* University of Minnesota Pamphlets on American Writers, no. 39. Minneapolis, 1964.

HOFFMAN, DANIEL G., and HYNES, SAMUEL, eds. *English Literary Criticism: Romantic and Victorian.* New York, 1963.

HOFFMAN, FREDERICK J. *The Twenties: American Writing in the Postwar Decade*, rev. ed. New York, 1962.

HOGGART, RICHARD. 'Big Dipper.' *The Listener*, LXXII (3 December 1964), 895–6.

—— 'The Dance of the Long-Legged Fly.' *Encounter*, XXVII (August 1966), 63–71.

HOLLOWAY, JOHN. 'The Critical Intimidation.' *HR*, V (Winter 1953), 474–95.

—— 'The Critical Zodiac of Northrop Frye.' *The Colours of Clarity: Essays on Contemporary Literature and Education*. London, 1964, pp. 153–160.

HOLMAN, C. HUGH. 'The Defense of Art: Criticism since 1930.' *The Development of American Literary Criticism*, ed. Floyd Stovall. Chapel Hill, 1955, pp. 199–245.

HOOK, SIDNEY. 'The New Failure of Nerve.' *Partisan Review*, X (January–February 1943), 2–23.

HORKHEIMER, MAX. 'Art and Mass Culture.' *Studies in Philosophy and Social Science*, published by the Institute of Social Research. Vol. IX. New York, 1941, pp. 290–304.

—— 'The End of Reason.' *Studies in Philosophy and Social Science*, pp. 366–88.

HOTOPF, W. H. N. *Language, Thought and Comprehension: A Case Study of the Writings of I. A. Richards*. London, 1965.

HOUGH, GRAHAM. *An Essay on Criticism*. London, 1966.

—— 'John Crowe Ransom: The Poet and the Critic.' *SR*, new series, I (January 1965), 1–21.

—— 'Marvell of the Deep South.' *The Listener*, LXIV (4 August 1960), 183–5.

HOWARD, DICK. 'Adorno.' *Telos*, no. 8 (Summer 1971), 146–9.

HULME, T. E. *Further Speculations*, ed. Sam Hynes. Minneapolis, 1955.

—— *Speculations: Essays on Humanism and the Philosophy of Art*, ed. Herbert Read, 2nd ed. London, 1936.

HUSSERL, EDMUND. *The Crisis of European Sciences and Transcendental Phenomenology*, trans. David Carr. Evanston, Ill., 1970.

HYMAN, STANLEY EDGAR. *The Armed Vision: A Study in the Methods of Modern Literary Criticism*, rev., abr. ed. New York, 1955.

HYNES, SAMUEL, ed. *English Literary Criticism: Restoration and Eighteenth Century*. New York, 1963.

INGLIS, FRED. 'Professor Northrop Frye and the Academic Study of Literature.' *The Centennial Review*, IX (Summer 1965), 319–31.

INNIS, HAROLD ADAMS. *The Bias of Communication*, introd. Marshall McLuhan. Toronto, 1964. First published 1951.

JACKSON, GEORGE. *Blood in My Eye*. London, 1972.

JARRELL, RANDALL. 'John Ransom's Poetry.' *SeR*, LVI (July 1948), 378–90.

JAY, MARTIN. *The Dialectical Imagination: A History of the Frankfurt School and the Institute of Social Research 1923–50*. Boston, 1973.

KAHN, SHOLOM J. 'What Does A Critic Analyze? (On a Phenomenological Approach to Literature.' *Philosophy and Phenomenological Research*, XIII (December 1952), 237–45.

KEPES, GYÖRGY, ed. *Education of Vision*. New York, 1965.

—— ed. *Sign, Image, Symbol*. New York, 1966.

KERMODE, FRANK. 'Contemplation and Method.' *SeR*, LXXII (January 1964), 124–31.
—— 'Frye Reconsidered.' *Continuities*. London, 1968, pp. 116–21.
—— 'Northrop Frye.' *Puzzles and Epiphanies: Essays and Reviews 1958–1961*. London, 1962, pp. 64–73.
—— 'Old Orders Changing.' *Encounter* XV (August 1960), 72–6.
—— *The Romantic Image*. London, 1961.
KEYNES, GEOFFREY. 'The Poetic Vision.' *Time & Tide*, XXVIII (27 December 1947), 1394.
KIBEL, ALVIN C. 'Academic Circles.' *KR*, XXVI (Spring 1964), 416–22.
—— 'The Imagination Goes to College.' *Partisan Review*, XXXII (Summer 1965), 461–6.
KNIGHT, KARL F. *The Poetry of John Crowe Ransom: A Study of Diction, Metaphor, and Symbol*. The Hague, 1964.
KOCH, VIVIENNE. 'The Achievement of John Crowe Ransom.' *SeR*, LVIII (April 1950), 227–61.
—— 'The Poetry of Allen Tate.' *The Kenyon Critics: Studies in Modern Literature from the Kenyon Review*, ed. John Crowe Ransom. Cleveland, 1951, pp. 169–81.
KOGAN, PAULINE. *Northrop Frye: The High Priest of Clerical Obscurantism*. Literature and Ideology Monographs, no. 1. Published by Progressive Books and Periodicals, Montreal, April 1969.
KOLAKOWSKI, LESZEK. *Marxism and Beyond: On Historical Understanding and Individual Responsibility*, trans. Jane Zielonko Peel. London, 1971.
KORSCH, KARL. *Marxism and Philosophy*. London, 1970.
KOSIK, KAREL. *Dialektik des Konkreten*, trans. from Czech by Marianne Hoffmann. Frankfurt-am-Main, 1967.
—— *La Dialectique du concret*, trans. from German by Roger Dangeville. Paris, 1970.
—— 'Reason and History.' *Telos*, no. 3 (Spring 1969), 64–71.
KRIEGER, MURRAY. *The New Apologists for Poetry*. Minneapolis, 1956.
—— ed. and intro. *Northrop Frye in Modern Criticism: Selected Papers from the English Institute*. New York, 1966. Introduction, 'Northrop Frye and Contemporary Criticism: Ariel and the Spirit of Gravity,' pp. 1–26.
—— *A Window to Criticism: Shakespeare's Sonnets and Modern Poetics*. Princeton, 1964.
KUHN, THOMAS S. *The Structure of Scientific Revolutions*. Chicago, 1962.
KUHNS, RICHARD. 'Professor Frye's Criticism.' *The Journal of Philosophy*, LVI (10 September 1959), 745–55.
LANE, MICHAEL, ed. *Structuralism: A Reader*. London, 1970.
LEACH, EDMUND. *Lévi-Strauss*. London, 1970.
LEDUC, VICTOR, ed. *Structuralisme et marxisme*. Paris, 1970.
LEFEBVRE, HENRI. *Au-delà du structuralisme*. Paris, 1971.

—— *Everyday Life in the Modern World*, trans. Sacha Rabinovitch. London, 1971.

—— *Le Langage et la société*. Paris, 1966.

LEMON, LEE T. *The Partial Critics*. London, 1965.

LENIN, V. I. *Philosophical Notebooks. Collected Works*, Vol. XXXVIII. Moscow, 1961.

LÉVI-STRAUSS, CLAUDE. *The Savage Mind*. Chicago, 1966.

—— *Structural Anthropology*, trans. Claire Jacobson and Brooke Grundfest Schoepf. Garden City, N.Y., 1967.

LICHTHEIM, GEORGE. 'The Concept of Ideology.' *Studies in the Philosophy of History*, ed. George H. Nadel. New York, 1965, pp. 148–79.

LILLEY, SAMUEL. *Men, Machines and History: The Story of Tools and Machines in Relation to Social Progress*, 2nd ed. New York, 1966.

LISSITSKY, EL. 'The Future of the Book.' *NLR*, no. 41 (January–February 1967), 31–43.

'Literary Dissection.' *TLS*, 14 February 1958, 81–2.

LLOYD, GEOFFREY E. R. *Polarity and Analogy: Two Types of Argumentation in Early Greek Thought*. Cambridge, 1966.

LONG, D. DAVID and BURR, MICHAEL R., eds. *John Crowe Ransom, Gentleman, Teacher, Poet, Editor Founder of the Kenyon Review: A Tribute from the Community of Letters*. Supplement to *The Kenyon Collegian*, LXXXX (1964). Gambier, Ohio.

LOWELL, ROBERT. 'John Ransom's Conversation.' *SeR*, LVI (July :948), 374–7.

LUKÁCS, GYÖRGY. 'The Dialectic of Labor: Beyond Causality and Teleology,' trans. Adolph W. Gucinski. *Telos*, no. 6 (Fall 1970), 162–74.

—— *Entretiens avec Georg Lukacs*, by Wolfgang Abendroth, Hans Heinz Holz, Leo Kofler, Theo Pinkus; trans. Marcel Ollivier. Paris, 1969.

—— *Az esztétikum sajátossága* [*The Specificity of the Aesthetic*], trans. István Eörsi. 2 vols. Budapest, 1965.

—— *History and Class Consciousness: Studies in Marxist Dialectics*, trans. Rodney Livingstone. London, 1971.

—— *A különösség mint esztétikai kategória* [*Peculiarity as an Aesthetic Category*]. Budapest, 1957.

—— 'N. Bukharin: Historical Materialism,' trans. Ben Brewster, in *Political Writings, 1919–1929: The Question of Parliamentarianism and Other Essays*, ed. Rodney Livingstone. London, 1972, pp. 134–42.

—— 'The Old Culture and the New Culture.' *Telos*, no. 5 (Spring 1970), 21–30.

—— *Political Writings, 1919–1929: The Question of Parliamentarianism and Other Essays*, ed. Rodney Livingstone; trans. Michael McColgan. London, 1972.

—— *Realism in Our Time: Literature and the Class Struggle*, trans. John and Necke Mander; preface by George Steiner. New York, 1962.

—— *A realizmus problémái* [*Problems of Realism*], trans. Endre Gaspar.

Budapest, n.d. [c. 1948].
—— *The Theory of the Novel: A Historico-philosophical Essay on the Forms of Great Epic Literature*, trans. Anna Bostock. London, 1971.
—— *Writer and Critic and Other Essays*, ed. and trans. Arthur Kahn. London, 1970.
LYNSKEY, WINIFRED. 'A Critic in Action: Mr. Ransom.' *College English*, V (February 1944), 239–49.
LYONS, JOHN. *Chomsky*. London, 1970.
LYTLE, ANDREW NELSON. 'The Hind Tit.' *I'll Take My Stand: The South and the Agrarian Tradition*, by Twelve Southerners. New York, 1930, pp. 201–45.
McDOWELL, FREDERICK P. W. 'After the New Criticism.' *The Western Review*, XXII (Summer 1958), 309–18.
MACHEREY, PIERRE. *Pour une théorie de la production littéraire*. Paris, 1966.
MacINTYRE, ALASDAIR. *Marcuse*. London, 1970.
MACKSEY, RICHARD, and DONATO, EUGENIO, eds. *The Languages of Criticism and the Sciences of Man: The Structuralist Controversy*. Baltimore and London, 1970.
MACPHERSON, C. B. *The Political Theory of Possessive Individualism: Hobbes to Locke*. Oxford, 1962.
MALLARMÉ, STÉPHANE. *Mallarmé: Selected Prose Poems, Essays and Letters*, trans. and intro. Bradford Cook. Baltimore, 1956.
MANDEL, ELI W. 'Frye's Anatomy of Criticism.' *The Canadian Forum*, XXXVIII (September 1958), 128–9.
—— 'The Language of Humanity: Three Books by Northrop Frye.' *The Tamarack Review*, Autumn 1963, 82–9.
—— 'Toward a Theory of Cultural Revolution: The Criticism of Northrop Frye.' *Canadian Literature*, no. 1 (Summer 1959), 58–67.
MANDEL, ERNEST. *Marxist Economic Theory*, trans. Brian Pearce. 2 vols. London, 1968.
MAO TSE-TUNG. *On Literature and Art*. Peking, 1967.
Marcuse, cet inconnu, by Lucien Goldmann, Henri Lefebvre, *et al.*, in *La Nef*, no. 36 (January–March 1969).
MARCUSE, HERBERT. 'Art and Revolution.' *Partisan Review*, July 1972, 174–87.
—— 'Art as Form of Reality.' *NLR*, no. 74 (July–August 1972), 51–8.
—— *Eros and Civilization: A Philosophical Inquiry into Freud*. New York, 1955.
—— *An Essay on Liberation*. London, 1969.
—— *Five Lectures: Psychoanalysis, Politics, and Utopia*, trans. Jeremy J. Shapiro and Shierry M. Weber. London, 1970.
—— *Negations: Essays in Critical Theory*, trans. Jeremy J. Shapiro. Boston, 1969.
—— *One-Dimensional Man: Studies in the Ideology of Advanced Industrial Society*. Boston, 1966.
—— *Reason and Revolution: Hegel and the Rise of Social Theory*, 3rd ed. Boston, 1960.

—— 'Repressive Tolerance.' *A Critique of Pure Tolerance*, by Robert Paul Wolff, Barrington Moore, Jr, and Herbert Marcuse. Boston, 1965.

—— 'Some Social Implications of Modern Technology.' *Studies in Philosophy and Social Science*, published by the Institute of Social Research. Vol. IX. New York, 1941, pp. 414–39.

—— *Studies in Critical Philosophy*, trans. Joris de Bres. London, 1972.

MÁRKUS, GYÖRGY. *Marxizmus és 'antropológia': az emberi lényeg fogalma Marx filozófiájában* [*Marxism and 'Anthropology': The Concept of Human Essence in Marx's Philosophy*], 2nd rev. ed. Budapest, 1971.

MARX, KARL. *Capital: A Critical Analysis of Capitalist Production*, trans. Samuel Moore and Edward Aveling, ed. Frederick Engels. 3 vols. Moscow, 1965–7.

—— *Economic and Philosophic Manuscripts of 1844*, ed. Dirk J. Struik. New York, 1964.

—— *Grundrisse: Foundations of the Critique of Political Economy* (*Rough Draft*), trans. Martin Nicolaus. Harmondsworth, 1973.

—— *The Poverty of Philosophy*. Moscow, 1955.

—— *Pre-Capitalist Economic Formations*, ed. E. J. Hobsbawm; trans. Jack Cohen. New York, 1965.

—— *Writings of the Young Marx on Philosophy and Society*, ed. and trans. Loyd D. Easton and Kurt H. Guddat. Garden City, N.Y., 1967.

—— and ENGELS, FREDERICK. *The German Ideology*. Moscow, 1964.

—— *A Handbook of Marxism*, ed. Emile Burns. London, 1935.

MATEJKA, LADISLAV and POMORSKA, KRYSTYNA, eds. *Readings in Russian Poetics: Formalist and Structuralist Views*. Cambridge, Mass., and London, 1971.

MATTHIESSEN, F. O. 'American Poetry, 1920–40.' *SeR*, LV (January 1947), 24–55.

—— 'Primarily Language.' *SeR*, LVI (July 1948), 391–401.

MATTICK, PAUL. *Marx and Keynes: The Limits of the Mixed Economy*. Boston, 1969.

MEAD, SHEPHERD. *The Big Ball of Wax*. London, 1955.

MERCIER, VIVIAN. 'A Synoptic View of Criticism.' *The Commonweal*, LXVI (20 September 1957), 618, 620.

MERLEAU-PONTY, MAURICE. *Phenomenology of Perception*, trans. Colin Smith. London, 1962.

—— 'Pravda.' *Telos*, no. 7 (Spring 1971), 112–21.

—— *The Primacy of Perception and Other Essays on Phenomenological Psychology, the Philosophy of Art, History and Politics*, ed. James M. Eadie. N.p., 1964.

—— *Sens et non-sens*, 3rd ed. Paris, 1948.

—— *Signes*. Paris, 1960.

—— *The Structure of Behaviour*, trans. Alden L. Fisher. London, 1965.

—— 'Western Marxism.' *Telos*, no. 6 (Fall 1970), 140–61.

MÉSZÁROS, ISTVÁN, ed. *Aspects of History and Class Consciousness*. London, 1971.

—— *Marx's Theory of Alienation*, London, 1970.

—— *The Necessity of Social Control*. London, 1971.

MILLER, JONATHAN. *McLuhan*. London, 1971.

MILLS, C. WRIGHT. *The Sociological Imagination*. New York, 1961.

MIZENER, ARTHUR. 'Recent Criticism.' *SR*, V (Autumn 1939), 376–400.

MONTAGU, M. F. ASHLEY, ed. *Man and Aggression*. New York, 1968.

MORRIS, RUDOLPH E. [Review of McLuhan.] *McLuhan: Hot and Cool*, ed. Gerald E. Stearn. New York, 1967, pp. 88–91.

MUGGERIDGE, MALCOLM. 'The Medium is McLuhan.' *New Statesman*, 1 September 1967, 253.

MULLER, HERBERT J. 'The Critic Behind Barbed Wire: If He Wishes, He Can End His Self-Imposed Internment.' *The Saturday Review of Literature*, XXVI (25 September 1943), 3–4, 18.

—— 'The New Criticism in Poetry.' *SR*, VI (Spring 1941), 811–39.

NAISON, MARK D. 'The Southern Tenant Farmers' Union and the CIO.' *Radical America*, II (September–October 1968), 36–56.

NEMEROV, HOWARD. 'The Current of the Frozen Stream.' *SeR*, LXVII (October 1959), 585–97.

Newsweek cover story, 'The Message of Marshall McLuhan,' 6 March 1967, 41–5.

NOTT, KATHLEEN. 'The Electronic Prophet.' *The Observer*, 7 August 1966, 20.

O'CONNOR, WILLIAM VAN. 'The Influence of the Metaphysicals on Modern Poetry.' *College English*, IX (January 1948), 180–7.

—— 'A Short View of the New Criticism.' *College English*, XI (November 1949), 63–71.

—— 'The World as Body.' *SeR*, LVI (July 1948), 435–41.

OGDEN, C. K. and RICHARDS, IVOR A. *The Meaning of Meaning: A Study of the Influence of Language upon Thought and of the Science of Symbolism*, 10th ed. London, 1949. First published 1923.

OLSON, ELDER. 'Recent Literary Criticism.' *Modern Philology*, XL (February 1943), 275–83.

O'NEILL, JOHN. *Sociology as a Skin Trade: Essays towards a Reflexive Sociology*. New York, 1972.

ONG, S. J., WALTER J. 'A Dialectic of Aural and Objective Correlatives.' *Perspectives on Poetry*, ed. James L. Calderwood and Harold E. Toliver. New York, 1968, pp. 119–31.

—— 'The Meaning of the "New Criticism,"' *Twentieth Century English*, ed. William S. Knickerbocker. New York, 1946, pp. 344–70.

—— 'A Modern Sensibility.' *McLuhan: Hot and Cool*, ed. Gerald E. Stearn. New York, 1967, pp. 92–101.

—— *The Presence of the Word: Some Prolegomena for Cultural and Religious History*. New Haven, 1967.

OWSLEY, FRANK LAWRENCE. 'The Irrepressible Conflict.' *I'll Take My Stand: The South and the Agrarian Tradition*, by Twelve Southerners. New York, 1930, pp. 61–91.

PALLOIX, CHRISTIAN. *L'Economie mondiale capitaliste*. 2 vols. Paris, 1971.

PARKINSON, G. H. R., ed. *Georg Lukács: The Man, His Work and His Ideas*. London, 1970.

—— 'Ransom and the Poetics of Monastic Ecstasy.' *Modern Language Quarterly*, XXVI (December 1965), 571–85.

PARSONS, THORNTON H. 'Ransom the Revisionist.' *SR*, new series, II (April 1966), 453–63.

PATER, WALTER. *Appreciations: with an Essay on Style*. London, 1899.

—— *Greek Studies*. London , 1895.

—— *Marius the Epicurean: His Sensations and Ideas*. London, 1891.

—— *Plato and Platonism*. London, 1893.

—— *The Renaissance: Studies in Art and Poetry*, 5th ed. London, 1912.

PERCIVAL, MILTON O. *William Blake's Circle of Destiny*. New York, 1938.

PERIGNON, SYLVAIN. 'Marxisme et positivisme.' *L'Homme et la société*, no. 7 (January–March 1968), 161–9.

PERLMAN, FREDY. 'Essay on Commodity Fetishism.' *Telos*, no. 6 (Fall 1970), 244–73.

PHILIPSON, MORRIS, ed. *Aesthetics Today*. Cleveland, 1961.

PICCONE, PAUL. 'Phenomenological Marxism.' *Telos*, no. 9 (Fall 1971), 3–31.

—— 'Reading the *Crisis*.' *Telos*, no. 8 (Summer 1971), 121–9.

—— 'Review of Gouldner's *The Dialectic of Ideology and Technology: The Origins, Grammar and Future of Ideology*.' 14 pp. Unpub. typescript, 1976.

—— 'Structuralist Marxism?' *Radical America*, III (September 1969), 25–32.

—— 'Towards an Understanding of Lenin's Philosophy.' *Radical America*, IV (September–October 1970), 3–20.

—— 'Towards a Socio-historical Interpretation of the Scientific Revolution.' *Telos*, no. 1 (Spring 1968), 16–26.

POITIER, RICHARD. 'The Great Tradition.' *The New York Review of Books*, I (12 December 1963), 20–1.

POULANTZAS, NICOS. 'The Problem of the Capitalist State.' *NLR*, no. 58 (November–December 1969), 67–78.

PRICE, MARTIN. 'Open and Shut: New Critical Essays.' *The Yale Review*, LIII (Summer 1964), 592–9.

PURDY, ROB ROY, ed. *Fugitives' Reunion: Conversations at Vanderbilt, May 3–5, 1956*. Introd. Louis D. Rubin, Jr. Nashville, 1959.

RAHV, PHILIP. 'Proletarian Literature: A Political Autopsy.' *SR*, IV (Winter 1939), 616–28.

RAINSBERRY, FREDERICK BEATTY. 'The Irony of Objectivity in the New Criticism.' Diss., Michigan State College of Agriculture and Applied Science, 1952.

RANK, OTTO. *The Myth of the Birth of the Hero and Other Writings*, ed. Philip Freund. New York, 1959.

RAWICK, GEORGE P. *The American Slave: A Composite Autobiography. I, From Sundown to Sunup: The Making of the Black Community*. Westport, Conn., 1972.

—— 'The Historical Roots of Black Liberation.' *Radical America*, II

(July–August 1968), 1–13.

REANEY, JAMES. 'Frye's Magnet.' *The Tamarack Review*, Autumn 1964, 72–8.

REICH, WILHELM. *Dialectical Materialism and Psychoanalysis*. Published by Socialist Reproduction, London, 1972. First published 1929.

—— *The Mass Psychology of Fascism*, trans. Vincent R. Carfagno. New York, 1970.

—— *Selected Writings: An Introduction to Orgonomy*. New York, 1960.

—— *What Is Class Consciousness?* Published by Socialist Reproduction, London, 1972. First published 1933.

RICHARDS, IVOR A. *Coleridge on Imagination*, 3rd ed. London, 1962. First published 1934.

—— *The Philosophy of Rhetoric*. New York, 1965. First published 1936.

—— *Poetries and Sciences: A Reissue of Science and Poetry (1926, 1935) with Commentary*. London, 1970.

—— *Practical Criticism: A Study of Literary Judgment*. London, 1964. First published 1929.

—— *Principles of Literary Criticism*. London, 1960. First published 1924.

RICKS, CHRISTOPHER. 'McLuhanism.' *McLuhan: Pro and Con*, ed. Raymond Rosenthal. Baltimore, 1969, pp. 100–5.

RIMBAUD, ARTHUR. *Complete Works, Selected Letters*, trans., intro., and notes by Wallace Fowlie. Chicago, 1966.

ROCKMAN, ARNOLD. 'McLuhanism: The Natural History of an Intellectual Fashion.' *Encounter*, XXXI (November 1968), 28–37.

ROELLINGER, FRANCIS X., JR. 'Two theories of Poetry as Knowledge.' *SR*, VII (Spring 1942), 690–705.

ROONEY, WILLIAM JOSEPH. 'The Problem of "Poetry and Belief" in Contemporary Criticism.' Diss., The Catholic University of America, Washington, D.C., 1949.

ROSE, J., ed. *Survey of Cybernetics: A Tribute to Dr. Norbert Wiener*. London, 1969.

ROSENTHAL, RAYMOND, ed. *McLuhan: Pro and Con*. Baltimore, 1969.

ROVIT, EARL. 'The Need for Engagement.' *Shenandoah*, XIV (Summer 1963), 62–5.

ROWNTREE, MICKEY, and ROWNTREE, JOHN. 'On Revolution in the Metropolis (Political Economy for Revolutionary Socialists).' Unpub. typescript. July 1970.

RUBIN, JERRY. *Do It: Scenarios of the Revolution*, introd. Eldridge Cleaver. New York, 1970.

RUBIN, LOUIS D., JR, and JACOBS, ROBERT D., eds. *South: Modern Southern Literature in Its Cultural Setting*. Garden City, N.Y., 1961.

RUDNER, RICHARD. 'On Semiotic Aesthetics.' *The Journal of Aesthetics and Art Criticism*, X (September 1951), 67–77.

RUSSETT, CYNTHIA EAGLE. *The Concept of Equilibrium in American Social Thought*. New Haven, 1966.

RYERSON, STANLEY. *The Open Society: Paradox and Challenge*. New York, 1965.

SARTRE, JEAN-PAUL. 'Replies to Structuralism: An Interview,' trans. Robert D'Amico. *Telos*, no. 9 (Fall 1971), 110–16.

—— 'The Risk of Spontaneity and the Logic of the Institution: An Interview,' conducted by Rossana Rossanda. *Telos*, no. 4 (Fall 1969), 191–205.

—— *Search for a Method*, trans. Hazel E. Barnes. New York, 1967.

SCHILLER, HERBERT I. *Mass Communications and American Empire*. New York, 1970.

SCHMIDT, ALFRED. *The Concept of Nature in Marx*. London, 1971.

SCHROYER, TRENT. 'Toward a Critical Theory for Advanced Industrial Society.' *Radical America*, IV (April 1970), 65–78.

SCHWARTZ, DELMORE. 'The Poetry of Allen Tate.' *SR*, V (Winter 1940), 419–38.

SHILS, EDWARD. 'Daydreams, and Nightmares: Reflections on the Criticism of Mass Culture.' *SeR*, LXV (October 1957), 587–608.

SKELTON, ROBIN. 'The House that Frye Built.' *Canadian Literature*, no. 24 (Spring 1965), 63–6.

SKLAR, MARTIN J. 'On the Proletarian Revolution and the End of Political-Economic Society.' *Radical America*, III (May–June 1969), 1–41.

SLADE, MARK. 'McLuhan: Magnetic Man.' *I.C.E.F. Review*, December 1966, 4–7.

SLAN, JON. 'Innis, McLuhan and Frye: Frontiers of Canadian Criticism.' *Canadian Dimension*, VIII (August 1972), 43–6.

SMITH, A. J. M. 'The Critic's Task: Frye's Latest Work.' *Canadian Literature*, no. 20 (Spring 1964), 6–14.

SMITH, BERNARD. *Forces in American Criticism: A Study in the History of American Literary Thought*. New York, 1939.

SOHN-RETHEL, ALFRED. 'Mental and Manual Labour and the Totality of Marxism.' Unpub. typescript, August 1971.

'Sons of New Critic.' *TLS*, 25 November 1965, 1078–9.

'Soothsayer of the Global Village.' *TLS*, 12 February 1971, 177.

SPARSHOTT, F. E. *The Structure of Aesthetics*. Toronto, 1963.

SPENCER, THEODORE. 'How To Criticize a Poem (In the Manner of Certain Contemporary Critics).' *NR*, CIX (6 December 1943), 816, 818.

STALLMAN, ROBERT WOOSTER, ed. *Critiques and Essays in Criticism 1920–1948: Representing the Achievement of Modern British and American Critics*, foreword by Cleanth Brooks. New York, 1949.

—— 'The New Critics.' *Critiques and Essays in Criticism*, pp. 488–506.

STAROBIN, ROBERT S. 'Racism and the American Experience.' *Radical America*, V (March–April 1971), 93–110.

—— and TOMICH, DALE. 'Black Liberation Historiography.' *Radical America*, II (September–October 1968), 24–8.

STAUFFER, DONALD A., ed. *The Intent of the Critic*, by Edmund Wilson, Norman Foerster, W. H. Auden and John Crowe Ransom. Princeton, 1941.

—— 'Portrait of the Critic-Poet as Equilibrist.' *SeR*, LVI (July 1948), 426–34.

STEARN, GERALD EMANUEL, ed. *McLuhan: Hot and Cool, A Primer for the Understanding of and A Critical Symposium with a Rebuttal by McLuhan*. New York, 1967.

STEINBERG, S. H. *Five Hundred Years of Printing*, 2nd ed. Harmondsworth, 1961.

STEINER, GEORGE. 'On Reading McLuhan.' *Language and Silence: Essays 1958–1966*. Harmondsworth, 1969.

STEWART, DOUGLAS J. 'Aristophanes and the Pleasures of Anarchy.' *The Antioch Review*, XXV (Spring 1965), 189–208.

STEWART, JOHN L. *The Burden of Time: The Fugitives and Agrarians—The Nashville Groups of the 1920's and 1930's, and the Writing of John Crowe Ransom, Allen Tate, and Robert Penn Warren*. Princeton, 1965.

—— *John Crowe Ransom*. University of Minnesota Pamphlets on American Writers, no. 18. Minneapolis, 1962.

STOVALL, FLOYD, ed. *The Development of American Literary Criticism*. Chapel Hill, 1955.

SUTTON, WALTER. 'The Contextualist Dilemma—Or Fallacy?' *The Journal of Aesthetics and Art Criticism*, XVII (December 1958), 219–29.

—— *Modern American Criticism*. Englewood Cliffs, N.J., 1963.

—— [Review of Frye's *Anatomy*] *Symposium*, XII (Spring–Fall 1958), 211–15.

SWEEZY, PAUL M. *The Theory of Capitalist Development: Principles of Marxian Political Economy*. New York, 1942.

TAAFE, GERALD. 'Marshall McLuhan—Electronic Medievalist.' *Parallel*, I (July–August 1966), 13–17.

TATE, ALLEN. 'Confusion and Poetry.' *SeR*, XXXVIII (April 1930), 133–49.

—— *Essays of Four Decades*. London, 1970.

—— 'The Fugitive 1922–1925: A Personal Recollection Twenty Years After.' *The Princeton University Library Chronicle*, III (April 1942), 75–84.

—— 'Gentleman in a Dustcoat.' *SeR*, LXXVI (July 1968), 375–81.

—— 'An Interview,' by Michael Millgate. *Shenandoah*, XII (Spring 1961), 27–34.

—— 'Mr. Burke and the Historical Environment.' *SR*, II (Autumn 1936), 363–72.

—— 'The Problem of the Unemployed: A Modest Proposal.' *AR*, I (May 1933), 129–49.

—— 'R. P. Blackmur and Others.' *SR*, II (Summer 1937), 183–98.

—— 'The State of Letters.' *SeR*, LII (October 1944), 608–14.

—— 'A Traditionalist Looks at Liberalism.' *SR*, I (Spring 1936), 731–44.

—— and AGAR, HERBERT., eds. *Who Owns America?* Boston, 1936.

TATE, CAROLYN. 'Pynchon's *V* and *The Crying of Lot 49*: History, Fiction and other Myths.' Unpub. typescript.

Telos. International Conference: 'The New Marxism,' Waterloo, Ontario, 8–11 October 1970. *Telos*, no. 6 (Fall 1970), 294–317.

289

THEALL, DONALD F. 'Education of the Senses.' *Canadian Art*, XXIII (April 1966), 8–10.

—— *The Medium is the Rear View Mirror: Understanding McLuhan*. Montreal, 1971.

—— 'T. S. Eliot.' Unpub. typescript.

THOMPSON, EDWARD P. *William Morris: Romantic to Revolutionary*. London, 1955.

TODOROV, TZVETAN, ed. *Théorie de la littérature: textes des formalistes russes*, trans. Tzvetan Todorov; preface by Roman Jakobson. Paris, 1965.

TRAN DUC THAO. *Phenoménologie et matérialisme dialectique*. Paris, 1951.

—— 'The Phenomenology of Mind and Its Real Content.' *Telos*, no. 8 (Summer 1971), 91–110.

—— 'The Rational Kernel in the Hegelian Dialectic.' *Telos*, no. 6 (Fall 1970), 118–39.

TROTSKY, LEON. *Literature and Revolution*. New York [1957].

TROWBRIDGE, HOYT. 'Aristotle and the "New Criticism." ' *SeR*, LII (October 1944), 537–55.

TURNER, BRIAN. 'Sociological Functionalism.' Unpub. typescript.

VAJDA, MIHÁLY. 'Marxism, Existentialism, Phenomenology: A Dialogue.' *Telos*, no. 7 (Spring 1971), 3–29.

—— 'Tömegmozgalom és diktatura: politikai és szociológiai tanulmány a fasizmusról' [Mass Movement and Dictatorship: A Political and Sociological Study of Fascism']. Unpub. typescript. Budapest, 1970. In English: *Fascism as a Mass Movement*. New York, 1976.

—— *Zárójelbe tett tudomány: a husserli fenomenológia tudományfelfogásának birálatához* [*Science in Brackets: Toward a Critique of the Conception of Science in Husserlian Phenomenology*]. Budapest, 1968.

VILLIERS DE L'ISLE-ADAM. *Axel*, trans. Marilyn Gaddis Rose. Dublin, 1970.

VIVAS, ELISEO. 'Literature and Knowledge.' *SeR*, LX (October 1952), 561–92.

—— 'Mi Ritrovai per una Selva Oscura.' *SeR*, LXVII (October 1959), 560–6.

WALSH, DOROTHY. 'The Cognitive Content of Art.' *The Philosophical Review*, LII (September 1943), 433–51.

WARREN, ROBERT PENN. 'John Crowe Ransom: A Study in Irony.' *The Virginia Quarterly Review*, XI (January 1935), 93–112.

—— 'Knowledge and the Image of Man.' *SeR*, LXIII (April 1955), 182–92.

—— 'A Note on Three Southern Poets,' *Poetry*, XL (May 1932), 103–13.

—— 'Pure and Impure Poetry.' *Perspectives on Poetry*, ed. James L. Calderwood and Harold E. Toliver. New York, 1968, pp. 69–92.

WATSON, GEORGE. *The Study of Literature*. London, 1969.

WATT, F. W. 'The Critic's Critic.' *Canadian Literature*, no. 19 (Winter 1964), 51–4.

'The Week.' *NR*, LXVII (29 July 1931), 270–2.

WEIMANN, ROBERT. 'Northrop Frye und das Ende des New Criticism.' *Sinn und Form: Beiträge zur Literatur*, XVII, 3–4 (1965), 621–30.

WEISINGER, HERBERT. 'Victories in a Lost War.' *The New Leader*, XLVI (13 May 1963), 18–19.

WELLEK, RENE. [Review of Frye's *Fearful Symmetry*.] *Modern Language Notes*, LXIV (January 1949), 62–3.

—— and WARREN, AUSTIN. *Theory of Literature*, 3rd ed. New York, 1962.

WEST, PAUL. *Robert Penn Warren*. University of Minnesota Pamphlets on American Writers, no. 44. Minneapolis, 1964.

WEST, RAY B., ed. *Essays in Modern Literary Criticism*. New York, 1952.

WEST, (DAME) REBECCA. *McLuhan and the Future of Literature*. Presidential Address to the English Association. London, 1969.

WHALLEY, GEORGE. 'Fry's [*sic*] *Anatomy of Criticism*.' *The Tamarack Review*, no. 8 (Summer 1958), 92–101.

—— [Review of Frye's *Anatomy*.] *The Modern Language Review*, LIV (January 1959), 107–9.

WIDMER, KINGSLEY. 'McLuhanism: A Libertarian View.' *Anarchy*, X (September 1970), 283–9.

WIENER, NORBERT. *The Human Use of Human Beings: Cybernetics and Society*, 2nd ed. London, 1954.

WILDE, OSCAR. *The Works of Oscar Wilde*. London, 1963.

WILLIAMS, BERNARD and MONTEFIORE, ALAN, eds. *British Analytical Philosophy*. London, 1966.

WILLIAMS, RAYMOND. *Communications*, rev. ed. Harmondsworth, 1966.

—— *Culture and Society 1780–1950*, 2nd ed. Harmondsworth, 1963.

—— *Drama from Ibsen to Brecht*, rev. and enlarg. ed. London, 1968.

—— 'Literature and Sociology: In Memory of Lucien Goldmann.' *NLR*, no. 67 (May–June 1971), 3–18.

—— *The Long Revolution*, rev. ed. New York, 1966.

—— 'The Magic System.' *NLR*, no. 4 (July–August 1960), 27–32.

—— ed. *May Day Manifesto 1968*. Harmondsworth, 1968.

—— *Modern Tragedy*. London, 1966.

—— *Orwell*. London, 1971.

WILSON, EDMUND. 'Tennessee Agrarians.' *NR*, LXVII (29 July 1931), 279–81.

—— 'The Tennessee Poets.' *NR*, LIV (7 March 1928), 103–4.

WILSON, W. A. 'Marshall McLuhan to Advise Trudeau.' *Montreal Star*, 22 October 1968, 55.

WIMSATT, W. K., JR. *Hateful Contraries: Studies in Literature and Criticism*. Lexington, 1966.

—— 'Northrop Frye: Criticism as Myth.' *Northrop Frye in Modern Criticism: Selected Papers from the English Institute*, ed. Murray Krieger. New York, 1966, pp. 75–107.

—— *The Verbal Icon: Studies in the Meaning of Poetry*, 5th ed. New York, 1965.

—— and BROOKS, CLEANTH. *Literary Criticism: A Short History*. 4 vols. London, 1970.

WINTERS, YVOR. *In Defense of Reason*. Denver, 1947.

WOODMAN, HAROLD D. *Slavery and the Southern Economy: Sources and Readings*. New York, 1966.

WYNN, DUDLEY. 'A Liberal Looks at Tradition.' *The Virginia Quarterly Review*, XII (January 1936), 59–79.

XXX. 'L'Idéologie technocratique et le teilhardisme.' *Les Temps Modernes*, XXII (August 1966), 254–95.

YOUNG, ROBERT M. 'Darwinism and the Division of Labour.' Draft of a talk for BBC Radio 3 in a series on 'Networks.' N.p., n.d. [Cambridge, *c.* 1971–2].

—— 'Evolutionary Biology and Ideology: Then and Now.' *Science Studies*, I (1971), 177–206.

—— 'The Historiographic and Ideological Contexts of the Nineteenth-Century Debate on Man's Place in Nature.' Typescript [Cambridge, 1972].

Index

Index

DATE DUE